A History of the United States for Newcomers

Expand Your Knowledge, Boost Your Confidence, and Thrive in the USA

Get your free gift

To help you acclimate to the USA, download **No Surprises in the USA**. This will help you adjust feel more confident in your new home

It contains cultural differences that newcomers often struggle with, including:

- Imperial vs Metric system – Distance, weight, temperature
- Tipping – How much and where
- Sales Tax – How much and where
- Terminology – Words and spellings
- School system – Grades and regulations
- AND MORE!

You can get a copy by visiting:
www.historyinaheartbeat.com/nosurprisesintheusa

Get another free gift

Get help passing your Citizenship Test. Download and use *Ace Your Citizenship Test with History in a Heartbeat*. This provides you with:

- All 100 questions and answers to the test
- Notes and pictures to help you remember
- Broken into categories of:
  - American Government
  - American History
  - Integrated Civics
- Updated yearly

You can get a copy by visiting:
www.historyinaheartbeat.com/aceyourtest

A History of the United States for Newcomers © Copyright <<2023>>
Charles Serocold

For more information, email contact@historyinaheartbeat.com

Published by: History in a Heartbeat

ISBN: 979-8-89109-204-4 - paperback

ISBN: 979-8-89109-205-1 - ebook

In loving memory of my parents

Contents

INTRODUCTION

One afternoon, I found out that a friend of mine, Josh, had decided to go home. And by home, he meant back to England. Permanently. He was frustrated and fed up; he had been in the US for a year, could not find a job, found it difficult to make new friends, and no longer believed the effort he was putting in to stay was worth it. I felt bad for him, but what bothered me most was that Josh was just the sort of guy that any country would love to have. He was intelligent, honest, and hardworking, and I wondered how I might have helped him had I known what he was going through.

Josh's story is not unique. In 2009, I moved to America to study at a business school where over 95 percent of the students had relocated from abroad. It was an exciting time, but it came with a new set of challenges. Many felt self-conscious and apprehensive, others struggled with bureaucracy or the language, and all of us missed the support system of our family and friends. We were eager to move beyond the "culture shock" that made us uncomfortable, and a lot of us hoped to stay and work in the US after we graduated. The consensus was that we just had to give it time.

But life does not wait, and most of my classmates returned to their own country at the end of the year. Their reasons varied, but I stayed on, determined to continue making a success of my time here. Setbacks happened, and I fought against problems common to any expat – getting a job, obtaining a visa, making new connections, finding an affordable apartment, etc. but I was intent on giving myself every chance – and that meant fully immersing myself in the society and culture of the country.

Today, over 50 million people living in the US were born in another country – more than the entire population of Canada – and it is home to more foreign-born immigrants, by far, than anywhere else in the world.[1] I have been lucky enough to have spoken with hundreds of them during my time here and discovered that all of them struggled to understand certain aspects of American life. Many scratch their heads over the lack of universal healthcare, the costs of college tuition, home prices and sales tax; and note that discussions with Americans about politics, gun control, abortion, immigration, and race relations can get very heated very quickly.

The roots of those problems can be traced back to the history of the United States: understand US history, understand these issues. And it can all be found in this book. Furthermore, by knowing US history, you will be demonstrating respect for the country's heritage, find it easier to develop better relationships, gain the ability to solve more complex problems, and grow your confidence. It is tempting to dismiss history as impractical and irrelevant, but the most successful people in America have an excellent grasp of it. Elon Musk, Arianna Huffington, and Henry Kissinger – who were born in South Africa, Greece, and Germany, respectively – reached the top of their fields, and have all cited the importance of history in order to learn from the lessons of the past.

---

1 As of 2023, the USA has the most foreign-born residents, with 50.6 million. Second is Germany, with 15.8 million; third is Saudi Arabia, with 13.5 million. Britain is fifth, with 9.4 million.

Also, the history of the US is fascinating. People occasionally claim that America's short life means that there is little to learn, but that is a myth that needs dispelling. Its history grew out of a period of profound global change at an extraordinarily rapid pace and is packed with dramatic stories of adventure, diplomacy, exploration, and warfare. Today, the US wields an outsized influence on global events, and it elicits a curious range of emotions from people who seek to leverage it, challenge it, or disabuse it. It is a status that is unlikely to change for generations to come.

This book differs from others on the market in several ways. It is written in a straightforward and informal style, and each chapter can be read chronologically or selectively – meaning you can skip to any chapter without having read the previous one and it will still make sense – and pictures and maps are placed within the text itself. It is also significantly shorter than many books about US history, some of which span over a thousand pages, so you could read this on a long-haul flight to America and, on touchdown, be ten times wiser and better prepared!

I would have loved to have given Josh and all my old classmates a copy of this book. It would have enriched their stay, helped them connect with the people and the country, and sped up their assimilation time. They would all have contributed greatly to American society, and my hope is that this book acts as the best jumping-off point that you can hope for when you move to the United States.

This book is part of the Newcomer series published by History in a Heartbeat. You can find more at:

www.historyinaheartbeat.com.

For the services I offer, you can email me at cserocold@historyinaheartbeat.com and find out more about me at www.historyinaheartbeat.com/charlesserocold.

You can find free gifts at:

- www.historyinaheartbeat.com/nosurprisesintheusa, and

- www.historyinaheartbeat.com/aceyourtest

You can sign up for new publications and news at: www.historyinaheartbeat.com/news.

Social Media	Name
X	@historyinbeat
Facebook	History in a Heartbeat
Youtube	@historyinaheartbeat
Instagram	@historyinbeat

Thank you, and enjoy!

Charlie

PART ONE:

ORIGINS

CHAPTER 1

PREHISTORIC AND PRECOLONIAL AMERICA (UNTIL 1607)

Pre-Columbian America

Approximately 13.8 billion years ago, everything in the universe was contained in a small singularity, a point of infinite denseness and heat. Suddenly it exploded with unimaginable force and, as it cooled, stars and galaxies began to form until, around 4.6 billion years ago, our own planet Earth was created.

Era	Years (millions of years ago)
Precambrian	4,600 – 540
Paleozoic	540 – 250
Mesozoic	250 – 66
Cenozoic	66 – today

Life gradually emerged on Earth during time divisions that are geologically classified into four eras: Precambrian, Paleozoic, Mesozoic, and Cenozoic, with a gigantic landmass called Pangaea developing in the Paleozoic era around 300 million years ago. Fauna and flora and marine and reptile life flourished until two mass extinction events occurred at the start of the Mesozoic era around 250 million years ago and at the end of the era, around 66 million years ago.

No one can be sure of what caused the first extinction event, but it was probably caused by volcanic eruptions that gave rise to intense global warming. It killed over 90 percent of all species on Earth. The other was caused when a six-mile-wide asteroid slammed into the waters off what is now Mexico (the Chicxulub crater), causing global wildfires and climate change to kill 75 percent of all life, including the dinosaurs. The Cenozoic era began after the extinction of the dinosaurs and continues today in a period also known as the Mammalian Age.

The supercontinent of Pangaea
as it existed around 175 million years ago

Between these two extinction events, the supercontinent of Pangaea began to break up. Bordered by the universal sea, Panthalassa, a three-pronged fissure grew between what is now Africa, South America, and North America, driving the supercontinent apart. Magma welled up through the weakness in the earth's crust and created a volcanic rift zone with dramatic eruptions and volcanic ash spewing debris across the landscape as the continents diverged. They continued to drift (and still do) in a process called plate tectonics, in which the North and South American continents are driven westwards.

Humans first evolved in Africa about 2 million years ago and ventured beyond that continent shortly afterwards. Exactly when they first reached North America is still debated, with the most likely answer being that they crossed the Bering Land Bridge (Beringia) – a strait between Asia (Siberia) and North America (Alaska) – anywhere between 33,000 and 15,000 years ago.

This is according to the "Clovis first theory" – so named for the distinct man-made tools estimated to be up to 11,000 years old that were discovered near Clovis, New Mexico. Based on the age of those tools,[2] humans would have journeyed across Beringia sometime before then, during the Last Glacial Period (which lasted from around 115,000 years ago to 12,000 years ago). The world's water supply was locked into massive continental ice sheets at the time, enabling humans to walk between the two continents.

Other possibilities exist, however. In 1996, human bones were discovered in Kennewick, Washington ("Kennewick Man") which gave scientists evidence to theorize that, based

---

2 Using radiocarbon dating techniques.

on the shape of his skull and other features, Kennewick Man and his forbears may have been Asian coastal seafarers. This means that a "coastal migration" may have occurred rather than a purely terrestrial one and that a wave, or waves, of people may have traveled by boats and lived along the coast of the American Pacific long before the Clovis-type tribes arrived. Further evidence reinforcing this theory emerged during recent excavations in Mexico where archaeologists claim to have found man-made stone tools that point to human occupation up to 31,500 years ago or even earlier. However, these claims have been disputed, with detractors arguing that these tools were produced by natural geological processes rather than by people.

In any event, however and whenever North America was populated, the mild climate, richness of the soil, and animal life gave rise to the growth of civilizations. This period is termed the pre-Columbian era – named for the period before Christopher Columbus arrived in America – and is traditionally classified into five categories as below.[3] The Lithic stage (or Paleo-Indian) is the earliest period of human occupation and the Post-Classic stage the latest.

---

3 As established by Gordon Willey and Philip Phillips in their 1958 book, *Method and Theory in American Archaeology.*

Period	Dates (circa)	Definition
Lithic (aka Paleo-Indian)	Before 8000 BC	Hunter-gatherer lifestyles and use of stone technology. Named after the first appearance of Lithic flaked stone tools.
Archaic	8000 BC – 1000 BC	Subsistence economies (aka moneyless) supported through the exploitation of nuts, seeds, and shellfish.
Formative	1000 BC – 500 AD	Agriculture and formation of permanent towns and villages. Theocracy or priestly class present or in development.
Classic	500 AD – 1200 AD	Craft specialization and beginnings of metal-lurgy, urbanism, and large ceremonial centers. Ideologically, the development of a theocracy.
Post-Classic	After 1200 AD	Possession of developed metallurgy and complex urbanism and militarism. A tendency towards the secularization of society.

Estimates of the number of Native Americans (or Indians[4]) that were living in North America by 1492 vary from between 900,000 to as many as 18 million or more. The challenge for researchers is that no census data or records of population size exist before 1492, so they are forced to rely on a combination of early European eyewitness accounts and records of "encomienda" – tribute payments set up during colonial times. Both metrics have their flaws. Early eyewitness accounts tended to overestimate population sizes, as they were eager to advertise the large scale of the riches available to their European investors; the encomienda system would underestimate the same populations as it was only put in place after the many disease epidemics and slaughters had run their course.

---

4 "Indians" used interchangeably with Native Americans in this text.

There is evidence that a vast number of languages were spoken – between 800 and 1,000 – that developed from as many as 30 language families. By contrast, at this time, Western Europe spoke between 40 and 70 languages which were developed from only two language families – Indo-European and Uralic. The Native Americans had also created numerous autonomous social systems which were radically different from one another depending on where they were based, which included nomadic hunting, farming, town-building, woodland, fishing, and coastal cultures.

The remains of the most sophisticated pre-Columbian native civilization north of Mexico can be found at the Cahokia Mounds in Collinsville, Illinois, about four miles from St. Louis, Missouri. This was, at the time, a huge city that existed between c. 600 and 1350 AD and housed around 20,000 people in a space of 3.5 square miles. It was complete with residential and leisure areas, farmland, a town center, and marketplaces.

The "Monks Mound" is the most obvious remnant of Cahokia, where archaeologists discovered postholes suggesting that a structure, such as a temple, may have sat on top. Less than half a mile south is "Mound 72" where the remains of 272 people were discovered – many of whom appear to have been sacrificed. One area indicates that 39 men and women had been sacrificed "on the spot," lined up, and "clubbed one by one so that their bodies fell sequentially into [the burial pit]."

Cahokia's population began to decline in the 13th century and was abandoned by around 1350. It is unclear as to why, with theories ranging from environmental changes, overhunting, and deforestation to disease, civil war, or invasion by outside peoples. Whatever it was, Cahokia provides us with remarkable evidence of early engineering and architectural developments in North America and reveals a society driven by economics and religion – two tenets that were also driving civilizations in Europe at the same time.

The Middle Ages

The period in Europe that preceded Columbus's voyages was known as the Middle Ages and is memorable for the rise of the Catholic Church and Islam, the Crusades, medieval architecture, feudalism, and the Black Death. Technological advancement drove trade, and increased manuscript production propelled intellectual inquiry and debate. These led to a fascination with, and a desire to explore, the world beyond its borders.

The Middle Ages began after the fall of Rome in 476 AD – a thousand-year-old empire which, at its peak in 117 AD, covered over 2.3 million square miles and reached into the continents of Europe, Africa, and Asia. But it was stretched thin and vulnerable to tribal attacks. Eventually, the 16-year-old emperor, Romulus Augustulus, succumbed to a raid by the German chieftain, Odoacer, who assumed the title of "King of Italy" rather than emperor, and the period of Imperial Rome came to an end.

Tribes formed in the new kingdoms in regions of the old Roman Empire.[5] But they had to endure attacks by Vikings from the north, Magyars (Hungarians) from the east, and Muslims from the south, and they struggled to defend themselves. To ensure greater safety, they developed a hierarchical system of authority called the feudal system. This was based on the exchange of land for loyalty and service and was structured

---

5 The eastern half of the Roman Empire (the Byzantine Empire) survived for 1,000 years after the Western Empire fell, eventually succumbing to the Ottoman Turks in 1453.

with kings at the top, followed by nobles, landlords, knights, and peasants who worked on the land.

The people's security was assured by the military and by the knights, who were wealthy enough to afford heavy armor and a horse. Some of these knights pledged their loyalty to the Christian church. In 1054, the church experienced the "Great Schism" out of which two branches developed – the Roman Catholic and the Eastern Orthodox – and the Catholic Church used its influence in the West to coordinate a campaign to recapture the Holy Land (Jerusalem) from Muslim control in 1095. Many knights and peasants joined up and ventured east in what came to be known as the First Crusade.

A further eight Crusades followed, with the final one occurring in 1291. Their primary aim was to secure control of holy sites, but they had the residual effect of providing the crusaders with a chance to trade with the people of the Middle East and the Orient, and crusaders brought back exciting foods and trinkets that Westerners had never seen before. Marco Polo, a Venetian merchant, sparked Western imaginations even further after he published *The Travels* around the year 1300,[6] and more and more goods were carried on ships going back and forth between the Black Sea and the Mediterranean. However, many questioned whether it was all worth it after a deadly disease was brought back that devastated the continent.

Rumors of a "Great Pestilence" in Asia had reached the ears of Europeans in the 1340s, and when 12 ships arrived at the port of Messina in Sicily, people were shocked to find the crew all either dead or gravely ill, covered in black boils that oozed blood and pus. The Sicilian authorities swiftly

---

6 He described meeting with Kublai Khan, the use of paper money, burning coal for heat, and a mail system along the Silk Road.

ordered the ships out of the harbor, but it was too late; the bubonic plague had escaped, and it spread all over Europe, killing more than 20 million people, almost one-third of the total population. Referred to as the Black Death, it was a precursor to the sort of devastation the Native Americans would endure when the Europeans arrived on their shores with their influenza, measles, and smallpox.

Yet wealth continued to flood in from Asia, and due to their fortuitous positioning between the Middle East and Western Europe, the Italian city-states of Venice, Pisa, and Genoa became increasingly affluent and influential. Western European kingdoms enviously eyed their riches and, hoping to land a similar windfall, started their own explorations to the south and to the west. By 1341, Portuguese sailors had explored the Canary Islands, and Henry the Navigator sponsored numerous expeditions along the western coast of Africa, aiming to spread Christianity and profit from gold, spices, and slaves. The Age of Discovery was about to begin.

Christopher Columbus (1451–1506)

Christopher Columbus, the "discoverer" of the New World in 1492, was an Italian explorer and navigator who made four trips across the Atlantic to America. He was born in Genoa and had three brothers, one of whom, Bartholomew, ran a cartography workshop in Lisbon and collaborated with Christopher to calculate the distance and plot the route across the ocean to the Orient.

Christopher Columbus in 1519, posthumously painted by
Sebastiano del Piombo.

In 1488, Columbus was in the audience as another explorer,
Bartolomeu Dias, shared the tales of his adventures to the
southern tip of Africa with the Portuguese court. Columbus,
who had been married to a Portuguese noblewoman (she
died in 1484), tried to interest the king in sailing west to find
a different route to the spice markets of India and Asia, but
the king thought that Columbus had underestimated the
distance across the ocean, so he turned him down.

However, in 1492, Columbus succeeded in obtaining sponsorship from a different king. He had approached King Ferdinand of Aragon and Queen Isabella of Castile, monarchs of modern-day Spain, many times since 1486, but now, having finally succeeded in defeating the Moors in Granada, the monarchs found themselves open to new adventures. They were eager to spread Christianity beyond European shores.

On August 3, 1492, Columbus and his crew set sail from Spain in three ships: the *Nina*, the *Pinta*, and the *Santa Maria*, and by October 12, they had found land. Columbus did not know it, but this was not the Orient. This was the island of San Salvador (Watling's Island) in the Caribbean – and, for five months, he sailed to other islands nearby, including Cuba and Hispaniola, where he met with people from the Lucayan, Taíno, and Arawak tribes. He erroneously labeled them *Indios*.

He set off back to Spain on January 16, 1493, leaving 39 men in Hispaniola (today's Haiti) to build a settlement called La Navidad. He took with him several Native Americans, small amounts of gold, a hammock, a turkey, a pineapple, and a tobacco plant, and created a sensation when he arrived home. Most people in Europe believed he had reached the Orient (this notion was dispelled by Amerigo Vespucci in 1502, who gave his name to the new continent), and Columbus was bestowed the titles of Admiral of the Ocean Sea and Governor of the Indies. The Spanish Crown financed a further three voyages (in 1493, 1498, and 1502), during which Columbus explored parts of the Central and South American mainland.

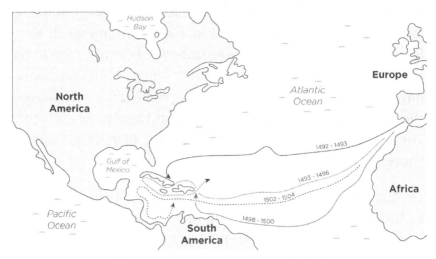

The four voyages of Christopher Columbus

But settlement and exploration of the New World was not easy. On Columbus's second voyage, he found the fort at La Navidad destroyed after the Taínos had rebelled against the Spaniards' demands for gold and women; and when Columbus sent Native Americans back to Queen Isabella in lieu of riches, she returned them, horrified at their enslavement. Columbus reached the South American mainland (Venezuela) on his third voyage, but when he returned to Hispaniola, he found the settlers staging a revolt against his and his brothers' heavy-handed rule. After a royal investigator was sent from Spain to review the situation, the investigator was greeted with the sight of six rebellious Spanish settlers hanging from a gibbet, and he sent Columbus back to Spain as a prisoner in 1500, having deemed him to have exceeded his authority.

Columbus begged for forgiveness and was eventually cleared of the most serious charges. He even managed to obtain funding for a final, fourth voyage in 1502 and was urged to find the Strait of Malacca into the Indian Ocean. He began an intensive search, landing on the coast of Panama, which was only 40 miles from the Pacific Ocean. But he did not venture overland and so never fully grasped the enormity of his discovery. He returned to Spain in November 1504, and, depressed and frustrated, died two years later at the age of 54 from Reiter's Syndrome (reactive arthritis).

Explorations by Spain and Portugal

Other Spanish and Portuguese explorers followed Columbus to the New World. In 1513, the Spanish explorer Vasco Núñez de Balboa crossed through the mountains of Panama and caught sight of the Pacific for the first time, calling it the South Sea. He went into the water and claimed the sea, its islands, and lands for Spain.

In 1519, the Portuguese navigator Ferdinand Magellan set out from Spain with five ships and 270 men. They sailed around South America (through the eponymously named Strait of Magellan) and into the Pacific Ocean, where they sailed for 99 days straight. During that time, they ran out of food and were eating leather, sawdust, and rats to keep themselves alive,[7] until they finally sighted land and arrived at Guam in March 1521. Magellan himself was killed one month later after he tried to lead an attack on a tribe in the Philippines, and only one ship and 18 men of the original crew made it back to Spain three years after they had set off.

Other explorers, such as John Cabot and Jacques Cartier, attempted to find a route through a northwest passage but were unsuccessful. Cabot explored parts of the east coast of Canada on his first voyage but either perished at sea or died somehow in Canada on his final trip, and Cartier's base camp up the Saint Lawrence River at Quebec proved unsustainable

---

7 19 of the sailors died of scurvy and other illnesses on the crossing.

after failing to endure a series of brutal winters, a lack of food, and hostile Indians.

European states became frustrated and began to lose interest in financing them further. The mantle passed on to adventurous individual freebooters, and in 1519 Hernan Cortés traveled to Mexico with 500 men, hoping to find a literal gold mine. Aided by a devastating smallpox outbreak to which the natives had no immunity, he used his superior weaponry, metal armor, and horses to conquer the Aztecs, killing their ruler, Moctezuma II,[8] and taking control of Tenochtitlan in 1521. Francisco Pizarro applied Cortés's playbook in 1533 and conquered the Incas in Peru, killing the last emperor, Atahualpa, and then raiding their camps for gold, silver, and emeralds.

Explorations into the North American continent occurred at around the same time. Juan Ponce de León led an expedition to an area he called "La Florida" (meaning "flowery" in Spanish) in 1513, but when he attempted to colonize it, the Indians killed him and drove the Spanish away. In 1539, Hernando de Soto, who had been one of Pizarro's lieutenants, landed in Tampa Bay, Florida, with 620 men and 220 horses. He traveled north and west over 4,000 miles, fending off Indian attacks in their search for gold before finally reaching the great Mississippi River three years later. There, de Soto contracted a fever and died, upon which his comrades buried him in the river itself.

Francisco Vázquez de Coronado also went north in 1540. He was looking for the rumored Seven Golden Cities of Cíbola which, according to Aztec legend, housed unlimited riches and could be found hundreds of miles to the north across the desert. He led a Spanish expedition up Mexico's

---

8 Also known as Montezuma.

western coast and into the southwest of what is now the United States, to the Grand Canyon and the Colorado River, where they clashed with local Indians and struggled through the oppressive heat and the rocky terrain. He returned to Mexico empty-handed two years later and died in 1554.

Spanish influence on place names in the US	
Current Name	**Translation from Spanish**
Los Angeles	The angels
Las Vegas	The meadows
Fresno	Ash tree
Nogales	Walnut trees
Rio Grande	Large river
San Francisco	Saint Francis
El Paso	The [mountain] pass

Successful expeditions promised much, but they were a huge gamble, and plenty could go wrong. Pánfilo de Narváez set off from Spain with 600 men in 1527, intending to build large settlements in northern Mexico. Before even reaching land, part of his crew had mutinied, two of his boats were damaged in hurricanes, and the expedition was blown off course, landing near Tampa. He led part of his crew inland, where he attacked the Indians, who retaliated, and within weeks, the remaining men were either starving to death or ravaged by disease.

Pánfilo decided to abort the mission and ordered rafts to be built so they could sail westwards to Mexico. However, after setting off, they ran into a storm that drowned most of the expedition including Pánfilo himself, although 80 crewmembers managed to scramble their way over to Malhado Island off what is now the Texas coast. Cabeza de Vaca picked up the story from there, describing how only 15 of the remaining crew survived starvation and disease that winter and how he was then left behind when they departed for Pánuco. He had been deemed too ill to travel but soon recovered, and he made a reputation for himself as a powerful medicine man after nursing several natives back to good health.

Cabeza de Vaca eventually left Malhado Island for the mainland and lived as a trader, whereupon he came across three of the other survivors, whom he discovered had since been enslaved by the Indians. They informed him that everyone else had been killed or had starved to death, and he set about helping them escape. Successful, the four of them then traveled west, healing Indians as they went, until they finally met up with other Spaniards in what is now the western part of Mexico, over nine years after they had first set out with Pánfilo.

Kings and queens in Europe watched on. Spain had set up formal governments (viceroyalties) loyal to the Spanish Crown, and incredible riches were sent back to the mother country, enabling it to become a world power in the 16th and 17th centuries. This newfound wealth was badly mismanaged however, and most of it was blown on religious wars, debt repayments, and propping up their states abroad – not least in the Spanish Netherlands, where they waged the Eighty Years' War (1568 – 1648) against the Dutch. Other European nations wondered if they could do better.

New France and New Netherland

Any French desire to explore the New World in the 16th century was hampered by the French Wars of Religion (1562–1598). These were a series of conflicts that were fought between Catholics and Protestants (also known as Huguenots) in a bid for power in the country, and they only ended after Henry IV granted certain rights and freedoms to the Huguenots under the Edict of Nantes. France then gained the capacity to look beyond its borders.

The French had, in fact, already engaged in some explorations of the New World. Giovanni da Verrazzano, an Italian explorer, had been commissioned by King Francis I to find a route to Cathay (China) in 1523 by going north, and he explored the coast of the Carolinas up to New York,[9] and Jacques Cartier had journeyed through the Gulf of Saint Lawrence and Quebec in 1540. The French Wars of Religion then intervened, and further explorations were put on hold.

They were now prepared to try again, and in 1608, Samuel de Champlain founded the city of Quebec, where Cartier had established his original settlement. The area was appealing to the French because, even though it was devoid of gold, it contained something else that sold for handsome profits in Europe: luxury furs (beaver, fox, lynx, and otter) – and they believed they could put the lessons learned by Cartier on his first exploration to good use.

In uncharted territory, de Champlain needed guides to build trading posts, so he worked to develop better relations with the local Indian tribes. The Algonquins, the Montagnais, and the Huron were prepared to help him, but in return, the French were asked to support them against their enemy, the Iroquois. De Champlain agreed, and in July 1609, he and his party of nine raided Iroquois territory, shot and killed two of their chiefs, and wounded a third. The Iroquois had never seen a white man or a firearm before, and they fled in terror, promptly resolving to make the French their mortal enemy for life and summarily aligning themselves with any European power that was not French.

---

9 Verrazzano was the first European to sail into New York Harbor. The bridge between Brooklyn and Staten Island is named after him.

French influence on place names in the US		
Current Name	Original French	Translation from French
Delaware	De la werre / guerre	Of the war
Oregon	Ouragon	Hurricane
Vermont	Vert mont	Green mountain
Juneau	Juneau	[Named after Joseph Juneau]
Baton Rouge	Baton rouge	Red stick
Boise	Boisé	Wooded
Detroit	Détroit	Strait

They made it difficult for the French to penetrate south of the Saint Lawrence River, so they ventured west instead. In 1682, Robert La Salle canoed all the way down the Mississippi River to the Gulf of Mexico and claimed the vast area of the Mississippi River basin for France, naming it "La Louisiane" in honor of Louis XIV. The first capital of New France was Mobile, Alabama (named after the local Mabila tribe) before it moved to New Orleans in 1723.

The area was enormously underpopulated however, and settlers in New France were vulnerable to raids and attacks by Indian tribes. This was partly due to Louis XIV's intransigence and continued persecution of the Huguenots, whom he sought to control by denying them emigration rights from France. Eventually, with the costs outweighing New France's returns, the French decided to focus on their holdings in the Far East and the Caribbean, and on gaining supremacy in Europe.

***

The United Provinces of the Netherlands seceded from Spanish rule in 1579 and was the first fully independent Dutch state. They distinguished themselves by shipbuilding and world trade, and the Dutch East India Company sought to capitalize on the fur trade by hiring an Englishman, Henry Hudson, to explore the northern part of America. They hoped to find that sought-after path to the Indies, and Hudson ventured up his eponymous river only to find that it led deeper and deeper into Canada. On his final expedition in 1611, he urged his crew to continue further north, but they had had enough and mutinied, casting Hudson, his son, and seven others adrift in the Canadian Arctic. They were never heard of again.

Painting by John Collier (1881) of Hudson cast adrift with his son into the Arctic.

The fur trade business led the Dutch to set up trading posts and plantations in a colony they called New Netherland in 1614. They constructed Fort Nassau on the Hudson River near present-day Albany and established relations with the Iroquois with whom they traded knives, metal cook pots, arrowheads, and firearms (which the Iroquois enthusiastically used on the French and the Algonquin). Peter Minuit purchased the islands of Manhattan and Staten from the Indians in exchange for trade goods worth $24 (around $1,150 today), and they established New Amsterdam on the southern tip of Manhattan Island in 1624.

Dutch influence on place names in New York		
Current Name	Original Dutch	Translation from Dutch
Coney Island	Konijn Eiland	Rabbit Island
Bowery	Bouwerij	Farm
Brooklyn	Breukelen	Broken land, or marshland
Harlem	Haarlem	[Named after a city in the Netherlands]
Greenwich Village	Grenen wijk	Pine wood quarter
Flushing	Vlissingen	Flushing
Staten Island	Staaten Eiland	States Island

Contrary to the Spanish or the French, the colony had little interest in spreading Christianity or any other religion. Instead, by focusing on commerce and profit, it attracted a wide array of immigrants and became the most diverse settlement in North America, with immigrants coming from France, Germany, England, Scandinavia, Ireland, Scotland, and Africa (some of them as slaves). They also tolerated Jews, Quakers, Lutherans, Presbyterians, and others, even though the Dutch themselves were Reformed Protestants. As many as 18 languages were spoken there by the 1630s.

The colony ultimately expanded into parts of what is now New York, New Jersey, Pennsylvania, Connecticut, Maryland,

and Delaware, but despite this, it was not a great success. Tempting immigrants from the Netherlands was difficult in the Dutch Golden Age, and at its peak in the 1650s, only around 9,000 people lived in New Netherland, most of whom came for the cheap land. People were encouraged to emigrate to the colony with the offer of a special land grant, of which they would become full owners ("patroons") after four years, but to qualify for the grant, they had to bring 50 people across the Atlantic with them. This proved too big a challenge for most.

For those at home, New Amsterdam was viewed primarily as a convenient supply port for Dutch ships raiding the Spanish, and in the end, neither the Dutch nor the French came close to what the Spaniards had achieved in the New World or, indeed, the English.

CHAPTER 2

THE COLONIAL PERIOD (1607–1765)

England and Virginia

Much like France, England had little capacity to explore the New World until it could pacify its own people first. A new royal house, the Tudors, had taken the throne after a series of civil wars ended in 1487, but the king, Henry VII, struggled with legitimacy thereafter and could do little else but work to reinforce his claim to the crown. He did commission an Italian, John Cabot, to find a northwest passage to the Orient, but after Cabot disappeared on his third voyage to Canada in 1499, no further English explorations followed for almost 100 years.

The country divided yet again when Henry VII's son, Henry VIII, unilaterally decided to split from the Catholic Church in 1534 after the Pope refused him a divorce. Persecutions followed, first of the Catholics by his Protestant son, Edward VI, and then of the Protestants by Henry's Catholic daughter, Mary I ("Bloody Mary"). It was only when Elizabeth I, who was Henry VIII's second Protestant daughter, came to the throne in 1558 that a real effort was made to unify the people. She pledged herself to the country as its "Virgin Queen," and although domestic issues persisted, she was able to consider new ventures into North America.

Queen Elizabeth happily licensed her Protestant sea captains, or "Sea Dogs," like Francis Drake and John Hawkins, to raid the treasure fleets of the great Catholic power, Spain, and it soon became evident that a foothold in North America would make such raids more effective. She tasked Humphrey Gilbert, an explorer and soldier, to establish a settlement in the New World, but when he drowned in a boating accident near the Azores in 1583, the charter passed on to his half-brother, Sir Walter Raleigh.

Raleigh had first come to the Queen's attention after playing a role in suppressing rebellions in Ireland in 1580 and soon became one of her favorites for his charm, wit, and good looks. In 1585 he directed a team to build a settlement on Roanoke Island located on the Outer Banks of North Carolina, but the settlers were not prepared for the brutal North American winters, so the project was abruptly discontinued.

The word "Croatoan" was found inscribed on a post, the only clue as to the fate of the early colonists.

But Raleigh tried again in 1587, putting the explorer, John White, in charge. The settlement was heavily reliant on supplies from England to sustain itself, and when White returned from Roanoke to collect some later in the year, he found that he was prohibited from sailing back. The Queen had placed a ban on any ship from leaving port due to an imminent attack from the Spanish Armada, and he settled in for a full three years until it was deemed that the coast was finally clear enough to venture out. White returned only to find the Roanoke colony abandoned, with the only clue to the settlers' whereabouts being the name of a nearby island, "Croatoan," carved into a palisade post. But he could not find anyone there either, and their fate became a mystery.

Wealthy individuals financing these settlements were put off by such a high-profile failure but found a way to continue their sponsorship by taking advantage of a new financial creation called a "joint-stock company."[10] In such a company, sponsors put money into one pot that was then invested on behalf of all of them, and it had the welcome effect of spreading the risk and enabling them to raise an even larger sum. The creation of the Virginia Company followed with the first lasting settlement, Jamestown (named after the King of England, James I), established on the Chesapeake Bay in 1607.

Life was not easy in Jamestown, however. Many perished during the "Starving Time" – the brutal winter of 1609–1610 – and they struggled to retain good relations with the local tribe, the Powhatans, on whom they became increasingly dependent for food. Relations improved in 1614 when one of the settlers, John Rolfe, married Pocahontas, the daughter of a Powhatan chief, but they deteriorated again after the

---

10   The Dutch East India Company, formed in 1602, was the first company to offer its shares to the public, effectively conducting the world's first initial public offering (IPO).

Powhatans judged the colony too brazen in its expansion into their lands. They decided to act and launched a surprise attack on the English in 1622, killing 347 settlers in the "Jamestown Massacre."

The king decided that more oversight was needed, and he revoked the Virginia Company's charter and assumed direct control himself. He appointed a royal governor to the colony, Sir Francis Wyatt, who set about raising taxes from the settlers in what was the first legislature of America, and the king sat back, adopting a policy of "benign (or salutary) neglect." This policy meant minimal royal interference, but in return required the colonists to supply raw materials for manufacture in England and act as markets for the finished products. From then on, the Crown would only intervene in the operations of the colonies when the situation truly demanded it.

This was an appealing notion to many in England, and several religious groups began to look towards the colonies as a possible way to live free from persecution for the practice of their faith. It was a big risk, however, as so little was known of what lay in store for them, although many felt that this was their opportunity to take hold of their own Promised Land.

New England

The Puritans were radical Protestants who believed that the Church of England (or Anglican Church) had not done enough to distinguish itself from Catholicism. They sought a "purer" form of worship and rejected the hierarchal structure, rituals, and ceremonies established by the Anglican Church. In turn, they adopted the ideology of John Calvin, a French theologian and reformer who taught that

God was all-powerful and completely sovereign and that all humans were depraved sinners, apart from a chosen few.

Another even more radical group, the Separatists, sought to form their own church – leading them to leave England (where they could be charged with the death penalty for pursuing such an ambition) and set up in Leiden in the Netherlands in 1609. Here, they were free to worship as they pleased, but after suffering economic hardship and fearing for their safety when the Thirty Years' War broke out, they decided to up sticks again and, this time, move to the colonies. A group of 102 of these Separatists – or Pilgrims as they came to be called – set out on the *Mayflower*, and after 66 days at sea, they landed in New England on November 11, 1620.

Dangerous shoals and poor winds meant that, instead of landing near the Hudson River in New York, they ended up at Plymouth, Massachusetts where they legitimized the colony by drafting the Mayflower Compact before even setting foot off the ship. This was a temporary set of laws that established a system of majority agreement and specified that the Pilgrims would:

1. Remain loyal subjects to King James, despite their need for self-governance

2. Create and enact "laws, ordinances, acts, constitutions and offices…" for the good of the colony, and abide by those laws

3. Create one society and work together to further it

4. Live in accordance with the Christian faith

The Compact was the first document to establish self-governance in the New World, and it affirmed the fundamental principle of the rule of law as a primary force in the creation of a new society. It remained active for over 70 years until the Plymouth Colony became part of the Massachusetts Bay Colony in 1691.

Other Puritans followed the Pilgrims. In 1630, 700 Puritan colonists led by a Sussex lawyer, John Winthrop, set out from England as part of the Massachusetts Bay Company, and they landed in a bay they called Boston, naming it after Boston, Lincolnshire. They brought the company charter with them, which had no mention of it requiring its headquarters to be in England, making the colony a self-governing body with its own court and council.

Winthrop alluded to Jesus's Sermon on the Mount by calling the colony a "City upon a Hill" in a sermon he wrote called *A Model of Christian Charity*. The phrase has since become synonymous with the idea of American exceptionalism and was used at the time by Winthrop to demonstrate how he wanted the colony to serve as an example to the rest of the world. He emphasized unity and self-sacrifice and envisioned the community submitting to his authority as governor and to the Court of Massachusetts Bay. Many of the colonists had other ideas though, and almost as soon as they landed, proceeded to set up their own communities, venturing as far out as Hartford, Connecticut.

Winthrop had to deal with certain troublesome individuals too. In 1631, a radical Puritan called Roger Williams arrived and began advocating for religious toleration and the separation of church and state — prompting Winthrop to exile Williams to Narragansett Bay. Williams set up his own colony from there, Rhode Island. Then, in 1634, Winthrop banished the daughter of an Anglican cleric and school-teacher, Anne Hutchinson, who preached that Heaven was attainable through a personal connection with God and that committing sins would not preclude them from going to Heaven. However, while it was relatively easy for Winthrop to exile one individual, it was much more difficult to exile entire church congregations, and before long, these began to develop their own divergent beliefs concurrent with demands for autonomy and self-governance.

John Winthrop died in 1649, representing the end of the first generation of English immigrants. The next one began pushing New England in a new direction and focused on increasing trade and commerce. Their families grew, and as the population increased (from 3,000 in 1630 to 68,000 in 1680), they began expanding beyond Massachusetts Bay – and onto land held by Indian tribes.

Early European traders had brought more than just copper bowls, metal items, and glassware. They had also brought death and disease, with one epidemic (believed to be smallpox or the bubonic plague) killing 50-90 percent of the people on the New England coast between 1616 and 1619. Indians had managed to put these concerns aside when the Pilgrims initially arrived and even shared the First Thanksgiving with them in 1621 when a bumper crop prompted a three-day celebration.[11] But as the numbers of the colonists grew, fears of their disruptive influence grew alongside it.

---

11   You can find more on Thanksgiving at https://historyinaheartbeat.com/thanksgiving/

King Metacom, aka King Philip.

In 1675, the Wampanoag chief, Metacom (also known as King Philip[12]), created an alliance between the Wampanoags and the other local tribes to prevent further encroachment. With tensions high, an interpreter was found dead after warning the colonists that the Indians planned to attack, and three of King Philip's warriors were found guilty of murder and hanged. This infuriated Philip, and the Indians attacked the settlements with tremendous force, sparking a brutal 14-month conflict known as King Philip's War. It left over 600 colonists dead, around 1,200 homes burned, and 12 out of 90 new settlements destroyed.

---

12 Many Indian Chiefs adopted English names to honor the relationship they developed with the new settlers.

But the colonists retaliated, and the Indians suffered far worse. Over 5,000 were killed or died through sickness and starvation, 1,000 were captured and sold into slavery, and another 2,000 fled west or north. King Philip himself was shot, hung, drawn, and quartered, and his head was displayed on a spike at the Plymouth Colony for over two decades – a warning to anyone with thoughts of revenge – and the war effectively ended any Indian threat to the colonists. They could now march unopposed into land previously held by the tribes.

Maryland, Carolina, and Georgia

Wealthy and influential people in England approached the king with ideas on how best to use the land in the New World. George Calvert, the first Lord Baltimore, was persistent in his requests to use some of it to house English and Irish Catholics who were being persecuted at home, and in 1632, the king finally consented in exchange for a share of income that could be derived from it.

George Calvert died just before the charter was granted, so it passed to his son, Cecil, who took full ownership of the land. This became the first proprietary colony, meaning that Cecil was free to establish his own rules and regulations, appoint officials and collect revenues. He called it the Province of Maryland, naming it in honor of the king's wife, Henrietta Maria (who was a Catholic), and he put his younger brother Leonard in place as governor. He then passed the Maryland Toleration Act in 1649, which required tolerance for all Christians in the colony.

Portrait of John Locke by Godfrey Kneller, 1697.

This freedom to make rules gave political thinkers an exciting opportunity to experiment with new political systems. England had just had a taste of republicanism after the English Civil War, and in 1663, after Charles II had been restored to the throne, a group of eight noblemen obtained a new charter from the king to the land below Virginia. They named it Carolina after the king and hired the philosopher John Locke to draft a constitution.[13] Locke took his inspiration from Greek philosophers like Aristotle and Cicero, and from modern thinkers like Isaac Newton and Francis Bacon, and he embraced the principle of basing government on a social

---

13   John Locke has historically received most of the credit for the Fundamental Constitutions, although some researchers have, over time, given more credit to the eight noblemen themselves, particularly to the Earl of Shaftesbury, Lord Anthony Ashley Cooper.

contract between the citizens and its rulers. This declared that the citizens would give up some of their rights in exchange for protection and promotion of their well-being, but if the government violated its terms by infringing upon their rights, the citizens had a right to rebel.

He developed a hierarchical system of government with the eight noblemen at the top (Lord Proprietors), followed by the gentry, the landowners, and the farmers at the bottom. Legislation was to be created by the Proprietors with assistance from a Grand Council (made up of the Proprietors and 42 councillors), and an elected parliament could veto regulations made by the Grand Council. Any religion that believed in God would be tolerated, and slavery would also be authorized and protected. He called it the Fundamental Constitutions (also the "Grand Model"), and the Crown was happy to permit its implementation since it did not have to foot the bill.

The Carolina experiment was then followed by an even more radical departure from conventional governing standards in Georgia. James Oglethorpe and his Board of Trustees proposed that debtors from the overcrowded London prisons be rehoused in the colony, where he believed their talents and skills could be put to more constructive use, and interviews were conducted with potential colonists to ensure they were worthy of the opportunity. Oglethorpe's trustees would govern the colony directly, and slavery, rum, lawyers, Jews, and Catholics were all banned.

Again, the Crown was happy for the trustees to implement this new style of government, and it remained a trustee colony for the next 20 years. But the charter was revoked in 1752 after it became clear that the experiment was not going to work. Some residents were assigned unfarmable land, the alcohol ban was openly flouted, and calls to permit slavery grew louder with many settlers simply fleeing the colony for the Carolinas. This utopia came to an abrupt, discouraging end.

Delaware, New York, New Jersey, and Pennsylvania

In 1638, the Delaware Bay and the Delaware River were settled by the Swedes,[14] one of Europe's great powers at the time. The Swedish South Company had been founded in 1626 with a mandate to establish a colony and cut into the fur trade business, and it put down roots on the Delaware Bay, spreading up the Delaware River into modern-day New Jersey.

French, English, Dutch, and Swedish Colonies
in Eastern North America in 1650

---

14 Delaware was originally named after the first governor of Virginia, Thomas West, Lord de la Warr.

But interest in immigrating to New Sweden was low among those at home, and the colony consisted of only a few hundred people. This made it easy for the Dutch to seize it in 1655 when their authoritarian one-legged governor, Peter Stuyvesant, sent a superior force of seven ships and several hundred troops down the Delaware River to take it over.

The Dutch suffered their own loss in 1664 when the English decided that they wanted to keep the profits of the shipping business for themselves and invaded New Netherland to assure it. The invasion was essentially peaceful: 300 English soldiers and four ships landed on Long Island and proceeded west through Brooklyn, offering fair treatment for those who surrendered, and despite Stuyvesant's heated protests, the English promptly took over. They changed the names of New Netherland and New Amsterdam to New York and New York City, respectively, after the sponsor of the conquest, the king's brother James, Duke of York. But, other than the names, the workings of the colony were largely left alone, including the patroon system, which eventually led to the creation of vast properties in upstate New York and beyond.

The old colony of New Sweden also changed hands in this conquest – from the Dutch to the English – and its workings were largely left alone too. But this changed in 1681 when King Charles II handed over a large piece of his North American holdings to William Penn in payment of a debt he owed to Penn's deceased father. The land would become the present-day states of Pennsylvania and Delaware, parts of which had been within New Sweden.

William Penn was the son of the aristocrat Sir William Penn, an admiral and staunch supporter of the royalty and the return of Charles II as King. When Penn Jr. was 22 years old, he met a Quaker missionary in Ireland, after which he claimed that the "Lord visited me and gave me divine impressions of Himself," and he converted to the Religious Society of Friends (or "Quakerism," named after their practice of trembling before God) in 1666.

Quakerism was created by George Fox, the son of a Leicestershire weaver, who had become disillusioned by the conventions of the church. It was one of several new religions established after the English Civil War, and it rejected rituals, opposed war, and assumed the presence of God within everyone. But Quakers began to develop an unpopular reputation as they openly defied the customs of the time. They refused to take off their hats or bow to those in authority or who were considered financially or socially superior, and would heckle and denounce speakers in public. Despite this, they managed to survive beyond 1660 when the Church of England was reestablished as the official religion, primarily because of their commitment to pacifism, and when Penn Jr. converted, he attempted to gain legal recognition for Quakerism through his aristocratic connections. But he was unsuccessful and began to look west, buying some land with his fellow Quakers in 1677 and 1682 in New Jersey. He then pressed the king to settle some of the debts that he owed his father.

The king owed £16,000 (around £3.5 million today) and, after listening to Penn's pleas, decided to duly pay up. At that, Penn became the world's largest private (non-royal) landowner in a single stroke. It is a curiosity as to why the king was content to make him so, and absent any official explanation, we are forced to speculate. Perhaps the king wanted to be rid of Penn and his fellow Quakers (along with other minority sects), or he felt the land was worthless and did not want the hassle of overseeing it. Maybe Penn had simply caught the king on a good day. But whatever the reason, Penn had secured himself an incredible deal. He called the land "Sylvania" – a derivation of the Latin for woods – although the king insisted on adding "Penn" to it in honor of Penn's father. This conflicted with Penn's practice of humility, but he agreed, and the land became Pennsylvania.[15]

Penn described Pennsylvania as his "Holy Experiment" and intended the land to be a haven for his fellow Quakers, envisioning fair treatment of the Native Americans, no military presence, and no persecution or dissension. Other minorities were attracted by these ideals of religious tolerance, and he sold land to Huguenots, Mennonites, Amish, Catholics, Lutherans, and Jews from all over Europe who spread out, together with his Quakers, into the Pennsylvanian countryside.

Penn arrived in Pennsylvania in 1682 and immediately found himself under pressure from the settlers to put a constitution in place.[16] He labored over several "Frameworks of Government" until 1701, developing a system of government with two houses of parliament; powers separated between the executive, legislative, and judiciary; religious tolerance; and fair trials for everyone, including an impeachment process that could be brought against the governor. All of these frameworks influenced the Founding Fathers when they worked on drafts of the Constitution in the years to follow.

Pennsylvania's population soon took off and, by the 1750s, outpaced New York to house the most diverse group of ethnicities and religions in the English-speaking world.

---

15 Penn named the capital Philadelphia, meaning the "City of Brotherly Love." It was a combination of the two Greek words: love (phileo) and brother (adelphos).

16 He only visited twice, from 1682–1684, and again from 1699–1701.

But the colony never turned a profit, and when Penn died penniless in 1718, the family was forced to turn the colony into another commercial venture. It remained in their hands until the American Revolution.

Some in England were uneasy about these political experiments. New systems had the potential to threaten the old, and by the 17th century, standards of living in the colonies were high. Regional trade patterns had developed, with New England building ships, Virginia and the Carolinas generating crops of tobacco and indigo, and New York and Pennsylvania providing other crops and furs. Part of this success was due to the abundance of natural resources within the colonies, and another part was due to their chosen labor force: indentured servants and African slaves.

Indentured Servants and Slavery

The dearth of labor was a constant problem for the colonists; there were just not enough hands to get the job done. Land was cheap in America, but labor was expensive – a problem that was the opposite of the one in the mother country, where land was expensive and labor cheap.

One way the Virginia Company found laborers was by paying the government a nominal fee for its prisoners and then selling the remainder of the prisoners' jail terms to farmers or merchants in America, where the prisoner would be put to work in the fields or the factory. Another way was through the practice of indentured servitude, which was a contract between a company and a laborer that required the laborer to work in the colonies for no salary in exchange for passage, board, and lodging. The contract would typically last for a period of between four and seven years, after which the laborer would earn his "freedom dues" – usually a piece of land, some supplies, and a gun – upon which he would be on his way. The laborer would often then set up his own farm, driving competition for labor even higher.

Landowners were acutely aware that once a jail or indenture term expired, a replacement laborer would need to be found, and they attempted to find ways to keep hold of their indentured servants for as long as possible. Sometimes the servant would literally be worked to death and die from exhaustion, and other times illness would kill them off. Penalties were put in place for breaking laws such as running away or becoming pregnant, and a laborer could find their indenture time doubled or more. The number of indentured servants grew to as much as 75 percent of the population at times, and landowners began to fear losing political power. They remedied this in Virginia in 1670 by restricting the right to vote to only those men who owned enough property to pay local taxes.

Bacon's Rebellion of 1676 was partly sparked by these laws after the governor had refused to allow the laborers to settle land beyond Virginia's borders. This would have given the laborers a chance to become landowners and potential voters themselves, but instead, the laws forced them to rely on work offered by the current landowners. They took up arms in revolt, on a level of violence so alarming to the landowners that, after it broke up, they looked to other sources for their labor.

Virginia had received their first slaves in 1619. The ships *White Lion* and *Treasurer* had arrived at port carrying 20-30 African (Angolan) captives each, seized from a Portuguese slave ship. They were sold as indentured servants, but their distinguishing skin color and captive status made them vulnerable to exploitation. Some of the Blacks from those ships did gain their freedom, but others were held in bondage for life, and with the white indentured servants growing more combative, the appeal of slave labor began to grow.

ON BOARD A SLAVE-SHIP.

Slaves aboard a ship being shackled Captives being brought on to a slave ship on the West Coast of Africa

The slave trade had already been established by the Spanish, Portuguese, and Dutch, so diverting ships to the colonies would take little effort, although the British eventually developed their own slave trading route – the notorious Middle Passage. This was a three-legged triangular trade route that took European goods to Africa, African slaves to America, and American goods back to Europe, with the slaves held in appalling conditions on the boats. As many as 700 slaves would be packed into the lower deck of a slave ship, with the men shackled together in pairs and kept separate from the women. The children were left completely naked, and with little airflow and sanitation, dysentery and smallpox could kill hundreds.

The Atlantic crossing usually lasted between two and three months, with slaves entirely subject to the vagaries of the crew. They could torture, kill, or sexually abuse slaves almost at will. Many suffered from such depression and despair that they threw themselves overboard, hanged themselves, or starved themselves to death. Any rebellious behavior was brutally suppressed by lashing the slaves with whips or torturing them with thumbscrews, and often as many as 20 percent of them would die in transit.

Slavery was a permanent condition, passed down from the mother. A slave had no identity, no rights, no political say, and no legal recourse. Marriage between them was not legally recognized and restrictive behavioral codes were put in place, with the slaves often prohibited from learning to read or write.

This system was easy to implement for the colonists because of the slaves' distinctive black skin. It made them identifiable in case of escape but ultimately raised the question of why a man's skin color should preclude him from the rights and freedoms of the white man. To answer this, slave owners had to forge false notions of the superiority of the white man, that it had existed throughout history, and that it was "supported" by the Bible.

In all, around 11 million slaves were taken from Africa. Around 40 percent of them went to Portugal's single giant colony of Brazil; 50 percent to the islands of the West Indies to work in the English, French, and Spanish sugar planta-tions; and less than 10 percent to North America. But even this relatively small amount became the bedrock of the

American economy, producing nearly 80 percent of the goods – tobacco, indigo, rice, rum, and cotton – that were exported back to Europe.

Slaves became a vital saleable commodity, and the forced migration of them into America outnumbered white immigration until as late as the 1840s. They brought much-needed stability to the economy, but it came at a horrific price, and any American claims of social parity with their English counterparts were dismissed out of hand – for in England, slavery did not exist, and the true freedom of its citizens was preserved.[17] It is a discrepancy that still haunts America today.

The Great Awakening

Many of America's early settlers were driven to move to the colonies to escape religious persecution, and one's faith was a prominent force in many people's lives. But this early period also coincided with revolutionary thinking in Western Europe that demoted God and promoted science and rationalism – the Scientific Revolution and the Age of Enlightenment. It was this thinking that had the most effect on the Founding Fathers.

Harvard University had been established to educate the clergy and was faced with a challenge after the philosopher Francis Bacon published his 1620 book, *Novum Organum*.[18] Within it, Bacon described a new form of thinking, empiricism, which argued that all knowledge comes from experience and observation obtained through our senses, and that knowledge was not innate or present in the mind from birth.

---

17 A position that was tested in the courts when a Jamaican slave, James Somerset, landed on English soil in 1771. He was deemed, by the court, to be a free man as no law authorized slavery in England.

18 The title referenced Aristotle's Organon (meaning "tool"), which was a treatise on logic and reasoning.

This was an idea that conflicted with the Christian values of faith, revelation, and divine inspiration (they could not be directly observed or measured through empirical methods), leaving Harvard to decide whether or not to accept Baconian thought.

Benjamin Franklin Drawing Electricity from the Sky (1816), by Benjamin West.

The issue with empiricism was the suggestion that God was no longer actively controlling the universe. He would not interfere through miracles or divine intervention; it was left to run by itself according to the systems He had put in place. This idea was too extreme for many, but not to a group called the "deists," and by the late 18th century, Deism had become an accepted religious position among both European and American educated classes. One deist was Benjamin Franklin.

Franklin was a true polymath who excelled at everything he tried his hand at. He first made his name, and his fortune, in the printing and newspaper business, and in 1752 conducted an experiment that involved sending a kite and a metal key into a rainstorm. He hoped that the key would pick up an electrical charge from the lightning, which it did, providing him with proof that one of God's most mysterious systems could be manipulated if only we fully understood it. The experiment won him the first honorary Master of Arts from Harvard and the prestigious Copley Medal from the Royal Society, although it took over another hundred years for electricity to be used practically when incandescent light-bulbs were invented by Thomas Edison.

But many rejected these new ideas and preferred to accept God as a supernatural force that could not be explained. In 1692, a "witchcraft craze" took hold of Salem (now Danvers), Massachusetts after several young girls accused more than 200 people of being witches, resulting in the hanging of 19 people. And in 1734, Northampton, Massachusetts suddenly found itself the center of an outburst of religious energy as crowds flocked to hear Northampton's minister, Jonathan Edwards. He stridently asserted the Calvinist principles of predestination and the authority of the Bible, utilizing a preaching style known as the "jeremiad" that urged people to repent of their sins and warned of impending doom unless a return was made to religious piety and righteousness.

The movement was significantly strengthened when George Whitefield, an Anglican priest from England, arrived with his own theatrical and expressive preaching style. Whitefield had attended Oxford University where he had been part of the "Holy Club," and he delighted his listeners by trembling, weeping, and waving his arms about dramatically during sermons. In 1738, the trustees of Georgia sent Whitefield off to Savannah, tasking him to raise money for an orphanage.

Word spread as he traveled through the colonies, and before long he was a sensation. Crowds became so large that he was forced to preach outdoors, sometimes to as many as 25,000, with even the esteemed Benjamin Franklin so moved that he emptied his pocket "wholly into the collector's dish, gold and all." In 1740, Jonathan Edwards invited Whitefield to preach in Northampton, and the religious revival grew even more intense. Edwards himself gave his most famous sermon entitled *Sinners in the Hands of an Angry God* in 1741. Bellowing in "fire and brimstone" style, he declared:

> *The God that holds you over the pit of hell, much as one holds a spider or some loathsome insect over the fire, abhors you, and is dreadfully provoked; his wrath towards you burns like fire; he looks upon you as worthy of nothing else, but to be cast into the fire... you are ten thousand times so abominable in his eyes, as the most hateful and venomous serpent is in ours.*

Dramatic as it was, such a style also had its detractors. They argued that it fomented fanaticism and would increase the number of impostors and charlatans. Before long, a split grew between Edwards's and Whitefield's "New Lights" and traditionalists' "Old Lights." Edwards published a series of texts including *A Treatise Concerning Religious Affections* (1746) as he strived to explain and understand people's behavior during mass conversions in this period. He argued that "converting grace," a spontaneous gift from God, was the cause of Christian awakening, and he laid out 12 tests of what constituted a true conversion and 12 signs of what constituted a false one.

In two years during the Great Awakening, new memberships in churches in New England grew from 25,000 to 50,000. New schools and colleges were built including Princeton, Rutgers, Brown, and Dartmouth, and people joined missions to Native American communities. Hundreds of new churches were formed and, for the first time, the colonies had commonality with other colonies.

But the Awakening was unsustainable in the hands of just a few men, and enthusiasm eventually waned. Jonathan Edwards was fired as pastor of Northampton in 1750 by those who disagreed with his formal approach for conversion, and he eventually accepted the position of president of Princeton College in 1757 but died of smallpox a year later. George Whitefield built his orphanage in Georgia and continued to preach, shuttling back and forth between America and England (13 times in all) before finally dying from either asthma or heart failure in 1770. He was buried in Newburyport, Massachusetts.

The Great Awakening was a significant milestone in American history. The movement paved the way for new religious denominations and the growth of evangelical Christianity, and it represented the first time Americans united to defy authority and established conventions. They would soon come together again – but this time it would be to challenge the absolutist principles of the British monarchy and, ultimately, the authority of the mother country.

The French and Indian War

The population of the colonies had surged from just over 250,000 people in 1700 to over 2.1 million by 1770. Exports had grown from $539,000 per annum to upwards of $4.1 million in the same period. These were thrilling numbers to the English, but equally concerning, as a mounting threat to the mother country appeared to be emerging.

Mercantilism vs. Capitalism	
Mercantilism	**Capitalism**
Focused on building a nation's strength	Focused on earning profits
Government-controlled trade	Free trade
Aims to increase net exports to create wealth, often through colonization	Aims to increase productivity to create wealth

England sought to incorporate the colonies' growth by applying the dominant economic theory of the time, mercantilism. This theory was formulated on the belief that there was a finite amount of wealth in the world and that it was, therefore, the duty of the government to gather as much wealth as possible while protecting what it had. Strategy for growth involved acquiring wealth through war or restraining imports (primarily through tariffs) while promoting exports. It would all be coordinated by a central government that would fund corporate, military, and national development.

The purpose of the colonies was to grow the wealth of the mother country. The colonies exclusively purchased goods from England, and the Navigation Act was passed in 1651 to ensure that all goods shipped to and from the American colonies were carried on English ships. Parliament then passed a series of other acts[19] that taxed the goods carried on ships, aiming to undermine the economic growth of the Netherlands and France. These led to conflicts and wars, with fighting spilling over into the colonies.

Enforcing these regulations was difficult, however. England was a long way away, and a timely bribe would satisfy some of the more overbearing enforcers. Sometimes the regulations could even help the local economy (for example, the Navigation Acts helped grow the shipbuilding industry of New England), and as the colonies sought to become more respected by the British social elite, they took any involvement in European wars as an affirmation, albeit backhanded, of their status.

They would soon have a major role as imperial competition between Britain and France reached a new level of intensity in the 1740s. They fought each other in the War of Austrian Succession (called King George's War in North America) which ended in 1748 but left the boundary between New France and the English colonies unclear. The French planned to rectify this by building a line of barrier forts from Lake Erie to the Alabama River, but these forts would have to pass through land that Virginia claimed as its own. In 1754, 300 Virginia militiamen under the charge of one George Washington were dispatched to Fort Duquesne to compel the French to abandon their construction. But the French were ready for them, and they forced the British back to Virginia on two occasions.

---

19 These included the Staple Act (1663) and Sugar Act (1733).

Map of British, French, and Spanish Settlements in North America in 1750, before the French and Indian War began (1754-1763)

Hostilities between the two nations escalated in 1756 when a massive conflict began in Europe called the Seven Years' War (the French and Indian War in North America), during which the British and French battled it out in North America, the Caribbean, and India. The British effort in North America began badly, hampered by lack of interest at home, rivalries among the American colonies, and France's greater success in winning the support of the Indians. But things began to improve once King George II appointed William Pitt the Elder to the office of Prime Minister in 1757.

Pitt changed strategies by targeting America and India. Robert Clive decisively defeated the French in India at the Battle of Plassey in 1757, and British fleets seized the French West Indian Islands and Cuba in the Caribbean. His main expeditions, however, were sent to North America under Generals Jeffery Amherst, Lord George Howe, and James Wolfe. In June 1758, Amherst won Britain's first great victory at Louisbourg near the mouth of the Saint Lawrence River, and in September, General John Forbes captured Fort Duquesne, renaming it Fort Pitt (now Pittsburgh) after the British Prime Minister.

The following year, 1759, was even more glorious for the British, as they won a string of high-profile victories. Fort Niagara was taken by William Johnson (helped by nearly 1,000 Iroquois warriors); General Amherst took Fort Carillon at Ticonderoga; and on September 13, 1759, James Wolfe achieved the most astonishing victory at Quebec – although both he and the French commander, the Marquis of Montcalm, were killed in battle.

The French lost their last foothold in Canada after Amherst captured Montreal the following year, and the war ended with a resounding victory for Britain, with the coronation of Britain's new king, George III, celebrated just as enthusiastically in the colonies as in the motherland. Britain was granted East Florida from the Spanish and the eastern half of French Louisiana (the area from the Mississippi River to the Appalachian Mountains not including New Orleans) at the Treaty of Paris in 1763.

However, the war had left the government with massive debt and spiraling costs. Its debt had doubled from £75 million in 1756 to over £133 million in 1763, and all the additional land Britain had acquired at the Treaty of Paris needed policing with a standing army. Britain was challenged to find ways to finance it.

CHAPTER 3

AMERICAN REVOLUTIONARY ERA (1765–1783)

Build Up to the Revolutionary War

The economic challenge of repaying debts was one problem, but it coincided with a political one too: the doctrine of absolutism. This was the practice of vesting unlimited power and authority into the hands of the monarch and had been exemplified by Louis XIV of France during his 72-year rule between 1643 and 1715. It subjected the king to no challenge or check by any other agency of power and was intended to prevent power struggles, maintain stability, and foster national unity. But it carried the risk of abuse with it too.

Louis XIV had presided over a golden age of art and literature, and by annexing key territories, had established France as the dominant European power at the time. The Stuart family in England had attempted to replicate it by proclaiming that God, rather than the people, had given the monarch a "divine right" to rule, and although this led to revolutions in 1642 and 1688, the absolutist argument in Britain remained strong. The two political parties were split between the Tories, who supported it, and the Whigs, who did not.

The Whigs had begun life as a political faction in 1678 and were strongly influenced by the ideology of John Locke.

Locke believed that the government had a duty to protect the three natural rights of its citizens – "life, liberty, and estate" – and the Whigs wished to see this implemented through the supremacy of Parliament and the constraint of governmental powers by law, custom, and humane principles. The most radical Whigs even suggested replacing the monarchy with a republic.

Taxes imposed on the colonies. The Stamp Act of 1765 was the first internal tax levied.		
Year	Tax Name	Effect
1651	Navigation Act	All exports were to be carried on English ships and have English crews, and the ships had to pay duties on the goods.
1663	Staple Act	Any goods picked up in foreign ports had to be taken back to England, paid for in duties, and then shipped to the colonies.
1764	Revenue Act (Sugar Act)	Placed a tax on sugar and molasses imported into the colonies.
1765	Stamp Act	Required that a revenue stamp be placed on all newspapers, pamphlets, almanacs, legal documents, liquor licenses, college diplomas, playing cards, and dice. Without the stamp, the document was not legal or admissible in court cases. Repealed in 1766.
1767	Townshend Acts	Added duties to the importation of paper, lead, painters' colors, and tea. With the exception of tea tax, the Acts were repealed in 1770.
1773	Tea Act	Gave the East India Company direct access to the American market, but colonists argued that it granted a monopoly injurious to American Trade. The Boston Tea Party followed.
1774	Coercive Acts (Intolerable Acts)	A series of Acts in response to the Boston Tea Party including the Port Act, which closed the port of Boston until the loss of the East India's tea was repaid.
1775	Prohibitory Act	Cut off all trade between the colonies and Britain, and removed the colonies from the King's protection.

In 1763, George Grenville took over as Prime Minister of the Whig Party after Pitt's resignation and immediately set to work resolving the debt crisis. His solution was to tax the colonists directly, and he passed the first internal tax, the

Stamp Act, in 1765. This charged a tax for stamping certain documents without which they were not legal or admissible in court,[20] but the colonists had traditionally raised money for administration through their own legislatures, and they reacted with dismay. The British Parliament argued that the colonists enjoyed virtual representation in Britain, thereby making the colonial legislatures illegitimate, but the colonists did not see it that way, and resistance to this new tax began to grow.

In Boston, a group calling itself the "Sons of Liberty" set fire to an effigy of the stamp distributor, and a riotous mob looted and smashed up his home. The Virginia House of Burgesses passed resolutions denying the British Parliament's authority to tax the colonies, and a convention composed of delegates from nine colonies assembled in New York. They wrote a petition to the king with the message that only the colonial legislatures had the constitutional authority to tax the colonists, triggering a political crisis in Britain that saw the collapse of the Grenville government.

Grenville was succeeded by the Marquis of Rockingham, whose government repealed the Stamp Act. However, the entire incident sparked a shift in colonial thinking towards the Whig principles of natural rights, limited government, and self-determination, and they began viewing themselves as not only British subjects but as Americans with unique rights and interests. They anticipated more challenges to come.

The repeal of the Stamp Act quieted the protestors for a time, but they were set off again when Charles Townshend, the Chancellor of the Exchequer, created new taxes (the

---

20 Including newspapers, wills, deeds, pamphlets, almanacs, legal documents, liquor licenses, college diplomas, playing cards, and dice.

Townshend Acts) that taxed exports to America such as glass, paint, paper, and tea. Rallying around the cry of "no taxation without representation," the colonists agreed to boycott British goods, and this time the British sent troops to quell the unrest. But this added fuel to the fire: skirmishes between the colonists and the British soldiers escalated on March 5, 1770, when British soldiers shot into an angry mob and killed five Americans in the Boston Massacre.

The Townshend Acts were repealed the following month, apart from the tax on tea. But for the colonists, the whole affair had reinforced their fears of British authoritarianism, and they were now fully prepared to fight back. In 1773, the government of Lord North passed the Tea Act, which gave the financially struggling East India Company a monopoly on the tea trade in North America and was intended to bail them out of bankruptcy. But with the tax on tea still in place, this was viewed as an underhanded tactic to obtain support for and legitimize said tax and, more broadly, indirectly acknowledge that Britain had the right to tax its colonies. Ships carrying the tea were turned back to Britain, and in Charleston, the cargo was left to rot on the docks.

The Boston Tea Party.

In Boston, however, the governor, Thomas Hutchinson, refused to allow the ships to return to England, and he ordered the tea tariff to be paid and the tea unloaded. This was like a red rag to a bull, and on the night of December 16, 1773, over 100 colonists, many of whom disguised as Mohawk Indians, boarded the docked ships and threw 342 chests of tea into the waters of Boston Harbor. The event became known as the Boston Tea Party.

The British were outraged and defiantly passed a series of punitive acts – collectively called the Intolerable Acts – which closed the port of Boston, demanded compensation to the East India Company, and put martial law in place under the British army's commander in chief, General Thomas Gage. These acts did nothing to reduce tensions, and all colonial legislatures (except Georgia) sent representatives to Philadelphia to discuss how to respond. The First Continental Congress convened in September 1774 in Carpenters' Hall where they endorsed the Suffolk Resolves. These ordered the citizens not to obey the Intolerable Acts and officially declared that the colonies had the right to govern independently of Britain.

Gage sensed rebellion and tried to persuade the British government to repeal the Intolerable Acts. But Parliament was in no mood for compromise. Upon learning that a large cache of war supplies had been hidden in the town of Concord and that two of the leaders of the Sons of Liberty (John Hancock and Samuel Adams) were hiding in nearby Lexington, General Gage was given orders to organize a force of 800 British troops and strike at Concord and Lexington on April 19.

A local silversmith, Paul Revere, got wind of Gage's plan and tipped off the Lexington militia. Under the command of Captain John Parker, the militia met the British upon the town green, and facing off against a vastly superior force, Parker ordered his 77 militiamen to disperse – but a shot rang out (no one knows by whom), and the nervous British unleashed a volley, killing eight and wounding ten others. Leaving the dead men in their wake, they looked for Samuel Adams and John Hancock, neither of whom they could find, and then continued to Concord. Here they encountered thousands of militiamen and were routed back to Boston, ambushed continually, suffering 300 killed or wounded. Britain was sent into crisis mode.

The Revolutionary War (1775–1783)

With the disaster of Lexington and Concord ringing in their ears, Britain had reached a key decision point. One option would have been to apologize and pledge to work with the colonists for mutual gain. Such a display of humility could have penetrated the divided sensibilities of the Americans, many of whom were unsure of what the Bostonian and

Philadelphian elite had in mind for them, and it may have nipped any revolutionary fervor in the bud. But the British never seemed to have considered such an approach, whether because of a sense of entitlement, a belief that their army could suppress them, or general indignation. Whatever the reason, compromise was not on their agenda.

In June 1775, the New England militia gathered themselves on Bunker Hill and Breed's Hill, just outside of Boston. A disturbed General Gage ordered his commanders to remove them, but the British were forced back twice and only managed to overwhelm the militia after the colonists had run out of powder and shot. A total of 1,054 British were killed or wounded, compared with the colonists' 450, in a Pyrrhic victory for the British.

That summer at the Second Continental Congress, George Washington, the Virginian veteran of the French and Indian War, was authorized to raise a Continental Army – into which the 22,000-strong militia in Boston folded[21] – and approval was granted to launch an invasion of Canada. The British bombarded and burned the coastal towns of Falmouth and Norfolk in Massachusetts and Virginia respectively, and following these raids, Thomas Paine anonymously published his pamphlet, *Common Sense*, advocating independence from Britain.

Paine was an English-born political philosopher and writer, and the pamphlet was met with critical acclaim, selling 150,000 copies in its first year (and remaining in print today). He argued for the benefits of a representational government over a monarchical one and pointed out that since America is related to Europe as a whole, it needed the ability to trade freely with every European nation, not just with Britain.

---

21   June 14th is still celebrated as the birthday of the US Army.

Not everyone in Congress wanted war, however, and the more conservative amongst them authorized the Olive Branch Petition to emphasize the colonies' loyalty to the Crown. But this was considered invalidated after the British declared the colonists to be in open rebellion in August 1775, and in December of the same year, Britain removed the colonies from the protection of the Crown, enabling its representatives to seize American ships at sea. Forced to bulk up their sparse troop numbers in North America, Britain also hired German mercenaries, mainly from Hesse-Kassel ("Hessians"), to help in combat.

These steps infuriated the colonists and drove them into the arms of the radicals. By May 1776, Congress had recommended that the colonies establish new governments based on the authority of the people rather than the Crown, and the Virginian Richard Henry Lee formally offered a resolution stating that the colonies "are, and of right ought to be, free and independent States." A committee was established (the "Committee of Five"), comprised of John Adams, Robert R. Livingston, Roger Sherman, Benjamin Franklin, and Thomas Jefferson, and they were tasked with drafting a statement to present the case for the colonies' independence. This eventually became the United States Declaration of Independence and was adopted by Congress on July 4 of that year.

Its principal author was Thomas Jefferson, who had previously published *A Summary View of the Rights of British America* in 1774. Strongly influenced by John Locke, the Enlightenment, and Whig political thought, he stressed the universal laws of nature, equality between men, and the "unalienable" rights of man to life, liberty, and the pursuit of happiness. He categorically rejected Absolutism and the Divine Right of Kings and identified the primary role of government as the protector of the rights of man – rights Britain had violated, and which had given the Americans license to revolt.

The Declaration was a landmark in the history of democracy. More than half of the 193 nations represented at the United Nations today have a founding document that can be called a declaration of independence, and many borrow language very similar to the American's, including countries as varied as Venezuela, Liberia, Vietnam, Hungary, and France.[22] Together with the Constitution and the Bill of Rights, the Declaration of Independence was one of the three essential founding documents of the United States government, and it holds a special place in the hearts of Americans, who celebrate Independence Day every year on July 4.[23]

Separately, the Constitution was written by John Dickinson and presented to Congress on July 12 as the Articles of Confederation and Perpetual Union. But this document sparked long debates about how much power Congress should have, how states should be represented in Congress, what taxes it had the right to implement, and who owned the land west of the Appalachians. In the end, since each state had its own system of government, a Confederacy was created that bound the states together for limited purposes, and each state was to be given an equal vote (as such, tiny Delaware had as much political power as Virginia or Pennsylvania).

---

22 France drafted the "Declaration of the Rights of Man and the Citizen" in their own revolution in 1789.

23 You can find more on Independence Day at https://historyinaheartbeat.com/the-declaration-of-independence/

The Continental Congress also established a Committee on Foreign Affairs to solicit help from Britons and other Europeans sympathetic to their cause. Led by Benjamin Franklin, they met with the French foreign minister Comte de Vergennes in Paris. He was in favor of an alliance but hesitated when he heard news of Washington's defeats in New York in 1776 and, at that point, would only commit to providing a secret loan and some military equipment (primarily gunpowder). The Patriots were left to do the fighting on their own.

***

The Americans had had a strong start to the war at Lexington, Concord, and Bunker Hill, but whether they could keep such momentum going against what was arguably the finest army in the world was open to question. British troop levels in the colonies amounted to 8,500 men in 1775, but they could call on many more, and their numbers rose to around 50,000 at the height of the war.

With most of the British army stationed in Boston in August 1775, General Thomas Gage suggested that they should be removed to the more strategic New York City. London agreed, and the British first moved to Canada to regroup. But Gage, who had overseen those early battles, had lost the confidence of the British government, and he was replaced with General William Howe.

After the British had evacuated Boston, George Washington, the commander of the Continental Army, shifted his troops to New York in anticipation of a British attack. Washington had served as a colonel in the French and Indian War and had resigned his commission when that war ended. He had since spent most of his time farming on Mount Vernon, a vast property on the Potomac River that he had inherited from his half-brother. His original goal was to become an officer in the British army, but he had been turned down, which prompts the counterfactual question of what might have happened in the war had he been accepted. For Washington was a natural leader – charismatic, principled, and patient – and his experience in the French and Indian War provided him with the lessons he needed to understand the importance of tactics, organization, and logistics on American soil.

He was initially up against significantly larger forces, and in June and July 1776 the British sent 34,000 troops and a fleet of 130 ships across the Atlantic to support General Howe. Together they attacked Washington and the Continental Army in New York, routing them at the Battle of Long Island, and the Americans were pushed back across the Delaware River. Popular support wavered.

Washington Crossing the Delaware (1851) by Emmanuel Leutze.

Washington's army numbered only around 5,000 troops, but they received a morale boost in December after Washington made a surprise attack on the Hessians at Trenton, New Jersey. He crossed back over the Delaware (immortalized in the Emmanuel Leutze painting *Washington Crossing the Delaware*) and captured around 1,000 prisoners, some cannons and provisions, and followed this success with a victory at Princeton a week later. Hostilities were then put on hold as the armies focused their energy on braving the winter.

The British changed their strategy when combat resumed in 1777. With loyalist support believed to be stronger in the south, they decided to focus their efforts on isolating the north, which they planned to achieve by taking control of the Hudson River. Generals John Burgoyne and Barry St. Leger were tasked to lead two forces down from Canada (from Montreal and Lake Ontario, respectively) and meet at Albany where General Howe could potentially join them.

It started well enough as Burgoyne defeated the Americans at the Siege of Fort Ticonderoga. But St. Leger was forced to retreat to Quebec, and Howe never even ventured north, unilaterally deciding to attack Philadelphia instead. Burgoyne continued to Albany but suddenly found his troops exposed, and General Horatio Gates took advantage, leading the American forces to victory at two Battles of Saratoga, in September and October. Over 6,000 British troops were captured.

News of Saratoga reached the ears of the French. Eager to see Britain defeated, they signed a treaty with the United States at the beginning of 1778, formally recognizing the United States as an independent nation and openly allowing them to provide the Americans with supplies, arms, ammunition, troops, and naval support. The British hastily reviewed their options, and the Prime Minister, Lord North, made an offer to the Americans to sue for peace based on home rule within the Empire. But with the British on the back foot, this offer, which would have been very appealing in 1775, was rejected.

Howe had set up his army's winter quarters in Philadelphia, and Washington withdrew to Valley Forge, only 20 miles away. There, the Patriots endured a particularly brutal winter, running so low on food and clothing that diseases ran rampant, resulting in the loss of 2,000 of the 12,000 soldiers over six months. Washington's leadership was tested, but the alliance with France bolstered him with two new officers from Europe – the French aristocrat Marquis de Lafayette and the Prussian military officer Baron Friedrich von Steuben – and he was able to retain the loyalty of his men.

Von Steuben was shocked by the state of the Continental Army when he arrived, and Washington permitted him to train and condition the troops. He initiated a system of drills, military tactics, and discipline, and by the spring of 1778, the army had been radically transformed. His lessons became the official military guide when they were codified in 1812 in the *Regulations for the Order and Discipline of the Troops of the United States* (known as the "Army's Blue Book"). Parts of it still influence US Army training today.

***

Howe was severely criticized by the British press after Saratoga, and he resigned, replaced by Sir Henry Clinton. Clinton decided to relocate the British forces from Philadelphia to New York where, for the remainder of the war, a stalemate ensued. But in the south, the British launched successful missions to capture Savannah, Georgia, and Charleston, South Carolina, the siege of which Clinton came down personally to oversee in May 1780.

The war in the south grew bitter and bloody at the end of May at the Battle of Waxhaws. Here, Banastre Tarleton's British Legion chose to ignore a flag of truce with an offer for surrender and massacred a detachment of Virginia Continentals, killing 113 soldiers. Tarleton was furiously condemned by the Patriots and given the nickname "Bloody Ban." The incident fueled anti-British sentiment and served as a rallying point for their cause.

The British took Charleston, and Clinton returned to New York, leaving General Cornwallis (with whom he was barely on speaking terms) with the responsibility of crushing the rebellion in South Carolina. Congress sent Horatio Gates, one of the victors of Saratoga, to head it off, but he was soundly beaten at the Battle of Camden, and he abandoned his army and rode nearly 200 miles in three days in a desperate escape from the battlefield. Washington had been somewhat skeptical of Gates's achievements at Saratoga from the start, and Gates was accused of cowardice and removed from command later that year.

Cornwallis held Charleston, but he was undermanned, and when he sent a force to North Carolina, they were routed at the Battle of King's Mountain. The British lost over 1,000 men to the Patriots' 90, and avenging Banastre Tarleton's massacre at Waxhaws, the Americans hung nine captured loyalists, terrifying southern loyalists and forcing the British to pull back.

In the north, Clinton had no soldiers to spare for Cornwallis. He had captured forts at Paulus Hook and Stony Point only to see them recaptured by Washington and, frustrated by the impasse, Clinton tried to bribe a senior American general, Benedict Arnold, to betray the Continental Army's outpost at West Point. Arnold had felt underappreciated for his efforts at Saratoga, was married to a loyalist wife, and was deep in debt, so he agreed. And the plan nearly worked until John André, a major in the British army, was captured by the Continental Army with detailed papers from Arnold outlining how the British could capture the fort. André was hanged, but Arnold escaped to New York City where he led a raid on Richmond and helped to burn New London in 1781.

Clinton also got wind of a mutiny that had occurred within the Continental Army in the winter of 1780 – 1781. Certain troops of the Pennsylvania Line believed that their three-year enlistment term had expired and were embittered by their pay, which was only a fraction of that paid to soldiers from other states, so 1,500 men departed the camp and set up in Princeton, demanding more money and better housing conditions. When Clinton heard of it, he offered them backpay from the British coffers and a full pardon provided they gave up the rebel cause. But the mutineers had no interest in turning coat and came to an agreement with Congress to either accept a discharge or a furlough coupled with a bonus for reenlistment.

***

At the start of 1781, in the south, British General Cornwallis found himself with only 1,300 men ready for duty and no more than 3,000 under his immediate command. He desperately needed supplies and planned to set up a new base at Wilmington, where he hoped the Royal Navy could provide support. But he now had to contend with Horatio Gates's replacement, General Nathanael Greene – one of Washington's most trusted military subordinates and one of the Continental Army's finest military strategists.

Greene sent a detachment led by Daniel Morgan into the highlands of South Carolina, and Cornwallis responded by dividing his troops. He led his main force towards Greene and sent Tarleton's British Legion after Morgan, but Tarleton was lured into Cowpens Pasture and was enveloped in a pincer movement by over 2,000 Continental Army troops and militiamen who utterly routed his army. Of the 1,000 British soldiers, only 140 mounted troops, including Tarleton himself, managed to escape.

Surrender of Lord Cornwallis (1820) by John Trumbull.

Cornwallis and his 2,100 troops were teetering on the brink when they engaged with Greene at the Battle of Guildford Court House in March. The British were victorious but suffered another 532 casualties, and Cornwallis withdrew to Yorktown, Virginia, on the James River peninsula. Washington, smelling blood, led 14,000 troops down to Yorktown from New York as Cornwallis waited for reinforcements to be provided by sea. But the Comte de Grasse and the French fleet had sailed up from the West Indies and engaged with the Royal Navy at the Battle of the Chesapeake, forcing the British ships back up north and leaving Cornwallis stranded. After three weeks under siege, during which he watched his supplies dwindle to dangerous levels, he finally surrendered on October 19, 1781.

American independence was effectively won at Yorktown that day, but at the time was not fully acknowledged. British troops remained in Charleston, Savannah, and New York, and although they were in no position to attack, the war labored on for another two years as neither side took decisive action to end it. It was costing Britain £12 million a year, and with exports (particularly wool) to the colonies having fallen off a cliff, Parliament finally voted to suspend the war on February 7, 1782, with Lord North resigning a month later.

The new British Prime Minister, Lord Shelburne, met Benjamin Franklin in Paris and signed a formal peace treaty in 1783. It recognized the existence of the United States and ceded claims on most of the lands east of the Mississippi River – including Ohio, Michigan, Indiana, Illinois, Wisconsin, and parts of Minnesota – doubling the size of the nation. Benjamin Franklin attempted to get the British to give them the Province of Quebec and other Canadian territories but was unsuccessful.

The American economy was also totally devastated. They had borrowed over $10 million from France, Spain, and the Netherlands, and their total debt exceeded $43 million, which they tried to manage by printing money, resulting in hyperinflation. Thousands of loyalists had been imprisoned, thousands of slaves had deserted, and a significant portion of the colonial elite had been killed.

New state constitutions were written up in which most states granted all taxpaying, free men the right to vote (New

Jersey's even contained an accidental phrase that allowed women to vote) and the Continental Army was demobilized. It was a key moment in American history as George Washington, the hero of the Revolution and who retained the full backing of the Continental troops, had every opportunity to take the full power of the nation directly into his own hands. But he chose not to. Instead, he set an example of virtuous Whig republicanism and resigned his commission in 1783, desirous of a return to private life. Upon hearing the news, George III cried in disbelief: "If he does that, he will be the greatest man in the world." But he did, and maybe he was.

PART TWO

INDEPENDENCE

CHAPTER 4

THE CONFEDERATION PERIOD (1783–1790)

The Constitution and the Bill of Rights

The Articles of Confederation and Perpetual Union had been ratified in 1781 and acted as the nation's first constitution. But most power was given to the states rather than to Congress, and Congress was hampered in its abilities, particularly concerning its immediate problem of paying down debts incurred from the war.

Alexander Hamilton, by John Trumbull.

Article VIII proclaimed that only the states could tax their citizens, but the states were providing little evidence of making a success of their finances or politics. In 1784, four counties in western North Carolina, concerned that Congress would sell the territory to pay off some of its debt, declared their independence as the state of Franklin and set up their own parallel government independent of the union.[24] In Massachusetts, Daniel Shays (who had fought at Bunker Hill) led a group of rebels protesting state taxes. They marched on Springfield and attempted to seize the federal arsenal, but were routed by the state militia, and Shays fled to Vermont.

The states filled their committees and assemblies with local tradesmen — mechanics, artisans, and militiamen — who had stepped into leadership positions after the loyalists had disappeared. Many of these men defined liberty as protection of individual rights and limited government. But by 1785, calls grew louder from a group who believed that the nation's health trumped that of the states' and that a stronger federal government was fundamental to providing the political and economic stability the US needed to thrive. The New York delegate Alexander Hamilton soon emerged as this group's champion.

Born in the British West Indies on the island of Nevis in 1757,[25] Hamilton was the son of a Scottish merchant and a British West Indian mother. His father abandoned the family when Alexander was young, and his mother died when he was around 13 years old, leaving him to be provided for by the sponsorship of local patrons. He moved to New York City just before the revolution to study at King's College, and

---

24 They rejoined North Carolina in 1789 after repeated attacks by Indian tribes. The counties eventually became part of Tennessee.

25 This birth year is according to Hamilton himself. Official documents from Nevis list Hamilton's birthdate as 1755.

when war broke out, he sided with the revolutionaries, rising up through the army and eventually serving as lieutenant colonel to George Washington.

Hamilton was critical of the states' small-mindedness and believed a powerful federal government would bring the people together. When the states drafted their own constitutions, they had to consider key questions, including the structure of the legislature, the selection of the judiciary, and the appropriateness of veto powers. These questions focused the minds and drew attention to the areas that needed reforming in the Federal Constitution itself.

In March 1785, commissioners from Virginia and Maryland met to discuss fishing rights and to regulate commerce on the Chesapeake Bay, and they quickly recognized the value of obtaining agreement from more states in the area. They called a convention in Annapolis, and Hamilton spotted an opportunity to have the matter considered on a federal level. Congress agreed, and a convention was scheduled to be held in Philadelphia.

The delegates attending the Philadelphia Convention in 1787 were eager to make the Federal Constitution work. The first open question was how the federal government should be structured, and James Madison presented his Virginia Plan, which proposed separating the government into three branches: legislative (split between two houses), executive, and judiciary. The plan further recommended that representation in the legislature be apportioned by population size, but this would give states like Virginia a larger voice in government. The New Jersey Plan countered it by proposing that each state have an equal number of delegates in one of the houses of the legislature (the Senate).

The convention created a powerful chief executive in the form of the president. He would be elected by the people, ensure that legislation was executed, and act as commander in chief of the army and navy. The unspoken assumption was that the position would go to George Washington, although objections were raised to the proposal that he be directly elected by the people. A compromise was offered in the form of the so-called Electoral College, a device that enabled the people to indirectly elect the president by voting directly for state electors, the number of which would vary by state according to its population size. The state electors would, in turn, cast their vote for president as a representative of the people.

Since its inception, the Electoral College has been a topic of much debate, particularly when the outcome of the election comes as a surprise. It does have its advantages, however: it keeps the smaller states relevant, ensures that a candidate obtains voters' support in several different regions, and gives more certainty to the election result. Since almost all states operate on a winner-takes-all basis, if one state has voting issues or the result is especially close, a recount can just be done in that state, and the potential trauma of a nationwide recount is averted.[26] The disadvantages are that swing states hold an outsized influence, and it makes some people's vote feel irrelevant, especially when a result conflicts with the popular vote – which has happened five times as of this writing (John Quincy Adams in 1824, Rutherford B Hayes in 1876, Benjamin Harrison in 1888, George W Bush in 2000, and Donald J Trump in 2016).

---

26 Nebraska and Maine use the "congressional district method" to distribute their electoral votes, which allocates two electoral votes to the state winner, and then one electoral vote to the popular vote winner in each Congressional district (2 in Maine, 3 in Nebraska).

Congress was authorized to levy taxes, declare war, raise an army, and regulate interstate commerce. The Supreme Court would adjudicate disputes between states, and states would retain powers that included their citizens' civil rights. Priority was given to the unity of the United States, which meant that slavery, which had the potential to critically divide the delegates, was put to one side, although many of the Founding Fathers were particularly conflicted about its practice. George Washington described his ownership of slaves as "the unavoidable subject of regret" and freed them in his will when he died. Benjamin Franklin later became president of the first abolitionist society in the United States, and Thomas Jefferson (who wrote the words "all men are equal" and who owned hundreds of slaves himself) wrote how he wished the institution were abolished and that it was a political and moral evil. But it was the bedrock of the Southern economy, and so slave labor remained in place.

It took just over four months to draft the Constitution with ratification required by nine out of 13 states. Debates followed between "Federalists" in favor of it and "Antifederalists" against it. Delaware ratified it first on December 7, 1787, followed by Pennsylvania, New Jersey, Georgia, and Connecticut. But the states of Massachusetts, New York, and Virginia wanted assurances that the federal government would not exceed its authority and called for greater constitutional protection for individual liberties.

To obtain their ratification, Hamilton, James Madison, and John Jay wrote a series of 85 essays entitled *The Federalist Papers* that they published anonymously. The essays were written in clear and succinct prose and detailed how the Constitution would bring stability to the Union and enable the fledgling country to effectively conduct foreign relations.

They described how the "separation" of powers provided safeguards against a tyrannical national government from forming and, along with the promise to consider adding amendments in the form of the American Bill of Rights,[27] the Federalists achieved their goal. The last state, Rhode Island, approved the Constitution on May 29, 1790.

The Bill of Rights was partly inspired by the English Bill of Rights (1689), which limited the power of the monarchy and laid out specific freedoms for individuals. These included freedom of speech, freedom to bear arms for self-defense, and freedom from royal interference with the law. Yet few members of Congress were eager to amend the Constitution and Hamilton was reluctant to include a similar bill for the US. He argued that any powers not given to the federal government automatically devolved to the people and the states and was concerned that if certain rights were drafted vaguely, they risked being misinterpreted or violated. But Jefferson and Madison (who drafted it) were insistent, and the American Bill of Rights was ratified by three-fourths of the states on December 15, 1791.

Freedom of religion, of speech, and of the press, and the right to a fair trial and to bear arms all became enshrined in US law – and for over 100 years, the Supreme Court saw few cases related to them. It was only in 1920 that the American Civil Liberties Union was formed to hold the government accountable for its promises in the Bill of Rights, and individuals began to point to the Bill to protect themselves from the reach of government.

---

27 Ratification was in danger in the key state of Massachusetts until the governor, John Hancock, proposed adding a Bill of Rights.

Since then, Bill of Rights claims have made up many of the highest-profile cases in the Supreme Court. The right to privacy implied in the 14th Amendment gave women the right to have an abortion in the case of *Roe v Wade* (1973),[28] and the right to bear arms in the 2nd Amendment gave citizens the right to possess a gun at home even when there is no relationship to the local militia (*District of Columbia v Heller* (2008)). The interpretation of the rights within the Bill remains a source of debate and discussion and shows little sign of slowing.

---

28   This decision was overturned in *Dobbs v Jackson Women's Health Organization* (2022).

CHAPTER 5

THE FEDERALIST ERA (1790–1801)

Hamilton's Reports

This era is named after the party that dominated American politics at this time. It ran for ten years – from the ratification of the Constitution in 1790, to when Thomas Jefferson's Democratic-Republican Party won the election of 1800. The period became known for the development of a stronger central government, a deepening of nationalism, and the promotion of good trade and diplomatic relations with Britain.

After the Constitution was ratified, Congress authorized the president, George Washington, to create four cabinet positions to manage the duties of the Executive Office. Thomas Jefferson became Secretary of State, Alexander Hamilton became Secretary of the Treasury, Henry Knox became Secretary of War, and Edmund Randolph became the Attorney General.

Hamilton immediately set to work. The United States had continued to accumulate debt which by now amounted to over $77 million, $40 million of which was owed to its citizens in the forms of securities and Treasury bonds (IOUs). Debate raged about how to deal with this debt, with recommendations being to divide it between the states or repudiate part or even all of it. The arguments for repudiating all of it were that it did not survive into this new government. It had been generated by the previous two, and by lending money to anyone, including the government, one ran the risk of not having it paid back.

Hamilton rejected these suggestions and argued for proper treatment of the debt. The debtors had taken the debt in good faith, and by treating it fairly, it would establish trustworthiness among creditors and the financial markets abroad. In January 1790, he presented a detailed analysis of American finances with recommendations on how to organize it in his *First Report on the Public Credit*. He suggested full federal repayment at face value to holders of government debt ("redemption"), with the federal government assuming the war debt owed by the states ("assumption"). To pay for this, Hamilton proposed to raise federal taxes on imports, and impose a 25 percent excise (sales) tax on whiskey. To administer it, he suggested the creation of a national bank.

This last suggestion sparked much debate. The idea had come from the British, who had created their own national bank in 1694. This had been partly to provide economic and political stability to the country following the Glorious Revolution of 1688, and partly to provide itself with a reliable way to obtain funds for its military campaigns. In British North America, however, no banks had existed before 1776 and many feared the concentration of financial and economic power that a national bank would produce.[29]

Hamilton detailed his plan for a national bank in his *Second Report on the Public Credit* (also referred to as *The Report on a National Bank*). He recommended that it be a joint

---

29 Britain refused the formation of banks in North America out of fear that large concentrations of wealth would build up and threaten the wealth and power of the mother country. Colonial Americans had to obtain credit from one another or from merchants and banks in Britain.

private and public venture in which the federal government would hold one-fifth of its capital and would use the bank as its agency for receipt and disbursement of funds. Profits generated from loans to businessmen and entrepreneurs would be used to pay off the debt in proportion to the government's holding. Hamilton also proposed a national currency in the form of bank notes, which would be redeemable on demand for gold and silver ("specie").

The arguments against a national bank were put forward by Thomas Jefferson. He feared that its creation would create a culture of speculative borrowing, long-term debt, and the monopolization of entire industries. He believed that since the bank could, theoretically, lend out more paper notes than it had available in gold and silver, the economy would be built on an illusory form of wealth leading to economic inequality and corruption. But Hamilton was adamant that without large-scale pooling of wealth, there could be no significant economic growth, and the questions of where this economic growth would occur and who would profit then followed.

The answers were found in Hamilton's third major report and magnum opus, *The Report on the Subject of Manufactures* (1791), in which he pushed for large-scale investment into the manufacturing economy. He argued that the United States needed to diversify from its agricultural foundations and that the development of a manufacturing economy could only improve and complement the current agrarian one. The manufacture of American products would ensure America's independence from Britain (and other nations), provide employment, and promote immigration to a country that needed labor, and the new tariff system would increase the costs to Americans for imported goods, thereby making American-made ones more attractive.

The reports were bold and creative but were a direct challenge to Jefferson and the agriculturalists. Jeffersonians argued that only the merchants would benefit, that farmers would bear the brunt of the taxes, and that corruption would be rife. They foresaw women and children being forced to leave their farms to work in dirty, gloomy factories and worried that the increased focus on manufacturing would create a trade imbalance and make the US overly reliant on imports. They also argued on the technicality that the Constitution gave Congress no authority to create a national bank.

Despite these objections, Hamilton successfully negotiated the passage of all three reports through Congress. The debt redemption proposal passed largely because many congressmen held much of the war debt themselves and wanted what they were owed, and the assumption proposal passed only after Jefferson agreed to support it in return for Hamilton's agreement to move the capital from Philadelphia to somewhere on the border between Virginia and Maryland.

Hamilton's other major asset was George Washington himself, who had full trust in Hamilton. When the Jeffersonians argued that Congress had no power to create a national bank and that Washington should use his power of veto, Washington listened to Hamilton's counterargument that the Constitution implied the right to create a national bank since it had the broader right to regulate the currency and bankruptcy of the nation. Washington signed the Bank Bill of 1791 into law, thus creating a 20-year charter for a national bank.

Between 1791 and 1792, 36 new corporations were chartered including 11 banks. Infrastructure such as canals, turnpikes, bridges, and roads was capitalized by the banknotes issued through the Bank of the United States, and abroad, US bonds and securities received the highest rating on the Amsterdam financial markets, encouraging foreign investment. Jefferson was furious and resigned as Secretary of State in 1793. But he would be back.

The Federalists and the Democratic-Republicans

The division between Hamilton and Jefferson had grown wider and more bitter, and the Constitution had not considered the effects such a division could have. No thought had gone into the prospect of the creation of separate political parties, with the Founding Fathers taking the view that separate political parties acted out of self-interest and that they would serve to generate polarization within the country and hinder their ability to govern. But individuals in Congress soon found themselves having to choose between one side or the other.

Hamilton organized himself and his supporters under the name Federalists. They stood for a united central government, good relations with Britain, a centralized banking system, and close ties between government and men of wealth. The Antifederalists, who branded themselves the Democratic-Republican Party,[30] were led by Thomas Jefferson and James Madison, and they championed states' rights, agrarianism, and political equality. Each promoted their ideas in newspapers they created, such as the Federalists' *Gazette of the United States* and the Democrat-Republicans' *National Gazette* and the *Philadelphia Aurora*.

The Democratic-Republicans almost lost credibility immediately, however. The French Revolution of 1789 seemed to mirror much of what the American Revolution had stood for and appeared deserving of American support, which

---

30 This party eventually formed the core of the modern Democratic Party.

it received from the Democratic-Republicans. But it soon descended into an orgy of violence and became a complete embarrassment for the party. Robespierre led the French into a "Reign of Terror," guillotining Louis XVI and his wife, Marie Antoinette, and summarily executing any "enemies of the revolution." Thousands of people, including aristocrats, priests, and members of the middle class, were beheaded.

The French minister to the United States, Edmond Genêt, almost caused an even bigger problem when he began issuing privateering commissions from Charleston, South Carolina. These authorized the bearers to seize British ships and their cargo for personal profit, and with the Revolutionary Wars raging, could easily be interpreted as a direct American attack on Britain. The US government was so appalled that they appealed to the French government to recall Genêt, who (under the control of the radical Jacobins) initially refused and argued that the US should show solidarity with them in their fight against the monarchies of Europe. But eventually they backed down, and the United States was able to stay neutral in a huge conflict that they could ill afford to be drawn into.

The Federalists, however, failed to obtain the support of grassroots voters. Many farmers on the frontier refused to pay the tax on whiskey, which was made by using the surplus grain they could not get to market in the east, and they tarred and feathered several tax collectors who requested they pay up. In January 1794, farmers and distillers led a mob of around 400 people in Western Pennsylvania to march on the tax collector's home, which they shot at and set on fire, and George Washington organized a militia to put the uprising down. He rode out with a huge force of 12,000 men, but once he arrived, the mob was nowhere to be found, making laughingstocks of Washington and Hamilton.

Similarly unpopular was John Jay's Treaty (1794–1795) with Britain. John Jay was sent to Britain to settle outstanding issues that had been left unresolved since the revolution, which he partly achieved by maintaining peace and preserving US neutrality. But matters such as the Canadian-Maine boundary, compensation for pre-revolutionary debts, and British seizures of American ships were left unresolved. He also made concessions allowing the British to seize US goods bound for France if they paid for them, and confiscate French goods on American ships without payment.

Hamilton left the government in 1795 to join the New York Bar, and George Washington, the Federalists' ace up the sleeve, announced that he would not be seeking a third term. Democratic-Republicans in Congress nominated Jefferson as their presidential candidate and Aaron Burr as his running mate, and the Federalists nominated John Adams (Washington's vice president) and Thomas Pinckney, respectively. Adams won by a margin of 3 votes (71 to 68), and since the Constitution had not accounted for political parties, Thomas Jefferson became vice president owing to his larger vote count over Pinckney (68 to 59). After the bitterness of the last few years, Jefferson soon made it clear that he had no plans to accommodate the agenda of the Adams administration.

The John Adams Administration

John Adams, by Gilbert Stuart.

At 61 years old, John Adams became the second president of the United States. Born in Quincy, Massachusetts, he had attended Harvard College, had been a delegate in the First and Second Continental Congress, and had served eight years as Washington's vice president. Short, paunchy, and temperamental, he was not, however, a popular member of Congress, and Hamilton doubted Adams's loyalty to his financial program. In the end, Adams was chosen as the Federalists' candidate more by default than by any strong desire to put him there.

His first crisis concerned France, a gift given their status as a favorite of the Jeffersonian Republicans. The French Revolution had entered a more moderate phase after the execution of Robespierre, but the French Revolutionary Wars raged on and, upon learning of the terms of the Jay Treaty – specifically that French goods could be confiscated by the British on American ships – the French retaliated by seizing American ships carrying British goods.

Adams sent a three-man delegation to Paris to negotiate. Once they arrived, however, they were treated disrespectfully and made to wait for weeks under the pretext that Charles Maurice de Talleyrand, the Foreign Minister of France, was not ready to receive them. Intermediaries then tried to bribe the Americans by requesting a $250,000 payment to Talleyrand personally, along with a loan of $10 million from the US coffers. A shocked Thomas Pinckney wrote "No; no; not a sixpence," and the Americans left, skeptical as to whether any agreements from negotiations would have been honored at all.

Once the delegation had safely returned to America, Adams revealed the full story to the newspapers, anonymizing the names of the French intermediaries with the letters X, Y, and Z, and the public reacted furiously. Adams canceled all treaties with France that had been agreed to during the Revolutionary War, asked Congress to appropriate funds to build up the army and the navy, and brought George Washington out of retirement as commander in chief. In what became known as the Quasi-War with France, Adams's popularity rose to new heights, and the Democratic-Republicans were accused of being Jacobins and French sympathizers.

Adams sensed an opportunity to crush the Democratic-Republicans for good, and he passed the Alien and Sedition

Acts in 1798. These gave him special powers to imprison and deport hostile non-citizens, restricted speech that was critical of the federal government, and increased the residency requirement for American citizenship from five to 14 years.

At best, one could argue that wartime demanded increased vigilance to ensure national security, but the reality was that these laws were designed to keep the Democratic-Republicans out of government. Suddenly any criticism against Adams's government was a potential violation of the acts, and congressmen themselves were arrested – Matthew Lyon for recommending that Adams be sent to a madhouse, and Jedediah Peck for simply criticizing the acts. In 1798, Madison and Jefferson condemned the acts in the *Virginia and Kentucky Resolutions*, claiming that the federal government had overstepped its authority.

In 1798, the British navy decisively defeated the French in Egypt, and the French government was overthrown by Napoleon Bonaparte the following year. With the French threat removed, the real purpose of the acts was exposed. Adams sent a peace mission to France to reopen negotiations, which so enraged Hamilton that he wrote a highly critical letter attacking Adams's policies and character. Intended to remain private, it soon became public knowledge thanks to Aaron Burr and dealt a significant blow to Adams's reelection campaign. Jefferson and the Democratic-Republicans ("Republicans") won the election in 1800 by a margin of 73 to 65, and the Federalist Party was all but finished for good.

CHAPTER 6

JEFFERSONIAN ERA (1801–1817)

Overview of the Jeffersonian Era

Thomas Jefferson, by Rembrandt Peale.

The Jeffersonian Era is named after its principal advocate, Thomas Jefferson, and was a period defined by a commitment to agrarianism and opposition to elitism and corruption. It was the first time power had passed from one party to another, and with the Constitution silent on such an event, Adams could have argued that Jefferson had no authority or legitimacy to become president. But he set a crucial precedent when, at 4 a.m. on March 4, 1801, he left Washington, DC under cover of darkness to take the stage-coach to Baltimore in what was a peaceful transition of power to the new president.

Thomas Jefferson called his election the "Revolution of 1800." He planned to shift the focus from the manufacturing industry towards farming and agriculture, pay more regard to the authority of the individual states, and cut federal debts. But Jefferson was not as revolutionary as many expected, and he struck a note of reconciliation with his rivals when he said in his inaugural address, "We are all Republicans, we are all Federalists," and in many areas, little changed. He did reduce the number of employees in government, discard the Alien and Sedition Acts, and repeal the Whiskey Tax, and he was able to cut the size of the national debt from $83 million to $57 million, partly by scaling down the size of the army and navy owing to the end of hostilities with France.

Voting rights (which were mostly limited to white males who owned at least 50 acres of land) were not expanded, and in some states, they were even taken away. Free Black men had their vote taken away in several states,[31] and women had their right to vote taken away in New Jersey. Jefferson attempted to expand it by introducing the Land Law of 1800, which reduced the minimum individual purchase of land in the Northwest Territory from 640 acres to 320 and allowed settlers to pay in installments over four years.[32] With a blind eye turned to squatters, the population in the West grew dramatically. The first census, in 1790, counted 100,000

---

31 Massachusetts, New Hampshire, Vermont, and Maine.
32 The Northwest Territory spanned all or part of the eventual states of Ohio, Indiana, Illinois, Michigan, Wisconsin, and the northeastern part of Minnesota.

settlers between the Appalachians and the Mississippi; the second census, of 1800, saw their numbers quadruple to 400,000, twice as fast as the general population growth.

Jefferson was wary of tampering with Hamilton's financial plan, so he left the national bank in place, but he experienced the fallout of his own economic policies in 1807. In an effort to stop the ongoing harassment of US merchant ships by the British and French, he passed the Embargo Act, which banned trade with all foreign nations. But this resulted in exports declining by 75 percent and imports by 50 percent. It also put 30,000 sailors out of a job. It was a disaster, and the legislation was eventually repealed in 1809, just three days before Jefferson left office.

The Supreme Court passed a series of decisions during Jefferson's terms that laid the groundwork for federal power going forward. In the cases of *Marbury v Madison*,[33] *Martin v Hunter's Lessee*,[34] and *McCulloch v Maryland*,[35] the Court, under Chief Justice John Marshall (who had been appointed by John Adams), respectively established the principles of judicial review, the authority of the federal courts over state courts, and the existence of "implied powers" that enabled Congress to charter the national bank. These decisions left Jefferson fuming, but he could do nothing. Marshall was a distant cousin of Jefferson's and a fellow Virginian, but their

---

33 *Marbury v Madison*: James Madison refused to deliver signed letters appointing Marbury as a new judge. The Supreme Court ruled that Madison had no right to do that.

34 *Martin v Hunter's Lessee*: Denny Martin inherited land from his uncle, a loyalist in the war. The Virginia legislature voided the land grant and transferred a portion of it to David Hunter. Martin appealed the transfer, and the court held that a federal treaty dictating that Martin was entitled to it superseded Virginia state law.

35 *McCulloch v Maryland*: The state of Maryland passed legislation that imposed a stamp tax on the banknotes provided by the Bank of the United States. McCulloch refused to pay them, and the state of Maryland appealed, arguing the Bank was unconstitutional. The Supreme Court decided that the Bank is legal, as the end justified the means, and that it was unreasonable to expect every detail containing the means to be in the Constitution.

similarities ended there, and they often fiercely argued. Marshall was eager to see national rights prevail over those of the states, and his Court represented an early example of judicial activism that still prevails in the US today.

The Louisiana Purchase

The biggest success of Jefferson's two administrations came in 1803 with the Louisiana Purchase. Settlers to the west were a long way from the markets of the eastern seaboard, and some chose to sail down the Mississippi to the port of New Orleans, where grain could be sold and exported faster and for less. But New Orleans was held by the hawkish Napoleonic France, and the US considered how it might be able to wrest control of the coastal city for itself.

Napoleon had dreams of reviving the old colonialist empire in North America. After a slave rebellion broke out in Saint Domingue (now Haiti and the Dominican Republic), he sent 20,000 men under the leadership of his brother-in-law, Charles Leclerc, to subdue it. He gave him instructions to reaffirm French domination and power in the region, but the expedition turned into a disaster, as yellow fever ravaged the French forces, killing around half of them including Leclerc himself, and the rebels took back control of the island. Napoleon was left to reevaluate his goals for America.

Under the counsel of his finance minister, he doubted Louisiana's value without Saint Domingue. The US representatives Robert Livingston and James Monroe were in Paris attempting to buy New Orleans when the French Foreign Minister Charles Maurice de Talleyrand abruptly informed them that France was, upon reflection, now willing to sell the whole of Louisiana for a fee of $15 million.

They almost choked and asked for time to discuss the offer with Jefferson. But Talleyrand was in a hurry, and after some debate between them, the two sides agreed. Livingston and Monroe worried about how Jefferson would react, but when they told him, he was thrilled. The surface area of the United States had doubled in one fell swoop, adding 827,000 square miles of territory, in what was the most incredible real estate transaction of all time and one that the French must have questioned in no short order.

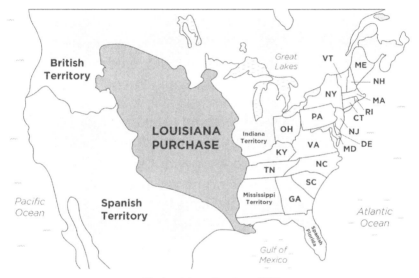

The Louisiana Purchase 1803

The Louisiana Purchase represented a huge chunk of land, but it was not exactly clear what the boundaries of the area were or indeed what was actually in it. Jefferson commissioned army captains Meriwether Lewis and William Clark to map out the territory, study its plant and animal life, and establish trade with the local Indian tribes. They set off on May 21, 1804, with a team of 45, and after no word from them was heard for over two years, they suddenly arrived back on August 12, 1806, having lost only one man. They had traveled 8,000 miles, drafted invaluable maps, filled notebooks with geographical information, identified at least 120 animal specimens and 200 botanical samples, and initiated relations with dozens of Indian tribes.

Zebulon Pike then led two further expeditions into the Louisiana territory to explore the northern reaches of the Mississippi and the Southwest. He traveled over the Rockies, lending his name to Pike's Peak in Colorado and getting himself arrested in New Mexico when he crossed the border, although he was let go unharmed. Entrepreneurs such as John Jacob Astor expanded his fur trading business into the Pacific Northwest, and freelance trappers such as Jim Bridger and John Colter followed, with middlemen, brokers, and dealers also finding ways to capitalize on this new land.

The acquisition also presented opportunities for deals of a rather more duplicitous nature. Aaron Burr, son of a Presbyterian minister and whose mother was the daughter of Jonathan Edwards, was orphaned at the age of two and raised by his wealthy maternal uncle. He began a career in New York politics and won a seat in the Senate, beating off the challenge of General Philip Schuyler, Alexander Hamilton's father-in-law. In 1800, he became vice president in the Jefferson administration.

But Burr was not popular in the administration and was even dropped from the ticket entirely in the 1804 election. He provoked Hamilton into a duel and killed him in July 1804, sparking denunciations from both Federalists and Democratic-Republicans, and he fled to the South to avoid arrest, his political career in tatters. He contacted the British ambassador, Anthony Merry, and claimed he could, with money and ships, pry the Louisiana territory away from the United States and create a new, sovereign nation. Merry responded that he would consider it.

Burr then recruited a ragtag band of followers including the governor of northern Louisiana, James Wilkinson, and planned to set up his force at New Madrid with the intent of capturing Baton Rouge and making it his headquarters. But Wilkinson lost his nerve and betrayed Burr's scheme, and when Burr realized the jig was up, he deserted his army only to be arrested as he tried to escape to Spanish West Florida.

On trial for treason with John Marshall presiding, Burr had covered his tracks well, and his lawyers skillfully managed to turn the trial into a referendum on the Thomas Jefferson administration itself. The judge, no friend of Jefferson, quashed the charge on a technicality, and Burr was suddenly a free man again, although he smuggled himself to England as a precaution. From there, he tried to gain English support to generate a Mexican revolution against Spanish rule, but the English were not interested, and when he was sure he would not be arrested, he returned to the US in 1812. He changed his last name to "Edwards" and set up a law office in New York where, after losing his and his new wife's wealth in speculative land deals,[36] he died in 1836 at the age of 80, an iconic American villain.

Go West

Manifest Destiny is a phrase originally coined by the journalist John O'Sullivan and was given to the idea that it was the destiny of the United States to expand its borders into the far reaches of the North American continent. Farmers continued to need land, and with rural families often producing up to six children or more, each would need an easy way to own land the way their fathers had done. The only way was west – and that meant onto lands held by Indian tribes.

---

36 She divorced him after four months, finalized on the same day of his death.

Many tribes were structured in ways that were similar to Jefferson's agrarian societies. They were domestic and patri-archal, and labor was divided by gender and age, with certain tribes grouped together to form a main tribe or a nation, such as the Iroquois or the Algonquian. Some had found ways to integrate into the white man's commercial world by acting as guides and middlemen in the fur trade, but they were wary of American westward expansion. They hoped their support of the French in the French and Indian War, and of the British in the Revolutionary War would prevent it, but they had been left disappointed on both occasions.

As the Americans started to pour into the Northwest Territory, Indians had to choose between two options: accept it and change ("accommodationists"), or refuse it and resist ("traditionalists"). Accommodationist tribes would sell or sign over their land for guarantees of protection or resettlement elsewhere, and the Iroquois, the Cherokee, and the Muscogee all signed separate treaties with the US government in the hope that the boundaries established would prevent further encroachment.

Accommodation sometimes meant assimilating tribal ways to white ones. The Cherokee nation adopted a consti-tution in 1827 that established a three-branch system of government and even included terms legalizing Black slavery and preventing Blacks from voting or holding any office. Cultural clashes led the Seneca tribe to fall victim to alcoholism, illness, and poverty, and they almost died out completely had Handsome Lake not experienced a dramatic vision that led to the formation of the Longhouse Religion. This combined Quaker values with traditional Seneca ones, and Lake secured the survival of the tribe by denouncing alcohol and urging the men to take up farming instead of hunting and waging war.

JEFFERSONIAN ERA (1801–1817)

The traditionalists, on the other hand, practiced resistance. In 1805, the Shawnee leader Lalawethika had a series of religious visions that prompted him to change his name to Tenskwatawa ("Open Door") and emphatically preach against accommodation. He developed a following that included his brother, Tecumseh, and they began organizing a pan-Indian resistance that included thousands of Indians from 14 distinct tribes. They founded a new village along the Tippecanoe River (north of present-day Lafayette, Indiana) and received support from the British Canadians who also feared American encroachment further north. Tenskwatawa's language grew increasingly militant, and William Henry Harrison, the main official in the Northwest, decided to pre-emptively attack the group in 1811 to prevent a strike of their own.

While Tecumseh was away in the South recruiting more tribes to his cause, a US military force approached Tippecanoe, and the Indians readied themselves for an attack. Tenskwatawa tried to reassure his followers by asserting he would cast spells that would make them immune from bullets, and they initially surprised Harrison's men, but the Americans regrouped and repelled them. Tenskwatawa was forced to retreat, and the Americans burned the village to the ground, brutally killing any Indian they captured.

This led Tecumseh to ally with the British in the War of 1812 and they played an integral part in the British successes in the Great Lakes region in the coming year. Tecumseh was killed in the Battle of the Thames in 1813, and Tenskwatawa himself moved back to the United States from Canada in 1824, dying in obscurity in 1836.

After the Battle of Tippecanoe and the War of 1812, the US had little trouble bending Indian tribes to its will. In 1828, the Sauk and Fox tribes of Illinois were ordered to vacate the Saukenuk area (present-day Rock Island, Illinois) and move west of the Mississippi – which caused a split between accommodationists and traditionalists. The accommodationists, led by Sauk Chief Keokuk, moved with most of the tribal members west; but the traditionalists, led by Black Hawk, chose to resist.

In 1832, a large force of US soldiers forced Black Hawk west, but he returned a few months later. He fought with the Americans at the Battle of Bad Axe, but was decisively defeated, captured, and humiliatingly paraded on a tour of the major eastern cities to demonstrate the futility of resistance. He was then relocated to an Iowa Indian agency, where he lived the remaining six years of his life under the supervision of a Sauk chief who had cooperated with the US.

The forced removal of Indian tribes was fully embraced during the presidency of Andrew Jackson (1829 – 1837), and he began floating the idea of uprooting the entire Cherokee tribe from Georgia. When Georgians began squatting on Cherokee land, the Cherokees took the state to court, arguing that it was in violation of agreements they had made with the Americans. The Marshall Court agreed (in the cases of *Cherokee Nation v Georgia* in 1831 and *Worcester v Georgia* in 1832), but Jackson had no time for technicalities. Under threat of invasion by the US Army, the Cherokee, Creeks, Chickasaw, Choctaw, and Seminole were forcibly removed from their lands to live in "Indian Territory" west of the Mississippi.[37]

The mass exodus became known as the Trail of Tears and saw approximately 100,000 Native Americans uprooted. In

---

37 The Indian Territory included parts of Kansas, Nebraska, and Oklahoma and was established in the Indian Removal Act of 1830.

the summer of 1838, the Cherokees were ejected from their homes at gunpoint and held in internment camps, where they were given little to eat and drink. Many succumbed to illnesses such as cholera and dysentery, and beginning in October, they were forced to march on foot for more than 1,200 miles over four months. The weather turned increasingly cold and bitter, and given little food or shelter, over 4,000 of the 16,000 who had set off died en route from exposure to the elements, malnutrition, whooping cough, and disease.

The United States, upon appropriating the Indian lands, became the new steward of an extraordinarily fertile, habitable farmland. This only encouraged them further, and even the Indian Territory was considered lost when, in 1907, Oklahoma became a state. Ownership of the Territory remains contentious, however: rulings by the Supreme Court in 2020 and 2022 first indicated that part of it was Indian tribal land and was subject to tribal authority, but then almost immediately handed power back to the states. In any event, there is little doubt that to the Native Americans, the arrival of the Europeans was an unmitigated disaster.

The War of 1812

The War of 1812 was fought between the United States and Britain from 1812–1815 primarily over disputes regarding maritime rights. Jefferson's Embargo Act had been passed to punish the British and French for their continued harassment of American merchant ships but did next to nothing to prevent it. Between 1793 and 1812, up to 15,000 American sailors had been "impressed" by the British – a practice of accusing American sailors of deserting their posts in order to force them into the Royal Navy's service, and by the time Jefferson left office in 1809, the situation remained unresolved.

Jefferson handpicked James Madison for president in 1809, and several new Republicans in Congress felt the United States needed to be much tougher with Britain. The new Speaker of the House, Henry Clay, struck a particularly anti-Federalist, anti-British tone and heatedly argued against rechartering the national bank on the grounds of its unconstitutionality. Regarding the British, he believed they deliberately fomented Indian disturbances on the frontier to slow American growth and became the leader of a group of Republicans called the War Hawks who wanted to strike back by invading Canada, even potentially assuming some of its lands.

Madison's Secretary of State, James Monroe, then obtained letters between John Henry, a former US Army captain, and Sir James Craig, the Governor General of Canada. These letters documented efforts between them to gauge whether New England Federalists would secede from the Union and join Britain were there to be a war, and when Congress was shown copies of the letters, the flames of the War Hawks' fire were stoked even more. It was later discovered that the letters were fraudulent, but the damage had been done.

In mid-May, the Republicans met to select the presidential nominee for the autumn of 1812. Speaker of the House Clay informed Madison that to secure the nomination, he would need to show the courage to declare war, and Madison duly steeled himself and sent the request to Congress. Despite vehement protests from representatives of New England (which had suffered the most from Jefferson's Embargo Act), Congress approved the declaration on June 17, 1812.

However, the US was in no fit state to conduct a war. The budget for the army and navy had been reduced over the 12 years of Republican rule, and the regular army consisted of fewer than 7,000 men commanded either by inexperienced, young officers or experienced, old, and senile ones. Congress authorized the army's expansion to 35,000, but service was voluntary and unpopular, and militias had no desire to leave their home states. The US Navy consisted of 16 ships compared to the Royal Navy's 500 – but the British ships were spread all over the world, and of its 240,000 regular army troops, only around 6,000 were in Canada.

The War Hawks were confident that a three-pronged invasion of Canada would undo the British. One prong, under General William Hull, would leap from Fort Detroit into lower Canada and take Fort Malden; the second, under General Stephen Van Rensselaer, would assault Queenston Heights on the Canadian side of the Niagara and move west to join Hull; and a third, under General Henry Dearborn, would travel up Lake Champlain and capture Montreal.

The results, however, were disastrous. Hull led his men to Fort Malden, but his supply train was intercepted, and he returned to Detroit. From there, he was informed in a bogus document that large numbers of Indians were on their way, and he surrendered his entire army and Detroit itself. Van Rensselaer crossed the Niagara and took Queenston Heights, but when he requested support from the New York State militia who had stayed on the other side of the Niagara, they refused to leave American territory, and he was forced to surrender. General Dearborn moved his forces up to the shore of Lake Champlain, but once again, militiamen refused to leave the United States, and Dearborn never even entered Canadian territory.

In 1813, General William Henry Harrison took command of the Army of the Northwest and set out to retake Detroit, but the first force he sent was stopped by a mixture of British and

Indians who massacred them along the River Raisin. Harrison lost over 900 men, with hundreds shot, tomahawked, and scalped during their withdrawal. In April, Dearborn and Zebulon Pike crossed Lake Ontario and captured the town of York (present-day Toronto), but Pike was killed, and the US troops burned down and looted government buildings before withdrawing. This destructive act was reciprocated by the British when they attacked Washington City the following year.

The Navy was more successful. Oliver Hazard Perry was sent to Lake Erie and engaged the British in a day-long battle on September 10, 1813, defeating and capturing six British vessels, and with the US in control of the lake, the British retreated from Detroit. Harrison launched another invasion into Canada where Tecumseh, who was helping the British, persuaded them to take a stand against the Americans at the Thames River. But Harrison's Kentucky militia broke through their lines, scattering the British and leaving the Indians to fight by themselves, where they were defeated by the Americans, and Tecumseh was killed in battle.

The Americans seemed to have the advantage, but they struggled to exploit their gains. In July 1814, General Jacob Brown crossed the Niagara and pushed north beyond Fort Erie and Chippawa. He engaged with the British at the Battle of Lundy's Lane, but both sides sustained such high casualties that Brown was forced to withdraw back to the United States. Then, after the defeat of Napoleon at Waterloo, the British reinforced their troop numbers by 15,000.

Fort McHenry still flies a replica of the same flag from the war of 1812 with 15 stars and 15 stripes.

The British planned to attack New York, raid the eastern American coastline, and attack New Orleans in the South. They began with the eastern coastline, looting and destroying buildings (including the White House and the Capitol) as they sailed up the Chesapeake Bay and on to Baltimore, where they encountered stubborn resistance. Baltimore citizens had worked on the city's defenses for more than a year, and the harbor entrance was blocked by a large chain and scuttled hulls. After two days of repelling British infantry and naval attacks, the British withdrew. It inspired the American lawyer and poet, Francis Scott Key, to write the poem "The Defense of Fort McHenry" which was eventually set to music and became the United States' national anthem, "The Star-Spangled Banner."

The British invasion of New York was also a failure. It was successfully repelled by Master Commandant Thomas

Macdonough at the Battle of Plattsburgh on September 11, 1814, moving Theodore Roosevelt to refer to it as the "greatest naval battle of the war." The American Navy also scored a notable single-ship success when the USS *Constitution* captured the British frigate the HMS *Guerriere*.

The British enjoyed some success in the south when the "Red Stick" Creek Indians attacked Fort Mimms, north of Mobile, Alabama. Roused by Tecumseh's traditionalist faction in the north, they killed hundreds of settlers including women and children, but the state militias of Georgia, Mississippi, and Tennessee soon rallied and repelled them. The Tennessee militia, under General Andrew Jackson, defeated the Red Sticks at the Battle of Horseshoe Bend, forced them to cede 23 million acres of land (half of central Alabama and part of southern Georgia), and aggressively pursued them into Pensacola, Spanish West Florida, claiming Spanish Florida for the United States.

Jackson then got word of Major General Sir Edward Pakenham's proposed attack on New Orleans, and he doubled back in January 1815. By this time, however, Madison had informed Congress that the United States was effectively bankrupt, and the dissolution of the national bank made it impossible to obtain more loans. The British, exhausted from their war in Europe, offered to negotiate a peace treaty in the Netherlands, and Madison sent five commissioners, including Henry Clay, where they agreed that all conquered territory would be returned and planned commissions to settle the boundary between the United States and Canada.

The treaty had been signed, but the news had not reached Andrew Jackson, who defeated a superior British force in New Orleans in a stunning victory. It made the public feel like the war had been won, even though it was technically a draw, and heralded the start of a career that would make Jackson a national hero and put him on the road to the White House.

The War of 1812 is often treated as a footnote in American history, but it did achieve a few notable results. It was the start of peaceful relations with the British that have lasted to this day; it destroyed the Indians' ability to resist American expansion, and it eventually drove Spain to abandon Florida in 1819, in an acknowledgement of the increasing strength of the United States. Politically, the War of 1812 dealt a death blow to the Federalist Party. Many of them believed the war had been waged to indirectly help Napoleon in Europe by forcing British troops abroad, and they opposed it by refusing to pay taxes or provide troops, and by boycotting war loans. They even suggested seceding from the Union at the Hartford Convention in 1814, but when the public discovered this, the Federalists were labeled as traitors, their brand tainted for good.

CHAPTER 7

THE ERA OF GOOD FEELINGS (1817–1825)

The American System

The Era of Good Feelings owes its name to the general sense of optimism and positivity that prevailed in the US at the time. The War of 1812 had ended; the Democratic-Republicans were in total control and free to concentrate on internal growth and security, and Americans liberally expanded west across the continent.

The Treaty of Ghent had ended the war, and while it restored territory and prisoners of war to the status quo as it had been before the war, it contained nothing about the impressment of sailors and the neutrality of American trading rights at sea, two of the main issues that had started it. Madison proposed investments to fortify the coast, enlarge the army and navy, and construct a national road system. Funding would be provided through protective tariffs, land taxes, and a recharter of the national bank.

Henry Clay in 1858, by Henry Darby.

These economic policies were termed the "American System," and they represented a significant departure from the traditional Jeffersonian thinking. They had, ironically, first been proposed by the Federalists in the 1790s, and Madison found surprising support from Henry Clay and John Calhoun, who were perhaps hoping to atone for driving the US to war in the first place. Clay eventually led a faction of the Democratic-Republicans into the National Republican Party in 1824 when Andrew Jackson appeared set to become president.

In 1817, James Monroe became the fifth US president. He set to work on a series of infrastructure projects including the development of turnpikes (toll roads), canals, railroads, and steamboats, built by private corporations or by the states. New York built a 363-mile canal between Albany and Buffalo called the Erie Canal, which transformed New York City into the nation's principal seaport; and the first commercial railway was built in 1830, with the *Tom Thumb* locomotive hauling a group of passengers on the Baltimore and Ohio Railroad. It eventually developed into a 73-mile track.

Costs of transporting goods on land fell by 95 percent between the years 1825 and 1855 which had dramatic effects on the communities inland. Markets for goods penetrated areas of the country that had previously been cut off, and a new consumer economy was launched as farming households used the profits from the sales of their crops to buy items such as furniture and clothing that they would traditionally have made at home.

New immigrants arrived and made their way west. They were attracted to the United States by the cheap land, and there was no military draft, censorship, or aristocrats. They were not required to have a passport upon entry, and taxes were a fraction of what they were in England or other European countries. In 1790, there were fewer than 4 million people in the country; by 1850, there were 23 million. To encourage migration west and raise revenues through sales, the government reduced the minimum allotment of land for sale from 320 acres to 80 acres and the price per acre from $2 to $1.25. Some did not pay anything at all and simply squatted on the land; others bought it off land speculators such as Moses Cleaveland (whose name is still attached to the city), who had bought it off the government and sold it for a profit.

Urban populations also grew. In 1800, only six cities had a population of more than 10,000; 50 years later, there were 64. As the industrialization model began to take hold, artisans and independent manufacturers were gradually turned into wage earners. Companies kept profits for themselves and their shareholders, and the gap between rich and poor grew wider. In New York, Boston, and Philadelphia, the top 1 percent of earners owned 25 percent of the wealth in 1825. Not much has changed in that regard. Today the top 1 percent own over 32 percent of the nation's wealth.

The Panic of 1819

The US endured its first widespread financial panic in 1819. The nation had undergone two smaller economic crises since its inception – one in 1797 that resulted from the bursting of a land speculation bubble and another in 1807 caused by the Embargo Act – but this one was nationwide and gave the country its first experience in bankruptcies, foreclosures, and unemployment. There would be plenty more in the years ahead.

It began with the death of the First National Bank in 1811. Constitutional questions and general suspicion of banks and their investors meant that the Bank's charter was not renewed, albeit by just one vote, and the War of 1812 was therefore financed by borrowing $16 million from private individuals. They proposed that these loans be exchangeable for stock in a new central bank, the Second Bank of the United States, which would operate under the same mandate as the First National Bank enabling the Treasury to manage its debt to them, create a common currency, and extend credit to entrepreneurs and corporations.

Legislation to recharter the Second Bank squeaked past the "old" Democratic-Republicans by a margin of nine votes (80 to 71) in 1816, and it led to the growth of state-chartered banks across the country. They issued their own paper banknotes against the gold and silver ("specie") they held in their vaults, but with the expansion into the West presenting an abundance of opportunities to offer loans and mortgages, they soon found themselves overextended.

The United States export markets then experienced a sudden drop in business when Britain and France, who had been at war for several years, ended hostilities and resumed their own agricultural production. Britain looked for cheaper alternatives to importing American goods and started importing cotton from India, sparking a 25 percent drop in the price of cotton in a single day and leaving US merchants asking for loans to finance the difference. Banks were unable to provide them, and a run on the banks took place, leading the state banks to call in their loans and mortgages and demand the borrowers repay them in gold and silver. They also sought to restock their own gold reserves by redeeming their paper money with the National Bank, but the National Bank was overextended too, and by July 1818, it had demand liabilities exceeding $22.4 million while its specie fund stood at $2.4 million. Companies were unable to pay their employees, and unemployment rose. New York's property values fell from $315 million to $256 million in 1820, and land values in Pennsylvania fell from $150 an acre in 1815 to $35 an acre in 1819.

The crisis unleashed a storm of protest and caused much soul-searching in the hearts and minds of the National Republicans. It was ultimately contained with the passage of various debt relief legislation that pushed out the date of debt repayments and allowed debtors to give land back to the government for which they would receive a credit in return. States also passed debtor relief laws that postponed payment on debts, and other laws that prevented creditors from creating undue hardship when calling in their loans.

One of the biggest impacts of the crisis, however, was voter reform. Voting was limited in most states to white males who owned property, but the panic had impacted so many people that other demographics started to demand a say in economic policy decisions. In 1826, New York changed its voter requirements to allow any white male to vote, and by 1840, almost every state had followed suit, enfranchising more than 90 percent of adult white males. The nationwide voting procedure also changed with the establishment of a nominating convention at which all voters could have a say, replacing the previous method wherein state legislatures selected candidates. Voter turnout soared. In 1821, voter participation was less than 30 percent, but by 1840, it had rocketed to 80 percent.

For Thomas Jefferson, the period was a gross betrayal of Democratic-Republican principles. He crowed, "I see nothing in this renewal... but a general demoralization of the nation." But America had turned a corner, and the deaths of Thomas Jefferson and John Adams within hours of each other on July 4, 1826, only served to emphasize the point.

The Industrial Revolution

The growth of manufacturing was one of the biggest changes in American society. The Industrial Revolution had begun in Britain in the mid-18th century, but it did not arrive on American shores until 50 years later due to wars, embargoes, and the obstructionism of the British. The British had developed the most powerful capitalist economy in the world by the end of the 19th century, and they greedily guarded the tools that had gotten them there, including forbidding operators and designers from sharing their knowledge with foreign agents.

An engraving of a Spinning Jenny.

The Industrial Revolution began with the development of large, complex machines that dramatically multiplied the output of a single person. The textile industry was transformed in England by machines such as the "Spinning Jenny," developed in 1764, which enabled one person to increase production by up to 30 times; and when James Watt invented the steam engine in 1765, a further revolution occurred in power. No longer reliant on human and animal muscle, steam engines were installed in cotton mills that drove the cotton spinning machinery so that by 1860, the cost of producing textiles had dropped to less than 1 percent of what it had been in the 1780s.

In 1793, Samuel Slater (called "the father of the American Industrial Revolution," by Andrew Jackson) landed in America and rebuilt the spinning machines. He had memorized their designs from those that he had used in England and developed the first textile mills in Rhode Island, establishing a template for others to follow. Francis Cabot

Lowell, on a two-year visit to see family in Britain, also spent time memorizing spinning machines and, upon his return to America, leveraged the revolution in capital to establish the Boston Manufacturing Company in 1814. By selling shares of the stock, he raised $100,000 and built his first textile factory at Waltham, Massachusetts. He then sold more stock to fund expansion into East Chelmsford where the Merrimack River fell 32 feet and promised unlimited power. The town grew to such an extent that it now bears his name, Lowell, and by 1821, the company was so successful that it was paying dividends of 27.5 percent to its shareholders.

Labor was no longer confined to skilled artisans – a simple "operative" would do. Lowell chose to use single women aged between 16 and 30 ("Lowell Girls") who were placed into the "Waltham System" of living in boarding houses provided by the company and supervised by older women. They would work six days a week on a strict schedule that included waking to the factory bell at 4:40 a.m., reporting to work at 5 a.m., taking half-hour breaks for breakfast and lunch, and finishing work at 7 p.m. Discipline was paternalistic, and the women were encouraged to use the library and attend lectures. They benefited by avoiding the claustrophobia and dirtiness that came with living in the slums and tenements of the cities and were glad to earn their own wages (which amounted to between $3 and $4 per week).[38] By 1840, over 8,000 women had worked for Lowell textile mills, making up over 75 percent of the workforce.

News of the success of the mills began to spread, and competition grew throughout the country. By 1860, there were 49 mills and workshops along a five-mile stretch of the Connecticut River alone. Mass manufacture was extended to

---

38 These 1840 wages are worth around $102–$137 today.

clocks, tools, sewing machines, and muskets, and managers soon had to find ways to keep sales up as prices incrementally decreased. Many smaller artisanal shops were put out of business, and employees were forced to accept wage cuts or work longer hours. In February 1834, Lowell Mills proposed a 15 percent wage cut, and nearly 2,000 women walked out, although they returned a few days later.

The exploitation of workers began manifesting in new ways, and the Northeastern states saw 172 strikes between 1833 and 1836. Working men protected themselves by forming trade unions, hoping to find sympathy from the courts. But the Supreme Court prioritized the rights of property and contract over arguments for fairness, and if working men chose to strike, the corporation would threaten mass firing or the prospect of being replaced with cheap immigrant labor. The time of paternalism was over; the fight between labor and capital was just beginning.

CHAPTER 8

JACKSONIAN ERA (1825–1849)

The Election of 1824

The US Constitution had not anticipated the development of separate political parties, and provided no guidance for nominating presidential candidates. When the two-party system developed, each party's congressional caucus would select its presidential nominee – the Federalists in Congress would select theirs, and the Democratic-Republicans theirs – and the nominees would be presented to the eligible voters.

After the Federalists' demise, the nomination by the Democratic-Republican caucus (dubbed "King Caucus" by its critics) was tantamount to election as president, and James Monroe ran unopposed in 1820. Under this process, the next in line was the Secretary of State (in this case, John Quincy Adams), but the voter reforms of the 1820s meant that 18 of the 24 states were now electing their presidential candidates by popular vote, and political factions developed within the Democratic-Republican Party that offered up different policy options to the voters.

Quincy Adams represented a faction that called itself the National Republicans. He was the son of John Adams, a Federalist, and although he had strived to distance himself from his father, working under both Madison and Monroe, his policies of protective tariffs, federally financed internal improvements, and support of the national bank had distinct Federalist tendencies. It gave him the backing of the New England states, and he counted James Monroe and Henry Clay, the Speaker of the House (who ran a separate campaign), as members.

In February 1824, the Congressional caucus convened in the House Chamber, but the active presidential candidates had encouraged their supporters to boycott the caucus system. When only one-quarter of the members turned up, they gave their nomination to the Treasury Secretary, William Crawford, despite a stroke he had suffered in 1823 that left him speechless and nearly blind. But as a former Georgia senator and "old" Republican, he was deemed preferable over either Quincy Adams or Clay. There was, however, one other candidate in the running too: Andrew Jackson.

***

Andrew Jackson was born in South Carolina in 1767 to Scots-Irish subsistence farmers. His father died in a logging accident just weeks before he was born, and his mother and two brothers died during the Revolutionary War (his mother to cholera, and his brothers to heatstroke and smallpox, respectively), leaving him with smoldering rage towards the British.

He studied law and moved to the frontier town of Nashville, Tennessee, in 1788 to work as a public prosecutor. He built up a successful law practice, lived in a mansion, bought slaves, and was elected to the House of Representatives. He served briefly in the Senate. He also became involved with Rachel Donelson Robards, who was married but had separated from her husband, Lewis. Jackson married Rachel in 1791 after he had heard that she had obtained a divorce, but Lewis then denied the divorce and filed a separate claim on the grounds of adultery. This left Jackson humiliated and hypersensitive, and when Charles Dickinson, an attorney and horse breeder, called Rachel a bigamist, Jackson was furious and challenged him to a duel.

Dickinson, an expert shot, accepted and fired first on the day, hitting Jackson in the chest. But Jackson stayed on his feet and fired back, also hitting Dickinson in the chest. Only this shot was fatal, and Dickinson died a few hours later. It turned out that bullet that Dickinson had fired deflected off Jackson's brass button, broke two ribs, and lodged inches from his heart. It was impossible to remove, and for the rest of his life, it caused Jackson to cough up blood and gave him intermittent bouts of fever. But he never complained, having gained his satisfaction.

The incident gave Jackson a reputation for violence and vengefulness in Tennessee, and his conduct in the War of 1812 compounded it. He was compared with the toughness of a hickory nut and known as "Old Hickory" by his troops, from whom he demanded absolute loyalty, shooting any for insubordination. He found enemies everywhere – the British in battle, the Spanish in Florida, and the Indians on the borders. He turned his victory over the Red Stick Indians at the Battle of Horseshoe Bend into a slaughter, with no exemptions for women and children.

He was subsequently named major general, and he scored his most spectacular victory against the British at the Battle of New Orleans. By that time in 1815, the war was essentially over, but the news had not reached the belligerents in the south, and he inflicted over 2,000 casualties on a much larger British force while suffering less than 70 himself. The date of the victory, January 8, was marked by celebrations every year until 1861, and Jackson was hailed as a national hero.

He remained in the army after the war and in 1818, received orders to subdue the Seminole Indians. They were raiding American territory from Spanish Florida, and liberally interpreting his orders, Jackson captured the Spanish military post of St. Marks and the town of Pensacola and hung two British subjects for aiding and abetting the Indians. He thought Monroe would be pleased, but it created a diplomatic incident with Britain, prompting the Secretary of War, John Calhoun, to urge Monroe to punish Jackson. But Monroe hesitated, and Congress was left to pass a resolution condemning the hangings, averting a crisis. In the end, Spain recognized its tenuous hold on Florida and sold it for $5 million to the United States in 1819. Jackson briefly served as the first territorial Governor of Florida in 1821, but he clashed with the outgoing Spanish governor and returned to Tennessee, citing his wife's poor health.

In the financial panic of 1819, Jackson found himself struggling to pay his debts and grew to despise the Second National Bank. He blamed the corruption of the Monroe administration for the panic itself and accepted the nomination for president by the Tennessee legislature in 1822, portraying himself as a Jeffersonian Republican and a defender of the people against those with special interests in government.

Capitol Hill looked on Jackson with foreboding but did not take his candidacy seriously at first. His reputation for dueling had revealed a questionable temperament, his successes had all come on the battlefield rather than the House, and Jefferson described him as a "dangerous man," noting the contempt Jackson appeared to show for laws and institutions. But in 1824, the radical section of the Democratic-Republican Party was running out of options, and with Crawford viewed as a desperate alternative, Jackson soon began to emerge as the only candidate with a true national following.

Initial Result of 1824 Election		
Candidate	Popular Vote %	Electoral Vote
Andrew Jackson	41.36%	99
John Quincy Adams	30.92%	84
William Crawford	11.21%	41
Henry Clay	12.99%	37

On the day of the election, Jackson won more votes than any other candidate but did not win the majority, having won 99 of the necessary 131 in the Electoral College. And so, under the rules of the 12th Amendment, the choice of the president would defer to the House of Representatives in a contingent election – an unprecedented event that had all the makings of trouble.

The House was limited to choosing from the three candidates who had received the most votes, so Clay was immediately eliminated. An absolute majority of 13 was required for victory and each of the 24 states had a single vote, but no member was bound or required to vote the way his state had voted, so there was no guarantee that Jackson, as the leading candidate, would win.

Clay despised Jackson and, as the Speaker of the House, saw an opportunity to influence those states that had voted for him to cast their ballots the way he wanted. He had previously denounced Jackson for his invasion of Spanish Florida in 1818 and questioned Jackson's commitment to his American System, which Clay considered crucial to the economic growth of the United States. Quincy Adams, however, did support it, and Clay and Adams arranged to meet on January 9, 1825. Here, Clay allegedly agreed to support Adams for the presidency in return for the position of Secretary of State, which would put Clay in a prime position for his own presidency once Adams's terms expired.

Their purported deal became known as the "corrupt bargain" – so called because after the meeting, Kentucky's 12 representatives, who had initially voted for Jackson, suddenly changed their vote for Adams - and so did Ohio, and then New York. Adams had somehow accumulated the votes he needed, and when Clay announced one week later that he had accepted an offer to be Secretary of State, the public reacted with outrage. The mere offer of the Secretary of State position to Clay had made the presidency look like a bargain, and Jackson was furious, vowing to win the election of 1828. The affair also split the party into the National Republicans and the Democratic-Republican Party, and the present-day two-party system was created.

In his first Annual Message in 1825, Adams announced a spectacular national program with federal sponsorship for a network of highways and canals, arts and sciences, and the creation of a national university and astronomical observatory. But he was mocked by critics for haughtily assuming his agenda would be embraced after such a controversial and divisive election, and Jackson watched on, seething.

Jackson recruited Martin Van Buren and John Calhoun into his ranks; held rallies, barbecues, and parades; and published anti-Adams newspapers. Adams responded by holding his own fundraisers and raking up charges of adultery against Jackson, but his cause was doomed. All the momentum was with Jackson, and there was nothing Adams could do to undo it. Jackson won the 1828 election by a landslide (178 to 83 in the electoral vote) in a true watershed moment that signaled the shift in political conscience from classical republicanism to democracy.[39]

Jacksonian Democracy

On Jackson's inauguration day, which was the first to take place on the east portico of the Capitol (they were moved to the west in 1981), the crowd swelled to more than 20,000. Feelings were running high with respect to both the 1824 and 1828 elections, and with the White House open to all for the post-inaugural reception, hundreds poured in. The fragile furniture was damaged as attendees pushed their way past servants carrying food and drinks, and eventually, servants had to set up washtubs of juice and whiskey on the White House Lawn to draw the crowd outside and restore order.

Andrew Jackson in 1845, aged 78.

---

39 Classical republicanism places the emphasis on representation by elected officials acting as intermediaries between the people and the government. These representatives make decisions on behalf of the citizens based on their judgment and expertise. Democracy places the emphasis on direct participation by the people themselves.

Jackson himself was numb to all this fanfare, however. His wife, Rachel, whom he loved deeply, had died in December 1828 of a massive heart attack after failing to endure the stresses of the campaign and the personal attacks on her in the press. It left him devastated, vowing never to forgive his political enemies, whom he felt had caused her death.

Jackson proceeded to make sweeping changes to the administration. He dismissed 10 percent of the federal employees, including all of Adams's cabinet appointees, bureau chiefs, land and customs officers, and federal marshals and attorneys. Known as the "spoils system," he installed Martin Van Buren as Secretary of State, despite the latter's inexperience in foreign policy, and those who had championed his cause in other positions. This removed valuable skills and experience but ultimately placed accountability for Jackson's campaign promises directly on his shoulders.

Jackson wanted to rid Washington of perceived corruption and reestablish the dominance of farmers in the republic, so he set about taking down the American System. He terminated the transportation subsidies and vetoed the Maysville Road bill in 1830 – a bill that had authorized Congress to purchase stock in a turnpike in Kentucky. He claimed it was unconstitutional as it gave the federal government too much power in state matters.

He then turned his attention to tariffs. The Tariff of 1828 had been signed into law by his predecessor, John Quincy Adams, and imposed duties on manufactured products and various imported raw materials. It was deeply unpopular in the South, and the senator from South Carolina, Robert Hayne, denounced the duties as unconstitutional and even threatened secession in 1830. John Calhoun, Jackson's vice president, supported Hayne's position and argued that a state could nullify a law and refuse to enforce it, although Jackson remained silent.

Jackson soon made his position clear however, at a dinner honoring Thomas Jefferson's birthday. Rising to make a toast, he purposefully looked at the attendees around the table dead in the eyes and said, "Our Union, it must be preserved," publicly embarrassing Calhoun and prompting him to resign as vice president in the summer of 1832.

Calhoun continued to rail against the tariffs after his resignation and supported the passage of South Carolina's Ordinance of Nullification which annulled the tariff laws in the state. The situation threatened to get out of hand when the governor of South Carolina began organizing armed resistance to the collection of the tariff, to which the president angrily cited treason and prepared to send troops in response. In the end, a compromise Tariff of 1833 was negotiated by Henry Clay, Daniel Webster, and John Calhoun; both sides backed down, and South Carolina repealed the Ordinance.

***

One of the tenets of Jacksonian democracy was a general opposition to banking, and more particularly, to the Second Bank of the United States. Among the Bank's responsibilities was its requirement to redeem state-issued banknotes that they received from individuals in gold and silver ("specie"), which they would request in return from the state banks. This effectively prevented the state banks from printing too many notes as they always had to have specie on hand to meet such a request from the Second Bank, and it indirectly gave the Second Bank the power to control the economy as it could make demands as often or as little as it suited them.

Another responsibility of the Second Bank was national investment. One-fifth of the Bank was capitalized by the federal government, and the Bank could invest in infrastructure projects that did not need the states' approval, leaving Jackson to rail against how the people were left out of the decision-making process.

The Bank could have alleviated some of these concerns, but the first president of the Bank, William Jones, had few political skills and even went bankrupt himself. It had been under his watch that the Panic of 1819 had begun, and his replacement, Langdon Cheves, implemented credit contraction policies that had only made the Panic worse. In 1823 however, Cheves was replaced by Nicholas Biddle, an outstanding financier who nursed the economy back to health by increasing the number of banknotes issued by the National Bank and putting restraints on the expansion of the number of state banknotes.

But the Bank openly offered generous loans and stipends to congressmen including Henry Clay, who was its legal advisor, and Jackson believed it put too much power in too few hands. He called the Bank a "many-headed monster," but he could do nothing about it until its charter expired in 1836, and with John Marshall sitting as Chief Justice and Congress filled with National Republicans whose savings and loans were tied up with the Bank, there was little chance of winning a battle to bring it down.

Anticipating what was to come, Henry Clay, a consummate politician, decided to make the first move. He convinced Biddle the charter should be brought forward to 1832, prior to the presidential election, as he believed it was more likely to pass the current Congress than the next one. Assuming it did pass Congress, he did not expect Jackson to use his power of veto against it, although if he were to do so, Clay further believed that Congress would pass it anyway. Conversely, if Jackson signed it, the Bank would be rechartered, and certain Democrats would accuse Jackson of betraying their principles. All in all, it would be a win for the National Republicans.

So, the petition went to Congress, and they voted 107-85 to reauthorize it, leaving Biddle anxiously awaiting Jackson's response while Clay sat back with his feet up. Contrary to Clay's initial assumption, Jackson did veto it, declaring furiously that the Bank "pitted the planters, the farmers, the mechanic, and the laborer" against the "monied interest," and that "the Bank [was] unauthorized by the Constitution, subversive to the rights of States, and dangerous to the liberties of the people." Jackson argued that the Bank was the very embodiment of the corrupt political elite and called on his supporters to side with him as he championed the rights of the common man.

Democrats were thrilled by this rhetoric. Clay sat back up and argued that Jackson was acting out of personal and political motives rather than in the best interests of the country – but his arguments were in vain, and an attempted override of the veto in the Senate only achieved a 22-19 vote, fewer than the two-thirds required.

This turned the 1832 presidential election into a disaster for Clay. He was defeated in a landslide by Jackson who then went on the offensive against the Bank with a plan to destroy it by demanding the government's $10 million be withdrawn and placed in seven select state banks (he eventually increased this to 300). The Secretary of the Treasury, Louis McLane, refused to follow Jackson's orders fearing the economic instability it would cause, and Jackson replaced him with

William J Duane, who also refused, so Jackson replaced him with Roger Taney. Taney duly complied, and Biddle fought back by restricting loans given by the Bank in an effort to generate public outrage towards Jackson's policies. But this caused more financial hardship, and people took their anger out on the Bank itself.

With the Bank dead, Jackson vetoed every spending bill, most of which were designed to improve the infrastructure of the country. He then started selling off government-owned Western land and, by 1835, the federal debt, which was $58 million when he came to power, was completely paid off – the first and only time in the nation's history that it was totally free of debt.

But the good times were short-lived. The last stockholder meeting of the Bank took place on February 19, 1836, which was followed almost immediately by the most severe economic depression in American history: the Panic of 1837. This was partly due to a real estate bubble that had been enabled by Jackson when he terminated the Bank, for it had indirectly given license to the state banks to go on a reckless spending and borrowing spree without oversight. The American economy would suffer for decades in this "free-banking" era until, finally, the Federal Reserve was established 77 years later, in 1913.

The Whig Party

The National Republicans' broader policy of national economic union and development was personified by the Second National Bank and when the Bank collapsed, the National Republicans collapsed with it. The United States' first national convention took place in 1831, during which the Democratic-Republican Party formally adopted the name Democratic Party and a new party was established in place of the National Republicans – the Whig Party.

"King Andrew the First," used in campaign posters, 1833.

The Whig name echoed England's recent history and substituted Andrew Jackson for the king as the personification of political tyranny and absolutist power. The Whigs believed in protective tariffs, national banking, and federal aid for internal improvements – which largely reflected the National Republicans' American System – and their party attracted urban businesses, financiers, and large-scale commercial farmers.

The Whig Party also promoted moral reforms, which appealed to evangelical protestants, and drew antislavery advocates and reformers calling for less harsh treatment of the Indians. Clay believed that the abolition of slavery in

129

Kentucky could act as a template for other slave states to follow and condemned the cruel treatment of the Indians under Jackson's Indian Removal Act of 1830.

At the end of Jackson's second term, his vice president, Martin Van Buren, swept into the White House in 1836. The destruction of the Second Bank and the "Specie Circular" (an executive order issued by Jackson demanding public lands be paid for in gold or silver rather than paper money) had put the American economy front and center during the election, but as soon as Van Buren arrived in office, he was tasked with stemming the financial crisis that was the Panic of 1837 – something he was wholly incapable of doing.

The panic was primarily driven by a real estate bubble and the erratic nature of the American banking policy. After the Second National Bank lost its charter, the nation's 850 banks issued banknotes with little restraint, but these notes depreciated rapidly after the Specie Circular, and within months, banks found themselves unable to redeem the notes they had printed. Trade came to a standstill, and people were left holding banknotes that were effectively worthless.

Hundreds of banks and businesses failed, and thousands of people lost their land. Book assets of all state banks fell by 45 percent, and railroad stocks fell by 63 percent. Food riots occurred in Baltimore, Boston, Albany, and New York City, and many debtors fled to Texas, an independent republic that had no extradition laws with the United States.

Van Buren moved government funds from the state banks into an independent treasury – which ensured the funds were safe but had the effect of locking up valuable gold and silver that could have been used to help remedy the situation. Van Buren also had a reputation for enjoying an extravagant lifestyle that included hiring expensively decorated carriages and demanding he be served with gold spoons at the White House. When the Whig candidate, William Henry Harrison, was mocked by a Democrat newspaper for being "a simple frontier Indian fighter, living in a log cabin and drinking cider," the Whigs pounced.

Van Buren had no chance, and Harrison crushed him in the election of 1840 by 234 electoral votes to 60. After three decades of rule by Jefferson and his heirs, an opposition party that was dedicated to market growth was in charge, although it would not be long before one of Jackson's protégés took it back.

The Second Great Awakening

A Second Great Awakening occurred during this period that began around the year 1795 and lasted through the 1830s. Generally considered a milder form of the First Great Awakening, it arose out of a pushback against the secular nature of the new nation, which had explicitly separated church from state in its First Amendment and had made no mention of God in its constitution. Skeptical and secular movements had grown in popularity, including Deism, Unitarianism, and Freemasonry, and Thomas Paine's *Age of Reason* (1794) even denounced the Old Testament for its "obscene stories, voluptuous debauches, cruel and tortuous executions, [and] the unrelenting vindictiveness."

The Second Great Awakening consisted of three phases. The first phase (1795–1810) was led by preachers such as James McGready, John McGee, and Barton Stone, who held "camp meetings" with as many as 20,000 people in attendance. With the lessons of Jonathan Edwards and George Whitefield ringing in his ears, McGready thundered on about Hell and its torments so vividly that people would wail and cry, and the revival spread to Kentucky, New York, and Ohio, before eventually expanding all over the country.

The second phase (1810–1825) was more conservative and was led by theologians such as Timothy Dwight and Lyman Beecher. Timothy Dwight was the president of Yale College and the grandson of Jonathan Edwards, and he promoted religious revivalism at the College as a reaction against the Enlightenment's anti-Christian philosophy. His passionate sermons prompted half the senior class to enter the pastoral ministry.

The third phase (1825–1835) was driven by the Presbyterian minister and abolitionist, Charles Grandison Finney, who converted thousands during revivalist meetings in upstate New York and emphasized personal conversion and social reform. In the South, thousands more – slaves and slave-holders alike – converted to Baptism and Methodism, which became the fastest-growing religions in the country.

The Second Great Awakening impacted the country in profound ways. The differences between the North and South were accentuated by the lessons given by the churches in each – the North taught abolition; the South taught submission. Women were allowed to pray alongside men and vote on church matters for the first time, giving them newfound confidence that they leveraged to form movements such as the Women's Temperance Organization and the Women's Suffrage Movement. Schools and colleges were founded to teach children to read, and the country's literacy rate increased.

The Age of Reform

Following the Second Great Awakening, a reform spirit took hold of the country during the years 1830–1850. Many women found themselves within a rising middle class, able to purchase goods and read newspapers (the number of which had increased by 180 percent between 1830 and 1850) for the first time. They now had time to assess their prescribed role in society and perhaps even change it, and Lucretia Mott and Elizabeth Cady Stanton started a campaign for, among other things, the right to vote and equal pay. They held the first women's rights convention at Seneca Falls in 1848.

A daguerreotype claimed to be of Joseph Smith, 1844.

New spiritual and communal living communities grew in popularity. These included the Shakers, the Millerites (now the Seventh-Day Adventists), and the Mormons. These last were founded by Joseph Smith after he claimed to have received visions of God and Jesus during the height of the Second Great Awakening in 1820, and in 1823 claimed to have had another vision from an angel called Moroni. The angel told him of an ancient record, inscribed on golden plates, that told of three tribes of Israelites who had traveled to America and had been rewarded with their own visitation by Christ. Eventually, the tribes had gone to war, and the Nephite tribe was reduced to just one man, Mormon, who had buried the plates.

Smith retrieved these plates from the Hill Cumorah, New York, and translated and published them in 1830 in the *Book of Mormon*. He founded his own church that year and, persecuted partly due to his preaching of polygamy, left New York with his followers, ending up in Illinois. An anti-Mormon lynch mob found and killed Smith and his brother Hyrum in 1844, and Brigham Young arose as Smith's successor, leading the Mormons to Utah, where they settled in Salt Lake City and lived apart from society. They now number over 16 million members worldwide.

A philosophical movement called Transcendentalism also developed at this time, led by Ralph Waldo Emerson. Closely linked to English and German Romanticism, its core beliefs included the concepts that people are inherently good and that one's potential was limitless, and the movement took progressive stances on various topics including women's rights, abolition, and education. Based in Boston, the Transcendental Club included Henry David Thoreau, Margaret Fuller, and Amos Bronson Alcott. Thoreau attempted to put Transcendentalist thought into practice by living self-sufficiently, alone in a cabin in the woods for two years. He wrote a chronicle of his experience published in 1854 called *Walden*, a classic piece of American literature within which he explores themes of nature, politics, and philosophy.

An early abolitionist movement emerged when Evangelical Christian groups in the Northeast began using the Bible to decry slavery. William Lloyd Garrison – a prominent Christian and journalist – published the first issue of his newspaper, *The Liberator*, in 1831, which supported the immediate freeing of all slaves. Frederick Douglass escaped from slavery in 1838 (by disguising himself as a sailor and boarding a train to the North), attended abolitionist meetings, and gave speeches denouncing slavery across the North and Midwest. He published his autobiography, *Narrative of the Life of Frederick Douglass*, in 1845 and soon became one of the leading figures in the abolitionist cause.

The various reform movements drew both praise and criticism. None of the major movements had large followings, few people participated in the activities they held, and the abolitionist cause was no vote-winner. But the reform movements reflected the sensitivity of certain people to the inequalities of American life. Alexis de Tocqueville, the French political thinker who wrote *Democracy in America* (1835 and 1840), recognized these reform movements as the signs of a healthy society, writing, "the gradual development of the equality of conditions... possesses all the characteristics of a divine decree." The American Dream may not yet have been a reality, but it was certainly being pursued.

The Mexican–American War (1846–1848)

The Northwest Ordinance of 1787 made it easy for territories to become states. When a territory reached a population size of 60,000, the government would take a referendum on statehood and present it to Congress for approval. In 1818, Missouri applied for statehood, and it would become the first state west of the Mississippi in 1821.

Missouri, however, sought to be recognized as a slave state, and a political crisis was triggered in Congress. If it were accepted on these terms, it would upset the balance of slave states to free states, and the additional two senators and an indeterminate number of congressmen could disrupt the northern campaign of tariffs, infrastructure investment, and defense of manufacturing. In response, the New York Congressman, James Tallmadge, proposed that as a condition of Missouri's admission, no further slaves were to be imported into the state, and all children born after Missouri's admission were to be born free, thereby setting out a plan for gradual emancipation.

The South erupted in rage. In Congress, Representative William Cobb of Georgia looked Tallmadge dead in the eye and declared, "You have kindled a fire which all the waters in the ocean cannot put out, which seas of blood can only extinguish" and continued, "if a dissolution of the Union must take place, let it be so!" And in a moment, all the underlying tensions of the slavery issue threatened to snap.

The moderates in the House duly took note, and Congress was divided completely on sectional lines (the North for, the South against). The Tallmadge Amendment passed the House but died in the Senate, where the Southern senators held greater influence, but its death did nothing to allay the fears it had sparked. Thomas Jefferson wrote to John Holmes, "This momentous question, like a fire bell in the night, awakened and filled me with terror. I considered it at once as the knell of the Union."

Henry Clay, working with the president, James Monroe, offered up a compromise. They suggested that Missouri be admitted as a slave state and Maine, who had also petitioned for statehood, as a free state, with slavery to be prohibited in the remainder of the Louisiana Purchase territory north of the 36°30' parallel (Missouri's southern boundary). Enough northern congressmen supported this compromise for it to pass, as it was evident that the territory above the 36°30' parallel was far bigger than the lands below it. That is unless one counted land farther west in the Viceroyalty of New Spain and in the area that is now Texas.

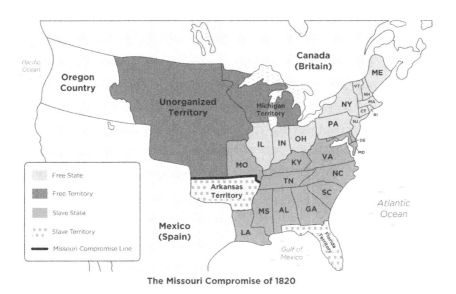

The Missouri Compromise of 1820

The Viceroyalty of New Spain had been founded in 1535, and Spain had clung on to it for almost three centuries. When Napoleon invaded Spain in 1808 and the Spanish monarch, Charles IV, was forced to abdicate, it triggered a crisis that led to demands for reform that reached into the Spanish empire and resulted in the Mexican War of Independence (1810 – 1821). This ended when Mexico established an independent constitutional monarchy, but it was short-lived, and Guadalupe Victoria set up a republic a year later.

Texas itself was part of the Mexican state of Coahuila y Tejas. The area was so large and underpopulated that the Mexican government appointed "empresarios" in 1824 to encourage American settlers to emigrate to the state, hoping that, because Mexico could not provide a military presence, the increased number of Americans would help prevent raids from Indian tribes. Stephen Austin, an empresario originally from Virginia, brought 300 families and their slaves to Texas in 1825, and between 1821 and 1836, an estimated 38,000 settlers trekked from the US into the region.

The land was perfect for livestock, farming, and growing cotton, and once word spread, Mexico grew concerned that the United States would try to annex the state. Mexico issued the Law of April 6, 1830, which banned further immigration from the US, angering the settlers and causing a series of skirmishes between them and the Mexicans. This happened to coincide with a revolt in Mexico itself led by General Antonio Lopez de Santa Anna who, upon taking over the presidency in 1834, attempted to centralize and consolidate his power by dismissing state legislatures and disbanding militias.

Fearing the loss of Texas, Santa Anna sent 500 soldiers under the leadership of his brother-in-law, General Martín Perfecto de Cos, to stabilize the region. But they were fought back to the south of the Rio Grande, leaving Santa Anna furious, and taking personal command, he marched north and reached the Alamo Mission (near modern-day San Antonio, Texas) on February 23, 1836. Here, he oversaw a siege of the compound during which approximately 200 Texans held them off for 13 days until they were finally overwhelmed. The Mexicans then executed every man, woman, and child in the mission, stacking and burning the bodies.

This outraged and terrified the Texans, motivating many of them to join the army. Texas had declared itself an independent republic during the siege (on March 2), retaliating at the Battle of San Jacinto under their commander, Sam Houston. Vengeful cries of "Remember the Alamo" rang out as the Texan army surprised and routed the Mexicans, capturing Santa Anna himself and making him sign the Treaties of Velasco. These recognized Texas as an independent republic and ended the war, but Santa Anna had been deposed in his absence, and the new government refused to acknowledge the treaties, and skirmishes continued into the 1840s.

Texas remained a republic and looked for annexation into the United States, applying for statehood as early as 1836. But Andrew Jackson blocked the request, as he wished to avoid the antislavery issue, and his successor, Martin Van Buren, also blocked it, as he feared starting a war with Mexico. The first Whig president, William Henry Harrison, took over in 1840, but he died of pneumonia only 32 days into his presidency and was replaced by John Tyler.

Tyler's views were at odds with many in the Whig Party, including Henry Clay and Daniel Webster, and he vetoed several bills (including one to reestablish the National Bank) that drove the party to expel him from it in 1841. He was an advocate of states' rights and slavery, and he assembled his own power base, turning the annexation of Texas into a campaign issue for the 1844 election. But Tyler eventually dropped out, and the Whig Party, led by Henry Clay, lost the election to the Democrats. The little-known protégé of Andrew Jackson, James Polk, then came to power.

***

James Polk, 1845.

James Knox Polk was born in Pineville, North Carolina in 1795, the first of ten children of parents of Scots-Irish descent. After graduating from North Carolina University, he moved to Tennessee to study law, where he befriended Andrew Jackson, even earning himself the nickname "Young Hickory." Polk won a seat in Congress in 1824 as a representative for Tennessee, spoke out against the corrupt bargain that had put Quincy Adams in the White House, and was a prominent ally to Jackson during the war against the Second National Bank.

He became governor of Tennessee in 1839 after the Democrats lost the White House, only to lose it in 1841, and any promise of a political career appeared to be drifting away. But in 1844, the Democrats were looking for a suitable presidential candidate after ruling out Martin Van Buren, so they turned to the "dark horse," James Polk.

The annexation of Texas quickly became a central political issue. Henry Clay, the Whig candidate, confused the public after it was revealed that he personally supported annexation but was afraid for the state of the Union were it approved. This upset both the Northern Whigs, who feared annexation would expand slavery, and the Southern Whigs, by implying that they wanted to break up the Union. Polk, on the other hand, displayed no such ambivalence and ran on a platform embracing expansionism and manifest destiny, and it won him the election – if only by the thinnest of margins (winning by just over 38,000 votes of a total of 2.64 million). It simultaneously ended Clay's presidential hopes for good.

On December 29, 1845, Polk signed the bill that annexed Texas as the 28th state of the Union. This was immediately rejected by the acting President of Mexico, José Joaquín de Herrera, who pledged to defend the land. But he was ousted in a coup, and in a period of political upheaval, the Mexican presidency changed hands four times in 1846. In the meantime, Polk ordered troops under General Zachary Taylor into Texas to establish the border.

Taylor directed them south from Corpus Christi to enforce the Rio Grande boundary, and when some of his men were attacked north of the river in April 1846, Polk declared war. Owing to the Americans' superior artillery and armaments, Taylor defeated a much larger Mexican force in two battles – the Battle of Palo Alto and the Battle of Resaca de la Palma – and the Mexicans were pushed back over the Rio Grande.

The US regular army only numbered around 8,000 men at this time, compared to the Mexicans' 30,000, but Mexico had no armaments industry of its own; its artillery was in a derelict state, and its gunpowder was of such poor quality that it could barely power cannonballs – often the US troops merely had to step to one side to avoid them.

The United States authorized the call-up of 50,000 volunteers under the auspices of the state militias to increase its presence on the battlefield, with the first of these arriving in July 1846. Taylor aimed to capture Monterrey and attacked it on September 21. As they gained ground, the Mexicans pulled back into the city, engaging in house-to-house fighting that finally forced the Mexican general, Pedro de Ampudia, to ask for a parley after three days. Taylor allowed Ampudia's troops to take their ammunition with them as they evacuated the city, and an eight-week armistice was signed, within which it was agreed that Taylor would not advance more than 50 miles farther to the south.

Meantime, Santa Anna, who had been living in exile in Cuba, was scheming to find a way back into Mexico. He convinced Polk that he would end the war on favorable terms to the United States if he were allowed to return, so the US let him slip back in. But as soon as Santa Anna arrived, he offered his services to a panicking Mexican government and was given command of the army. He led 15,000 troops into battle against 5,000 Americans at the Battle of Buena Vista on February 22, 1847, but, once again, the US artillery proved too powerful, and the Mexicans were forced to withdraw.

Polk then ordered Colonel Stephen W Kearny and his Army of the West (around 1,700 men) to march from Fort Leavenworth (in modern-day Kansas) to Santa Fe in New Mexico. The journey spanned almost 850 miles of some of the driest land in the United States, and Kearny and his troops showed extraordinary perseverance to push through it, for which they were rewarded by taking Santa Fe without a shot being fired. The Mexicans had laid down their arms upon their arrival, and Kearny then took 300 men on to California, where he planned to meet up with the US Navy under Commodore Robert Stockton in San Diego.

Simplifying matters, John Frémont, a military officer and explorer, had followed the Texas playbook by leading a group of Californians to declare independence from Mexico as the "Bear Flag Republic." With their goal to become part of the United States, they looked on as Kearny and Stockton defeated a small army of Mexicans at the Battle of Río San Gabriel on January 8, 1847, and California was in American hands. To cap it off, the Missouri volunteers left in Santa Fe had, under Alexander Doniphan, continued into modern-day northwest Mexico and captured El Paso, Texas, at the Battle of El Brazito.

Winfield Scott, by Robert Walter Weir (1855).

The greatest success, however, occurred two weeks after the Battle of Buena Vista on the other side of Mexico, in the east.

Here, Polk had sent a second army under General Winfield Scott to invade the Mexican heartland from the coast to take Mexico City. Scott landed with 12,000 volunteers and regular soldiers (which included the future generals Robert E. Lee, George Meade, Ulysses S. Grant, and Thomas "Stonewall" Jackson), and attacked Veracruz on March 24, 1847, claiming it after a 12-day siege.

Santa Anna had not arrived in time to provide support for his compatriots at Veracruz, and hoping that yellow fever and other diseases would reduce the American numbers, he moved his army south, allowing Scott to march inland. He set up fortifications at Cerro Gordo, but after his position was spotted by American scouts, his army was totally routed, and Scott continued to Puebla where the inhabitants offered no resistance. He then proceeded to Mexico City itself, and in a series of battles culminating in the Battle of Chapultepec and the storming of the city gates, the capital was occupied by the US, upon which Scott became military governor.

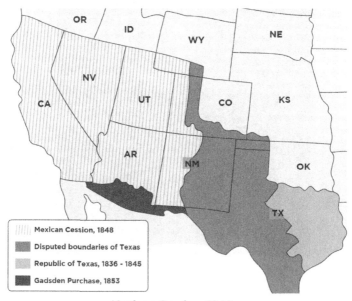

Mexican Cession, 1848

It was a disaster for Mexico. It signed the Treaty of Guadalupe Hidalgo on February 2, 1848, and ceded 55 percent of its territory to the United States. This included the modern-day states of California, New Mexico, Utah, Nevada, and most of Arizona and Colorado, and it recognized the Rio Grande as the border with Texas (disputes arose between Texas and the US government as to the westerly and northerly boundaries of the state). In return, Congress paid $15 million to settle all Mexican claims and debts to the US.

Then, in a classic case of "to the victors belong the spoils," gold was found in Sutter Creek near Coloma, California, on January 24, 1848. This was nine days before the treaty was signed, but news of it had not arrived, and it served to set off the world's most incredible gold rush. "Forty-niners," named for the year the prospectors made their way to California, came from all over the country to try to make their fortunes, and the resentment felt by Mexico for the war was made more bitter by the boomtown conditions now unfolding in its old territory. The events still resonate today, and relations between Mexico and the United States have never fully recovered.

## PART THREE

CIVIL WAR AND RECONSTRUCTION

CHAPTER 9

THE CIVIL WAR ERA (1850–1865)

Slavery before the Civil War

For a country established on the principles of the Enlightenment, slaves must have wondered why overtures about liberty and equality reached only so far. Indeed, at one point during the Revolution, it seemed slavery was on its way out. Vermont banned slavery outright in 1777, followed by Pennsylvania and Massachusetts, and the British abolished the slave trade in 1807, freeing more than 800,000 enslaved Blacks in the British West Indies. They sent slave ship patrols in the Atlantic to enforce the new laws.

Some slaves were deported after emancipation. High numbers of immigrants from Europe had brought down the cost of labor, and following the example set by the British who had resettled former slaves in Sierra Leone, the American Colonization Society founded the colony of Liberia for the same purpose. Between 1822 and 1867, around 13,000 African Americans settled in Liberia – but the policy was never popular, either with the former slaves or with American abolitionists. They argued that deportation provided slaveholders with a way to rid themselves of the "problem" of free African Americans and that it was a form of racism itself.

Certain religious groups and evangelists openly denounced slavery. Jonathan Edwards may have owned slaves, but he authored *Freedom of the Will,* a book that inspired Samuel Hopkins and other radical congregationalist ministers to condemn slavery based on the concept of free will. The Quakers were prohibited from owning slaves and even petitioned for the abolition of slavery in 1790. Charles Grandison Finney used his platform in the Second Great Awakening to add his voice to the cause.

Just after the Revolution, many Southerners were comfortable with a decline in the practice of owning slaves, and no fight was made to include slavery in the Constitution partly because it was becoming a less cost-effective labor resource. Overproduction and shipping disruptions dramatically affected the price of their main cash crop, tobacco, and in the first year of the Revolution, tobacco production in Virginia dropped to less than 25 percent of its annual prewar output. In 1792, Virginia passed a law permitting slave owners to formally emancipate their slaves.

But this tendency away from slavery was reversed by two inventions. The first was the Spinning Jenny which enabled textiles to be mass-produced, creating a huge demand for cotton ("white gold"). The second was the "cotton gin" (short for cotton engine), developed by Eli Whitney in 1793, which separated cotton fibers from their seeds, increasing production by up to 25 times. Within a decade, cotton production had increased from 2 million pounds to more than 60 million pounds, and by the 1830s, it had become the largest American agricultural export. But the cotton still needed picking, so slave numbers shot up, growing from 700,000 in 1790 to over 3 million by 1850.

The growth in the cotton industry was not the only reason to continue with slavery – fear also played a role. In August 1791, a former slave, François-Dominique Toussaint Louverture, led a massive rebellion against his masters in Haiti, leading the slaves in "pillage, rape, torture, mutilation, and death" in revenge for their enslavement. Slaveowners were dragged from their beds to be tortured and killed, and the heads of slaveowners' children were displayed on pikes at the front of the rebel columns.

Nat Turner's Slave Rebellion.

Slave revolts had occurred in the United States before – in South Carolina (1739), New York (1741), Virginia (1800), Louisiana (1811), and most disturbingly in Southampton County, Virginia, in 1831. This was Nat Turner's Rebellion which began when Turner, who claimed he was chosen by God to lead the enslaved Blacks from bondage, set off with about 70 armed slaves and free Blacks to slaughter the white neighbors who had enslaved them. They bludgeoned Turner's master, along with his wife and children, to death with axes and attacked about 15 homes in the area, killing between 55 and 60 whites. The militia retaliated, and the rebellion broke up. Turner initially managed to escape, although he

149

was tracked down and sentenced to death by hanging with 21 of his followers. This event led to a general feeling of hysteria and paranoia, resulting in another 200 slaves killed by white mobs and militias afterwards. Virginia and several other states passed laws that made it illegal to teach Blacks to read or write and forbade Blacks from preaching.

More drama occurred at sea. In 1839, 53 slaves aboard the *Amistad* managed to pick or break their locks before killing all the crew members apart from two, whom they instructed to return to Africa. The crew appeared to comply, but after first heading east, they turned north, and after 63 days at sea during which several Africans died of dehydration and dysentery, the ship grounded on Long Island, New York. Charged with piracy and murder, the case against the slaves became highly politicized and gave local abolitionist groups a powerful stage to denounce slavery. The case eventually made its way to the Supreme Court, which granted the Africans their freedom, and they were later returned to Africa.

Slave uprisings forced the whites to develop arguments to justify slavery, such as claiming there were fundamental differences between the races that went beyond skin color. One argument, presented by Joseph Arthur de Gobineau, asserted that a distinct hierarchy of races existed in which white Aryans sat at the top and Blacks at the bottom. Josiah Nott, an American surgeon, declared that there had been multiple creations (a theory known as polygenesis) that had produced superior and inferior races. Some proclaimed that slaves lived like another family alongside their master, although the question of why a family would happily sell one of its members remained unanswered. Others asserted that slavery was a legitimate institution supported by God and that it had existed throughout history or that slavery was just punishment for African Americans as the descendants of Noah's son Ham.

Arguments for slavery were also developed on economic grounds. James Henry Hammond, the governor of South Carolina, declared, "There must be a class to do the menial duties, to perform the drudgery of life." George Fitzhugh, a sociologist, proclaimed that all labor was a form of enslavement, pointing an accusatory finger at the wage slave society of the North. He said that the slaves were, in fact, more cared for in old age than any other working group, making them, in some senses, the freest people in the land.

It was impossible, however, for slaveowners not to be conscious of the exploitation they were guilty of. But with huge profits rolling in and the possibilities of expanding west, they suppressed any guilt and fear they might have felt and were afraid of losing the capital investment they had made in their slaves.

In the North, the emancipation movement enjoyed a rebirth in the 1830s. William Lloyd Garrison's newspaper, *The Liberator*, advocated for the immediate emancipation of all enslaved men and women, to which Georgia reacted by offering $5,000 for Garrison's arrest and conviction. The North considered him something of a radical too, as he pronounced the Constitution illegal (seeing that it allowed for slavery), and he attacked the church for its refusal to condemn slavery.

But the Southerners feared these noises from the North. At their request, President Andrew Jackson banned the post office from delivering abolitionist literature in the South, and a "gag rule" was passed that forbade the discussion of bills that restricted slavery. The battle lines were being drawn.

The Compromise of 1850

After the Mexican–American War, expansionism remained popular within the US, with some Southerners going so far as to imagine a great slave-owning republic that would stretch across the Caribbean to Brazil. But such dreams took a backseat to reality as Congress debated whether and to what extent slavery would be permitted in its new territory.

Polk had signed the Treaty of Oregon with Britain in 1846, which accepted the border between the US and British North America at the 49th parallel, except for Vancouver Island, which was retained entirely by the British. US expansionists were surprised that Polk had not sought to push the border further north, but he wanted to avoid fighting two wars at once, especially against a military power as mighty as Britain.

Such humility was in no way evident at the Treaty of Guadalupe Hidalgo however: deliberation about how to treat the land in the southwest began even before the Mexican–American War ended. On August 8, 1846, David Wilmot, a Democrat representative from Pennsylvania, introduced legislation declaring that "neither slavery nor involuntary servitude shall ever exist" in lands won in the Mexican–American War (the "Wilmot Proviso"), upon which both the House and the Senate immediately split on sectional, rather than party, lines. But the legislation could not gain the necessary majority in the Senate, and the proposal went no further. Wilmot was not an abolitionist, but he wanted a place where free white Pennsylvanians could work without the competition of slave labor, and like him, many Northern Democrats were unhappy that Southern interests appeared to take priority over their own.

The administration put forward the idea of extending the Missouri Compromise line of 1820 westward, but this proposal also failed. The debate shifted as to whether Congress was empowered to determine the status of slavery in any territory. John Calhoun argued that the territories belonged to all the states, and so a citizen from any state could take their property, including slaves, into them. The Democrat Lewis Cass of Michigan counterargued, suggesting the people of the territories be allowed to decide for themselves whether or not to permit slavery.

Cass's solution was termed "popular sovereignty," but this option was not enough for some Northern Democrats who formed a third party, the "Free Soil" Party, in 1848. They opposed any further expansion of slavery into the western territories and based their arguments on the threat to free labor and the economic livelihoods of white workers, rather than on the morality of slavery. They nominated Martin Van Buren as their presidential candidate.

The split within the Democrats presented a massive opportunity for the Whigs, who nominated Zachary Taylor as their presidential candidate. He was a slaveowner himself but a hero of the Mexican–American War, and he ran on a platform that did not commit him to any position regarding slavery in the new territories. The strategy worked, and Taylor and the Whigs took the White House in 1848.

By this time, the California Gold Rush was in full swing. California's population had grown by 100,000, and $10 million[40] worth of gold was pulled from the ground in 1849. Taylor urged California and New Mexico to write constitutions and apply for statehood immediately, bypassing the territorial stage as he assumed (correctly) that both consti-

[40]   Around $400 million today.

tutions would reject slavery. Since taking the White House, Taylor had taken a firm antislavery position, and he was eager to make gains.

California submitted its application as a free state in 1850, which would make it the 31st state – and would upset the delicate ratio of 15:15 between free states and slave states. This would enable free states to dominate legislation, so many Southern Democrats called for a secession convention, which Taylor responded to by warning a group of Southern leaders that he would hang anyone who tried to disrupt the Union by force or conspiracy.

A compromise was urgently needed, and the indomitable Henry Clay, by now 73 years old, leapt into action. He put forth a set of eight proposals in an "omnibus bill" that included accepting California as a free state, allowing popular sovereignty in the territories of New Mexico and Utah, abolishing the slave trade in Washington, DC, and passing a Fugitive Slave Act that would require citizens to assist in the recovery of fugitive slaves.

Clay strove for six months to find the requisite number of supporters, but its structure as one giant package caused the omnibus bill to fail in the Senate. John Calhoun, dying from consumption, argued the compromises would betray the South and threatened secession, and, in a surprising turn, Daniel Webster spoke for three days as he urged Northerners to forgo antislavery measures for the good of the Union. This speech obliterated Webster's support in New England, where it was interpreted as an attempt to win Southern support for a run at the presidency, and Henry Clay saw his omnibus bill hacked into pieces. With extraordinary careers behind them, both Clay and Webster died in 1852, doubtless harboring regrets for some missed opportunities along the way.

Two years prior, Zachary Taylor had also died (within five days of contracting a stomach virus – believed to be cholera, although it remains uncertain), and his vice president, Millard Fillmore, took office. He made it clear that he supported the resolutions in Clay's bill, and the forthright Illinois senator, Stephen Douglas, decided that each resolution needed to be considered separately for it to have a chance of passing. He then set out tirelessly to build support for each; by mid-September, he had succeeded, and the Compromise of 1850 became law.

The Compromise of 1850	
North benefits	**South benefits**
California admitted as a free state	No slavery restrictions in Utah or New Mexico territories
Slave trade prohibited in Washington, DC	Slaveholding permitted in Washington, DC
	Texas gets $10 million
Texas loses boundary dispute with New Mexico	Fugitive Slave Law

People celebrated in the streets, talk of secession was averted in the Capitol, and Douglas was hailed throughout the country. But it was not long before cracks started to appear; this time, there would be no compromise.

Build Up to War

The US tried to move on after the Compromise of 1850. In 1853, Congress purchased a strip of land from Mexico along the Gila River for $10 million (the Gadsden Purchase), which they planned to use for a transcontinental railroad. They also hoped the payment might soothe some of the bad feelings that lingered from the war.

The country greeted over 1.7 million new immigrants between 1841 and 1850. They mainly came from Ireland, Germany, and Britain, and they flocked to the cities to take jobs in the manufacturing industry. Another financial panic, due partly to inflation caused by the discovery of gold in California, struck the nation in 1857, with the telegraph (invented by Samuel Morse in 1844) helping to spread it faster than ever before. Most of the harm was felt in the North, as the South's cotton market had remained relatively stable, and over 5,000 banks failed, and unemployment rocketed upwards.

The compromises that had been reached in 1850 remained controversial. Harriet Beecher Stowe wrote *Uncle Tom's Cabin* in 1852 in response to the Fugitive Slave Act, and it became an instant classic, selling over 300,000 copies in its first year. It told the story of a gentle, dignified slave who was brutally whipped to death by his new owner after refusing to reveal the whereabouts of other runaway slaves, and it used the death of Christ as a metaphor. The book changed many people's perceptions of slavery in the North and was eagerly paraded by abolitionists. It outraged the South, where mere possession of the book could lead to incarceration and where Stowe was furiously denounced by politicians and newspapers. But its impact was immense, and when Abraham Lincoln met Stowe in 1863, he reportedly asked her, "Is this the little woman who made this great war?"

Opposition to the Fugitive Slave Act grew when a runaway slave, Anthony Burns, was captured and put on trial in Boston. The act was despised in the city, and groups had formed to actively resist its enforcement. But the court applied the law and sent Burns back to Virginia with crowds jeering and booing as he was marched in shackles to the

THE CIVIL WAR ERA (1850-1865)

waterfront. As a result of the trial, Massachusetts passed the most progressive liberty law the nation had seen up to 1854 by prohibiting state officers from aiding slave catchers at any step in the process of fugitive slave removal. It also laid the burden of the proof of ownership and escape of the slave squarely on the shoulders of the slaveholder.

The slavery issue was so divisive that it soon completely tore apart the Whig Party. At the 1852 Whig National Convention, the party was torn between selecting Millard Fillmore – a "doughface" (a Northerner not opposed to slavery) – and Winfield Scott, the hero of the Mexican–American War who endorsed the Compromise of 1850. After an astonishing 53 ballots, Scott was nominated, but he suffered a crushing defeat to the Democrat, Franklin Pierce (another doughface), in the election of 1852.

Then, in 1854, Stephen Douglas presented the Kansas-Nebraska Act to organize the Territory of Nebraska – an area covering the present-day states of Kansas, Nebraska, Montana, and the Dakotas – according to popular sovereignty. But this contradicted the Missouri Compromise (which banned slavery above the 36°30' line), and the House erupted. Free Soilers, Northern Whigs, and certain Northern Democrats opposed it, with the Ohio senator Salmon Chase condemning it as a "gross violation of a sacred pledge." But it passed in the Senate by 37-14 and did repeal the Missouri Compromise, creating two new territories (Nebraska and Kansas) which allowed for popular sovereignty.

The church in Ripon, Wisconsin, where the
Republican Party was founded.

Divisions in the Whig Party could not be resolved after
the passage of the Kansas-Nebraska Act, and the party
collapsed. Representatives looked around for another party
to join, with some opting for the Know Nothing Party (an
anti-immigrant, anti-Catholic party that was popular with
working men), but it split sectionally in 1855 and faded
away. Another option was the creation of a new party, and
on March 20, 1854, a group of abolitionists, antislavery
individuals, and Northern Whigs came together in Ripon,
Wisconsin to discuss its formation. This one would oppose
both the spread of slavery into the western territories and
the terms of the Kansas-Nebraska Act, and then, paying
homage to Jefferson's Democratic-Republican Party of the
past, they gave themselves a name: the Republican Party.
Before long, Free Soilers and many Know Nothings had also

joined, and in 1856, they nominated John C Frémont as their presidential candidate.

In the meantime, the Democrat Party had judged that the incumbent president, Franklin Pierce, was too unpopular in the North, so they unceremoniously dumped him and replaced him with the long-serving doughface senator from Pennsylvania, James Buchanan. This decision paid off, winning the Democrats the election of 1856,[41] which was decided entirely along sectional lines.

Even religious groups failed to find a compromise. Methodists, Baptists, and Presbyterians all split between North and South, and other groups such as the Episcopal Church and Catholic Church struggled to keep their members together, either by stressing political realities or remaining silent on the whole debate. Some Congregationalists were so infuriated that they provided rifles (so-called Beecher's Bibles, named after Henry Ward Beecher – the minister, abolitionist, and brother of Harriet Beecher Stowe) for use by antislavery combatants in Kansas between 1854 and 1861.

These were the years of "Bleeding Kansas" – outbreaks of guerilla warfare between pro-slavery and antislavery forces that saw the killing of 55 people and put the slavery issue front and center. Kansas bordered both slave and free states, and pro-slavery "border ruffians" crossed into the state to take up arms against its antislavery forces, destroying property, intimidating voters, and rigging elections.

Franklin Pierce, the president in 1854, took a pro-slavery position which angered many in Congress, including the Massachusetts senator, Charles Sumner. He delivered an

---

41   This remains the only time in US history when a party denied the renomination of an incumbent who yet still won the election.

impassioned five-hour speech over two days ("The Crime Against Kansas") to decry the supporters of slavery, and with tensions at boiling point, a representative from South Carolina, Preston Brooks, waited until the Senate had adjourned before attacking and viciously beating Sumner with his cane. He collapsed into a bloody mess and was unable to return to the Senate for three years due to his injuries. The Massachusetts legislature chose to leave his seat empty as a gesture against the savagery of the South.

In 1857, the new president, James Buchanan, revealed his own pro-slavery position by endorsing the new Kansas constitution, the Lecompton Constitution, which approved slavery in the territory. But the constitution had been supported by no more than 20 percent of the state and had been boycotted by antislavery groups, so Congress called for resubmission of the territory's constitution to the state's voters. The North noted Buchanan's position with regret, and with no hope of finding support from the legislature, they looked to the judiciary for support.

The case of *Dred Scott v Sandford* found its way to the Supreme Court in 1857, two days after President Buchanan took office. Scott had sued for freedom on the basis that because his owners had taken him from a slave state (Missouri) to the "free" territory of Illinois and Wisconsin, he could no longer be classified as a slave. After retrials and reversals of decisions from lower courts over a period of eleven years, a decision on his status was finally due to be made by the highest court in the land.

Buchanan was aware of the impact it could have, and he called on American citizens to respect the Supreme Court's decision. This breached the protocol of the executive office remaining aloof of the judiciary, but Buchanan had no time for etiquette, and followed this up by putting pressure on the Court to provide a ruling that would broadly settle the slavery issue. In a 7-2 ruling, the Court first stated that enslaved Blacks were not citizens under the Constitution, so could therefore not bring a suit – which should have brought the whole case to an early conclusion. But it then went on to declare that, even if he were allowed to bring a suit, he would still have lost because the Missouri Compromise of 1820 was unconstitutional, and Congress did not have the authority to prohibit slavery in the territories. Consequently, US citizens could take their property (including slaves) into any state, free or not.

The Court had announced itself as pro-slavery, to the delight of the South. But the North and the Republican Party were incensed. The Republicans' whole platform rested on preventing the extension of slavery into the territories, and when the Supreme Court upheld the constitutionality of the Fugitive Slave Act in its ruling in *Ableman v Booth* (1859), the North began to envision a nation without the South.

These issues provided the canvas for the 1858 Illinois senatorial contest between Stephen Douglas of the Democrats and Abraham Lincoln of the Republicans. Douglas, standing at 5'4", was known as the "little giant," and was the most famous and most popular Democrat in the country. But he had opposed the Kansas Lecompton Constitution, which alienated him from the South, and had to be careful not to alienate them further with a strong stand against the *Dred Scott* decision. Abraham Lincoln, not quite 50 years old and standing at 6'4", was largely unknown at the time but had a very successful law practice and had served one term in the House of Representatives as a Whig representative.

The two met in a series of seven debates that were covered nationally by the press and were attended by crowds of up to 20,000 people. Douglas supported popular sovereignty, which Lincoln claimed would be impossible to sustain, and he stressed the moral injustice of slavery and that Douglas was part of a conspiracy to nationalize it. Douglas responded by saying that he disagreed with the *Dred Scott* decision and claimed that Lincoln was an abolitionist looking for equality between the races. This was an incendiary accusation in Illinois, and Lincoln replied that Blacks had the "right to eat the bread, without leave of anybody else, which his own hand earns," and declared that he was not looking to abolish slavery where it currently existed. In the end, Douglas won the election by a very slim margin, but his comments on *Dred Scott* drove away the South. The Republican Party had, on the other hand, found itself a new star.

***

A year after the Douglas-Lincoln debates, the abolitionist John Brown planned to lead a slave revolt that would overwhelm the South and rid the country of slavery once and for all. Brown himself was something of a drifter, having been jailed at one point for attempting to take back property he had lost in the Panic of 1837. But he fully embraced the fight against slavery, and in the 1850s he traveled to Kansas with five of his sons to fight against the pro-slavery forces in the contest for the territory.

In 1856, he killed five pro-slavers which triggered a summer of guerrilla warfare, and he returned east a year later to carry out his vision of a mass slave uprising. He secured the support of six prominent abolitionists, assembled an invasion force of 22 men, five of them Black, and plotted to seize the armory at Harper's Ferry in Virginia and go on a rampage across the country. But word spread, and a company of marines led by Robert E Lee surrounded them and killed ten, two of whom were Brown's sons.

Badly wounded himself, Brown was found guilty of treason and sent to the gallows, and although the raid was a total failure, Brown was held up as a martyr, and the whole event electrified the country. Ralph Waldo Emerson praised him for being prepared to act, and a song in his honor – "John Brown's Body" – was written and used as a marching song by the Union soldiers during the Civil War.

The South was horrified and condemned Brown as a lunatic and a criminal. The Southerners feared a slave revolt, but they feared a revolt led by a white man just as much, maybe more, and their fears were exacerbated when Hinton Rowan Helper's *The Impending Crisis of the South* (1857) called on non-slaveholders of the South to repudiate slavery. Helper argued that it hurt the economy by concentrating wealth in the hands of the few, but the South said that he was acting as an agent of the North and was attempting to split the Southerners along class lines. They banned its possession and distribution and burned all the copies they could get their hands on.

The Democrats met in April 1860 in Charleston, South Carolina to prepare for the election. It was chaos. Charleston was the most pro-slavery city in the US and was filled with "Fire-Eaters" who considered Stephen Douglas, the Democrat frontrunner, a traitor for his opposition to *Dred Scott* and his support of popular sovereignty. Fifty delegates walked out in protest, and Douglas failed to obtain the two-thirds majority required to win the nomination before the convention adjourned.

Six weeks later, the Democrats reconvened in Baltimore, Maryland, but delegates from the Deep South walked out again. This time the Southern Democrats set up their own rival nomination convention and selected John C Breckinridge of Kentucky, a former vice president of James Buchanan, as their nominee, running on a platform of expansion of slavery into the territories, strong enforcement of the Fugitive Slave Act, federal protection of the rights of slaveholders, and the annexation of Cuba. Douglas was nominated by Northern Democrats on a platform of popular sovereignty.

The Democrat split was an opportunity for the Republicans. They met in Chicago in May and acknowledged that they needed a candidate who would take the Northern states that Buchanan had carried – New Jersey, Illinois, Indiana, and Pennsylvania – with William H Seward emerging as the frontrunner. But he spoke of an irrepressible and inevitable conflict, and moderates were put off, looking around for other options.

Two other candidates, Salman Chase and Edward Bates, did not do enough to unite the discrete factions of the party, so Republicans turned to a fourth candidate, Abraham Lincoln. Lincoln had been quietly considering a run for the presidency since his contest with Douglas in 1858, and had ensured that the debates had been widely published. He was an excellent speaker, and he appealed to the delegates for his moderate position of keeping slavery out of the territories but accepting it where it existed. To attract the swing states, his platform also included import tariffs, internal improvements, a transcontinental railroad, and a Homestead Act to encourage migration west. After the third ballot, Lincoln won the nomination.

In addition to the Northern Democrats, Southern Democrats, and Republicans, a fourth party also ran in the election: the Constitutional Union Party. They chose not to mention slavery at all, nominating John Bell (a slaveowner) of Tennessee as their candidate. With four candidates on the field, it came down to a battle in the North between Lincoln and Douglas, and a battle in the South between Breckinridge and Bell. Lincoln did not even feature on the ballot in ten slave states, but with the Democrats totally divided and the vote completely sectional, Lincoln won every Northern state except New Jersey and won in the Electoral College with a landslide of 180 votes.[42]

The South were beside themselves. With the White House now full of supporters of John Brown, abolition, and liberty laws, they anticipated the loss of the Supreme Court and questioned what they could do. Privately, the governor of South Carolina, William H Gist, had informed the other Southern governors of his state's intention to secede if Lincoln won the election, and on December 6, 1860, they voted to withdraw from the Union. This was followed by Mississippi, Florida, Alabama, Georgia, and Louisiana. Sam Houston, the governor of Texas, opposed secession, whereupon he was removed from his position, paving the way for Texas to follow.

The Constitution had made no provisions for a withdrawal of a state, and the legality of seceding was debatable – which would give the North, and the Republicans, the right to put down any rebellion. But the South cared little for technicalities. Delegates from six of the seven seceded states (Texas arrived late) drafted a new constitution for the Confederate Nation in Montgomery, Alabama, on March

---

42 The North had many more people than the South, hence many more Electors in the Electoral College.

11, 1861, which was almost identical to the US Constitution but added passages that protected slavery and the rights of slaveowners.

The Confederates elected Jefferson Davis, the Mississippian senator and hero of the Mexican–American War, as its first president and the Georgian Alexander Stephens as vice president. Stephens underlined the role of slavery in his Cornerstone Speech of March 21, 1861, saying that the new government is "founded upon the great truth that the negro is not equal to the white man; that slavery subordination to the superior race is his natural and normal condition."

But this was a gamble for the South. They played their hand anticipating that Congress would outlaw slavery in the near future and believed that by making the first move, they would gain an advantage. James Buchanan, president when the South seceded, believed secession to be illegal but did nothing, and Congress debated how to keep the Southern states in the Union. They argued for extending the Missouri Compromise line of 1820 or amending the Constitution to incorporate slavery, but the Republicans' platform had been based on the refusal to extend slavery, and they had no wish to alter it. Lincoln himself, who had stayed relatively quiet during the whole process, now pronounced his opposition to anything that would expand slavery – and so the North and South came to an impasse.

In his first inaugural address on March 4, 1861, Lincoln was eager to appear accommodating. He said that the government would "hold, occupy, and possess the property and places belonging to the Government... but beyond what may be necessary for these objects, there will be no invasion, no using of force against or among the people anywhere." But this raised the question of what property, exactly, the government held in the Confederate states.

The answer to this question was four military forts, including two key ones – Fort Pickens in Pensacola, Florida, and Fort Sumter in Charleston, South Carolina. The Confederacy sent a delegate to Washington, DC demanding the surrender of Fort Sumter to South Carolina in its status as a newly independent republic, but President Buchanan refused, upon which 6,000 South Carolina militiamen surrounded the fort. Buchanan, in one of his last acts as president, authorized an unarmed merchant ship containing 200 men and supplies to sail to the fort on January 9, but it was fired on by South Carolina cadets, and the ship abandoned its mission.

Lincoln, now president, had to decide whether to give it up or resupply it. After discussions with his Secretary of State, William Seward, and General Winfield Scott, he decided to resupply it, conscious of how it would look if he chose to back down. On April 4, he informed Southern delegates that he intended to resupply the fort at a certain date and time and that he would send no troops or weapons. But Jefferson Davis and the Confederate cabinet decided this amounted to a hostile act and sent forces to the fort to demand capitulation.

Major Robert Anderson of the Union stood firm, and the Confederate cannons began to fire. After nearly 36 hours, the Union forces ran out of resources and were forced to surrender, and two days later, on April 15, Lincoln called for 75,000 militiamen to put down the "insurrection." Four more states joined the Confederacy – Virginia, Arkansas, North Carolina, and Tennessee – and the Confederacy moved its capital from Montgomery, Alabama, to Richmond, Virginia. The war had begun.

First Years of the Civil War (1861–1863)

In retrospect, it is easy to claim that the Union was destined to win. It had larger resources, exceptional political and military leaders, and a moralistic cause – but the reality was that, at the beginning of the war, there were no certainties at all. The Union did have some important advantages, however. It had more people – in 1860, 18.5 million people lived in the Union compared to 5.5 million free men and 3.5 million slaves in the Confederacy.[43] It also had more manufacturing capabilities – 101,000 factories compared to the Confederacy's 21,000; and 20,000 miles of railroad compared to the 9,000 miles of the Confederacy's. They also had twice as many draft animals, a professional army and navy, and a first-rate president in the form of Abraham Lincoln.

But Jefferson Davis was also an excellent leader, and the Confederacy had other advantages. For one, it did not need to invade the North or capture any Northern state or city – it simply needed to hold off any Union advance. Conversely, the Union had to invade, and the Confederate area was huge, consisting of over 750,000 square miles and more than 3,500 miles of coastline. Militarily, the North had fine generals in Ulysses S Grant and William Tecumseh Sherman, but Robert E Lee and Thomas Jonathan "Stonewall" Jackson were equally capable, and both the North and the South had similar numbers of generals and officers who had been trained at West Point and had had experience in the Mexican–American War.

The one wildcard was whether any foreign nation, particularly Britain or France, would intervene. France's intervention in the Revolutionary War had had an instrumental effect on

---

43 The border states held 2.5 million free people and 500,000 slaves.

the outcome of that conflict, but there was less at stake for either Britain or France now, so their involvement seemed unlikely. In the end, the closest Britain and the United States came to war was in 1861 when the US Navy captured two Confederate envoys aboard a British mail ship. Britain demanded their release together with a formal apology and even sent troops to Canada in indignation. Lincoln obliged, and the crisis was averted.

Attention first turned to the border states: Delaware, Kentucky, Missouri, and Maryland. Delaware's status as a Union state was never in doubt – slavery was rare, and the state was already economically integrated into the Northern economy. But the others were hoping to remain neutral, however hard that may be.

Regarding Kentucky, the Confederacy viewed the Ohio River as a valuable defensive barrier between themselves and the North. The birthplace of both Lincoln and Davis, Kentucky had the most divided loyalties of all the states (three of Henry Clay's grandsons fought for the Union, four for the Confederacy), and the state became a hotbed of guerilla warfare.

Missouri had seen plenty of guerilla warfare during the "Bleeding Kansas" era. Battles now took place between pro-Southern forces led by the state's governor, Claiborne Fox Jackson, and Union troops, and Jackson was defeated and exiled from the state in March 1862. The Union spent the remainder of the war fending off guerilla attacks from the likes of William Quantrill, "Bloody Bill" Anderson, Cole Younger, and Jesse and Frank James, who had picked up the pro-Southern baton.

Maryland was home to the White House itself, which prompted Lincoln to take political as well as military measures to keep the state in the Union. He suspended the writ of habeas corpus, which meant that anyone suspected of Southern sympathizing could be arrested and detained without being given a hearing in court, and it resulted in the arrest of 19 members of the legislature. His administration then imposed martial law on the state, ordering the seizure of property owned by Confederate sympathizers, including their slaves.

A fifth border state, West Virginia, was created in 1861 when 50 counties broke off from Virginia in support of the Union. It was admitted to the Union as a state in 1863, and had an economy dominated by self-sufficient farmers in the rugged western counties. It had far fewer slaves and conducted most of its trade with Ohio and Pennsylvania, so its split from Virginia was understandable. All five border states stayed within the Union, but the divided loyalties within them saw much bloodshed during the war.

Focus turned toward the capitals of the Confederacy and the Union, which were only 100 miles apart. Washington, DC was especially vulnerable, being located opposite Virginia across the Potomac, and the Union Army secured it by crossing the river and capturing the high ground in Arlington and Alexandria. Lincoln looked to the ageing general-in-chief, Winfield Scott, to develop a strategy for winning the war, and he proposed the "Anaconda Plan." This consisted of a joint army and navy force of 80,000 men pushing down the Mississippi to split the Confederacy in two, with the US Navy blockading the southern coastline to disable the South's economy and prevent them from obtaining supplies. If this were to fail, a final step, which Scott anticipated as two to three years away, was to attack Richmond directly with 300,000 men.

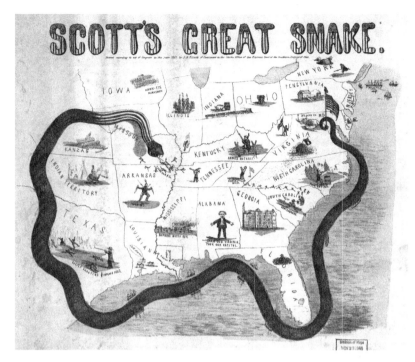

Winfield Scott's "Anaconda Plan."

The timeframe was concerning. No one wanted a long, drawn-out war, so Scott was pushed into executing the final step of his plan first, and he ordered General Irvin McDowell to advance on Confederate troops at Manassas Junction, Virginia, resulting in the First Battle of Bull Run.[44] Just 25 miles from Washington, men, women, and children from the Union watched the battle from high ground with picnic baskets and opera glasses and were pleased to see the Union army initially performing well. But, by the afternoon, the Confederates had brought in reinforcements led by Stonewall Jackson, and the Union was forced into a retreat. Suddenly, frightened soldiers raced past the

---

44   Battles in the Civil War sometimes have two names – one given by the Union (named for nearby natural landmarks) and one given by the Confederacy (named after nearby towns). This battle is known as the Battle of Bull Run by the Union and the Battle of Manassas by the Confederacy.

onlookers, and chaos ensued as the civilians got caught up in the flight, grabbing what they could and running home. The Confederates had won but did not know how to capitalize, and a shocked Union was forced to confront the reality that there would be no swift victory.

Under pressure and in poor health, Winfield Scott retired and George McClellan took his place as Commanding General of the Union Army; Robert E Lee was appointed commander of the Confederate Army of Northern Virginia. The Union then commenced a series of offensives in 1862 – one struck west towards the Mississippi River and Ohio River valleys, and one struck east towards Richmond.

In the West, General Henry Halleck ordered Ulysses S Grant to attack Fort Henry and Fort Donelson in Tennessee, and on February 23, Nashville fell, becoming the first Southern state capital to pass into enemy hands. Halleck then ordered Grant to go south to the border of Mississippi. Here, the Confederates launched a full-force attack on Grant's troops at the Battle of Shiloh on April 6, 1862. In a huge battle that pitted 65,000 Union forces against 45,000 Confederates, the Union won a victory that cost a shocking 13,000 casualties (the Confederacy suffered 10,000). The Union followed this up by capturing New Orleans and Memphis in the spring.

In the East, however, the principal offensive against Richmond was a failure. Commander George McClellan, arrogant and contemptuous of Lincoln, had built a huge army – the Army of the Potomac – that consisted of over 105,000 men whom he had shipped down the Chesapeake Bay to the southeast of Richmond. He then marched them back up overland, but in a series of six battles over the course of seven days (Seven Days Battles), the Confederate commander, Robert E Lee, used his 92,000-strong army to repel them.

Lee followed this up by crushing the Union forces led by General John Pope at the Second Battle of Bull Run. Total casualties amounted to almost 22,000, with most on the Union side, and Pope and McClellan found themselves summoned to Washington, both having failed in their respective objectives. The Union Army was in disarray in the East, in marked contrast to its success in the West, and Northern morale was dropping sharply. Lincoln dismissed Pope, whose army merged with McClellan's.

It was the only time in the war that the foreign powers came close to recognizing the Confederacy as a separate state. France and Napoleon III leaned towards supporting the Confederacy but were reluctant to do so without Britain following suit, and Britain considered making an offer to mediate between the United States and the Confederacy. This would lead to recognition of the Confederacy as an independent nation. But the proposal was eventually tabled, and the war continued.

***

Robert E Lee believed in retaining the initiative, and he invaded the North in September. He hoped that Marylanders would rally to the Confederate flag and that Republican support would be damaged in the upcoming elections, considering this moment "the most propitious time since the commencement of the war... to enter Maryland."

Part of the Confederate Army under Stonewall Jackson laid siege to the 13,000-man Union garrison at Harpers Ferry. The garrison surrendered after four days (the largest surrender of American troops until the Philippines in the Second World War), and Jackson reunited with Lee at Sharpsburg where Lee was readying for battle. McClellan had actually managed to obtain a copy of the Confederates' battle plan for the Maryland campaign,[45] but his naturally cautious approach meant that he failed to take full advantage. He chose not to commit his full force when he engaged Lee in battle on September 17 at the Battle of Antietam.

Aftermath of the Battle of Antietam, by Alexander Gardner (1862)

Antietam was the bloodiest one-day battle in American military history, resulting in over 22,000 casualties. Fighting occurred at close range, and with 15,000 casualties after eight hours, doctors on the battlefield were completely overwhelmed. Both armies tended to their dead and wounded that evening. Lee skirmished with McClellan the following day but then retreated across the Potomac, and McClellan and his much larger force decided not to pursue. If he had, he might have ended the war, and an immensely

---

45   One general wrapped a copy of Robert E Lee's battle plan around several cigars, which he later lost. A Union soldier discovered the cigars and the plan, and sent it to McClellan.

frustrated Lincoln replaced McClellan with General Ambrose E Burnside a few weeks later.

In the West, the Confederates mounted a counteroffensive (the Kentucky Campaign) under General Braxton Bragg, driving through Tennessee into Kentucky. Bragg hoped to rally civilians to the Confederate flag, but he failed to obtain the civilian numbers he needed, and he was forced to retreat at the Battle of Chaplin Hills. Again, the Union (led by General Don Carlos Buell) did not pursue the Confederate forces, but it ended the Confederacy's offensive in the West, which would not be reattempted for the remainder of the war.

Offensives by the Confederate forces in the West and the East had been pushed back by mid-October, but the refusal to pursue by the Union troops was a real disappointment to the United States. Lincoln, however, skillfully changed the nature of the war after the Battle of Antietam by issuing the Emancipation Proclamation. This officially identified the United States as antislavery and made it impossible for Britain and France to publicly support the Confederacy. Both had formally banned slavery from their colonies years before the Civil War had begun.

At the time, the Emancipation Proclamation was no great watershed moment, and focus remained on the battlefield. The Confederacy became increasingly reliant on Lee, and on the Union side, a frustrated Lincoln replaced Buell with General William S Rosecrans and put pressure on him and Burnside to do something proactive. This was the winter of 1862 – traditionally a time when campaigning settled down due to the difficulties of obtaining supplies – but this was hardly a traditional time, and the Union generals considered how best to respond.

In the West, Rosecrans marched south from Nashville with 44,000 men (leaving 40,000 behind) where they were surprised by Confederate forces at Stones River. After engaging in battle for two and a half days, and with both sides suffering huge casualties, the Confederate forces withdrew, allowing Rosecrans to proclaim victory although, again, he also chose not to pursue them. Grant, proceeding according to the Anaconda Plan, began his Vicksburg campaign by taking one part of his army down the Mississippi Central Railroad and advancing the other, led by General William Tecumseh Sherman, to the Yazoo River. But both initiatives failed, and a stalemate ensued into the spring.

In the East, things went even worse for the Union. Burnside planned to move south, defeat Lee, and capture Richmond, so he moved his 123,000-man army to Falmouth, a riverport town opposite Fredericksburg on the north side of the Rappahannock River. With the bridges across the river destroyed, Burnside ordered pontoon bridges to be built, but delays meant that Lee caught on to the Union's plan and placed his armies in strategic positions. As the Union troops advanced, waves of their soldiers were shot down on open ground, and they lost over 12,500 men in a crushing defeat. Lincoln was moved to exclaim, "If there is a worse place than hell, I am in it."

He responded by removing Burnside from command and replacing him with General Joseph Hooker, now the fourth commander of the Army. Hooker orchestrated a "perfect plan" in May 1863 to trap Lee between two pincers and drive him from Fredericksburg. He confronted Lee's 57,000-strong army with his 97,000 and Lee was initially surprised, but he hurriedly gathered his army together and retaliated at Chancellorsville, forcing the Union back and delivering another devastating defeat to the Union Army. The

Confederates did, however, suffer the loss of their general, Stonewall Jackson, who was shot three times and had his arm amputated. But pneumonia set in, and he died days later.

Robert E Lee in 1869.

Lee seemed unbeatable, having secured two extraordinary victories at Fredericksburg and Chancellorsville. Morale in the North was at its lowest level yet, and Lincoln was found shaking his head, pacing back and forth, repeating, "My God! My God! What will the country say?" The Emancipation Proclamation was perceived by many as too radical, and the "Copperheads" (Northerners who opposed the war) were growing in strength. The economy was teetering, inflation was rocketing, and gold prices were fluctuating dramatically.

On top of this, the United States had passed a deeply unpopular Conscription Act in March 1863 calling for the registration of all males between the ages of 20 and 45.[46] Both sides had initially found men by signing up volunteers, and the Conscription Act did help to persuade more to sign up. But exemptions to conscription could be bought for $300 or by finding a substitute draftee, and accusations were made that it was a war fought by the poor. New York saw five days of rioting by mainly Irish and Irish Americans who, after initially attacking military and government buildings, moved on to assaulting, lynching, and beating Black citizens. They looted their homes and businesses and even set fire to the Colored Orphan Asylum on Fifth Avenue, which housed 200 children.

Overall, the United States put 2.4 million white soldiers, 180,000 African Americans, and 3,500 Native Americans into battle. To escape the draft, about 90,000 Northerners fled to Canada, and others fled into the mountains of Pennsylvania. Notable figures among these draft dodgers included Grover Cleveland, Mark Twain, and John D Rockefeller.

The Confederacy, where the draft was similarly unpopular, put between 750,000 and 1.25 million men into combat.[47] Their original force was also made up of volunteers, but their term expired after a year, so a conscription act was passed (ironically, given the Confederacy's promotion of individual and states' rights) which brought recruits in for a term of three years and, rather harshly, extended the terms of the original volunteers. Around 80 percent of white men of military age were conscripted by the Confederacy, and draftees could evade service by paying someone to take their place.

---

46 The Confederacy also passed a Conscription Act at around the same time.
47 Demographics are not available due to incomplete or destroyed enlistment records.

***

Lee drove into Pennsylvania after the Battle of Chancellorsville. General Hooker had resigned after his defeat, and Lincoln replaced him with General George Meade (ignoring requests to bring back McClellan), who moved his army in line with Lee's to prevent a direct attack on Washington. Lee was informed that the Union Army was close, and he decided to engage with them at Gettysburg. After the Union repelled a dramatic infantry assault on Cemetery Ridge led by General George Pickett, the Union decimated the Confederates and forced Lee back into Virginia on July 4. Suffering casualties of over 28,000 (to the Union's 23,000), Lee was again allowed to retreat, with Lincoln lamenting that "we had only to stretch forth our hands and they were ours."

On the same day in the West, Grant, after a 47-day siege, finally forced the surrender of 30,000 Confederate troops at Vicksburg, Mississippi. Situated halfway between Memphis and New Orleans, his victory gave control of the Mississippi River to the Union and split the Confederacy in two. The Confederates responded in September by striking back at Rosecrans's forces at the Battle of Chickamauga, after which Rosecrans retreated to Chattanooga where his troops were put under siege by the Confederate General Bragg.

Lincoln replaced Rosecrans with Grant, who managed to engineer an extraordinary turnaround. He brought in reinforcements (including his favorite general, William Tecumseh Sherman), re-secured the supply lines, and broke the Union forces out of Chattanooga. Charging up the Missionary Ridge, Union soldiers managed to surround the Confederates over the course of three days in November and forced them to retreat. This cleared the way for Sherman's March to the Sea a year later.

Victories at Gettysburg, Vicksburg and Chattanooga picked up Northern morale and are often considered turning points in the war. But Lee had only withdrawn, and the Confederate forces could yet stage a comeback in both the West and the East. Gettysburg may be the most visited battlefield in the United States nowadays, but nothing was certain at this stage, and come the summer of 1864, Northern morale was even lower than it had been after the Battle of Chancellorsville.

North and South in the War

At the start of the war, the Confederates briefly enjoyed a period of political unity. But the Unionist tendencies of areas such as East Tennessee and West Virginia and the economic and military demands of the war required the Confederacy to centralize power. Ultimately, the Confederacy became the most intrusive government the United States had ever seen, and it remained that way until the mid-20th century.

There were no political parties in the Confederacy, but factions developed that ultimately became pro- or anti-Jefferson Davis. Davis was difficult to work with, and he surrounded himself with stooges, which alienated his subordinates and constituents. His own vice president, Alexander Hamilton Stephens, spent most of the war away from Richmond, writing scathing letters critical of Davis.

	North	South
Taxes	21%	5%
Loans	66%	35%
Paper Money	13%	60%

Economically, the Confederacy financed the war in much the same way as the United States – they both raised taxes, borrowed money, and printed paper money – but in different proportions. The US government issued $432 million in paper money compared to the Confederacy's $1.5 billion, which led to inflation running at 12 percent per month by the end of the war in the South.

This made the cost of basic consumer staples in the South too high for many, and they resorted to a barter economy as paper money became worthless. Problems were compounded by refugees pouring into towns and cities to escape the Union armies, and the South soon struggled to produce enough food and find ways to distribute it, which incited riots in Mobile, Atlanta, and Richmond between 1863 and 1864.

Desertions from the army were a problem for both sides. Around 103,000 Confederate soldiers and 200,000 Union soldiers deserted (around 13 percent for both), but desertion was felt more keenly on the Confederate side where the population was smaller. Women wrote to their husbands, fathers, and brothers, urging them to come home to help; and many men avoided the draft by hiding from government agents, sometimes even assisted by the state governors themselves. Often deserters and refugees would return to find their homes completely destroyed – either by the Union Army or as punishment for having deserted.

The Northerners experienced a different type of war as they were not being invaded. There was little to no dislocation, and as much as women missed their men, their routine was largely the same. The economy, in fact, took off during the war as additional demands were put on factories and laborers to produce clothes, munitions, and food (canned fruits and condensed milk among others). Lincoln signed the Pacific Railway Act into law in 1862, stimulating the building of railroads together with canals and roads. The economic disparity between the North and South that developed during the war would continue for decades.

Politically, the two-party system remained, and a heated 1864 presidential election was contested in the middle of the war. Fought between incumbent Abraham Lincoln of the National Union Party (essentially Republicans and War Democrats) and George McClellan of the Democrat Party, the South watched closely in the hope that Lincoln would be ousted from office. But Lincoln prevailed in one of the most crucial elections in American history. He secured a huge margin of victory in the Electoral College (212-21) and won 55 percent of the popular vote (nearly 80 percent of soldiers cast their vote for the Republican Party). The result was devastating to the Confederacy, and the Republicans remained the dominant party for 80 years until Franklin Roosevelt's Democrats of 1932.

Lincoln had to balance the varied views held by members of the Republican Party regarding emancipation. The radical wing of the party, who were in the minority but were vocal and held key roles in the Senate (Charles Sumner) and the House of Representatives (Thaddeus Stevens), wanted immediate emancipation of the slaves, and Lincoln, who had initially taken a moderate stance on slavery, eventually joined them. But only after he had exhausted his other options.

With Southern congressmen no longer on Capitol Hill, the Republicans passed a series of laws that reflected their capitalist tendencies. The National Bank Act was passed to administer a system of nationally chartered banks and a uniform national currency, and the Homestead Act allowed any citizen (or intended citizen) to claim 160 acres of government land which they could purchase for a small fee after five years.

The Morrill Land Grant College Act granted land to states to "benefit the agricultural and mechanical arts," eventually establishing the great universities of Penn State, Michigan State, Cornell, and Texas A&M. The Pacific Railroad Act was passed, intending to connect the Midwest (Omaha, Nebraska) to the West (Sacramento, California), which would provide the foundation required to create the manufacturing powerhouse envisioned by the United States. These changes generated great optimism in the North when the war ended – in marked contrast to the South, which was utterly defeated and would face serious economic and infrastructure issues.

Certain effects of the war were felt in equal measure by both sides. The grief of losing a loved one who had gone to battle; the trauma of life on the front line, seeing friends and colleagues killed or wounded; and living life under the strict routine of military discipline were the same for all. But the extraordinary differences between life in the North and the South made up a large part of the story of the US Civil War.

African Americans in the War

Lincoln needed men to win the war, and the government passed the first Confiscation Act in August 1861. This law allowed the federal government to seize property, including slaves, that was being used to support the Confederate war effort. The second Confiscation Act declared that slaves of Confederate officials would be free, giving slaves an incentive to run away and join the Union, and the Militia Act allowed African Americans to serve in the militias.

Lincoln was only prepared to deliver the Emancipation Proclamation after a victory on the battlefield, which occurred after the Battle of Antietam in September 1862. He proclaimed that slaves "shall be then, thenceforward and forever free," and although it only applied to those slaves in the Confederacy (not those in the border states), it directly stripped US citizens of their personal property – a dramatic violation of individuals' constitutional rights, but one that was required to end the war.

Union generals such as Benjamin Butler, John C Frémont, and David Hunter all reinforced the emancipation message on the battlefield. Butler identified slaves who ran into Union lines as "contraband of war" and refused to return them; Frémont proclaimed martial law in Missouri and announced the emancipation of slaves of citizens who fought against the Union; and Hunter declared the emancipation of slaves in South Carolina, Georgia, and Florida.[48]

Many Northern Democrats believed the Emancipation Proclamation was too radical. But, as the war continued, and more people saw friends and family killed, an increasing desire to punish the Confederacy developed. Because Lincoln presented the Proclamation as a military measure (rather than a moral one), it gained in popularity and was perceived as something that would directly weaken Southern war efforts. The status of "free" was assigned to all slaves who ran away (estimated to be around one-half to 1 million), enabling the army to recruit African American soldiers, and its numbers swelled by an additional 200,000 soldiers by the end of the war.

---

48 Lincoln had both orders from Frémont and Hunter rescinded (primarily because he was worried about losing support of the Democrats and the border states), but the emancipation movement remained forefront in his mind.

The Union Army was initially reluctant to take on Black soldiers. They were not believed to be as skilled as whites, although a cynical mentality developed that deemed it preferable to sacrifice Black soldiers over white ones. Further prejudice saw Black units used only moderately and employed as guards, cooks, and laborers (similar to how the Confederate army employed them), although some Black soldiers served with distinction in battle. They fought bravely at Milliken's Bend and Port Hudson in Louisiana and at Petersburg, Virginia, and Nashville, Tennessee. On July 18, 1863, they daringly stormed Fort Wagner in Charleston, South Carolina, under the leadership of Robert Gould Shaw. Almost half of them died that day, including Shaw himself, the events of which are dramatized in the film *Glory* (1989).

Black soldiers also faced severe consequences if captured in battle, and Jefferson Davis declared that any Black prisoners of war would be enslaved or executed on the spot. After the Union garrison surrendered at Fort Pillow in Tennessee in 1864, Confederate forces murdered 300 soldiers – most of whom were Black – in cold blood. At the First Battle of Saltville later that same year, the Confederate soldiers sought out every wounded Black soldier and summarily executed them, even those being treated in the field hospitals.

In 1865, the Confederacy approved using Black troops for its own purposes. Debates had raged in the South that claimed arming them was essentially the same as setting them free, and that it would lead to uprisings and undermine the control of the whites. Supporters argued it was better to arm them and win the war than not, and eventually, the Confederate Congress, which was becoming increasingly desperate by this stage, voted to arm them but stopped short of promising freedom.

By contrast, Black men who fought in the Civil War for the Union were able to establish an ironclad claim to freedom and citizenship, and in January 1865, the 13th Amendment passed through Congress, explicitly banning slavery.[49] Lincoln took an active role in ensuring it obtained the necessary votes in the House (many Democrats at first refused to support it), and when it passed, people cried and rejoiced wildly in the streets. Suddenly, 4 million slaves were free, and many former slaves found themselves grappling with a range of emotions that swung tortuously between happiness, shock, rage, and despair. The question of equality was tabled for the time being.

Later War Years (1864–1865)

Following Chattanooga, Lincoln promoted Ulysses S Grant to Lieutenant General of the Union armies in March 1864. This was the first time since 1798 that a general had been promoted to such a rank, left vacant in honor of the last Lieutenant General, George Washington.[50] Grant planned two major Union offensives. One, to be led by him, was to engage Lee's forces continuously in Virginia until they were fully defeated; the second was for Sherman to push south from Chattanooga and capture Atlanta, Georgia – a key southern city and manufacturing hub – and, from there, continue east to Savannah.

Sherman had spent part of his life in the South and was fond of it, but he despised secession and believed the South was committing treason. He applied a strategy of total war, famously saying that "war is cruelty... the crueler it is, the

---

49 The 13th Amendment banned slavery with the words "neither slavery nor involuntary servitude, except as a punishment for crime whereof the party shall have been duly convicted, shall exist within the United Sates, or any place subject to their jurisdiction."
50 Winfield Scott had briefly earned the rank but only as a temporary measure at the time.

sooner it will be over," and he thought nothing of laying waste to factories, farms, and railroads, and slaughtering livestock. The South hated him so much that he was compared to Ivan the Terrible and Genghis Khan.

In May 1864, Sherman arrived in Atlanta and laid siege to the city but could not break through. In the East, Grant waged the Overland Campaign against Lee, fighting a series of brutal battles in which neither side could claim victory and where casualties could reach up to 3,000 per day.[51] With no decisive victory, the North's morale was at its very lowest, and Lincoln looked ahead to the election of 1864 with foreboding.

But the tide finally began to turn in late August. Admiral David Farragut, 60 years old at the time, brazenly attacked the open port of Mobile which was defended by forts, mines, and barriers. Allegedly crying out, "Damn the torpedoes, full speed ahead!" he ploughed through a minefield and into the bay to victory. Then, on the night of September 1, Sherman captured Atlanta, sending shudders of fear through Confederate ranks. Grant dispatched General Philip H Sheridan to clear the Shenandoah, and he won a series of victories that gave the Union control in the valley and ensured a Republican triumph in the election.

Morale dropped precipitously in the Confederacy, and two major campaigns by the United States sought to end the war. Sherman took half of his forces (62,000 men) and headed east to Savannah, marching ten miles a day and "smashing things to the sea." He caused millions of dollars' worth of damage and terrible heartache to Confederate civilians by leaving

---

51   These included the Battle of the Wilderness, Spotsylvania Court House, Yellow Tavern, Meadow Bridge, North Anna, Wilson's Wharf, Across the Pamunkey, Haw's Shop, Totopotomoy Creek, Old Church, Cold Harbor, Crossing the James, Trevilian Station, and Saint Mary's Church.

a trail of dead animals, burned factories, and looted farms on his 285-mile March to the Sea, arriving in Savannah on December 21, 1864. He found it undefended and presented the city and its 25,000 bales of cotton to President Lincoln as a Christmas gift. He then turned north, burning and pillaging his way through South Carolina to Charleston, ending up outside Durham, North Carolina in April 1865.

Grant and Lee were mired in siege warfare. After the Overland Campaign had failed to capture Richmond or destroy the Confederate Army, Grant decided to cut off the supply and communication routes to Richmond, laying siege to the city of Petersburg. In one of the earliest examples of trench warfare, Grant extended his lines over 30 miles, choking Lee's army and the Confederate capital for nine months. Finally, on April 1, the Union Army broke through, and Lee abandoned Petersburg, heading west in an attempt to meet up with forces under the command of General Joseph E Johnston in North Carolina. In Richmond, President Davis and his cabinet abandoned the city and ordered the soldiers to burn the bridges, armory, and supply warehouses as they fled.

Grant followed Lee's army west and blocked any escape route by staying south of him. Finally, on April 9, an exhausted Lee acknowledged that his army was stretched too thin to break through and realized that further resistance would be futile. To avoid more destruction to the South and to his troops, he asked to discuss surrender terms with Grant. So, at the house of Wilmer McLean in Appomattox, Virginia, Grant offered not to prosecute Confederate soldiers should they surrender, and Lee accepted the terms, leaving Grant "sad and depressed." He said, "I felt like anything rather than rejoicing at the downfall of a foe who had fought so long and valiantly." The war was over.

***

Lincoln in 1858.

Lincoln in 1865.

Five days later, Abraham Lincoln attended *Our American Cousin*, a play being shown at Ford's Theatre in Washington, DC. Visibly ravaged and exhausted by the burdens of the war, and with his mind turning towards reconstruction, he was given a standing ovation upon his arrival as he settled into his box. During a raucous scene, John Wilkes Booth, a prominent actor and Southern sympathizer, quietly stepped into the box, raised his gun, and fired at Lincoln with a single shot in the back of the head. Booth jumped down from the box onto the stage, shouted the Virginia state motto, *sic semper tyrannis* ("Thus always to tyrants"), and rushed out of the theatre.

Lincoln was carried across the street to the house of a tailor, William Petersen, where he died at 7:22 a.m. on April 15. The North, the South, and the entire international community were left in shock and mourning. After 12 days on the run, Booth was tracked down, shot, and killed as he fled from a burning barn, and his co-conspirators were arrested and either imprisoned or sentenced to death by hanging. Booth had organized the conspiracy independently of the Confederacy, and as Lincoln's vice president, Andrew Johnson (who was also on the conspirators' list for assassination that day), became president, any joyous end-of-war celebrations were immediately snuffed out.

Lincoln's death may have been the most high-profile of all those killed during the Civil War, but he was just one of 1.1 million total casualties, with 620,000 killed (roughly 2 percent of the population). Government debt before the war stood at $64.8 million; now it stood at $5.2 billion, and the destruction to the South would be comparable to that of Europe in the World Wars. Cities and infrastructure still smoldered from the catastrophe, and an estimated two-thirds of the wealth was destroyed.

The Union, however, was guaranteed. Slavery was dead, and the superiority of federal power over local and state had been assured. But big questions remained as to how to heal the wounds, how to treat the Confederate states, and how to integrate African Americans into society.

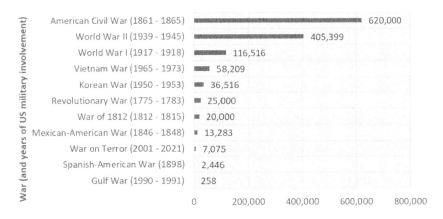

Number of Fatalities in US Wars

War (and years of US military involvement)	Fatalities
American Civil War (1861 - 1865)	620,000
World War II (1939 - 1945)	405,399
World War I (1917 - 1918)	116,516
Vietnam War (1965 - 1973)	58,209
Korean War (1950 - 1953)	36,516
Revolutionary War (1775 - 1783)	25,000
War of 1812 (1812 - 1815)	20,000
Mexican-American War (1846 - 1848)	13,283
War on Terror (2001 - 2021)	7,075
Spanish-American War (1898)	2,446
Gulf War (1990 - 1991)	258

CHAPTER 10

RECONSTRUCTION ERA (1865–1877)

Early Years of Reconstruction (1865–1870)

Debates about reconstructing the nation began while the war was still raging. In late 1863, Lincoln suggested the "Ten Percent Plan" which allowed for a Southern state to be readmitted to the Union once 10 percent of its voters (from the voter rolls for the election of 1860) had sworn an Oath of Allegiance to the Union, but radical Republicans opposed this plan. They believed it was too lenient on the South, and many, including Thaddeus Stevens, wanted to see a "radical reorganization of the Southern institutions, habits and manners." This included disbanding the plantation aristocracy, redistributing land, developing industry, and guaranteeing civil liberties for former slaves.

Other radicals in Congress developed their own plan in 1864. The Wade Davis Bill (named for Senator Benjamin Wade and Representative Henry Davis) provided for readmission of the rebel states provided 50 percent of white males in the state swore an oath that they had never in the past fought for the Confederacy and that the states would extend voting rights to all African American men. But many Southern men could not take that oath, and even though the Bill passed the House of Representatives and the Senate, Lincoln used his pocket veto to prevent it from becoming law – essentially not signing it until Congress adjourned for the session.

This infuriated the Radicals, who attacked him in a manifesto titled *To the Supporters of the Government* and called for the president to "confine himself to his executive duties – to obey and execute, not to make the laws."

By 1865, Lincoln appeared to move closer to the radical Republicans. But before he had a chance to make any further suggestions, he was assassinated, and his vice president, Andrew Johnson – a Democrat from eastern Tennessee who revered Andrew Jackson – took his place in the White House.

Andrew Johnson, c.1870.

Johnson had been added to the ticket in 1864 to ensure Democrat votes. He had little formal education, having taught himself to read and write late in life, and he harbored a passionate hatred for the plantation aristocracy of the South. He seemed to side with the Radicals at first and talked about the treasonous and traitorous acts of the South, but before long, his true feelings came to the surface. He was a staunch racist, with Frederick Douglass noting his expression as one of "bitter contempt and aversion" when he met him, and while Congress was in recess, Johnson formulated his own reconstruction plan based on Lincoln's Ten Percent Plan.

Johnson's plan allowed for the readmission of a state if 10 percent of the men who had voted in the 1860 election took an oath of allegiance, and for any ex-Confederate to petition him personally for a presidential pardon. He granted these pardons freely, exempting only a handful of senior Confederate leaders (Jefferson Davis was held in prison for two years; Robert E Lee was granted a pardon), and he allowed states to send their representatives to Washington provided they upheld the 13th Amendment and paid their war debts. There was no mention of Black rights at all.

Radicals were outraged but powerless to do anything, as the Congress elected in 1864 was not yet in session. Southern states were emboldened. South Carolina refused to condemn its act of secession, Mississippi and Kentucky resisted ratifying the 13th Amendment, and several states even began to talk about states' rights again. In Mississippi, "black codes" were enacted that restricted the right of Black people to own property, the type of job they could hold, whom they could marry, and even whether they could move freely through public spaces.

Johnson did nothing to put a stop to this and was flattered when he received requests for pardons by former Confederates, granting 13,500 of 15,000. Obtaining a pardon enabled them to resume leadership positions in the Southern states, and Johnson began to align himself with the Southern Democrats, building up his own coalition of loyalists within the National Union Party. Even Conservative Republicans, who favored a sympathetic approach towards the South, found themselves horrified by his approach.

Congress met in December 1865 and refused to seat the Congressional representatives from the former Confederate states who had been elected under Johnson's plan. Radical Republicans then acted in January 1866 by broadening the scope of the Freedman's Bureau Act. This act had been initially drafted to help with the transition of once-slaves to freed Blacks in the former Confederate states, and radical Republicans expanded it to include every state in the US, and increased the power of the military governors to protect African Americans. Congress passed the bill only to see it vetoed by Johnson, who claimed that it infringed on states' rights and that Congress could not legislate for states unrepresented in the House. An enraged Congress passed the bill over Johnson's veto.

Congress then passed a Civil Rights Act in April which, although it did not give the vote to African Americans, was designed to reinforce their right to make contracts, sue, give evidence in court, and purchase and sell property. Again, Johnson vetoed it for the same reasons, and again, Congress passed it over his veto.

The Democrats were thrilled with Johnson's tactics, but it served to push Moderate Republicans towards the Radicals. Congress then proposed a constitutional amendment – the 14th Amendment – that would guarantee the citizenship of all African Americans (but not the vote) and would prohibit former Confederate public servants from holding office. It was implied that ratification of the Amendment by a state would mean acceptance back into the Union, and Johnson urged Southern legislatures to reject it, arguing again that because the Southern states were not represented, the amendment was unconstitutional.

A violent summer of rioting and intimidation occurred in 1866 as whites resisted the cause of Black citizenship. They killed and wounded hundreds of African Americans in Memphis and New Orleans, which only served to convince the North that more needed to be done to protect Black people. Johnson, furious with Congress, tried to build support by applying the Andrew Jackson playbook and going straight to the people, so he set out on a speaking tour (the "Swing around the Circle") during the midterm elections of 1866. But he often appeared drunk and used vile and abusive language to attack his Republican opponents, and he was met with heckling, protests, and hostile crowds. It was a disaster.

The Republicans were quick to capitalize and they won a majority in both houses of Congress. This assured them of enough votes to override any presidential veto, and Johnson saw his National Union Party collapse. The elections of 1866 demonstrated that the North was fully behind the 14th Amendment, but for it to become law, four Confederate states would have to ratify it to make up part of the three-fourths majority required. Johnson encouraged Southern states to vote against it, and one by one, they did; Tennessee was the only one that did not.

Johnson's defiance and the South's stubbornness pushed the Moderates and the Radicals towards a desire to enfranchise African Americans. This would give the Republicans a solid support base in the South, and they passed two Reconstruction Acts – both of which were vetoed by Johnson, and both of which Congress upheld – that provided for a "Radical Reconstruction."

The first act nullified the state governments in all the former Confederate states and divided the South into five military districts. These were to be led by military governors until Congress could approve the state constitutions, and the new state constitutions themselves had to meet two requirements: provide for Black suffrage and ratify the 14th Amendment. The second act gave the responsibility of registering voters to the military governors and disenfranchised those Southern officeholders who had taken up their posts before the Civil War (and so had not taken the oath of allegiance).

Congress also wanted to ensure these policies were enforced effectively, so they passed the Tenure of Office Act. This prevented the president from removing certain officeholders without the approval of the Senate and was specifically intended to stop Johnson from replacing Edwin Stanton from his position as Secretary of War. Stanton frequently clashed with Johnson and was charged with enforcing the policies within the acts. The constitutionality of such legislation was questionable, and Johnson tried to veto it,[52] but Congress again passed it over his head.

Many white Southerners hoped Johnson would protect them from Radical Reconstruction, but Congress members were, by now, thinking about how they could remove Johnson entirely through a process of impeachment. This would require the Senate to convict the president for "Treason, Bribery, or other high Crimes and Misdemeanors," and Johnson gave them a pretext when he violated the Tenure of Office Act by removing Edwin Stanton from his position. Johnson was happy to put the constitutionality of the act to the test, and the House obliged, adopting 11 articles of impeachment

---

52 It was repealed by the Supreme Court in 1926 in the case of *Myers v United States* with the Court ruling that the president has the exclusive power to remove executive branch officials.

against him – eight of which dealt with the violation of the act, and three of other alleged transgressions.

Johnson's trial began on March 4, 1868, and continued for 11 weeks. His counsel argued that his actions constituted neither a high crime nor a misdemeanor and that impeachment proceedings had been used as a political weapon to dismiss him. Galleries were packed over the course of the trial, and with a two-thirds majority required to convict him, he was, in a moment of high drama, finally acquitted by a single vote (35 to 19; 36 to 18 would have convicted him).

During the trial, Johnson had conducted himself with a great deal more decorum than he had done over the last few years, and he also promised to enforce the Reconstruction Acts and to give no more speeches attacking Congress. Some senators were reluctant to convict him because the Radical Benjamin Franklin Wade would be promoted to the presidency, and his pro-labor views were too extreme for many; others feared the precedent that would be set if Johnson were convicted. Johnson ended up completing his term and chose not to seek reelection on the Democratic ticket in 1868. In 1875, he even won reelection to Congress as a senator for Tennessee but died of a stroke less than four months after taking office at the age of 66.

Reconstruction proceeded apace in the South with 703,000 African Americans now registered as voters, making up a majority in five states (Alabama, Florida, Mississippi, Louisiana, and South Carolina). Constitutional conventions were held at which many states drafted progressive constitutions that included funding for free public schools, roads, prisons, and hospitals, and by the summer of 1868, all but three former Confederate states had ratified the 14th Amendment and were readmitted to the Union.[53]

---

53 All except Mississippi, Texas, and Virginia, who were readmitted in 1870.

Tensions remained high, however. Democrats in the Georgia legislature expelled their Black members on the grounds that the new state constitution made them ineligible to hold office, and Congress reimposed military rule. In the election of 1868, Ulysses S Grant won the presidency by only 306,000 votes, relying on the 500,000 Black votes to win, while the Democrat candidate, Horatio Seymour, campaigned under the slogan "This is a White Man's Country. Let White Men Rule." In the South, domestic terrorist groups like the Ku Klux Klan banded together to threaten and intimidate Black men away from the polls, and in Louisiana, 200 African Americans were massacred on local plantations to prevent them from voting. Others were kept inside by the sound of gunfire, and one parish saw every single vote cast for Seymour.

But Grant carried 55 percent of the vote in the North (the same as Lincoln in 1860). He drew up the 15th Amendment permitting all citizens the right to vote, not to be denied by "any State on account of race, color, or previous condition of servitude," and it was passed by Congress and ratified in March 1870. His opponents had accused him of hypocrisy because only eight Northern states allowed Blacks to vote, and many women felt let down, hoping their moment for enfranchisement might also have come. But Republicans feared it was too radical a step, and so women were forced to wait.

Later Years of Reconstruction (1870–1877)

All the Confederate states had been admitted back into the Union by 1870, and the Republican Party controlled the governments of almost all of them. Few were popular, however, and many of its members were inexperienced or corrupt. Northerners were labeled "carpetbaggers" if they were perceived to be exploiting the South for personal gain. Southern whites were called "scalawags" if they supported the policies of Reconstruction.

Group of Klansmen surround freedman Gus (played by white actor Walter Long in blackface) in Birth of a Nation (1915).

The Ku Klux Klan and other similar groups were applauded for trying to "liberate" the South from Republican rule. The films *Birth of a Nation* and *Gone with the Wind* – both hugely popular, made in 1915 and 1939, respectively – portrayed governments overrun with carpetbagging Republicans, scalawags, abolitionists, and conniving African Americans. *Birth of a Nation* even presents the Ku Klux Klan as heroes and African Americans (played in blackface by white actors) as sexual predators. *Gone with the Wind* includes an offscreen political meeting that implies a Ku Klux Klan gathering.

In reality, Southern corruption was no worse than that of the Northern state and municipal governments. Boss Tweed's Tammany Hall political machine of New York plundered more money from its citizens than any government in the South. Carpetbaggers were mostly Northern middle-class migrants with idealistic visions for the South, and scalawags were non-slaveholding farmers who had remained loyal to the Union. African Americans themselves were rarely elected to the legislature despite holding majorities in several states – no Black man was nominated as governor, and only 16 Black politicians were elected to Congress and two to the Senate (Hiram Revels and Blanche K Bruce from Mississippi). White politicians still dominated government.

The problems for the Republican Party were rooted in the fact that it historically had little support from whites in the South and no track record at all of working together with the newly freed African Americans. The party gradually began to fracture. Taxes had gone up to levels never before seen in the South, and voter intimidation at the polling booths increased. People were often too scared to report it, and in some cases, when it was reported, witnesses were murdered before they could testify at trial. It became increasingly hard for white Southerners to remain allied to the Republican Party, and between 1869 and 1874, seven states were "redeemed" – a term meaning they returned power to white Democratic rule.[54]

In the election of 1872, the Republican Party faced a split. Internal corruption tainted the party, and many wanted to move on from Reconstruction to focus on other matters. A faction calling itself the Liberal Republicans hoped to attract more principled adherents, promoting civil service reform and an end to Reconstruction. They nominated the *New York Tribune* publisher, Horace Greeley, as their presidential candidate whereupon the Democrats, sensing an

---

54 Virginia, North Carolina, Tennessee, Alabama, Georgia, Texas and Arkansas.

opportunity, also nominated Greeley at their own national convention. But Greeley was eccentric and often displayed conflicting opinions, and Grant won 31 of 37 states and 56 percent of the vote.

Nonetheless, momentum was with those who wanted to put Reconstruction aside. Up to 150 African Americans were killed after the 1872 election for governor in the Louisiana Colfax Massacre, and with violence increasing and white perpetrators escaping punishment, disillusionment among the Northerners set in. The fact was that support for the Blacks and the emancipation of the slaves had never really been that strong. The goal had been to bring the Confederate states back into the Union, and with that accomplished, plus another economic crisis to handle (the Panic of 1873), the Republicans' attention strayed elsewhere.

For the first time in 18 years, the Democrats won a majority in the House of Representatives, and Massachusetts even elected a Democratic governor in the midterm elections of 1874. Democrat Southerners had escalated intimidation tactics by applying the "Mississippi Plan" – sending armed patrols throughout towns and cities to stop African Americans from voting – and up to 300 Blacks were killed in the Vicksburg riots in 1874. By 1875, Republicans controlled only four Southern state governments.

The election of 1876 and the Compromise of 1877 signaled the end of Reconstruction. The Grant administration was rocked by more scandals, opening up another opportunity for the Democrats, whose candidate, Samuel Tilden, ran on a platform of honest government and an end to the "rapacity of carpetbag tyrannies." The Republicans nominated Rutherford B Hayes, a moderate Republican and governor of Ohio. The ensuing election was marred by violence.

The Democrats used paramilitary groups such as the Red Shirts and the White League to enforce the Mississippi Plan, and by the end of election day, no clear winner had emerged. Tilden had won the popular vote, but each party claimed victory in the states of Louisiana, South Carolina, and Florida, and Republican-controlled commissions were selected to review the votes and determine a winner. The commission argued that fraud, intimidation, and violence had invalidated the outcome and voted to award all three states to Hayes (winning in the Electoral College by 185 to 184), to which the Democrats responded by threatening adjournments and filibusters to delegitimize the result.

Before long, Hayes's Republicans and the moderate Democrats decided it was in everyone's best interest to come to an arrangement. Hayes agreed to remove federal troops from the South, subsidize internal improvements (notably a railroad through Texas), and name Southerners into his cabinet. In return, the Democrats were expected to respect Black rights. Hayes kept his promises, but the Democrats reneged on theirs, and through a process of poll taxes, literacy tests, and intimidation, they systematically continued their efforts to disenfranchise Black voters across the South.

The success of the Reconstruction era is debatable. It succeeded in that the Union had been restored, new state governments had been formed, and African Americans were freed from slavery and their rights cemented with the 13th, 14th, and 15th Amendments. But Reconstruction failed in that those rights were not enforced, and Black people were compelled to live as unequal partners under a system of racial segregation that lasted for another 90 years.

PART FOUR

INDUSTRIALIZATION TO 1917

CHAPTER 11
THE GILDED AGE (1877–1895)

American Tycoons

Once the turmoil of the Civil War era came to an end, a period of unprecedented growth in industry and technology occurred in a period termed the "Gilded Age."[55] Massive corporations were created, with their owners able to take advantage of new technologies, modern management techniques, and an astonishingly sympathetic government to develop monopolies in entire sectors of the economy. Individuals accumulated wealth on a vast scale, and new products were developed that drastically changed the lives of millions of people.

The first industries to be transformed were iron and steel, pioneered by Andrew Carnegie. Carnegie was born in Scotland in 1835 and, at age 12, moved with his family to Allegheny, Pennsylvania, after his father lost his job as a handloom weaver. This had been due to the revolutionary new technologies in the textile industry, giving the young Carnegie a valuable first lesson in business, and after stints in a cotton mill and a telegraph company, he ended up at the Pennsylvania Railroad Company where he rose to a managerial position.

---

55 The moniker comes from the title of the book *The Gilded Age: A Tale of Today* (1873), written by Mark Twain and Charles Dudley Warner. "Gilded" means covered in a thin layer of gold, and the title suggests a lack of substance within it.

There he nurtured relationships with influential owners and investors and in 1872 set up his own steel manufacturing business called the Edgar Thomson Steel Works, named after his former boss and head of the Pennsylvania Railroad Company. Carnegie was one of the first businessmen to apply modern managerial innovations including vertical integration (buying sources of raw materials and distribution networks) and to use new technologies (Bessemer Process and open-hearth furnaces) which significantly increased production and reduced costs.

Carnegie rarely used credit, and he tightly controlled expenses. With cash on hand, he purchased goods at cheap prices during economic downturns, and after the railroad boom slowed, he switched to providing steel for skyscrapers. Steel production in the United States rose from 13,000 tons a year in 1860 to over 11 million tons by 1900, and Carnegie eventually sold his company in 1901 to John Pierpont Morgan for just over $480 million,[56] making him one of the world's richest men. JP Morgan merged with Carnegie Steel later that year to form US Steel, the world's first billion-dollar corporation and the company that forms the bedrock of the one that still operates today.

---

56   Over $17 billion today.

The Chase of the Bowhead Whale (1909), by Clifford Warren Ashley.

The other industry that was transformed in this period was oil. Settlers had used oil as lamp fuel, for greasing wagons and tools, or to make soap and candles, with whale blubber providing the principal source. But the whaling business was extraordinarily dangerous with crews sometimes spending up to four years at sea searching for whales. The process, upon finding one, consisted of lowering a rowboat into the water and getting close enough to harpoon the whale, who would inevitably charge off in anger, sparking what became known as the "Nantucket sleigh ride." When the whale tired itself out, the crew would continue to harpoon it to death, and the main ship would then haul it in. They would cut and peel off its skin, and boil it down to make whale oil.[57]

By the 1850s, overfishing had caused the price of whale oil to rise substantially, and the dangers involved in whaling cried

---

57 Herman Melville drew on his experience as a sailor on a whaling ship when he wrote *Moby Dick*, published in 1851.

out for an alternative option. This came in the form of rock oil (or crude oil), which could be found in such abundance in Titusville, Pennsylvania, that it seeped up from the earth to form puddles on the surface. Much like the California Gold Rush of 1849, people poured into the town to make their fortune, although it was not long before the puddles were harvested, necessitating more complicated and expensive equipment to extract the oil from the ground.

John D Rockefeller in 1914.

Once extracted, the oil would need refining into usable petroleum products, such as kerosene, and John Davison Rockefeller recognized that a bottleneck developed at this stage. He moved from New York to Cleveland, Ohio, and worked to partner with or buy out competitors, giving him the power to adjust the price of oil as he saw fit and to negotiate preferred rates with railroad companies for transporting it. Rockefeller called his company Standard Oil (indicating the high standard it set), and like Carnegie was a superb organizer and an early proponent of vertical integration. He bought the oil fields themselves and developed the barrels, containers, pipelines, and train cars for distribution.

Rockefeller lived for almost a hundred years (1839–1937) and was a sober, God-fearing man who read the Bible daily, even leading his own Bible study with his wife. He abhorred waste and devoted huge amounts of time to increasing the efficiency of his business, driven in part by a fear the oil might run out.[58] His company was a pioneer in universal marketing and distribution, using red "Standard" wagons driving through town every week to top off consumers' oil cans, and in time, he managed to reduce the price of kerosene to the consumer and improve the quality of the product itself. When automobiles were invented in the 1890s, a whole new market developed that generated extraordinary expansion in the business.

American society also experienced a remarkable boom in innovative new products at this time. Thomas Edison made a science of developing and testing new devices and inventions at his laboratory in Menlo Park, New Jersey. Dozens of assistants helped him tinker with experimental combinations of electricity, wiring, and metals, and he developed numerous products including the incandescent light bulb in 1879, the phonograph (or gramophone) in 1877, and the motion picture camera in 1896 – which all had huge impacts on the modern world. By the time of his death, he held 1,328 patents.

---

58 This fear was put to rest in 1901 when the Spindletop oil field was discovered in Texas about 85 miles east of Houston.

One of his rivals was the inventor Alexander Graham Bell (1847–1922), a Scottish-born inventor whose mother and wife were both deaf, profoundly influencing his life's work. He created the first telephone in 1876, which amazed the American public, and he founded the American Telephone and Telegraph Company (AT&T) in 1885, creating a near monopoly in the industry.

Labor and Capital

Congress and the Supreme Court were sympathetic to corporations, and a division began to emerge between owners and employees. Startup costs were just too high for most people, and they began to reconcile that they would be workingmen all their lives. They came to understand that by banding together, they would have more leverage when making demands, and they sought to improve their lot by requesting higher wages, job security, and workplace safety. Employers argued that if they raised salaries, they would become uncompetitive, which would eventually mean having to close operations completely.

Industrial accidents were a real hazard for workers. Before George Westinghouse invented the airbrakes, railroad engineers would stop trains by cutting power and using the whistle to signal the brakemen, who would then walk along the top of the train, jumping from one carriage to the next to apply the brakes by hand. Brakemen could get killed or maimed by being thrown off around a sharp bend or knocked off by a bridge. Icy, windy, or wet weather would make their job even more dangerous.

An estimated 20 percent of deaths among men in Pittsburgh during the 1880s was due to accidents at the Carnegie Steel Works. Tired men would fall into blast furnaces, get struck by falling steel, or be asphyxiated by the fumes. In 1911, 146 women were burned to death at the Triangle Shirtwaist factory in New York. They were mostly teenage girls, and the combination of locked doors, inoperative elevators, and a lack of fire escapes meant they could not get out. The accident remains one of the worst in American industrial history.

Breaker Boys, photographed by Lewis Hine (1911). Children were hired to use a coal breaker to separate slate and other impurities from coal.

States that regulated work standards – such as Massachusetts, which passed several laws relating to factory safety and child labor – would see entire industries relocate to more lenient ones. Its textile industry moved to North Carolina and Georgia where factory owners employed children because they were cheaper and considered easier to manage. Employed in cotton mills, factories, and coal mines, children would sometimes work 14-hour days during which they could be beaten or whipped by a manager, were forbidden from talking or singing, and risked losing limbs or dying in accidents. They had little to no opportunity for attending school, and many could not write their own names, spell the street they lived on, or speak English.

Trade unions developed slowly, primarily because most failed to establish a common binding interest to unite them. The Knights of Labor, founded in 1869 by Uriah S Stephens, brought together workers from every industry (although they excluded bankers, lawyers, gamblers, and saloon keepers) and attempted to generate commitment to the union by swearing members to secrecy and following rituals comparable to Masonry. Under Terrence Powderly's leadership from 1879, the Knights achieved some successes, primarily against the railroad companies, as they advocated for an eight-hour workday, health and safety laws, and compensation for injuries on the job. However, the 1886 Haymarket Square Riot led to a plummet in membership numbers when a rally turned violent. A bomb was thrown into a group of police that saw seven of them killed and one civilian, and even though the bomb-thrower was never identified, eight men were rounded up, labeled anarchists, and convicted in a sensational trial where no solid evidence was produced against them.

Workers within the railroad companies were dispersed over vast distances and divided by job type, but they had huge numbers of employees and the ability to severely impact the economy. The Great Railroad Strike of 1877 started in Martinsburg, West Virginia, after workers' wages were cut. It spread all the way to Chicago, with pitched battles fought between the police, the National Guard, the US Army, and angry mobs throughout the country. A riot erupted in

Pittsburgh, 20 people were killed, and the railroad's engines, cars, and buildings were looted and set on fire. But the violence prevented the wider public from supporting them, and they ultimately achieved nothing.

Strikes were most effective in highly skilled trades because strikebreakers could not provide the services of the tradesmen. In December 1886 (the same year of the Haymarket Square riot), Samuel Gompers, a British Jew who worked in the cigar trade, formed the American Federation of Labor (AFL) – a loose grouping of smaller craft unions including the masons' union, the hatmakers' union, and the cigarmakers' union. Gompers did not believe in radical socialist or anarchist movements, which appealed to the government and the public. By 1900, the AFL counted over 500,000 tradespeople as members.

Employers tried to prevent unionization by hiring an ethnically diverse workforce, banning strike leaders, and hiring strikebreakers. They assumed English managers overseeing Irish workers would not lead to a natural camaraderie, and they would exploit language barriers by hiring and grouping people from different countries. Strike leaders were banned, and "birds of passage" were used to replace strikers – workers who came to the US with the intention of returning home at the end of a season.

In 1892, workers at Carnegie Steel went on strike at the Homestead steel mill following a pay cut made by the chairman of the company, Henry Clay Frick. Frick shuttered the mill, locked out the 3,800 workers, and eventually called in the Pinkerton National Detective Agency to break up the strike. As 300 Pinkerton detectives were sailing up the Monongahela River, thousands of workers rushed down to prevent them from coming ashore before exchanging gunfire. Nine people were killed, including three Pinkerton men, and the remaining Pinkertons were beaten out of town by the workers. It appeared that the strikers might win this round until, at Frick's request, the governor of Pennsylvania sent 8,500 National Guard forces to take control of the town and the mill. The movement broke up, and in the years to come, Carnegie slashed wages, implemented a 12-hour workday, and cut hundreds of jobs. Unionizing ended among steelworkers for the next 26 years, only making a comeback after the First World War.

The Pullman strike of 1894 was even bigger. George Pullman laid off three-quarters of his workforce and then rehired many at a reduced salary, while refusing to lower rents or store prices in the company town. The American Railway Union (ARU), headed by Eugene Debs, announced a boycott of all trains carrying Pullman cars, shutting down rail travel in 27 states. Again, it appeared that the strike may work, but a court injunction was issued against the strikers, and the president sent in 10,000 federal troops to suppress it, sending many strikers, including Debs, to jail. Debs spent his time in jail reading Karl Marx's *Das Kapital* and emerged a convinced socialist spouting apocalyptic, doom-laden rhetoric.

The owners of these corporations did somehow develop a philanthropic side. Andrew Carnegie wrote in his essay, *The Gospel of Wealth*, in 1889 that the rich should use their fortunes for the "general good," and he built over 2,500 libraries, financed the Carnegie Mellon University and Carnegie Hall, and donated to churches and to funds for teaching and education. The Rockefeller Foundation endowed education, cultural projects, and medical research, and many universities were named after the industrialists of the time (Duke, Stanford, and Vanderbilt Universities, for example).

The principle of philanthropy became established in American life and culture. But the oppressive way of life forced on the workingmen sharply contrasted with the freedoms pronounced by the US Constitution and the values the country purported to represent. The period reflected the difficulties inherent in trying to advance too quickly.

Life on the Frontier

The High Plains, in the 19th century, was referred to as the Great American Desert, and the Homestead Act of 1862 was passed to encourage its settlement. The legislation remained active for 114 years (until 1976) and gave Americans the opportunity to buy a 160-acre plot of public land for a small filing fee if they could demonstrate that they had occupied it and improved it after a five-year period.

A new transcontinental railroad provided the necessities that had been lacking on the plains and provided an opportunity for many to take advantage and move west. The railroad had been completed in 1869 after a four-year construction period and stretched 1,911 miles from Sacramento, California in the West to Omaha, Nebraska in the Midwest. It had been an immense engineering challenge, as it passed through mountain ranges, deserts, rivers, and valleys, and workers had to face life-threatening conditions, including avalanches in the mountains, the thick heat of the desert, and the Indian attacks on the plains. General William Tecumseh Sherman warned the Indians that "you cannot stop the locomotive any more than you can stop the sun or the moon."

Leland Stanford, one of the investors in the Central Pacific Railroad company (and whose name is synonymous with the university), tapped the gold "last spike" of the railway track with a silver hammer at Promontory Point, Utah on May 10,

1869, completing the construction. Suddenly, journeys were reduced from three months to one week, new towns were built along the line, and businesses and consumers could access the Asian markets. One day after the railroad opened, the first freight train rumbled out of California to the East Coast, carrying a shipment of Japanese teas.

A family in a sod house (1886).

But life was tough on the plains. Among the hardships families endured were lack of wood, a harsh climate, isolation, and loneliness. The lack of wood forced them to build houses from mud, sod, and thatch or to live in caves dug out of a hill. In sod houses, rain would cause mud to infiltrate food stores, and vermin, particularly lice, would scamper across the bedding. Without wood, buffalo chips (dried buffalo dung) would keep the fire burning, which was unappealing to many. Doors and windows among other items were purchased from the Sears and Roebuck company, whose first customers were settlers.

Harsh winters, tornadoes, droughts, fires, and blizzards could wipe out a whole crop. As farmers began moving from subsistence farming to commercial, they would choose to grow just one crop – usually corn or wheat – which would create perfect conditions for locusts and grasshoppers. From 1873 to 1877, grasshopper plagues infested Minnesota, causing bankruptcies across the state.

Finally, many people could not cope with the isolation and loneliness on the plains. Sometimes a family might emigrate with their wider community as a whole,[59] which would help to sustain healthy social bonds and a sense of security, but if not, the vastness of the plains could trigger a desperate longing for what they had left behind. Ole Rølvaag's *Giants in the Earth* (1927) depicts a Norwegian farmer's wife becoming intensely religious in her efforts to adjust, gradually descending into madness. In *My Ántonia* (1918) by Willa Cather, Antonia's father commits suicide when he loses hope during a brutal plains winter.

The cattle industry boomed at this time, with cowboys tasked with driving cattle from Texas to be sold in railhead towns in Kansas such as Abilene, Dodge City, and Ellsworth. Hollywood's depiction of them as skilled marksmen, lawless and independent, was entertaining but imprecise, as their job consisted mostly of slowly and patiently driving cattle north, and making frequent stops to ensure the cattle ate as much as they liked to retain their weight. One of their biggest fears was of a stampede, so cowboys would sing to soothe them. It took several weeks to round them up from the open range[60] and brand them before setting off, and the

---

59 Most would come from Britain, Ireland, Germany, Norway, or Sweden.

60 The age of the open range ended after Joseph Glidden invented barbed wire in 1874. Farmers used it to prevent animals from running off, separate them from crops, and to undertake selective breeding.

lasso, rather than the gun, was used to keep them in line. The cowboys' reputation came primarily from the rowdy drinking sessions they would engage in once they had delivered the cattle and collected their pay at their destination.

In 1878, John Wesley Powell identified a line that went roughly down the middle of the United States: the 100th meridian west. It separated the humid eastern part of the country from the arid western part where drought conditions prevailed. Powell tried to persuade the federal government that the aridity of the West required watersheds and irrigation so farmers could grow crops. Initially reluctant, the government eventually passed the Newlands Reclamation Act in 1902 authorizing federal funds to build dams and channels to irrigate the land. Most notably, the Theodore Roosevelt Dam in Arizona – one of the Act's first projects – was built between 1905 and 1911, and plenty more followed.

Some farmers were hugely successful, and many merged or were bought out by speculators to create large commercial farms, which became known as "bonanza farms." An abundance of cattle, wheat, and corn drove prices down for consumers, and enough food was produced in the country to feed its people forever. Americans' diets also improved, and when refrigerated railroad cars were developed in the late 1800s, fresh meat and vegetables became accessible to everyone.

Plains Indians

One problem for farmers, cowboys, and railway constructors was the Indians living in the plains. These consisted of more than thirty separate tribes, many of whom were nomadic and survived by following and hunting the American bison (also known as the buffalo). Others were semi-nomadic tribes, sometimes called Prairie Indians, and they spent part of the year farming and raising crops and the other part hunting bison.

The Plains Indians' first encounter with European immigrants occurred 200 years before they had even met a white man when they found feral horses roaming the plains. These had been brought over by the conquistadors and would escape, run off into the interior, and breed rapidly. The Indians would track them down, domesticate them, and ride them to hunt bison. This made the Indians more carnivorous and more belligerent, and they now competed with other tribes for the right to hunt.

In 1846, Francis Parkman set out on a tour to understand how the Indians lived, sensing their way of life would soon be lost. He described their virtuoso horsemanship while killing bison in *The Oregon Trail* and how every inch of the animal would be put to use – parts would be eaten; their hides would be made into clothing or covering for their tepees; their muscles fashioned into bowstrings or moccasins; their hoofs made into glue; their bones shaped into tools or ornaments; and their dung would be used as fuel.

As Hollywood has done for cowboys, the life of Plains Indians is commonly romanticized, but theirs was a warrior culture rooted in raiding, hunting, and killing. In one of the last hostilities between the Pawnee and the Sioux in 1873, they fought each other at the Massacre Canyon battle in Nebraska, where the Sioux killed over 150 Pawnees – men, women, and children – mutilated them, and set many on fire. These types of attacks and warfare between tribes had been practiced for decades.

Plains Indians tribes circa 1820

Certain Indian tribes demanded that, in order to reach adulthood, younger tribesmen needed to demonstrate their bravery and prowess in battle, and they would push their chiefs to go to war with the whites instead of making treaties. Within other tribes, the symbolic passage to adulthood took place through brutal rituals. For example, in the Mandan tribal culture, a young man would starve himself for three days in advance of the coming-of-age ceremony, whereupon he would be hung in the air from splints that would be hammered into his chest, shoulders, and back muscles. More splints would be hammered into his legs and arms, and the skulls of his ancestors were hung on the ends of them. He would eventually faint, either from loss of blood or sheer pain, and when he awoke, his left pinky finger would be chopped off as a sacrifice to the gods. Finally, he would run around in a circle as the villagers tore out the splints still embedded in his body.

The Plains Indians watched in astonishment at the thousands of whites making their way through on the Oregon Trail. Occasionally they would ambush them or raid them for supplies, and they hoped to live separately from them. But the sheer number of white settlers, their technologies, and the diseases they brought with them made a life independent of them impossible. Entire Indian Plains tribes were wiped out by disease, with as many as 90 percent of Indians killed by illnesses to which they had no immunity. The 1837 Great Plains smallpox epidemic alone killed over 17,000 Indians between 1837 and 1840, including many of the Mandan tribe who were reduced to as few as 125 people.

United States government policy towards the Plains Indians varied. One policy was to destroy their way of life, which they tried to do by decimating the herds of bison on the plains. Between 1872 and 1873, over 3 million bison were killed as white hunters slaughtered thousands every day (William Cody, known as Buffalo Bill, could kill up to 100 in a day). Sometimes they would take the bison's tongues and hides, but often they would just leave their carcasses to rot on the plains.

Another policy was to make treaties with the Indians and confine them to certain areas, or reservations, but land disputes became common and sometimes descended into brutal violence. When Chief Black Kettle of the Cheyenne camped his 750 people in a bend of the Big Sandy Creek,[61] he was preparing them to move to Fort Lyon under orders by the American military and even flew a United States flag with a white flag beneath it as a gesture of goodwill. But Colonel John Chivington and his cavalry ignored orders and marched in, killing as many men, women, and children as they could in cold blood. Known as the Sand Creek Massacre (1864), it remains one of the most highly charged and controversial events in American history and is one of the worst atrocities ever committed against the Indians. Estimates of the dead range between 100 and 600, and with the victims unarmed, Chivington's men took time to scalp them and cut out their unborn babies, taking those and other body parts – such as the male and female genitalia – as trophies which they publicly displayed in Denver's Apollo Theatre. The event is dramatized in the film *Soldier Blue* (1970).

Atrocities were committed on both sides, however. The Indians attacked isolated army posts and settlers' cabins and staged ambushes against US soldiers. In 1866, the Lakota Chief, Red Cloud, led US forces into a trap where 1,000 Indians lay in wait and massacred all 80 of them, mutilating the bodies by cutting off their noses, ears, hands, and feet, and tearing out their eyes and brains to lay them on rocks. Many had their faces smashed into bloody pulps, and others were struck by over 100 arrows.

---

61 In present-day Colorado.

In the East, the president, Rutherford B Hayes, favored assimilation over extermination. He acknowledged the wrongs committed by the Americans, saying that "many, if not most, of our Indian wars have had their origins in broken promises and acts of injustice on our part," and encouraged efforts to help the Indians adjust. Schools were set up[62] to specifically provide Native Americans with an Americanized education, and a group of wealthy philanthropists, who referred to themselves as Friends of the Indian, met annually at what became known as the Lake Mohonk Conference. In 1896, they called for the abolition of the tribal system and for Indians to become American citizens, but as settlers ventured farther into Indian lands, the differences between the two cultures would do more to keep them apart than bring them together.

This was especially the case if settlers anticipated finding gold on Indian land. Once a treaty had been made with a tribe, the US Army was supposed to defend Indian rights, but they found it hard not to side with the whites or to respect the cultural differences of the Indians, most of whom they viewed as hostile and uncivilized. The Bald Hills War and the Owens Valley Indian War occurred in California during the gold rush, and the Great Sioux War of 1876 began after General George Custer reported the existence of gold in the Black Hills of South Dakota. This prompted a huge gold rush that violated the Treaty of Fort Laramie.[63]

Prospectors and the US Army flocked into the Black Hills, and with the treaties ignored, the Indians felt within their rights to fight back. Sitting Bull predicted a great victory for the Lakota tribes after he performed a Sun Dance (a ceremonial

---

62 The Carlisle Indian Industrial School (established in 1879), for example.

63 In 1876, thousands of gold-seekers flocked to the new town of Deadwood, South Dakota, although the town was still within Indian land.

tradition among the Plains tribes), during which he made 50 sacrificial cuts into each arm and danced for hours. He fell into a trance and claimed he saw soldiers tumbling into his camp like grasshoppers falling from the sky, and the Indians, looking for any pretext to attack, interpreted it as a great victory and prepared for battle.

A few weeks later, when several tribes missed a federal deadline to move onto reservations, the US Army was dispatched to confront them. Custer ignored orders to wait for reinforcements and underestimated the number of Indians in the area, and his 210 men were attacked by as many as 3,000 Indians. Within an hour, he and all of his soldiers were dead.[64] Custer himself was killed by two bullet wounds, and after the battle, the Indians stripped, scalped, and dismembered the US troops' corpses on the battlefield. This was the Battle of Little Bighorn (or Custer's Last Stand), the most decisive Indian victory in the Plains Indian War, and it shook up the eastern communities in Washington and Philadelphia, which were just about to celebrate the centenary of the founding of the United States.

The US military intensified its efforts to subdue the Indians in its aftermath. In the winter of 1876, in a battle known as the Dull Knife Fight, Colonel Ranald Mackenzie led 1,000 soldiers into a Cheyenne camp and surprised them in a dawn attack, forcing many to flee without clothes or blankets into the freezing countryside. Many of the Cheyenne died from frostbite (including 11 babies), and the battle effectively ended Cheyenne resistance to the whites.

Crazy Horse, a Sioux Indian chief who had fought at the Battle of Little Bighorn and had led raids and attacks on US soldiers

---

64 It was witnessed by Black Elk and described (albeit 60 years after the event) in the book *Black Elk Speaks*, recorded by the writer John Neihardt in 1932.

for years, surrendered in Nebraska where he was later killed by a US soldier in 1877. Sitting Bull surrendered a few years later and was shot dead by an Indian agent policeman after an altercation at his house in 1890.

There were scattered conflicts in the 1870s and 1880s, such as against the Nez Percé tribe led by Chief Joseph. When Chief Joseph finally surrendered, he gave one of the most famous speeches of the American West when he proclaimed, "The little children are freezing to death. My people, some of them, have run away to the hills and have no blankets, no food; no one knows where they are – perhaps freezing to death. I want to have time to look for my children and see how many I can find. Maybe I shall find them among the dead. Hear me, my chiefs. I am tired; my heart is sick and sad. From where the sun now stands, I will fight no more forever."

Indians on the Plains (1901).

Geronimo, an Apache leader whose wife, three children, and mother were killed by Mexican soldiers in 1851, devoted his life to avenging them and violently resisted American settlers coming onto his land in Gila, Arizona. He was put on a reservation in San Carlos and broke out on three separate occasions, making the US authorities look ridiculous. He was finally captured for good in 1886 and forced to live on a reservation at Fort Sill, Oklahoma until his death in 1909.

The final desperate end to Indian resistance occurred at the Battle of Wounded Knee in South Dakota in 1890. A Paiute prophet named Wovoka was said to have had a vision from the Creator that an Indian messiah would come and free the world of the white man. He and his followers performed the "ghost dance," which encouraged them to believe that the shirts they wore had the power to repel bullets. On the morning of December 29, 1890, the US Army surrounded the dancers and tried to force them to surrender their weapons and, at some point, a shot was fired (it is unclear by whom), provoking the massacre of 150 Indians,[65] many of them women and children. The site of Wounded Knee remains a sacrosanct place for Native Americans.

The policy of placing Indian tribes on reservations was intended as a temporary measure, designed to encourage them to become more like farmers and homestead settlers. But the Indians had little experience in living that way and were often put on unfarmable land, falling prey to speculators and sharks who would cheat them out of it. In 1881, the poet and writer Helen Hunt Jackson wrote *A Century of Dishonor* in an attempt to draw attention to the plight of the Indians, sending a copy of the book to every member of Congress at her own expense, but it had little impact. Today 325 reservations remain in the United States.

---

65   Some historians put this number twice as high.

The Populists

Economic state	Debt	Earning power / bushel	Must sell (bushels)
Spot	$5,000	$1	5,000
Deflation	$5,000	$0.5	10,000
Inflation	$5,000	$3	1,666

After the Civil War, farmers' fortunes dwindled. Most farmers were heavily in debt, and overproduction and the limited money supply created a deflationary economic environment which drove commodity prices down. This meant farmers had to sell more to earn the same amount of money (*see box*), and farmers angrily pointed at the owners of railroads and grain elevators, arguing that the monopolies they held enabled them to charge predatory prices. Frank Norris's classic novel *The Octopus: A Story of California* (1901) portrayed the railroad as an octopus with its tentacles reaching all over the country, and the farmers as oppressed and mistreated.

Farmers began to organize themselves to address their problems together, founding the Grange Movement in 1867 to share farming and agricultural practices, and the Farmers' Alliance to lobby the government for economic policies that would benefit them. They also formed cooperatives to find ways to store grain without having to pay grain elevator fees.

In 1892, the farmers created the Populist Party (also known as the People's Party) to challenge the Republicans and Democrats alike. They held their first presidential nomination convention on July 4 in Omaha, Nebraska, during which Ignatius Donnelly, a Minnesotan congressman who had written a dystopian novel called *Caesar's Column*, was chosen to write the preamble. *Caesar's Column* depicts a proletarian society that deposes a tyrannical oligarchy after a brutal, violent rebellion, and his preamble acted as a veiled warning to the wealthy, corrupt elite.

The Populist Party platform ran on the direct election of senators, nationalization of the railroads, a graduated income tax, an eight-hour workday, a ban on immigration, and a ban on foreign land ownership. They also campaigned for free coinage of silver at a ratio of 16:1 which was designed to create inflation. Many miners and farmers owned silver and relied on selling it to make a living, but the Coinage Act of 1873 had effectively ended the use of silver as a form of currency,[66] and its value plummeted after passage of the act, which they referred to as the "Crime of 1873." During the financial depression of the 1890s, the Populists promoted a broadly antisemitic theory that the depression was caused by bankers themselves, starting a trend of populist parties pushing conspiracy theories that continues to this day.

The Populist Party carried five states and just over 1 million votes in the 1892 election, losing to the Democrats, led by Grover Cleveland. The following year, a severe economic depression struck the country, and the Democrats, aware of the Populists' demands to bring silver back as a form of currency, debated whether to take up the same policy. They split between "silverites" and "goldbugs," with William Jennings Bryan, an attorney from Nebraska and defender of farmers' rights, taking up the silverite mantle in his famous "Cross of Gold" speech. A superb orator, his flair for drama and use of religious symbolism whipped the crowd into a fervor, whooping and cheering as he closed with the words, "You shall not press down upon the brow of labor this crown of thorns. You shall not crucify mankind upon a cross of gold."

---

66 The Coinage Act of 1792 had established a bimetallic standard, meaning that both gold and silver were recognized as official forms of currency in the country.

It earned Bryan the Democrat nomination for the election of 1896, which officially split the party between his followers and the "goldbug" National Democrats – within which Grover Cleveland remained, although his two terms were now up as president. It also created a dilemma within the Populist Party who were torn between simply pivoting their support towards the Democrats or continuing to fight on for their other causes.

Eventually, they decided to continue, nominating Bryan as well. Bryan and the Democrats knew this would split the vote between themselves and the Populists, so he disavowed his nomination to the Populist Party, but the Populists could not agree on an alternative option, and Bryan remained on the ticket. This led to the inevitable defeat of both the Populist and Democrat parties in the election, and the Republican Party's William McKinley entered the White House.

The anomaly of the 1896 election led many to interpret L Frank Baum's The Wonderful Wizard of Oz (1900) as an allegory for the election itself. The Scarecrow was said to represent the farmers (no brain), the Tin Man as the industrial worker (no heart), and the Lion (no courage) to represent William Jennings Bryan. The Wizard was McKinley, Oz was an abbreviation for ounce, and the gold road represented the gold standard. The primary difference between the film and the book is that in the film Dorothy wears ruby shoes, whereas in the book she wears silver ones – silver being the key to her, and the dollar's, security.

The Populist Party gradually died out after 1896, but many of their proposals found their way into law. The 16th and 17th Constitutional Amendments gave power to Congress to set an income tax and gave voters the right to elect senators directly, and the Hepburn Act of 1906 regulated maximum railroad rates. Farmers became less profitable owing to the growth of new technologies and commercial farming, and their numbers reduced (partly out of bankruptcy). The industry became a less visible feature of American life: in 1850, 64 percent of Americans lived or worked on farms, but by 1920, it was only 30 percent, and farmers switched their strategy from running on their own platform to lobbying politicians and enacting legislation in Washington.[67]

Another legacy of the Populist Party was the term "populist" itself. It originally referred to the party and the related left-wing movements that followed it, although later it expanded to include any anti-establishment movement. Still today, with little attempt to control or limit the term's reference, politicians such as Bernie Sanders and Donald Trump have both been labeled populists despite standing for very different things.

---

67 An attempt to highlight the importance of the farmer was developed by the Granger Movement in 1875 with a picture of a farmer in a red shirt with the caption "I feed you all."

CHAPTER 12

THE PROGRESSIVE ERA (1896–1916)

Overview of the Progressives

Progressivism in the early 20th century was a social and political reform movement spurred by changes in US society generated by industrial labor, urban growth, women's movements, immigration, and religious and racial division. It was urban-based, and its members generally came from the Northeast. They were well-educated, Protestant, and middle class, although almost all politicians and public figures were quick to appropriate the "progressive" label for its implied forward-thinking characteristics.

Progressives wanted to make America more meritocratic, and they believed in the strength of democracy, introducing the 17th Amendment in 1912. This established direct elections of senators, replacing the previous model of senatorial appointment by state legislatures, and the Progressives sought to increase accountability and reduce corruption with an increased focus on political processes.

Progressivism did have a more sinister side, however, in that it accepted racial superiority and promoted discriminatory policies. New immigration and sterilization laws were introduced, and segregation intensified (particularly in the South under Woodrow Wilson's administration), leading to a revival of the Ku Klux Klan in 1915.

The definition of progressivism has changed over the years and is today primarily associated with the left-leaning faction of the Democrat Party. That faction emphasizes racial equality and minority rights, advocates for universal healthcare, decries US imperialism, pronounces the dangers of climate change, and supports taxing the rich. Its platform is partly in response to the role played by the banks in the Global Financial Crisis of 2008 and the huge wealth that accumulated in the hands of technology and financial tycoons at a time when many people were losing their jobs and struggling to pay their bills. The progressives of the early 20th century would have understood those fears, for their own platform was a reaction to the wealth of the industrial tycoons and the growing gap between the rich and the poor.

African Americans in the Progressive Era

After 1876, segregation in the South continued as Southern Redeemers took control. A "New South" campaign was launched by Southern elites to develop it into a modern, industrialized society to mirror that of the North. Birmingham, Alabama became a manufacturing hub for iron and steel; the Duke family took advantage of the newly-invented cigarette rolling machine to create the American Tobacco Company in Durham, North Carolina; and textile mills flourished in the southern Appalachian foothills of the Carolinas and Georgia (although they became known for their use of child labor).

But the New South vision was only a partial success. Redeemer governments gradually reduced or eliminated state government programs that benefited poor people, most of whom were Black. By 1890, the per capita expenditure in the South for public education was only 97 cents compared to $2.24 in the country.

The 15th Amendment specified that African Americans could not be denied the right to vote on account of their race. But states sought ways to circumvent it by ruling that men had to pass a literacy test and pay a poll tax. Most African Americans were illiterate,[68] and few could afford to pay a poll tax, so on these grounds, they were excluded from the vote. Governments realized these rules might also exclude poor, uneducated, white people, so to solve that problem, they added a clause that allowed men to vote if they were descended from men who had voted before 1867 ("grand-father clause").

State governments in the South began to introduce legislation that legalized racial segregation. These were the so-called Jim Crow laws, named after a Black stage character, that denied African Americans certain jobs and education and created separate areas in railway cars, hotels, restaurants, hospitals, schools, and parks. Those who defied the Jim Crow laws faced arrest, fines, jail sentences, or death.

The Supreme Court was tested by these new laws when the case of *Plessy v Ferguson* reached it in 1896. Homer Plessy – who was seven-eighths white yet classified as Black under Louisiana law – had sat in the "whites only" car of a train and was arrested for refusing to vacate it. The railroad itself sided with Plessy (as upholding segregation would mean incurring the expense of adding more cars to the train) and hoped the Court would rule against the law – but it did not, and Plessy was convicted. In an 8-1 verdict, the dissenting Justice John Marshall Harlan (who, ironically, was a former slave owner from Kentucky) predicted that segregation would plant the "seeds of race hate," into state law.

---

68 It had been illegal for slaves to learn to read or write in the antebellum years.

Most African Americans in the South worked as cotton farmers, often as sharecroppers. This meant they lived as tenants on a farm and gave part of each crop to the landlord as rent. A sharecropper would often have to borrow equipment, seed, and fertilizer at the start of a season and hope the harvest would be bountiful enough to provide him with the means to pay his lenders back. But high interest rates, unpredictable harvests, and unscrupulous landlords kept most sharecroppers in a permanent state of indebtedness. Moreover, cotton farming was backbreaking work: the plants needed careful tending, and working in the oppressive summer sun was exhausting – although this generated little compassion from the landlord.

"The Waco Horror" photo essay in The Crisis published this photo of the lynching of Jesse Washington (1916).

Most white Southerners unashamedly supported segregation. Black subordination was underlined by violent white groups who vandalized Black schools and attacked, tortured, and lynched Black citizens in the night. The most ruthless group was the Ku Klux Klan, some of whose members worked in the highest levels of government. State governments mostly ignored lynchings, which were used by whites to terrorize and control Black people and would consist of hanging them from trees, torturing, and mutilating them. From 1882 to 1968, over 4,700 lynchings occurred in the US, the brutality of which was on full display in a photo essay called "The Waco Horror" published in the 1916 issue of *The Crisis*, sharing graphic images of the lynching of Jesse Washington, a 17-year-old Black man in Waco, Texas accused of killing a white woman.[69]

African Americans debated how to respond. Memphis teacher Ida B Wells refused to leave a train car designated for white people, and when she was forcibly removed, she sued the railroad – which she won at first, but a higher court then overruled the decision. Rosa Parks would follow in her footsteps 72 years later. Wells became co-owner of the Memphis newspaper *Free Speech and Headlight* and used her position to write about school segregation, sexual harassment, and lynchings.

Booker T Washington (1856–1915) was one of the most prominent voices at the time, preferring (although not necessarily liking) to take an "accommodationist" approach to segregation. He was born into slavery in Virginia – his father was white; his mother a slave – and he was only permitted to go to school after he had worked from 4 a.m. to 9 a.m. each morning in a local salt works. He heard about a place where formerly enslaved people could get a fuller education, and Washington walked the 500-mile distance to

69 Sometimes a lynching victim was white, as in the case of Leo Frank – a Jewish man who was convicted of murdering a 13-year-old employee in Atlanta, Georgia – but most were Black.

the Hampton Institute where he convinced administrators to let him attend the school and took a job as a janitor to help pay his tuition. His studies so impressed its founder, General Samuel Armstrong, that Armstrong referred him as principal of a new school for African Americans in Alabama, the Tuskegee Normal and Industrial Institute (today known as the Tuskegee Institute).

An excellent orator, Washington emphasized economic self-determination over political and civil rights and urged Blacks to accept discrimination and focus on helping themselves. He made a speech at the Cotton States Exposition in September 1895 known as the "Atlanta Compromise" speech, wherein he outlined his accommodationist approach by encouraging Black people to become proficient in agriculture, mechanics, commerce, and domestic service, and to "dignify and glorify common labor." Of course, this was all music to white people's ears, and Washington simply asked them to trust Black people with opportunities.

A different approach to Washington's was offered by W E B Du Bois (1868–1963). Du Bois was a Black writer and intellectual from Massachusetts and had no connection to slavery, having been educated at Harvard and the University of Berlin (which was, at the time, arguably the best university in the world). He believed Washington's accommodationist model would serve only to perpetuate white oppression and took a professorship in 1897 at Atlanta University from where he wrote *The Souls of Black Folk* (1903) – a social study of the South and a classic of American literature. He introduced the concept of double consciousness, which challenged African Americans to consider both how they saw themselves, and how white people saw them.

Du Bois, calling for "ceaseless agitation and insistent demand for equality," advocated political action and a civil rights agenda. He was one of the founders of the National Association for the Advancement of Colored People (NAACP) and served as editor of the organization's monthly magazine, *The Crisis*, for 25 years. He also coined the phrase the "Talented Tenth" – the proposition that one in ten Black men could become leaders of the Black community by acquiring a college education, writing books, and directly involving themselves in social change.

At the time, the opposing viewpoints of Washington and Du Bois polarized African American leaders into "conservative" supporters of Washington and his "radical" critics. Du Bois later criticized Marcus Garvey's Back to Africa movement in the 1920s, and in the 1960s it was Du Bois's philosophy of agitation and protest that flowed directly into the Civil Rights movement.

Gender Spheres and the First Wave of Feminism

Differences between genders were emphasized in the late 19th century. The concept of "gender spheres" was rooted in the idea that the type of work men and women did was different – men were considered more rational but aggressive and less moral; women were considered nurturing but emotional and more volatile. The ideal woman was considered an "angel in the house," devoted and submissive to her husband, self-sacrificing, and pure – and many women, such as the authors Lydia Sigourney and Sarah Hale (who wrote the nursery rhyme *Mary Had a Little Lamb*), promoted this vision.

There were certainly some women who aspired to stay at home, but the reality was that many women were too poor not to work. Chores and tasks on the farm had historically been split between husband and wife, and as cities increased in size and population, work opportunities for women grew beyond the farm, and they took jobs as domestic servants, laborers in factories and mills, teachers, nurses, secretaries, and department store clerks.

Men, on the other hand, were bucketed into a category that identified them as aggressive and competitive. Herbert Spencer, the English philosopher, drew from Darwin's theory of survival of the fittest to argue that humans needed to be ruthless to succeed, and as churches began to worry that Christianity was becoming too feminized, a movement known as Muscular Christianity developed. Originating in England with organizations such as the Young Men's Christian Association (YMCA) and the Boy Scouts, Muscular Christianity was applied in English public schools where it was thought to build character.[70]

In America, Muscular Christianity was expressed through American nationalism, discipline, and competitive sports. American (or gridiron) football was invented by Walter Camp in 1869, and basketball was invented by James Naismith of the YMCA in 1891. Champions of Muscular Christianity included Billy Sunday, the prominent evangelist, and the future president Theodore Roosevelt who, as a child, had suffered from asthma and other ailments. He worked to overcome them through boxing, hiking, and swimming.

Women took steps into social reform and politics. The Woman's Christian Temperance Union (WCTU) was founded in 1874 to promote the moderation of alcohol consumption. Its leader, Frances Willard, argued for female suffrage

---

70 Written about in Thomas Hughes's *Tom Brown's School Days* (1857), and William Farrar's *Eric, or, Little by Little* (1858).

in part to protect women from the violence a man may commit when drunk. Carry Nation, who described herself as a "bulldog running along at the feet of Jesus, barking at what He doesn't like," applied a more aggressive policy by attacking alcohol-serving establishments with an axe. Nation was beaten and jailed many times, and the WCTU stopped funding her after she became too outspoken and, in their eyes, too much of a liability.

Elizabeth Cady Stanton in 1880.

Women's suffrage in America got its start at the Seneca Falls Convention in 1847. There, the attendees signed a Declaration of Sentiments that laid out grievances and set the agenda for the women's rights movement. They were, however, left frustrated when their right to vote was overlooked in the 15th Amendment, and Elizabeth Cady Stanton and Susan B Anthony founded the National Woman

Suffrage Association in 1869. This saw its first success in the West when the territory of Wyoming granted women the right to vote, followed by Utah in 1870. However, it was not until 1917 that the first states east of the Mississippi granted women's suffrage (Rhode Island and New York).

The suffrage movement also pushed for more education opportunities for women, although they had to manage fears that if they became "overeducated," they would go insane. Matthew Vassar founded Vassar College in 1861 where women were monitored and supervised every minute of the day to prevent any overstimulation that might unhinge them. Ellen Richards was a Vassar student who in 1870 went on to become the first woman admitted to the Massachusetts Institute of Technology. She pioneered scientific education for women and laid the foundation for the new science of home economics.

The values of the "women's sphere" were further promoted through the Settlement House Movement – a home where destitute immigrants could go if they had nowhere else to turn. The House provided food, English lessons, and tips on how to survive American culture. The first one, called Hull House and founded by Jane Addams, opened in 1889 in Chicago and created a new kind of profession: social work.

For many poor families, having multiple children was a serious problem, so Margaret Sanger, a social reformer and activist, worked hard to provide contraception and planned parenting information. To do so violated the Comstock Act of 1873, which made it illegal to send "obscene, lewd or lascivious publications through the mail," and Sanger had to flee to Britain until public opinion settled down. In 1916, she opened the first birth control clinic in the United States and founded the American Birth Control League (which later became the Planned Parenthood Federation of America). She became one of the heroines of the feminist movement.

Sometimes women could profit from the prevailing notion of their gentleness. In 1892, Lizzie Borden was tried for the murder of her father and stepmother, chopping them up to 29 times with an axe. There was no alternative theory, but attributing such a heinous crime to a woman was tremendously difficult, and the defense simply rested on whether the jury really believed someone with such a delicate nature could commit it. Her attorneys encouraged her to act frail and gentle, and the jury – who were all men at the time – acquitted her. She lived out the rest of her life quietly until her death in 1927, although popular consensus felt she had gotten away with it.

By the beginning of the 20th century, the Victorian ideals of womanhood were breaking down, due in part to the women's suffrage movement along with their increased employment and educational opportunities. More progress would be made in the 1960s and 1970s in areas such as equal pay, equal rights, and an end to sexual harassment and discrimination – although this time women based their arguments on the similarities between themselves and men, rather than the differences. But the first wave of feminism was crucial to providing the women of the 1960s with the courage and inspiration they needed, and they leveraged many of the same strategies to fulfill their goals, including grassroots organizing, building coalitions, and campaigning through the media.

New Immigrants

The turn of the century saw a new wave of immigration into the US. Between 1900 and 1915, more than 15 million immigrants entered the country, mostly from Europe, where emigration was so high that by the eve of the First World War, 38 percent of the world's population was of European ancestry. Most went to the United States, but emigration to South America, South Africa, Canada, Australia, and New Zealand was also common.

People were primarily forced out of their home countries through persecution or economics. In Russia, Czar Alexander III blamed Jews for the assassination of his father, Alexander II, in 1881, and murderous pogroms were waged against them. Italians sought to leave the violence and ensuing poverty of the Italian Unification Wars, and the Chinese were escaping the Taiping Rebellion, a civil war between 1850 and 1864 that left an estimated 20 million people dead. For others, the availability of work, the higher salaries, and the cheap farmland were what attracted them to the United States. Work was needed mostly in coal or steel mines, textile mills, and construction; and railroad and land companies advertised the availability of farmland, with some providing subsidies to settle in the region.

The cost of emigrating kept the brunt of the globe's poor from entering the US, but moving also required courage and initiative. Before the mid-1800s, immigrants would board a sailing ship and spend between 40 and 90 days crossing the ocean. Hundreds of passengers would be crammed into tight quarters in steerage travel (the cheapest) where they would have to contend with lice and rats, and many died of typhus or dysentery contracted on the ship. By the late 19th century, things had improved with the introduction of steamships, which reduced the crossing to between seven and ten days, presenting opportunities for birds of passage.

Until 1855, migrants would sail into the docks on the east side of Manhattan, New York. However, as immigration surged, the city developed Castle Island (now Castle Clinton), the country's first immigration processing center, on the southern tip of Manhattan. It was then transferred to Ellis Island in 1890, and the federal government took over its administration.

Upon arrival, immigrants were tagged with information from their ship's registry and then waited in long lines for medical and legal inspections to determine whether they were fit for entry. Doctors checked those passing through for more than 60 diseases including mental illness and trachoma, a contagious eye condition that caused more detainments and deportations than any other ailment and required the examiner to turn an immigrant's eyelids inside out using a buttonhook to check for contamination.

Acceptance rates were high: 90 percent of people were admitted entry, and for most of the 19th century, the United States readily welcomed immigrants. "The New Colossus" is a poem written by Emma Lazarus inscribed on a bronze plaque inside the Statue of Liberty, which was a late 100-year birthday present from the government of France. It ends with the words:

> *"Keep, ancient lands, your storied pomp!" cries she*
>
> *With silent lips. "Give me your tired, your poor,*
>
> *Your huddled masses yearning to breathe free,*
>
> *The wretched refuse of your teeming shore.*
>
> *Send these, the homeless, tempest-tost to me,*
>
> *I lift my lamp beside the golden door!"*

The poem contains themes of mercy and protection, and the torch acts as a beacon welcoming those landing on US shores.

For some, adapting to life in America was easy. The British and Irish could speak the language, came from industrialized countries, and had in-demand skills. For others, blending in was more difficult, and they tended to cluster together in cities and rural communities. Many struggled with English, and some would never learn it at all, relying on their children (who were taught exclusively in English at public schools) to help them when needed. Still others struggled with the accelerated work rhythms of industrial labor and found themselves having to forgo certain religious traditions – for instance, Jews often had to work on Saturdays, and Catholics could not celebrate all their feast days.[71]

Various Americanization programs at public schools aimed to help immigrants assimilate and learn English. In New York, over 70 percent of children were from immigrant families in 1909, and some classrooms contained 150 children (three to a seat). World events also provided an incentive for people to speak English – many German immigrants stopped speaking their first language when America entered the First World War in 1917 out of fear of being targeted for disloyalty.

For immigrants of the era, upward mobility into the middle classes was achievable, although prejudice often had to be overcome. The Chinese and Blacks from the South were discriminated against for accepting lower wages, the Irish for Catholicism, and the Germans and the Russians for socialist politics or anarchism. Nativism (holding white Americans

---

71 Abraham Cahan's semi-autobiographical novel, *The Rise of David Levinsky* (1917), narrates some of the fears and the loneliness he experienced arriving as a Russian immigrant.

with older family trees in high regard) grew in popularity, and its supporters sought to restrict entry of certain "inferior" races into America, citing theories like social Darwinism and eugenics to support their claims.

As immigration grew, concerns about wage depression and job competition spurred the passage of legislation to contain it. The Chinese Exclusion Act provided an absolute ten-year ban on Chinese laborers immigrating to the United States, and the Emergency Immigration Act used a quota system that limited annual immigration from any given country. The National Origins Act of 1924 reduced that quota even further by restricting the numbers of immigrants to no more than 2 percent of the total number of each nationality who had been living in the US in 1890, which primarily impacted Southern and Eastern Europeans. The act also completely excluded immigrants from Asia (apart from Japan and the Philippines).

Immigration to the United States remained strict until the passage of the Immigration and Nationality Act of 1965. Immigration had plummeted during the Depression and the Second World War, but the civil rights movement, which stressed equality and fair treatment for all, called for the immigration system to be re-evaluated. The 1965 act abolished the quota system in favor of a preference system that enabled Americans to sponsor relatives from their country of origin, encouraged skilled workers and professionals, and allowed for refugees. This led to a huge shift in immigration patterns: today, most immigrants come from South America and Asia and immigration remains a hot-button issue for politicians.

Growth of the Cities

The scale of immigration growth at the start of the 20th century meant that the population sizes of US cities increased dramatically, and land values and rent went up. By 1900, two-thirds of New York's population were living in tenement housing on the Lower East Side, which was usually a cheaply constructed building of five to seven stories. As many as 12 adults would sleep in a room 13 feet across, and up to 20 people would share one toilet. People were vulnerable to fires and illnesses and the infant death rate was as high as one in ten.

How the Other Half Lives, by Jacob Riis (1889).

Jacob Riis, a journalist who emigrated from Denmark in 1870 when he was 21, documented and photographed life in tenement conditions in his pioneering book, *How the Other Half Lives*. He captured children sleeping on streets, babies being cared for by other children, and families crowded into cramped living spaces. With little public transport, people had to live near their place of work, and New York became one of the most densely populated places on the planet, housing 500,000 people per square mile.

The lack of city central planning meant there was little land set aside for park spaces, and water supplies were rare, especially in the South. In 1885, Baltimore, New Orleans, and Mobile still had open sewers, and Philadelphia had 82,000 cesspools. Every household had an open fire for heating and cooking, and many would use a kerosene lamp for lighting, causing innumerable fires. Before municipal fire depart-ments were created,[72] fire prevention consisted of gangs of adolescent boys rushing to fight them when they saw smoke and flames coming from a building. The Great Chicago Fire of 1871 killed an estimated 300 people and caused around $200 million in damages. Smoke from homes, factories, and plants generated a yellow hue in the air, and with winds tending to blow from the west to the east, the west side of cities became more affluent.

Cities were also home to animals, either used for transport or food, and urban planners worried about how cities could manage the accumulation of all the manure and buildup of animal carcasses. When horses died, they would often rot on the street. An event known as the "Great Epizootic" of 1872 affected one out of every four horses in the country, including 30,000 in New York. It was an outbreak of equine influenza, and it killed 1,400 horses in total.

Deaths and illnesses in the human population were often caused by food prepared in unsanitary conditions. Upton Sinclair's novel *The Jungle* (1906) was intended as a socialist tract exposing the drudgery of life as a "wage slave" but

---

72 The first municipal fire department in New York was established in 1865.

in fact prompted the establishment of the Food and Drug Administration (FDA). He wrote how food in a meat-packing plant was processed by men with skin and lung diseases, and that the meat for canning and sausage was piled on the floor before being carried off in carts containing sawdust, human spit and urine, rat dung, rat poison, and even dead rats. Theodore Roosevelt ordered an immediate investigation and Sinclair quipped, "I aimed at the public's heart and by accident hit it in the stomach."

City government was dominated by "political machines," so called for their efficiency and predictability. The most famous was Tammany Hall in New York, run by William Magear Tweed ("Boss Tweed"), and it traded votes for promises to provide jobs or housing. The machines were prone to massive corruption, with Tammany Hall plundering millions of dollars from the New York Treasury through devices such as faked leases, false vouchers, and overpriced goods and services. Reformers furiously tried to eliminate this type of theft but found it difficult as many of a machine's supporters were given something in return. But the reformers gradually made inroads, helped by a new breed of journalists called "muckrakers."

Muckrakers were investigative journalists who used interviews, photographs, and undercover reporting to expose and lampoon the corruption of political bosses in newspaper articles and books. Lincoln Steffens published *The Shame of the Cities* (1904) after he had investigated the workings of political machines in several major cities, including New York, Philadelphia, Pittsburgh, St. Louis, and Chicago. He pointed to businessmen as the primary source of corruption.

In time, horse-drawn cars were replaced by streetcars (also called trams or trolleys), bicycles, and automobiles. City density diminished as its geographical limits expanded and as people started commuting to work instead, and the visual aspect of cities changed with the invention of the steel girder skyscraper. Their first wide application was after the Great Chicago Fire when buildings of steel and plate glass were built by architects such as William Le Baron Jenney (who built the first modern-day skyscraper in the US[73]), Daniel Burnham, and Louis Sullivan from the Chicago School of Architecture.

Urban identity developed through sports and local newspapers. The railroad network facilitated the rise of major league sports (the National League of Professional Baseball Clubs was established in 1876; the National Football League was established in 1920), and newspapermen like Joseph Pulitzer and William Randolph Hearst published sensationalist and human interest stories read by millions of people. Their publications provided a shared cultural touchstone for residents and gave them conversation pieces and reasons to feel proud, which was vital for cities to attract workers and businesses.

Ethnic enclaves in cities gradually broke up as fewer first-generation immigrants ("greenhorns") arrived, and by the third generation, ethnic identification often became nothing more than a token interest. In broad terms, America has been astonishingly successful at integrating diverse nationalities, races, and religions, and one only has to look to the northern border to see how French Canadian demands can threaten the unity of a country.

Today, more than 80 percent of the American population lives in metropolitan areas, the largest of which are New

---

73 This was the Home Insurance Building in Chicago. Built in 1885, it was demolished in 1931.

York, Los Angeles, and Chicago. The reasons for living in a city today are not dissimilar to those from a century ago – job opportunities are broader and wider, wages are higher, and there are more diversions and opportunities to meet people. The United States is the fourth largest country in the world,[74] but its urban areas take up only 3 percent of its total land area, and a great deal of the country remains totally unpopulated, with just over 40 percent used for agriculture and forestry.

Religion in the United States

The various religions brought by new immigrants to the United States were allowed to flourish thanks to America's principle of religious freedom. Most Americans were of a Protestant denomination (it remains so), and this period saw Christianity in America pivoting away from the doctrinal, judgmental God of the First and Second Great Awakenings to be replaced with a more kindly, compassionate God and Jesus as one's companion.

Elizabeth Stuart Phelps's *The Gates Ajar* (1868) depicts the afterlife as a comfortable, homely place where families reunited with their loved ones (even their pets), singing songs around the piano. This new image of Heaven helped survivors of the Civil War manage their grief, and the book sold over 100,000 copies in the United States and England. The sequels, *Beyond the Gates* (1883) and *The Gates Between* (1887), are set in Heaven itself.

Another invocation of Jesus included asking the question "What would Jesus do?" first imagined in Charles Sheldon's *In His Steps* (1896). The book's plot revolves around a pastor who refuses to help a beggar who then dies, prompting

---

74 The three largest are Russia, Canada, and China.

the pastor to ask himself what Jesus would have done. Lew Wallace's *Ben Hur: A Tale of the Christ* (1880) is an adventure story set in the Roman Empire that portrays Jesus as a kindly man of love and forgiveness, providing help and encouragement to Ben Hur at key moments in the story, and saving his mother and sister from leprosy.

Protestant Revivalism continued to play a central role in the United States. Dwight Moody (1837–1899) converted to evangelical Christianity when he was 17 and toured the country with Ira Sankey, a gospel singer and composer. Moody preached the "old-fashioned gospel" which emphasized a literal interpretation of the Bible and anticipated the premillennial Second Coming. In Chicago, he built one of the nation's major evangelical centers – the Moody Church and Bible Institute – which is still active today.

American Protestantism divided into liberal and evangelical branches at the beginning of the 20th century. Charles Darwin's theory of evolution and Charles Lyell's geological surveys which indicated that the Earth was millions of years old were difficult for Christians to reconcile (Genesis puts the age of the Earth at around 6,000 years). Historical-critical Bible studies also revealed several contradictions and different writing styles, which muddied the waters even further.

The liberal branch that developed was prepared to accept these modern theories.[75] It tried to adapt Christian ethics to social problems such as poverty, crime, and alcoholism (the Social Gospel), and Henry Ward Beecher accepted Charles Darwin's theory of evolution. But as an ardent teetotaler and advocate of the temperance movement, he struggled to explain why Jesus would turn water into wine. One argument

---

75   Also known as Liberal Theology and, historically, Christian Modernism.

said Jesus had not actually made wine but rather grape juice, and another was that Jesus would never perform such a miracle today in light of all the problems alcohol had caused.

The American Catholic Church was predominantly made up of Irish who had been driven from their homeland as victims of the potato famine of the 1840s and 1850s. As huge numbers of Catholics poured into New York, Archbishop John Hughes argued for a Catholic school system separate from that of the public school system which was dominated by Protestants and Protestant teachings. The Third Plenary Council of Baltimore, so dissatisfied with public education, mandated that all parishes nationwide have a school and that all Catholic children be sent to those schools.

Catholics had to counter a great deal of bias against them. Certain Protestant leaders continued to believe Catholicism was the "Whore of Babylon" that had been written about in the Book of Revelation, and the cartoonist Thomas Nast depicted Catholic bishops as crocodiles emerging from the river into New York. Maria Monk's *Awful Disclosures* (1849) caused a public outcry as she described how Catholic nuns were forced to have sex with priests and how nuns' babies were immediately baptized, strangled, and dumped in a lime pit in the basement. Scholars now consider the book a hoax, but much damage was done.

Italian, Slavic, and Polish immigrants diversified the Catholic population after 1870 and brought their own rituals with them, which many bishops fought to prevent to preserve the uniformity of the Catholic faith. PP Cahensly's plan to create ethnically distinct parishes was rejected, and events such as the Madonna of 115th Street – an annual parade created by Italian immigrants in East Harlem, New York – was forced underground.

Jewish immigrants were mostly German Reform Jews. Rabbi Isaac Meyer Wise wanted Reform Judaism to fit in more with Protestant-style rituals and attempted to change some of its rules by counting women in forming a minyan (religious quorum), allowing men and women to sit together, eliminating the Bar Mitzvah, and even changing the Sabbath from Saturday to Sunday. In an incident known as the "Treifa Banquet," he allowed shrimp (a non-kosher food) to be served at Cincinnati's Plum Street Temple, and certain rabbis walked out in protest. This helped to inspire the creation of the Conservative Judaism movement (founded by Solomon Schechter) which sought to strike a balance between Reform Judaism and Orthodox Judaism.

After 1882, around 2 million Jews came to the US from Russia, Romania, and Austria-Hungary. Their close-knit Orthodox communities were so fringe compared to other American groups that Jewish leaders worried about a resurgence of antisemitism, although they managed to offset some of these fears through the charitable programs they engaged in. Today the biggest Jewish communities can be found in Brooklyn, New York, and Los Angeles, California.

America's homegrown religions also continued to flourish. Mormons began adapting to Victorian values, and Wilford Woodruff, the fourth president of the Latter Day Saints (LDS) Church, ended the public practice of polygamy in 1890. The Supreme Court ruled in the case of *Reynolds v US* (1879) that while Congress could not outlaw a belief in polygamy, it could outlaw its practice, to which Woodruff responded by claiming God had told him that polygamy was not necessary. Utah Territory's application for statehood was approved in 1896.

The Jehovah's Witnesses splintered from Charles Taze Russell's Bible Student movement in the late 1870s. They believed Armageddon was imminent and they were living in the last days, predicting the year 1914 as the end of the "Gentile Times," which would be replaced by the full establishment of God's Kingdom on Earth. When that did not happen in 1914, they interpreted the outbreak of the First World War as the beginning of the end. Today the Jehovah's Witnesses count over 8.5 million members.

Mary Baker Eddy created the Christian Scientist Church in 1875. This stated that the material world is an illusion and that reality is purely spiritual. Christian Scientists attributed all illnesses to one's state of mind, denied themselves any stimulants – including tea, coffee, and alcohol – and rejected medication. Eddy believed death was unnecessary and claimed her enemies were beaming a force called Malicious Animal Magnetism towards her which was causing her pain and illness (at the time, she was in fact dying of old age). Her beliefs may have been popular in an era when doctors could cause as much damage as illnesses themselves, although as medicine improved, the popularity of the Christian Scientist Church waned.

Other new religions developed in the 20th century that included the Nation of Islam, Scientology, and New Age Spirituality, although fears of cultism tainted many. After Jim Jones created the People's Temple in the 1960s, he took his church and its members to the jungle of Guyana where, after convincing them the community was being attacked by outside forces, he ordered them to carry out a mass suicide by drinking Kool-Aid laced with potassium cyanide. Over 900 people died, including 200 children.

Today, America remains the most ethnically and religiously diverse country in the world. Until as recently as the early 1990s, about 90 percent identified as Christians but, since then, the number of unaffiliated (which includes atheist, agnostic, and "nothing in particular") has increased from around 5 percent to 28 percent, and the impact of changing immigration laws is reflected in the increased number of Catholics, Hindus, Buddhists, and Muslims.

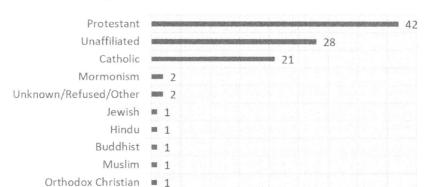

Religious Affiliation 2020 (Population %)

Theodore Roosevelt

Theodore Roosevelt embodied many of the era's progressivist principles. He was too young to have participated in the Civil War, but he longed to have been part of it, and he embraced Muscular Christianity as well as the concept of purification through violence.

He attended Harvard College and, conscious of his social class, believed it was his duty to involve himself in state politics. He contested the power of the political machines and was elected to the New York State Assembly in 1882. Initially considered something of a dandy for his high-pitched voice and his spectacles, he soon proved himself and leveraged the Roosevelt name (his father had been a prominent businessman and member of the Republican Party) to make sure he was a regular feature in the newspapers.

Roosevelt was loathed by the political machines of New York, but just as he was coming to prominence, he was struck by the tragedy of losing both his mother and his wife who died within hours of each other on February 14, 1884. Roosevelt was devastated and abandoned politics to withdraw onto a ranch in the Dakota territories, where he stayed for two years. He raised cattle, acted as a local lawman, and hunted prodigiously. He spent a great deal of time reading and writing, and after a blizzard destroyed his herd of cattle in 1885, he decided to return to politics and to the East, becoming a New York City police commissioner in 1894.

Roosevelt took a close interest in the Europeans scrambling for footholds in Africa, and with the Anglo-German naval arms race in full swing, he was appointed Assistant Secretary of the Navy under the McKinley administration in 1897. He was eager to see the United States compete as a world power and pushed for Spain's ejection from Cuba, which at the time, was seeking its independence. When the USS *Maine* was blown up in Havana, war on Spain was declared, and Roosevelt resigned from his post in order to form a volunteer regiment referred to by the press as the "Rough Riders."

Roosevelt and his "Rough Riders" (1898).

With just over 1,000 members, the Rough Riders was a ragtag band of cowboys from Dakota, gold and mining prospectors, hunters, gamblers, Native Americans, and friends of Roosevelt's from New York and Harvard. Roosevelt led a series of charges up Kettle Hill towards San Juan Heights on his horse, Texas, calling it "the great day of my life," glorying in the destruction and drama of the battlefield. The press enthusiastically covered his exploits (members of the regular army were less impressed and obtained their revenge by summarily rejecting Roosevelt for being too old when he sought service in the First World War), and he returned to New York a national hero.

He became governor of New York in 1898 and then vice president under McKinley in 1901. When McKinley was assassinated by an anarchist in New York, Roosevelt became the youngest president ever at the age of 42, reinvigo-rating the presidency with an energetic, idealistic style. He was the first president to encourage the United States to engage actively abroad, sending the US Navy to support Panamanian independence and overseeing the construction of the Panama Canal. Roosevelt also won the Nobel Peace Prize for helping to negotiate peace in the Russo–Japanese War of 1904–1905.

Domestically, Roosevelt became known as a trustbuster for his efforts at breaking up monopolistic and anticompetitive practices. He distinguished between good monopolies and bad monopolies, categorizing companies as "good" if they acted like they were in competition and provided services at reasonable rates, but "bad" if they jacked up rates and exploited consumers. He forced the Northern Securities railroad company, owned partly by JP Morgan, to break up and charge reasonable rates, but he left Morgan's US Steel Company alone.

Under Roosevelt's administration, the United States Forest Service and five National Parks[76] were established, along with 51 bird reserves, four game preserves, 150 National Forests, and numerous national monuments. He was reelected on his own ticket in 1904, but his announcement that he would not seek reelection in 1908 turned him into a lame-duck president as Congress anticipated his departure.

After he left office, Roosevelt went to Africa to hunt big game, leaving his handpicked successor, William Howard Taft, in the president's seat. But Taft increasingly came into conflict with corporations, and by 1912, Roosevelt had completely lost confidence in him, running an independent campaign

---

76 These are: Wind Cave, South Dakota; White Horse Hill, North Dakota; Mesa Verde, Colorado; Platt, Oklahoma; and Glacier, Montana.

as leader of the Progressive Party (known colloquially as the "Bull Moose" Party since Roosevelt claimed he was "as fit as a bull moose"). He engaged in a nationwide speaking tour, even surviving an assassination attempt in Wisconsin, but his party split the Republican vote, and Woodrow Wilson's Democrats won the election.

Wilson had run on a "New Freedom" platform (similar to Roosevelt's "New Nationalism") that included the creation of a Federal Reserve Bank, a Federal Trade Commission, and antitrust regulations. He also banned child labor, instituted maximum hours legislation for railroad workers, ratified the direct election of senators, and created a direct federal income tax. This was a total rejection of laissez-faire[77] government, but the Socialist Party had had a strong showing in the 1912 election under Eugene Debs winning 6 percent of the popular vote, and Wilson had to consider which of their policies he could afford to incorporate.

The Second Industrial Revolution

The first Industrial Revolution was in textiles, railroads, steel, and oil, but the second was in consumer goods. Business owners relentlessly searched for ways to increase efficiency and applied new technologies and scientific management thinking to their operations. The revolution evolved with mass production, investment in advertising and marketing, and the ability to purchase products on credit.

Mass production was first developed at Isaac Singer's Sewing Machine Company and Samuel Colt's Manufacturing Company. They applied the concept of interchangeable parts for products without the need for custom fitting or

---

77 "Laissez-faire" is a term borrowed from the French meaning "let do" or "let it be" and refers to a style of government that emphasizes minimal involvement or interference in individuals' economic and social lives.

adjustment, making repairs and replacements infinitely easier. Singer started mass-producing sewing machines, and by 1880, he was selling 500,000 a year. He employed traveling salesmen, using showrooms where people could watch a demonstration of the product and ask questions about how it worked. He also allowed customers to pay in installments.

Albert Pope applied the concept of the interchangeability of parts to bicycles which found him, at the height of the bicycle craze in the mid-1890s, manufacturing about 750,000 bicycles annually. He stratified the market by building different types of bicycles – a luxury model, a model for women, and another for children – and he applied new technologies such as the pneumatic tire, wire wheels, and spring suspension. Pope was also one of the founders of the League of American Wheelmen in 1880 who campaigned to improve the quality of the roads – which gained a huge boost in momentum when the automobile business took off.

Some of the technologies used by bicycle manufacturers were applied elsewhere. The Wright Brothers used knowledge gained from working as bicycle repairmen to build their first plane in 1903, and automobiles borrowed several features from bicycles. Originally, cars were custom-made and extremely expensive, but after Henry Ford saw workers in a meatpacking plant breaking down pigs and cows in a disassembly line, he considered how he could apply the same effort in reverse. He built an automobile plant at Highland Park just outside of Detroit next to railway yards that supplied it with the requisite parts and tools, and the first Model Ts were built in 1909. By the end of 1913, Ford was producing 200,000 cars a year.

Entire industries grew to support the demand for automobiles: lamps were needed for headlights, cowhides for seat covers, horsehair for seat padding, and glass for windows. Ford was lionized for his achievements as an industrialist in places as far-reaching as Bolshevik, Russia. Aldous Huxley's *Brave New World* (1931) substitutes Ford for God by referring to time as "After Ford" (in place of AD, anno domini) and replacing the sign of the cross by making the sign of the T (for Model T) on one's stomach.

Henry Ford with a Model T (1921).

Assembly line work was exceptionally tedious, however – so much so that Ford's annual turnover rate hit 370 percent in 1913. Losing workers at such high volumes increased cost and delays, so he took the radical, progressive step of doubling the basic rate of pay from $2.50 to $5 while reducing the standard workday hours from nine hours to eight. Labor turnover fell from 370 percent to 40 percent, production increased, and employees found themselves in the position of the consumer, able to buy the very product they were making.

Further efficiency was sought by applying knowledge obtained from a new kind of service: management consulting. Frederick Winslow Taylor, a laborer and machinist, scientifically analyzed how people and machines worked together to improve the symbiosis between them. After watching the way workers shoveled coal at Bethlehem Steel Corporation, he redesigned the shovel so that one man could move 47 tons of coal a day instead of 12, enabling the owner, Andrew Carnegie, to cut his labor force from 600 to 140 with no loss of output (he was not popular with the workers!). Taylor redesigned tennis rackets and golf clubs and wrote many publications with *The Principles of Scientific Management* (1911), voted the most influential management book of the 20th century by the Academy of Management in 2001.

Frank Gilbreth was another consultant who studied time and motion. He developed a new unit of motion that he called the "therblig," – his surname spelled backwards with the "th" transposed – which was designed to break down work tasks into their individual components. He created a set of 18 kinds of therbligs that included tasks like "Assemble (A): joining two parts together," and "Release Load (RL): releasing control of an object," and "Select (St.): choosing among several objects in a group." Gilbreth applied these to particular activities (like bricklaying), capturing the time it took to complete each therblig with the goal of identifying where he could improve it. He also wrote the novel *Cheaper by the Dozen* about his life growing up in a household of 12 children, which became a popular film in 1950 (remade in 2003).

Improving efficiency even extended into the effects a worker's environment might have on his psychology. The Australian-born Elton Mayo conducted his most famous experiment at the Hawthorne plant of Western Electric where workers assembled telephones. He noted that increasing the lighting, providing rest breaks, or changing the temperature all raised productivity – but productivity also went up for the control group, for whom nothing had been changed. Mayo concluded that the mere attention paid to the workers caused productivity to rise, and companies applied the results of these studies by creating clinics, small social groups, and regular private interviews in which employees could be heard.

Psychology-based advertising tactics also developed around the 1910s and 1920s. The idea of inducing an artificial need in a customer's mind was regularly employed, facilitated by celebrity endorsements. Sometimes entire budgets were spent on advertising – Ford Motor Company spent $2 million in one week when they built the Model A in 1927. That need led to a desire for instant gratification, and buying on credit became common and was used to buy cars, washing machines, radios, vacuum cleaners, and refrigerators.

In the second decade of the 20th century, European powers applied the lessons of the First and Second Industrial Revolutions to wage an extraordinarily savage war against each other. They used advancements in technological and management efficiency to build weapons, tanks, and aircraft; dig trenches; transport troops, and communicate with each other – all with the goal of killing as many people as they could on a battlefield. The US watched on in horror and hoped it would all end quickly. But it did not, and they soon found it impossible to remain a neutral observer.

## PART FIVE

FIRST WORLD WAR TO THE END OF THE SECOND WORLD WAR

CHAPTER 13

THE FIRST WORLD WAR (1917–1919)

Build up to Entry into the First World War

Germany invaded France in 1914 after a period of intense imperial expansionism by European powers in Africa, the Middle East, and Asia. Ostensibly, Germany's invasion was done in support of Austria-Hungary and their war with Russia, but the incredible growth and might of the German industrial engine led Kaiser Wilhelm II to believe he could colonize Europe and take Britain and France's imperial empires for himself.

The United States was traditionally isolationist, but since the Spanish–American War of 1898, it had adopted a more active foreign policy. Spain lost control of the remains of its overseas empire after the war, and the US assumed sovereignty of the Philippines, picking up the baton of the Spanish who had been fighting an insurrection of Filipino revolutionaries led by Emilio Aguinaldo. A brutal guerilla campaign followed as part of the Philippine–American War of 1899–1902 during which both sides committed massacres and atrocities. US Senator Albert Beveridge reflected the bombastic tone of the Imperial Era when the said in 1900, "The Philippines are ours forever… and just beyond the Philippines are China's illimitable markets. We will not retreat from either. We will not repudiate our duty in the archipelago. We will not abandon our opportunity in the Orient. We will not renounce our part in the mission of our race, trustee, under God, of the civilization of the world."

In 1903, Theodore Roosevelt helped a secessionist movement in Panama declare its independence from Colombia. He sent warships into Panamanian and Atlantic waters and removed American trains from the US-administered railroad, stranding Colombian troops who had been sent in to put down the insurrection. The new nation of Panama gave the United States exclusive and permanent possession of the Panama Canal Zone which, when construction was completed in 1914, gave the US Navy a crucial passageway from the West Coast to the East.

The United States also intervened during the Mexican Revolution of the 1910s, sending troops to Veracruz and to northern Mexico in a failed attempt to capture Pancho Villa. But when the First World War broke out, Wilson wanted no part in it, urging Americans to remain neutral "in thought as well as deed." The war was by far the most destructive the world had ever seen, with defenders holding the advantage over attackers by digging themselves into trenches protected by barbed wire, machine guns, mines, and cannons, and able to pick individuals off as they charged across no man's land. Whole economies were devoted to the war, and new methods of warfare were employed, including firing poison gas shells into enemy trenches, charging tanks, bombing cities, and targeting merchant vessels with submarines. Old methods of warfare like cavalry and bayonet charges would never be used again.

Wilson hoped that he could wait it out and that the European powers would come to their senses. Influential American figures like Andrew Carnegie and Jane Addams were ardent Pacifists, and the Women's Peace Parade of 1914 in New

York City reflected many Americans' desire to remain out of the conflict. America even continued to trade with all sides just as it had before the war, but Britain and France enjoyed naval supremacy,[78] and the geographic boundaries of Germany meant that it was easy for British ships to prevent American ones from getting through. Between 1914 and 1916, trade tripled between England and America, while American trade with Germany dropped by 90 percent.

Lusitania leaving New York Harbor for its last trip (1915).

American sentiment shifted after the sinking of the *Lusitania* by a German submarine in 1915. The ship was one of the great ocean liners of its day and was on its way from New York to Liverpool when it was struck by a German torpedo, sinking within 20 minutes. A total of 1,195 people died, including 128 Americans. It further appeared that the Germans had breached the protocols of war by neglecting to fire a warning shot that would have enabled passengers

---

78 The Battle of Jutland (1916) assured Britain and France's control of the seas.

to be hurried off the ship, which infuriated the US. Germany responded by saying the ship had been carrying war munitions, so no protocol had been required, but the British denied that (it has since been proven true), and Wilson sent a note of protest to the German government in extremely critical language. His secretary of state, William Jennings Bryan, believed the note was as close to a war declaration as one could get and resigned in protest, which removed one of the cabinet's most devout antiwar advocates.

Britain bought what it could from the United States, but its foreign exchange reserves diminished and it needed to borrow money. American bankers were happy to oblige, arguing that if they did not, demand would fall, and the economy would tip into a recession, and Wilson himself had no problem aiding the British war effort where he could. He was an Anglophile, as exhibited in his *Congressional Government: A Study in American Politics*, which complimented the British on their parliamentary system, and many of his cabinet members were even more pro-British, identifying Britain as America's best customer and a German victory as bad for business. The period also coincided with the concept of a common destiny of the Anglo-Saxon races.

Wilson won the 1916 presidential election under the slogan, "He kept us out of war," but even he admitted – somewhat disingenuously – that this was barely sustainable. By the time Wilson was inaugurated in 1917, Germany had decided to target all American ships at sea because of the help they were giving to the Allies, although Wilson delayed declaring war for as long as he could, recognizing there would be psychological consequences for a nation that had been isolationist for so long.

In early 1917, the British intercepted a message (the Zimmermann telegram) sent from Germany to Mexico. The message proposed a military alliance between Germany and Mexico with the offer to give Texas, Arizona, and New Mexico back to Mexico in the event of victory. When the press published news of this telegram on March 1, Americans (particularly those in the Southwest states) were outraged. As a result, on April 6, 1917, Congress approved a resolution declaring war on Germany. American isolationism had come to an end.

The United States in the First World War

No sooner had Wilson declared war than he found himself afraid of losing it. The Germans sank 250 tons of goods in ten days in the Atlantic, and when Wilson initiated a draft that required all males aged 21 to 30 to register for war, he found that many of the draftees were not fit to fight. Thousands failed the IQ test and physical exams, and of those who were drafted, urgent training was required. Military camps sprung up rapidly, and though the YMCA opened the doors of their clubs to soldiers for relaxation, recreation, and personal enrichment, many of them preferred drinking, gambling, and going to brothels instead.

Conscientious objectors were permitted to serve in noncombatant military roles, but absolute refusal to cooperate was not allowed by the US, and about 2,000 men were imprisoned for taking such a position. Usually, they gave their passivist religion as a reason (in the case of Mennonites and Quakers, for example), but many were accused of cowardice and were subjected to short rations, solitary confinement, and physical abuse in prison.

Wilson instituted a propaganda campaign (the Committee on Public Information) to sustain morale and manage news releases, putting George Creel in charge. "Four Minute Men" (they included Charlie Chaplin and Douglas Fairbanks) would speak at places like movie theatres, town restaurants, and fellowship halls for four minutes to keep morale up, encourage men to volunteer for the draft, or persuade people to buy war bonds. Legislation was passed that restricted open criticism of the war, which led to opponents commenting that America was unnecessarily curtailing civil rights. Eugene Debs was among those arrested for denouncing American participation, claiming it was a war between capitalist countries and had no significance for the workers.

Protestant and Catholic clergy spoke in apocalyptic terms, with Billy Sunday (the most influential evangelist at the time) saying, "If you turn hell upside down, you will find 'Made in Germany' stamped on the bottom." Rumors, not all true, abounded of drunk Germans committing large-scale massacres against residents in Belgium, raping and pillaging as they went. Many state governments and vigilante groups tried to prevent people from using German words (sauerkraut, for instance, was redubbed "liberty cabbage") and companies from selling German newspapers. Robert Prager, a German immigrant, was lynched by a mob of 300 people, forced to walk barefoot, wrapped in an American flag alone in downtown Collinsville, Illinois, and was then hanged to death.

The year 1917 saw not only the American entry into the war but also the Russian exit from it. Russia had sustained 5 million casualties in the war – more than any other nation – and, with the army beginning to mutiny, only the Bolsheviks (a faction of the Russian Social-Democratic Workers' Party) promised an end to the fighting. On March 3, 1918, they signed the Treaty of Brest–Litovsk which ceded large parts of the Russian Empire to Germany, prompting forces loyal to the assassinated czar, White Russians, to furiously fight back against the Bolsheviks. Britain and America both sent troops into Russia to support the White Russians, hoping they would reclaim power and bring Russia back into the war against Germany, and they remained there until 1920. They were ultimately unsuccessful, and it foreshadowed US foreign interventions in the century to come and sowed bitterness between American–Russian relations.

With operations ceasing on the Eastern Front, Germany moved their men and equipment to the West and launched a huge offensive in the spring. They came within 50 miles of Paris, making the deepest advances into France since the start of the war, and American troops arrived just in time to help stem the German advance at Château-Thierry and Belleau Wood. The American admiral William Sims also persuaded the Royal Navy to introduce a convoy system in the North Atlantic which helped to repel submarine attacks, and they assisted in laying a minefield in the North Sea to hem in German ships and submarines.

In September 1918, Americans enjoyed a major victory at the Battle of Saint-Mihiel and then took part in the Meuse-Argonne offensive. This was the largest battle in US military history and involved 1.2 million American troops as they attacked the Germans in the dense Argonne Forest. They suffered over 122,000 casualties (including 26,000 killed), and on the eleventh day of the American offensive, the Germans retreated, holding on for another month before suing for peace on November 11.

The United States had suffered 204,000 casualties in the war (with over 116,000 killed), which was substantial and yet merely a fraction of the global total of 40 million. The US now found itself with a new responsibility – that of a victor in a world war – whose burden Wilson felt keenly.

Wilson's Fourteen Points

Peace negotiations would be held in Versailles, just outside Paris, and Wilson decided to attend in person. Joyous crowds hailed him as a great liberator upon his arrival, and he approached the peace negotiations with a more idealistic perspective than that of the Allies. The US had seen limited battlefield engagement and had only been active in the war for a little over a year.

Woodrow Wilson being greeted in Paris (1919).

Wilson was desirous of no land or compensation and was just eager to see democratic principles and human rights respected in the world. He had appointed a committee of experts, known as The Inquiry, to draw up specific recommendations which were called the Fourteen Points, and he now sought to ratify them at the Treaty of Versailles. These Points included the surrender of all conquered territories (including the return of land to Russia that had been given to Germany at the Treaty of Brest–Litovsk), the requirement for open diplomacy without secret treaties, democratic self-determination for lands in Austria-Hungary and the Balkan regions, and the creation of a League of Nations that aimed to settle all future disputes peacefully.

The Germans had, in fact, been attempting to arrange an armistice through Wilson since early October and viewed the Fourteen Points as their best option for a judicious peace agreement. With Austria and Turkey dropping out of the war in early November, followed by the abdication of the Kaiser on November 9, the new German Republic agreed to peace, although it quickly became clear that the German view of peace was significantly different from the view held by the British and the French. They wanted the Germans to accept blame and pay reparations for all the suffering caused during the war, and the French president, Georges Clemenceau, drily commented on Wilson's Points by saying, "God gave us the Ten Commandments, and we broke them. Wilson gives us the Fourteen Points. We shall see."

In the end, Clemenceau and British Prime Minister David Lloyd George managed to get their way on a few things, including the addition of a humiliating section of the treaty that assigned all the blame to the Germans, known as the "War Guilt Clause." Germany was required to make hefty reparation payments (arguments were even made for Germany to pay British and French war pensions for disabled veterans and allowances for war widows) and transfer all its colonial possessions to the victors or to the League of Nations. Even the British delegation thought the terms too harsh, and the economist John Maynard Keynes remarked that Germany would be economically destroyed.

Germany felt betrayed by Wilson and was furious for being made to take sole responsibility for the war. The Germans had, after all, not been fully defeated on the battlefield, and they had chosen to negotiate partly because they were satisfied with the requirements of the Fourteen Points. But now, they were also required to give up 13 percent of their territory and 10 percent of their population. The Germans wrote a 443-page criticism of the Treaty of Versailles, pointing out where it had violated the Points, and Germany's foreign minister sarcastically remarked that the whole treaty could have been put more simply into one clause – "Germany renounces its existence." The German delegation read their response to the treaty without standing up, in a calculated display of discontent, and some Americans – such as Robert Lansing and William Bullitt – proclaimed that Wilson had compromised too much.

Wilson accepted the new terms of the treaty in the belief that the new League of Nations would ultimately work together to solve any further conflicts. Historians have since argued that his presence in Versailles had been counterproductive and that Wilson would have had more authority had he remained abroad, where he would have been removed from all the squabbling. But his in-person attendance demonstrated his commitment to peace and his compassion for the tragic nature of the events and helped elevate the US on the world stage.

At home, the country was reeling from a pandemic known as the Spanish Flu. This particular strain of the flu targeted young adults rather than the old or the very young, killing 675,000 in the US and over 50 million worldwide (even more than the war had killed). Many life insurance companies were completely bankrupt, hospitals and cemeteries overflowed, and people were fined for spitting in the streets as authorities struggled to contain the spread of disease.

Anxiety in the country was high, intensified by a fear of foreign radicals influenced by the Russian Revolution. After an anarchist blew up the front of the home of the new Attorney General A Mitchell Palmer, the Palmer Raids (1919–1920) were conducted, leading to the arrests of 350,000 people and the deportation of 556 of them. J Edgar Hoover, 24 years old at the time, was appointed by Palmer to a newly created Bureau of Investigation, which was given the responsibility of investigating the programs of radical groups and identifying their members. This was the first "Red Scare" to occur in the United States; the next would come after the Second World War, to be helmed by Senator Joseph McCarthy.

The First World War had discredited the Second International (the socialist parties of Europe) because its members had reneged on their promise not to fight for the capitalist governments. It was only in the US that they had not fought, but the Socialist Party's leader in the country, Eugene Debs, languished in prison.[79] Russia launched the Third International (also known as the Communist International) with the resolution to "struggle by all available means, including armed force, for the overthrow of the international bourgeoisie," and directed all socialists to join the International and to take orders only from the Russians.

---

79 Eugene Debs ran for president five times in all – in 1900, 1904, 1908, 1912, and 1920.

This caused a split in the Socialist Party of the US between those willing to accept such demands (thereby becoming members of the Communist Party) and those unwilling (remaining within the Socialist Party). Some socialist Christians refused to accept violence as a legitimate method of achieving power and so refused to join the communists, and the weakened position of both parties was evidenced by the fact that Debs was forced to run for the presidency while he was in jail in 1920. He was released by Warren Harding in 1921.

When Wilson returned, the US Senate refused to ratify the Treaty of Versailles. They argued that if the League of Nations were to form, the United States could be dragged into war by a smaller nation since each member's rights were of equal weight to the others'. This came as a shock to Wilson, but the Republicans had taken control of both Houses in the midterm elections of 1918, and he had failed to build the coalitions he needed. Many of them were also nervous about the state of the German economy, having internalized the warnings of Keynes in his *Economic Consequence of the Peace* (1919), which forecast potentially catastrophic implications for Europe and the world.

Henry Cabot Lodge, the Senate Majority Leader, wanted to see some recognition of the power differentials among would-be members of the proposed League. But Wilson ignored him and undertook a huge speaking tour to promote ratification of the treaty in its current form, covering 8,000 miles in 22 days during which he delivered 32 major addresses. But the stresses of the last few years caught up with him. Wilson suffered from constant headaches until he finally collapsed from exhaustion in Pueblo, Colorado, and suffered a near-fatal stroke on October 2, 1919. His wife, Edith, furiously blamed Republican intransigence for the deterioration of her husband's health and kept the true extent of Wilson's state from the press and his opponents. She even screened his paperwork and would issue bulletins in her own writing reading "the president says" thus.

Wilson gradually improved but remained partially paralyzed on one side. He failed to get the Senate to ratify the treaty, and the United States never joined the League of Nations, fatally compromising its operations from the start. The weakness of the treaty laid the groundwork for an even worse war 20 years later, and the other Points proved hard to apply. Czechoslovakia, for example, came into existence after the war, and the League of Nations could have helped mediate the political differences between the Czechs and the Slovaks; and the League could have provided a joint military response to Hitler's invasion of the Sudetenland, But, in the end, the League's influence was negligible.

CHAPTER 14

THE ROARING TWENTIES (1920–1929)

Overview of the 1920s

America emerged from the First World War as an undisputed world power. Factory production had risen during the war which led to the development of a new consumer society, with millions of households now able to own cars, spend their time going to the cinema, and dance their evenings away to jazz music. It was their spending and a general sense of optimism that gave the "Roaring Twenties" its moniker, and the years 1920–1929 saw the economy grow by 42 percent and the stock market more than quadruple in value. That would all come crashing down in 1929, but for now, the country reaped the rewards of mass production as it spun off new industries including advertising, vacationing, gas stations, rubber production, road construction, diners, and fast food, all of which increased job opportunities and boosted the economy.

It was also a time of social change. In 1920, women obtained the right to vote via the 19th Amendment, and the Volstead Act heralded the start of the Prohibition Era while simultaneously sparking an unprecedented growth of organized crime and an underground economy. African Americans, seeking work and escape from Jim Crow laws, made their way north in the "Great Migration." At the same time, millions of whites joined the Ku Klux Klan in the belief that it represented a return to the traditional values threatened by modernization.

Politically, and in stark contrast to what was occurring elsewhere in the world, the size of the federal government declined. It employed fewer people in 1930 than it did in 1920, and both Harding and Coolidge (who took over after Harding died from a heart attack two years into his term) believed that government should play a limited role in people's daily lives. Coolidge himself gained the nickname "Silent Cal," for his conduct during meetings, at which he merely listened without voicing his opinion. In an interview with advisor Bernard Baruch, Coolidge said his technique for dealing with visitors who wanted something was just to let them talk themselves out: "Well, Baruch," he said, "many times, I say only 'yes' or 'no' to people. Even that is too much. It winds them up for 20 minutes more." Elsewhere, Russia was being led by Lenin and then Stalin, Italy by Mussolini, and Germany by Hitler, all of whom made everything and everyone subordinate to the state.

Prohibition

The Prohibition Era started in 1919 when the 18th Amendment was ratified – banning the manufacture, transportation, and sale of intoxicating liquors – and only ended at the deepest point of the Great Depression in 1933. It was the culmination of a long campaign that began with the American Temperance Society in 1826 but was, in the end, a terrible disappointment. Openly abused and almost impossible to enforce, Prohibition proved to serve only criminal organizations, who amassed fortunes and committed heinous crimes.

It was initially motivated by the high social costs of alcohol. If a man's wages were spent on alcohol, his entire family could be left to starve or freeze, and the potential for violence and abuse in the home increased significantly. Drunken performance at work caused accidents and job loss, and alcohol itself led to physical and mental health problems.

Such concerns drove two main movements to call for anti-alcohol legislation: the Women's Christian Temperance Union (WCTU) and the Anti-Saloon League. The WCTU was founded in 1874 and was one of the first social reform movements that tried to apply Christian principles to current affairs, and the Anti-Saloon League drew support from Protestant ministers and congregations, and pressed for legislation and a constitutional amendment. The First World War provided anti-alcohol legislation with a solid springboard as President Wilson issued a temporary wartime prohibition, calling for grain to be used for food rather than for the manufacture of alcohol. Furthermore, since most alcohol manufacturers were German (such as Anheuser-Busch, Coors, and Pabst), it was a short hop to associate it with wrongdoing.

Wilson viewed Prohibition as a way to win votes, and many believed it would promote a moral social order. By 1917, the "dries" outnumbered the "wets" in both parties, and the 18th Amendment was ratified two years later. But enforcing it was immensely challenging. Responsibility was initially assigned to the Internal Revenue Service (IRS), but it lacked the effective means to do so, and widespread bribery of police as well as open violation of the laws by congressmen, senators, governors, and judges was commonplace. The Attorney General, Harry M Daugherty, was embroiled in bribery and bootlegging scandals; the mayor of Chicago, William Thompson, boasted how "wet" his city was, and Roy Olmstead, a former police lieutenant, became one of the most successful bootleggers in the Pacific Northwest.

Even the president, Warren G Harding, was known to drink whiskey and serve liquor to his guests in the White House.

Prohibition was more successful in rural areas and small towns, but it facilitated organized crime in the cities, the most notorious example of which was the Chicago gangster Al Capone. Capone had been born in Brooklyn, New York to Italian immigrants and moved to Chicago after his mob mentor, Johnny Torrio, invited him there to work in his gambling, prostitution, and bootlegging business. Torrio left the United States in 1925 after surviving an attempt on his life, and he turned the whole business over to Capone who developed the enterprise into a huge success, bringing in an estimated $60 million per year (over $1 billion in today's terms) from bootleg operations and speakeasies.

Al Capone, c.1935.

Competition among the organizations spurred gang violence, and turf wars and clashes with police became common. Any establishment that refused to purchase liquor from Capone was blown up, and Capone ordered the Saint Valentine's Day Massacre in 1929 in an attempt to kill a rival gang member, Bugs Moran of the North Side gang. Four members of Capone's organization, the Chicago Outfit, dressed themselves up as police officers and gunned down seven Irish North Siders in cold blood, and when the photos were released to the public, their opinion – much of which had been sympathetic towards Capone – turned against him. Under pressure to prosecute, the IRS jailed Capone for tax evasion in 1931, sentencing him to 11 years in prison, most of which he served in Alcatraz. He was released after eight years and died at age 48 of cardiac arrest after suffering for years from the debilitating effects of syphilis.

The economic effects of Prohibition had been disastrous. Before its implementation, approximately 14 percent of taxes had been derived from the alcohol business, and the agriculture, hospitality, and transportation businesses were all adversely impacted. In 1933, with the Great Depression at its worst, the government decided that the jobs and revenue that would be created by the alcohol industry outweighed the expenses they incurred, and the 21st Amendment was ratified, bringing an end to Prohibition for good.

The Amendment allowed for states to write their own laws governing alcohol, and Prohibition remained active in some states, with Mississippi the last to give it up in 1966. A few jurisdictions still enforce it (mainly in the Midwestern and Southern "Bible Belt"), and advocates of Prohibition point to a decrease in domestic violence, delinquency from work, and illnesses and deaths as some of the benefits of its implementation.

The Ku Klux Klan

The original Ku Klux Klan, or first generation, was founded by six Confederate veterans in Pulaski, Tennessee in 1865 who begrudged the changes brought about by Reconstruction after the Civil War. It quickly evolved into an organization that used violence and intimidation to terrorize the African American community and developed customs that included wearing masks and gowns, with its leader given the title of "Grand Wizard."[80]

With violence on the rise during the Reconstruction era, Congress passed three Enforcement Acts that made it a crime to interfere with the suffrage rights of African Americans; the third of these acts targeted the Ku Klux Klan directly (Ku Klux Klan Act 1871). This crushed the first generation of the KKK, but it was revived atop Stone Mountain, Georgia in 1915. Inspired by Thomas Dixon, Jr.'s book *The Clansman* (1905) and the film *Birth of a Nation* (1915), the revival was a reaction to the surge in immigration, and its members broadened its targets from African Americans to include Roman Catholics, Jews, foreigners, and organized laborers. This helped the organization grow beyond the Deep South, primarily into the Midwest, but also into Maine, Colorado, and Oregon.

---

80 The first Grand Wizard was Nathan Bedford Forrest, a former Confederate general appointed to the position in 1867.

The Ku Klux Klan at Harvard, 1924.

The new Klan developed its mythology, taking a burning cross as its symbol and wearing white robes and pointed hoods. They traveled by horseback and used words that began with the letter K (such as "Kloran" meaning handbook, and "Klavern," a local branch); charged an initiation fee, hired recruiters, and held a monopoly on sales of its costumes. At its peak in the 1920s, Klan membership exceeded 4 million people nationwide, and the money poured in.

For many, it was just an opportunity to join a fraternal society, and it was generally less violent than its first incarnation. But the Klan still had the capacity to strike fear in the community, and its official national newspaper, *The Searchlight*, declared that "race forms the basis for all human interactions and reactions," providing the pretext for many Klansmen to perpetrate lynchings, arson, beatings, and whippings.

The Klan helped to elect the governors of Alabama, California, Oregon, and Indiana, and many politicians were reluctant to alienate Klan members, but before long, its influence and membership collapsed. Opposing groups and individuals spoke out against it, newspapers printed graphic photographs of crimes its members had committed, and public education campaigns were launched to expose them. Finally, the Klan's claim of standing for morality was totally discredited when the Grand Dragon of Indiana, DC Stephenson, was convicted of the rape, kidnapping, and second-degree murder of his aide in 1925, following which membership in the Klan imploded.

A third incarnation of the Klan occurred during the Civil Rights movement of the 1960s. This time, however, they had no mainstream support whatsoever and committed some of the worst anti-Black violence of the period. This included the bombing of a Baptist church in Alabama where four young Black girls were killed and the murders of three civil rights workers in Mississippi (the "Mississippi Burning" murders[81]). Law enforcement and a cultural shift in the South ensured the Klan never gained the sort of following that it had seen in the 1920s, and although it still exists, other white supremacist groups such as the Aryan Brotherhood, the Proud Boys, and The Order rose to compete for the Klan's recruits.

Fundamentalist Protestants and the "Scopes Monkey Trial"

Fundamentalist Protestants also feared the impacts of changes in society. *The Fundamentals*, a set of 90 essays published between 1910 and 1915, declared the Bible sacrosanct in matters of science, history, and theology, and believed in the imminent return of Christ. In Tennessee, concerted

---

81 The 1988 film *Mississippi Burning* is loosely based on the event.

Fundamentalists managed to have the Butler Act passed, which made the teaching of evolution a misdemeanor.

This was almost immediately challenged in 1925 when a young high school teacher, John T Scopes, was taken to court for violating the act. The Fundamentalist politician and three-time presidential candidate William Jennings Bryan represented the prosecution, pitted against the agnostic lawyer Clarence Darrow. The "Scopes Monkey Trial" was the first to be broadcast live on the radio and was attended by thousands of spectators and journalists who eagerly reported on its confrontational and bizarre nature.

The most compelling moments came when Darrow called his opposing counsel, Bryan himself, as his sole witness. Darrow wanted to discredit Bryan by asking him about his literal interpretation of the Bible, bringing the crowds to the edge of their seats as they awaited his responses. Bryan amused many by bemoaning how evolution taught children that humans were descended "not even from American monkeys, but from Old World monkeys," and when Darrow asked him to explain geological evidence that identified the age of the Earth to be in the millions of years, Bryan replied by saying, "I am more interested in the Rock of Ages than in the age of rocks!" The trial was dramatized in the film *Inherit the Wind* (1960).

Scopes was ultimately found guilty, but to show there were no hard feelings, Bryan volunteered to pay the fine. The Fundamentalists had won the case, but they lost in the court of public opinion, and days after the trial ended, having been humiliated and ridiculed in front of the world, Bryan went to sleep and suffered a stroke. He never woke up.

After the Scopes Monkey Trial, enforcement of the Butler Act became increasingly rare, and laws prohibiting the teaching of evolution were defeated in 22 states. But it mattered not to Fundamentalist Christians, and evangelists such as Billy Sunday and Aimee Semple McPherson continued to preach to thousands, foreshadowing the future trend of televangelism – whose proponents could reach tens of millions of viewers.

The Great Migration

"The Great Migration" was a period when many African Americans made their way north and west. Looking to escape the Ku Klux Klan and the Jim Crow laws of the South, they answered the call from industrialists who had reached out for laborers during the First World War, and areas like Harlem in New York, the South Side in Chicago, and Detroit, Michigan became predominantly Black. In the period between the two world wars, an estimated 2 million Black people moved from the South, and social tensions increased in response.

Many whites reacted by moving out as Black people moved in ("white flight"), and some residential neighborhoods placed covenants requiring white property owners not to sell to Black people (these remained legal until 1948). Tensions boiled over in Chicago in the "Red Summer" of 1919. After police refused to arrest a white man who was seen killing a Black man, a week of rioting followed, leaving 15 white and 23 Black people dead. Around 1,000 Black families lost their homes, having been torched by the rioters.

Black community leaders called for action. Marcus Garvey, a powerful orator and Jamaican political activist, created the Universal Negro Improvement Association (UNIA) which attracted as many as 25,000 people into Carnegie Hall to hear him speak in 1923. The UNIA promoted a "Back to

Africa" campaign that called for all Black people to return to Africa and create a mighty race that would rule the continent and take it back from the white man. He tried to buy steamships for his shipping company, the Black Star Line, that would transport people across the Atlantic, but the company failed due to mismanagement and corruption. Garvey was eventually sentenced to jail for mail fraud in 1925 and deported to Jamaica.

W E B Du Bois was no supporter of Garvey's "Back to Africa" movement, and he continued to fight for Black rights as editor of *The Crisis*, the NAACP's monthly magazine. Based out of New York, he was a central figure in the Harlem Renaissance, an unprecedented outburst of creativity among African Americans in all fields of art that broke out in Manhattan at this time. Langston Hughes wrote *The Negro Speaks of Rivers*, Duke Ellington and Cab Calloway played in the Cotton Club (to exclusively white audiences), Aaron Douglas painted *Aspects of Negro Life*, and the first all-Black musical, *Shuffle Along*, was a smash hit on Broadway.

The Harlem Renaissance helped pave the way for better relations between Blacks and whites and gave the Black community a creative outlet for their emotions. But when the Depression hit, the movement was deprived of funding, and a line was drawn under the era when three African Americans were killed and 75 arrested in a race riot that broke out in Harlem in 1935.

CHAPTER 15

THE GREAT DEPRESSION (1929–1941)

The Wall Street Crash

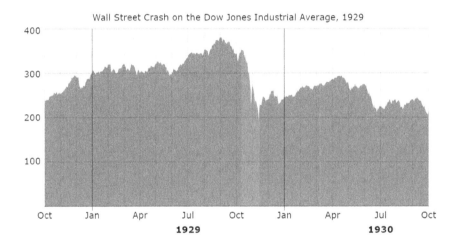

The Wall Street Crash, October 1929.

Boom conditions of the 1920s came to a complete stop in October 1929. The Federal Reserve began warning of excessive speculation in March of that year and a small crash occurred, with the National City Bank providing $25 million in credit to halt its decline. The stock market resumed climbing, although various economists were warning of a potential calamity, and by mid-September, the stock market was fluctuating wildly.

On October 24 ("Black Thursday"), the economic bubble burst. The market lost 11 percent of its value at the opening bell and continued into the following week, losing nearly 13 percent on Monday and another 12 percent on Tuesday. By mid-November, the Dow had lost almost half its value, and it would continue its descent for over another two years – until the summer of 1932 – when it closed at 89 percent below its all-time high. The event kicked off the Great Depression that lasted until 1939, leaving millions destitute and unemployed.

Multiple factors contributed to the crash, and historians continue to debate how much weight each one carried. These factors included irrational optimism, the ability to buy on margin, a credit boom, overproduction, agricultural recession, weaknesses in the banking system, and laissez-faire policies of the government and Federal Reserve.

First, the economic prosperity and technological advancements preceding the crash provided people with an overwhelming sense of optimism which unscrupulous individuals were quick to exploit. Charles Ponzi developed his eponymous scheme in the early 1920s. This maintained the illusion of a successful business by paying old investors off with new investors' money, while siphoning part of the new investment money for himself (the largest Ponzi scheme in history occurred in 2008 when Bernie Madoff defrauded his clients of more than $50 billion).

Companies also sought to take advantage of the public's optimistic nature, most notably in 1926 with the Florida land boom and bust. Miami had just been connected by railway lines, and mosquito control districts (using ditching and dredging techniques) had been created that led to a boom in tourism and residential development in the area. The population of Miami grew from around 5,000 in 1900 to 75,000 by 1925, and advertisements appeared in national newspapers encouraging people to buy and invest in land there.

George Merrick, a real estate developer, built Coral Gables in a Mediterranean Revival style, and Carl Fisher created the resort of Miami Beach, and Miami saw an unprecedented surge of business in its real estate sector. It had 25,000 real estate agents working out of 2,000 offices selling land at $200 an acre that once sold for $22. Slick advertising and marketing attracted investors from New York, Chicago, and San Francisco, and fantastic profits began fueling speculation. On one occasion an old man was committed to a sanatorium by his sons for spending his life savings of $1,700 on a piece of land in Pinellas County, but when the value of the land reached $300,000 in 1925, the man's lawyer got him released to sue his children for committing him.

At first, people were cautious, but as word spread about the profits, speculation grew – and to such an extent that many people even bought land sight unseen. Some were duped into buying swampland that they believed was on the coast but was miles from the ocean. This did not matter if the market rose and if one could find another buyer, but the gap between what was worth buying and what was not gradually began to grow.

The boom came to a dramatic halt when two hurricanes hit in 1926 and 1928. The first devastated Greater Miami and caused catastrophic damage to the area, killing 400 people and leaving 50,000 people homeless. Hundreds of buildings were underwater, electricity was out, and property prices immediately collapsed. When a second hurricane hit in 1928, it sealed shut any hope of a comeback.

In the stock market, prices began to exceed real values, and there was no legislation to discourage speculation. Margin trading enabled investors to pay only one-tenth of the value of the shares, which had the effect of artificially increasing the value of a stock as more money was pumped in. Dividend rates for a stock ranged between 1 percent and 3 percent, but with interest rates at around 12 percent, the buyer could not afford to wait long if he wanted to pay back the lender. Any dip in the market could be calamitous.

Additionally, credit was easily obtainable and investing in shares directly encouraged. The president of National City Bank (now Citibank) and director of the Federal Reserve Bank of New York, Charles E Mitchell, continued to encourage people to purchase stocks right into October, and 90 percent of the banks had invested in the stock market themselves. Many people refused to consider that a stock investment could turn out badly, putting their trust in the Federal Reserve (which had been created in 1913) to use its power and foresight to prevent the boom and bust cycles that had plagued the country since its birth.

Another problem the country faced was overproduction. Demand struggled to keep pace with supply as the improvement in production techniques meant that food and consumer goods were produced ever more efficiently. The ability to buy on credit kept products moving, but consumers would eventually have to decide between paying the interest on the loans or buying more products. If they stopped buying products, companies would have to report decreasing profits, and their share price would decline.

Furthermore, international trade was depressed due to the high tariffs the government had imposed on goods coming into the US. They were designed to protect American industries, but it meant that European nations were priced out, and they consequently imposed tariffs of their own as they attempted to keep up with their debt payments from the war. Farmers were particularly harmed as they could not export their products, and millions struggled with debt and defaulted on their loans. Between 1920 and 1929, more than 5,000 of the nation's 30,000 banks failed as they found themselves overextended.

Drought conditions then severely affected the southern plains region from 1930. Farmers had torn up millions of acres of prairie grassland to plant more crops to make up for the lower grain prices (caused by overproduction and resumption of the agricultural economy in Europe), and the drought exposed the bare, over-plowed farmland which simply blew away. "Dust to eat, and dust to breathe, and dust to drink. Dust in the bed and in the flour bin, on dishes and walls and windows, in hair and eyes and teeth and throats, to say nothing of the heaped-up accumulation on floors and window sills after one of the bad days," wrote Caroline Henderson in one of her *Letters from the Dust Bowl* (1936). Dirt was carried off by the wind, muddy rain could be seen pouring down over cities and even on ships at sea, and people would cover their faces with handkerchiefs only to find them black with dirt moments after exposure to it.

Migrant Mother, by Dorothea Lange (1936) – a photograph of a migratory family after the Dust Bowl travesty.

With so many farmers made bankrupt, migratory workers climbed aboard trains looking for work. They were known as "Okies" and "Arkies" according to their place of origin – Oklahoma or Arkansas – and they played the leading role in John Steinbeck's masterpiece set in the Great Depression, *The Grapes of Wrath* (1939). Hobo communities became common, many of which were dubbed Hooverville after the president, Herbert Hoover, who eventually became a scapegoat for the crisis.

It is common to hear about how many people were invested in the stock market in 1929, but it was only around 10 percent of the population. Yet those investors were crucial to the overall health of the economy, and with almost every bank also invested, millions were affected when they failed.

Around one-third of Americans lost their life savings, and as production ground to a halt, others were laid off or saw their wages cut. Unemployment tripled from 1.5 million at the end of 1929 to 4.5 million at the end of 1930, and the country's gross national product declined by over 25 percent within a year. The US would not fully recover until after the Second World War.

FDR and the New Deal

The magnitude of the crisis was unlike any the government had faced, and the president, Herbert Hoover, struggled with how to respond. He had been president for under a year and had come into office as one of the most popular and well-respected politicians in years. He had helped organize the evacuation of 120,000 Americans back to the United States from Europe during the First World War and had arranged for famine relief for Belgians who had been overrun by Germans. Keynes commented that Hoover was the only man to emerge from negotiations at Versailles with an enhanced reputation. He had been made Secretary of Commerce in 1921, with his department the only one to see growth in the eight years he held the post.

Hoover was, however, an avowed proponent of limited government, and in the first few months after the crash, his administration did nothing. When he did respond, it was against First World War veterans who had come to Washington to request their bonuses early to help alleviate some of their suffering. Instead of sympathizing with them and offering a solution, Hoover used military force (under General Douglas MacArthur) to drive them out of the city by setting fire to their camps.

His reaction to veterans came across as cruel and heavy-handed, and Hoover tried to pivot by passing legislation to help stem the crisis. The National Credit Corporation helped banks to stay open, and the establishment of the Reconstruction Finance Corporation steered much-needed funds to major US industries like banks, railroads, and manufacturers. He also approved the Glass-Steagall Act which aimed to protect depositors from potential losses caused by bank speculation in stocks. But these measures came too late to win the 1932 election, and the Democrats swept into office for the first time in 80 years under the leadership of Franklin Delano Roosevelt (FDR).

FDR in 1944.

FDR was the fifth cousin of Theodore Roosevelt. He had grown up in New York and had been educated at Groton and Harvard, declaring himself a Democrat while at Harvard and marrying another distant cousin, Eleanor Roosevelt (Theodore's niece), in 1905 – although their relationship became platonic in 1918 after she discovered he was having an affair.

Roosevelt joined the Wilson administration in 1913 as assistant secretary to the Navy and was the unsuccessful candidate for vice president in 1920. The following year, he contracted polio, a potentially lethal virus that was little understood at the time, which permanently paralyzed him from the waist down at the age of 39. During a time when the press was more accommodating towards presidents, they agreed not to publish photographs of Roosevelt in his wheelchair or struggling to walk or stand (they also agreed not to publish details of his extramarital affairs – a concession that would not be extended to certain future presidents), so the public never knew the extent of his disability. If a photographer were to take a photo of him that was too revealing, Secret Service Agents would tear up all the proofs.

Roosevelt became governor of New York in 1928, and Democrats turned to him in 1932, hoping his candidacy would unify the white South and the working-class groups of the North. It did just that, and he won 42 states out of 48 in the election, although this huge margin was primarily due to the disastrous economic conditions of the Depression.

Roosevelt was a progressive reformer, and although he had no grand strategy to fix the Depression, he was willing to try new ideas. He was reluctant to provide direct relief to citizens, likening such a practice to administering "a narcotic, a subtle destroyer of the human spirit," but in the first 100 days of his presidency, he introduced 15 major pieces of legislation to help combat the crisis, many of which still resonate today.

Legislation	Effect
Emergency Banking Act	Authorized the government to inspect all banks to reorganize and stabilize the banking system
Cullen-Harrison Act	Ended Prohibition
Economy Act	Cut salaries of federal workers and reduced benefit payments to veterans
Civilian Conservation Corps	Provided jobs for unemployed young men to work on conservation projects and improve national parks and forests
Federal Emergency Relief Act	Provided funding to state and local governments to help those in need and contribute towards public works projects
Agricultural Adjustment Act	Designed to boost agriculture prices whereby the government bought livestock for slaughter and paid farmers subsidies not to plant on part of their land
Emergency Farm Mortgage Act	Refinanced existing farm mortgages and issued new loans to farmers in need
Tennessee Valley Authority	Created a corporation to provide flood control, improve navigation, generate electric power, and promote economic development
Securities Act	Regulated the offer and sale of stocks
Abrogation of Gold Clauses	Eliminated contractual provisions that required payments to be made in gold or gold-backed currency
Homeowners' Refinancing Act	Provided mortgage assistance to homeowners or would-be homeowners by providing them with money or refinancing their mortgage
Glass-Steagall Act	Separated investment banking from commercial banking and guaranteed people's deposits up to $5,000 ($250,000) today
Farm Credit Act	Provided loans for agricultural purposes
Emergency Railroad Transport Act	Enabled the government to take control of the nation's railroads
National Industrial Recovery Act	Developed codes of fair competition that established minimum wages and maximum work hours, and prohibited child labor

Roosevelt was aware of the power of new technologies, and he used the radio to deliver "fireside chats" during which he tried to calm a worried nation. He greeted listeners as "my friends," referred to himself as "I" and the American people as "you," and employed a speaking style that was clear, compassionate, and personal.

Innovations continued beyond FDR's first 100 days. The Social Security Act of 1935 created a federal safety net for elderly, unemployed, and disadvantaged Americans, many of whom lived in fear of poverty and illness in old age. He also passed the National Labor Relations Act (NLRA), which strengthened American trade unions by providing employees the fundamental right to seek better working conditions. Memberships in trade unions grew in 1935 even though many people were unemployed, and in 1936, emboldened autoworkers at the General Motors factory in Flint, Michigan organized one of the first sit-down strikes. For 44 days, they refused to move, fed by their families who passed food through the windows. Eventually FDR intervened, urging GM to recognize the workers' demands, and upon securing a 5 percent pay raise, the plant reopened.

FDR and the New Deal suffered blows in 1935 and 1936 when the Supreme Court ruled that the National Recovery Administration (NRA) and the Agricultural Adjustment Administration (AAA) were unconstitutional, suddenly throwing Roosevelt into conflict with several colorful characters. As a blue blood, many Republicans despised him, casting him as a "traitor to his class," and they cited the Wealth Tax of 1935 and the Victory Tax Act of 1942 as direct evidence. The former taxed people who earned more than $5 million per year by up to 75 percent, and the latter required employers to withhold money from paychecks.

Father Charles Coughlin, the Catholic "Radio Priest," had initially supported FDR for president but soon changed his opinion. He accused Roosevelt of becoming too friendly with the bankers, particularly Jewish ones, and Coughlin's radio program – which was listened to by an estimated 30 million people – broadcasted antisemitic commentary and accused Jews of planning to seize control of the world. Jewish leaders were shocked by his rhetoric, and upon America's entry into the war, Coughlin's appeal greatly diminished.

Huey Long, a Louisiana senator, had also backed FDR in the 1932 election but abandoned him for being too conservative. Long was a fiery orator, totally devoid of scruples, and announced his "Share Our Wealth" program in 1934. This proposed to cap personal fortunes at $50 million each, restrict inheritances to $5 million, and annual incomes to $1 million. By February 1935, he had organized over 27,000 "Share Our Wealth" clubs. Roosevelt had to take Long seriously as his popularity grew, but on September 8, 1935, Long was shot in the abdomen by the son-in-law of a political enemy and died two days later.

The Communist Party also saw a rise in membership at this time – from below 20,000 in 1933 to 66,000 in 1939. People acknowledged Stalin's boasts about Russia's low unemployment rates and how conditions for Russians had improved due to the success of all the projects Stalin had implemented. But Roosevelt had made such dramatic changes in American society that he won the election of 1936 by one of the largest margins in history. He won 60.8 percent of the popular vote, losing only the states of Maine and Vermont to the Republican Party. With such a large mandate, Roosevelt felt empowered to ensure more of his legislation went through, and he then tried to reshape the Supreme Court.

Certain New Deal legislation was bottlenecked by a 5-4 vote against it, and Roosevelt sought to rectify this by increasing the number of pro-New Deal judges in the Supreme Court. Strictly speaking, Congress could decide the number of judges that could make up the Court, so Roosevelt's plan was not unconstitutional, but from 1869 the number of judges had settled at nine (where it remains today), and Congress was concerned that if one president were to tamper with the structure of the Court, the next one might be tempted to tamper with it further. FDR's problem suddenly went away, however, when one of the justices, the Hoover appointee Owen Roberts, started to vote in favor of New Deal legislation. There is no archival evidence explaining why he changed his mind, but as a result, support for FDR's Court-packing bill fell through, while New Deal legislation passed.

The New Deal restored some confidence in the health of the nation and its ability to survive a crisis. But it did little to reduce unemployment which remained high right into the 1940s, forcing millions to survive on charity and governmental handouts (a matter of indignity to many Americans). The New Deal also led to much greater responsibility for the federal government, whose role in the economy had traditionally been laissez-faire but which had now expanded into new areas of civilian life. It shaped the modern welfare state and created legislation in healthcare, education, infrastructure, and the environment, and many people argued that its reach now extended too far into individuals' rights and freedoms. It is an argument that persists today.

CHAPTER 16

THE SECOND WORLD WAR (1941–1945)

Build up to Entry into the Second World War

While the US struggled through the Depression, aggressive new colonialism was developing in Europe and Asia. Justified by language like "living space" in Germany and "co-prosperity sphere" in Japan, these two countries along with Italy sought to carve out vast new empires for themselves. The League of Nations was powerless to prevent Japan from invading Manchuria in 1931 and Italy from invading Ethiopia in 1935.

In Germany, Hitler won the elections of 1933 and then brazenly developed a cult of personality, presenting himself as a messiah who would restore Germany to its rightful place alongside the great nations of the past. He abolished the civil rights that had been established in the Weimar Constitution and ruthlessly persecuted the Jews, removing their citizenship and barring them from professional occupations and state schools. During the war, the Final Solution took full priority as Himmler ordered mobile gas vans into occupied territory, and scores of Jews were sent to death camps by rail, truck, or on foot on the pretext of being "resettled."

In 1936, Hitler directly contravened the Treaty of Versailles by ordering troops into the Rhineland, a demilitarized zone between Germany and France, but Britain and France did nothing to force them back out. Germany then annexed Austria in March 1938, and at the Munich Conference in September, Britain and France allowed Hitler to occupy the German-speaking area of the Sudetenland in Czechoslovakia.

Badly scarred by the First World War, Britain and France were desperately attempting to appease Hitler to avert another one, and initially, their inaction was applauded. But Churchill called the Munich Agreement an "unmitigated disaster," and it eventually came to be recognized as a sober warning not to allow one's hopes to take priority over reality.

Just under one year later, on September 1, 1939, Hitler invaded Poland, prompting Britain and France to at last declare war. The British Army was then sent across the English Channel to support the French, and until May 1940, both sides did little but build up their defenses in a period known as the "Phony War." A few skirmishes were fought, a naval blockade was imposed, and propaganda leaflets were dropped into Germany denouncing the evils of the Nazis while highlighting the country's vulnerability to bombing raids.

These tactics differed significantly from Hitler's "lightning war" (blitzkrieg) in Poland. There he completely overran the country in about a month by using a closely coordinated fleet of tanks, infantry forces, and air support. In mid-September, Russia's Red Army crossed into Poland, dividing the country between Russia and Germany.

Historians view this period as a lost opportunity to have brought the war to a swift conclusion, for Hitler had left only 23 divisions on the Western Front, whereas the Allies had 110 and held an 80:1 advantage in tanks over Germany. During the Nuremberg trials in 1945, General Alfred Jodl admitted that Germany would have been easily defeated if the Allies had invaded at that time, but they did not. When Hitler finally turned his attention west in May 1940, he overran France in six weeks, achieving that which the German army had failed to do in four years in the First World War.

France, a world power, had capitulated, and Britain evacuated its forces at Dunkirk in the summer of 1940. Britain remained Germany's sole undefeated foe in Europe, and Germany set about attacking it by air in a series of bombing raids – known as "the Blitz" in Britain – on such cities as London, Liverpool, Coventry, and Birmingham. The American journalist Edward Murrow reported from London on the stoicism and resilience of the British people, and during his radio broadcasts, bombs, sirens, and whistles could be heard live, which helped generate American support for the nation under siege.

Churchill was desperate for the US to intervene and appealed personally to Roosevelt. Americans were officially neutral and divided about what role, if any, they should play, but Roosevelt agreed to provide 50 outdated American destroyers in return for leases on British bases in the Caribbean and Newfoundland. The North Atlantic fast became a key battleground, and the USS *Reuben James* was sunk by a torpedo fired from a German submarine in October 1941, killing 100, as the Germans sought to prevent munitions and supplies from arriving in Britain. Roosevelt, however, remained cautious.

The US was aware of the Nazis' persecution of the Jews, but it was hard to believe the shocking details. Rumors of German atrocities in the First World War had since been discredited, and the memories of the First World War generated a strong isolationist mentality. Much of the clergy were pacificists and members of the Fellowship of Reconciliation, which promoted peace and nonviolence,[82] and personalities such as the aviator Charles Lindbergh, former president Herbert Hoover, and Father Charles Coughlin argued that American interests were not at stake. With the effects of the Depression still reverberating, they stressed that domestic issues needed to remain the priority.

In 1940, Roosevelt ran for an unprecedented third term. Every president since the country's founding had honored the principle of running for a maximum of two terms,[83] but this tradition had not yet been enshrined in the Constitution. With the geopolitical situation worsening, the Democrats wanted to retain some semblance of consistency, so Roosevelt was asked to run again. He agreed and won, partly by promising to keep America out of the war.

It was not, however, a promise easily kept, and in mid-December 1940, Roosevelt further helped the Allied cause with the Lend-Lease program which lent, rather than sold, military supplies to Britain and deferred the loan payments. This kept the US out of the war but provided support for defeating Germany, which had expanded the war by invading Russia in June 1941. Stalin was incredulous. Right up to the day of the invasion, he ignored his own spies who had been reporting with increasing urgency that the Nazis were about to strike, preferring to accept German reports that their troops were massing in the East to avoid British air raids and that any Luftwaffe planes they saw had simply lost their way.

---

82 Reinhold Niebuhr, a theologian and political preacher, left the Fellowship and railed against them traveling around the country in support of joining the Allies against Germany.

83 Two years after FDR's death, US lawmakers passed the 22nd Amendment limiting presidents to two terms.

Hitler's decision to invade Russia was a pivotal moment. It had been attempted before by European powers but had never succeeded. Charles XII of Sweden had tried it in 1708 and Napoleon in 1812, but Hitler believed his superior military technology would make all the difference and, not least, he wanted Russia's raw materials.

At first, Germany made significant progress, and by December 1941, the Red Army had suffered 4 million casualties. But as the Nazis progressed deeper into Russia and winter began to take hold, their supply lines became stretched, and the Nazis stalled in Stalingrad on their way to overtake Moscow. There, Germans and Russians battled it out for five months in some of the fiercest fighting of the war, and in the end, Germany suffered more casualties on the Eastern Front than on the Western (they suffered a total of around 6.5 million). But this number pales in comparison to the Russians, who suffered the most casualties of any country in the Second World War, with estimates of up to 27 million.

The United States Enters the Second World War

America's isolationist stance changed overnight – specifically on December 7, 1941 – when the Japanese attacked the US naval base in Pearl Harbor, Hawaii. Just before 8 a.m. on that Sunday morning, hundreds of Japanese fighter planes destroyed or damaged 20 American naval vessels including eight battleships, and over 300 airplanes. More than 2,400 Americans died in the attack, including civilians, and another 1,000 were wounded. The next day, Roosevelt asked Congress to declare war on Japan.[84]

---

84   You can find more on the attack at Pearl Harbor at https://historyinaheartbeat.com/7th-december-pearl-harbor-memorial-day/

The Japanese had been gradually expanding their empire in Asia since 1931. They had been the first Asian nation to industrialize, had fully invaded China in 1937, and overran Korea and French Indochina as they sought to create a Greater East Asia Co-Prosperity Sphere in the area. The US embargoed all oil exports to the country in 1940, which inflamed the Japanese who imported up to 90 percent of its oil, and they started to believe that their warrior and martial values would triumph over the softer democratic values of the United States. It was a fatal miscalculation.

The USS West Virginia burns after the attack
on Pearl Harbor, 1941.

The attack on Pearl Harbor was an audacious scheme conceived by the Japanese admiral Isoroku Yamamoto. 353 Japanese planes traveled on six aircraft carriers on a 3,500-mile voyage, reaching a staging area 230 miles away from the island of Oahu. From there, they set off in radio silence, flying at low altitude to avoid radar detection. US officials missed warning signs – including an intercepted message asking about berthing positions at Pearl Harbor and a radar sighting of planes on the morning of December 7 – and were ultimately caught by surprise. The Japanese were disappointed not to find aircraft carriers and submarines at the Hawaiian base, however, and lacked the fuel to track them down, and the US Navy would recover quickly. They raised the ships that had sunk in shallow water at Pearl Harbor, fixed them, and put them back into operation.

Japan followed up Pearl Harbor with attacks against British and US bases in the Philippines, Guam, Midway Island, Wake Island, Malaya, and Hong Kong and within days became masters of the Pacific. Germany and Italy declared war on the United States after the US declaration of war on Japan, and the US was now also formally engaged in Europe – which suited Roosevelt, as he felt Germany was the greater threat.

Panic on the West Coast followed as Californians feared a full Japanese invasion, and FDR pushed through what is considered one of the worst violations of American civil rights, Executive Order 9066. It forced people of Japanese descent who were living in the United States, including citizens who had been established there for one or two generations, to give away or sell their property and live in relocation centers in desert and mountain states for most of the war. About 120,000 people were uprooted to live in deplorable conditions, with some living in horse stalls with dirt floors, surrounded by guards, watchtowers, and barbed wire fences. To add insult to injury, those of fighting age could still be drafted by the War Office but would deliberately be sent to the European theatre rather than the Asian one.

The nation faced a formidable challenge. It was ill-equipped and wounded and suddenly found itself at war with three major powers on two distant, and very different, fronts. A massive government spending plan ensued as entire industries were converted to generate wartime products and restrictions on consumption were placed on citizens. At the time, the United States had a smaller army than Portugal, so it instituted a draft, and just as it had experienced in the First World War, the US found as many as 43 percent of draftees unfit to serve, mostly due to lack of access to basic medical care, poor vision, or poor diet.

The war did not start well for the United States. The Philippines was poorly defended, and an attack on Clark Field by the Japanese the day after Pearl Harbor took out all but one of the B-17s, which had been lined up in full view. Then, after the Battle of Bataan in the Philippines, which took place from January to April 1942, the Americans were forced to surrender and march with their captors to a prison camp through more than 65 miles of jungle without any medical care. Around 70,000 Filipino and American prisoners of war stumbled onward, some of whom were tortured and given nothing to eat or drink. Others were beaten with rifle butts and clubs, and hundreds were summarily killed on the way. Approximately 10,000 men died (9,000 Filipinos and 1,000 Americans) overall.

These actions embittered relations between the United States and Japan for many years to come. But, in the short term, the United States got a boost as General Douglas MacArthur escaped from the Philippines just in time, whereupon he made a promise to return. "Keep the flag flying," he said. "I'm coming back" – a mantra he enjoyed repeating over the coming years and which never failed to galvanize the US public.

The US in Europe

Winston Churchill arrived in Washington, DC ten days after the US declared war. He agreed with Roosevelt to pool military resources and prioritize defeating Germany in a "Germany First" policy, but from mid-1941, they held back and watched as almost the entire German army was fighting in Russia.

Stalin was desperate for the Allies to open a second front in the West to divert Hitler's forces, but the Allies dragged their feet. Churchill reminded Roosevelt that Stalin had been an ally of Hitler's until very recently and that another alliance between them could not be entirely ruled out. So, from the summer of 1941 through the summer of 1944, Russia did most of the fighting in the war. Churchill was happy to see these two vast empires battle it out, for however much he wanted Germany defeated, he was very wary of Stalin's Marxist dictatorship.

Roosevelt was no supporter of the Soviet Union himself, calling it a "dictatorship as absolute as any other dictatorship in the world," but Russia badly needed help. Roosevelt expanded the Lend-Lease program and sent goods via Arctic convoys for delivery in Archangel and Murmansk in northern Russia. This was an extremely dangerous run, as ships could only sail when ice permitted and would have to face fog, snow, and sleet at the same time as hoping to avoid drift ice, strong currents, and German planes and submarines. In the winter months, runs would be conducted in full darkness, and in the summer, in full daylight. A total of $11.3 billion ($180 billion in today's currency) in goods made it through, and when the Russians pushed west in 1944, they were driving Dodge and Studebaker trucks and eating spam made by Americans in the Midwest.

As much as Stalin wanted a second front opened in the West, an Anglo–American invasion would have been, at the time, very difficult to accomplish. The Germans had built a series of coastal defenses and fortifications known as the Atlantic Wall, which stretched 2,400 miles along the coast of continental Europe and north into Scandinavia. The first Americans to see combat in Europe tested these fortifications in August 1942 when a combined British, Canadian, and American force raided Dieppe. After being pummeled by the Germans on the beaches, the Allies withdrew after only ten hours with over 3,600 men (of 6,000) killed, wounded, or captured.

One of the lessons of the Dieppe Raid was to resist attempting another amphibious attack until they were better prepared, so in the meantime, the Allies concentrated their efforts on bombing raids. Roosevelt and Churchill agreed that Americans would fly during the day and the British at night, and they identified Hamburg as their target in August 1943. Code-named Operation Gomorrah, the Hamburg bombing was the heaviest assault in the history of aerial warfare, lasting eight days and seven nights, killing around 37,000 civilians and wounding another 180,000. Large parts of the city were completely destroyed after a firestorm engulfed the city in the dry August conditions.[85]

The bombing raids to the Germans, much like the Blitz to the British, did nothing to weaken their resolve. The Germans relocated many of their industrial operations into the countryside, compromising the precision of Allied bombing. Creep-back – the tendency to drop bombs early based on fires seen ahead – was common, hitting nothing but open fields.

---

85 A firestorm occurs when strong currents of air are drawn into the blaze, making it burn more fiercely.

Dresden after being bombed by the Allies in 1945.

Hamburg was a legitimate target. It was Germany's second-largest city and home to many factories and shipbuilding facilities, but Dresden, the next city targeted, was less so. It already housed thousands of refugees from Hamburg and from Russian advances in the East, yet the Allies sent 800 bombers over three days in February 1945, dropping 2,700 tons of explosives and incendiaries on the city.[86] The bombing came after many US troops had been killed at the Battle of the Bulge and the atrocities of Auschwitz had recently been discovered, so critics argued that the Allied mission was as much a revenge mission as it was a traditional bombing raid. It left the city known as "Florence on the Elbe," in complete ruins with around 25,000 people dead. Indeed, the two attacks on Hamburg and Dresden left more people dead than similar German air raids against the British in the whole length of the war (the British lost around 60,000 people).

---

86 Kurt Vonnegut was held captive in Dresden at the time, and wrote about his experience through his protagonist in *Slaughterhouse-Five* (1969).

At sea, the Battle of the North Atlantic lasted the duration of the war, as German U-boats targeted Allied warships and merchant ships taking supplies from America to Britain. British codebreakers cracked the Enigma cipher machine in 1941, which enabled them to read intercepted coded messages sent by German U-boats and gradually turned the battle in their favor. It raised an ethical issue of how best to use the decoded information, as they did not want the Germans to discover that their code had been broken but also wanted to prevent strikes, so the Allies had to choose between what information to act on and what to ignore.

In North Africa, Mussolini was reinforced in 1941 by German forces led by Erwin Rommel. Rommel scored some early notable successes, earning him the nickname "Desert Fox," but his defeat to British Commonwealth forces at the Battle of El Alamein in 1942 was a significant turning point. Just afterwards, the United States Army landed in West Africa, advancing eastwards as the British moved westwards. America's first engagement with Germany came at the Battle of Kasserine Pass in February 1943 at which they were pushed back and suffered over 3,000 casualties. Regrouping, they continued to push east, and facing a "two army" pincer, the Germans and Italians evacuated North Africa, yielding over 275,000 prisoners of war and surrendering their possessions.

An Anglo–American invasion of Sicily and Italy followed next, as they looked to eliminate Italy from the war and secure sea lanes in the Mediterranean. US forces landed at Salerno and Anzio in Italy in September where they encountered fierce German resistance and, as they advanced north, found the mountainous Apennine terrain increasingly difficult. They engaged with the Germans at the Battle of Monte Cassino for four brutal months between January and May 1944, which resulted in the destruction of the town and its historic Benedictine monastery.

The second front fully opened on June 6, 1944, with the D-Day landings, and the war ended eleven months later. General Dwight Eisenhower was appointed Supreme Commander and, in advance, had his military carry out deception operations to make the Germans believe the Allies would land at Calais, the narrowest point in the English Channel between England and France. A tremendous bombing campaign was conducted before the D-Day landings, targeting railroad bridges and roadways in northern France to prevent the Germans from bringing in reserves. Troops were parachuted behind enemy lines the night before to continue causing damage.

The landing zone was divided into five separate beaches that had different code names, with the Americans landing at Omaha and Utah. The fiercest fighting was at Omaha, where machine-gun fire greeted soldiers as soon as they stepped off the landing boats and continued as they raced to the bottom of the cliffs. About 35,000 men landed on the beaches, and 4,700 were killed, wounded, or missing by the time the Allies took control of the area. By nightfall, about 175,000 Allied troops and 50,000 vehicles were ashore with nearly 1 million more men on the way.

The Allies then proceeded to fight their way inland, and by the end of August 1944, they had reached the Seine and liberated Paris. Moving east, the US forces engaged with the Germans at the Battle of the Bulge in the Ardennes region of Belgium in the winter of 1944. It was Hitler's last major offensive on the Western Front, and Churchill termed it the "greatest American battle of the war" which the Germans, considering they must have known they were facing imminent defeat, fought with extraordinary tenacity. Hitler experimented with a Trojan Horse style of attack by forming a special unit of English-speaking men wearing American uniforms and driving captured US Army vehicles. They would go ahead, with the goal of infiltrating Allied lines and securing bridges, and others would create confusion by spreading disinformation and by changing road signs. After some of these men were captured, the Americans designed a method to thwart them by asking soldiers passing through checkpoints specific questions about American culture.[87]

The Battle of the Bulge was the costliest ever for the US, incurring over 19,000 deaths with another 70,500 wounded or missing. Many struggled with trench foot, pneumonia, and frostbite, and on Christmas Day 1944, they were finally given support by the Allied air forces as the weather conditions cleared enough to allow them through. The US arrived in Berlin in June.

In the east, the Germans finally succumbed to Russian forces at the Battle of Stalingrad. In what was one of the bloodiest battles in the history of warfare with an estimated 2 million casualties, Russian victory came in February 1943. Russia remained on the offensive, liberating most of Ukraine and virtually all of Russia and eastern Belorussia over the year. They then rolled into Poland, Bulgaria, and Romania and on into Germany in 1945.

As the Red Army moved west, the leaders of the United States, Russia, and Britain met at Yalta in February to discuss the postwar fate of Germany and Europe. Stalin, embittered by Roosevelt and Churchill's lethargy during the war, was determined to retain control of the eastern nations he

---

87 Omar Bradley recounts that he was asked to name the capital of Illinois and a position in American football in his memoirs, *A Soldier's Story*.

had reclaimed from Hitler, and with his troops consolidating their positions, Roosevelt and Churchill had little choice but to allow them to stay there. Hitler committed suicide in a bunker in Berlin on April 30, 1945, and his successor, Admiral Karl Dönitz, surrendered unconditionally a week later. The war in Europe was over.

The US in the Pacific

Just over four months after the attack on Pearl Harbor, the United States struck back against Japan with the Doolittle Raid of April 18, 1942. In much the same way as Japan had employed aircraft carriers to attack Pearl Harbor, the United States used the USS *Hornet*[88] to transport 16 B-25 bombers 650 miles east of Japan from where they set off to bomb industrial targets in Tokyo, Yokohama, Yokosuka, Nagoya, Kobe, and Osaka. They lacked the fuel to return and continued west, crash-landing in China (with one landing in Russia).

The attack horrified the Japanese high command. The damage done by the bombs was insignificant, but they were forced to accept their vulnerability to air attacks, and they retaliated by sending 180,000 Japanese troops to track down the American airmen, then punishing them and anyone else suspected of helping them. Known as the Zhejiang-Jiangxi campaign, the brutality of it was on par with anything the Japanese did in the war as they laid waste to an area of some 20,000 square miles.

They managed to capture eight US airmen, of whom they executed three, before taking their anger out on the Chinese. Father Wendelin Dunker reported on what he saw in the town of Ihwang: "They shot any man, woman, child,

---

88 Three aircraft carriers, the USS *Enterprise*, the USS *Lexington*, and the USS *Saratoga* were away from Pearl Harbor at the time of the attack.

cow, hog, or just about anything that moved, they raped any woman from the ages of 10-65, and before burning down the town, they thoroughly looted it... none of the humans shot were buried either."

American codebreakers cracked the Japanese naval codes in 1942, enabling them to intercept the Japanese fleet on its way to Tulagi and Port Moresby in May. They fought one another at the Battle of the Coral Sea, where the planes took off from aircraft carriers to conduct the fighting. It resulted in the loss of 70 Japanese warplanes to the Americans' 66 as well as the loss of the USS *Lexington*, but the battle proved that the United States could fight Japan on equal terms and forced Japan to put their Port Moresby invasion on hold, perhaps preventing a future invasion of Australia.

The staying power of the United States was demonstrated as the USS *Yorktown*, damaged in the Battle of the Coral Sea, was patched up and ready for battle in three days. Its captain had expected it to take 90 days, but it was repaired in time for the Battle of Midway, which took place a month later in June 1942. The Japanese wanted to use the island of Midway as a base to attack Pearl Harbor, but US Navy codebreakers deciphered the date they planned to invade and inflicted a devastating defeat on the Japanese fleet. The Japanese Imperial Navy lost four aircraft carriers in five minutes, and, as luck would have it, the Japanese planes had been refueling on the carriers when the US dive-bombers struck, and all the bombs, fuel, and electric devices ignited all at once, creating a huge inferno and killing hundreds on board in a crucial victory for the United States.

The distances of the crossings in the Pacific were so vast that they became a determining factor for Japan's defeat in the war. Neither fleet came over the other's horizon in the Battle of Midway (Midway itself was 2,000 miles away from the nearest continent), and aviators would have to contend with the fear that every time they flew off a carrier, they may get blown up, shot down, or lost at sea. Further, aviators risked being unable to find their way back to the carrier, after which they would be forced to circle around until they ran out of fuel. Many planes crashed into the sea when taking off or landing, like in the case of twenty-year-old George Bush Sr., who was shot down on a mission and bailed out over the ocean. He swam to a life raft, bleeding from his forehead and vomiting uncontrollably, but managed to remain afloat until a US submarine rescued him hours later.

The US scored a major psychological victory when codebreakers discovered that Admiral Yamamoto himself would be flying over Bougainville Island on the morning of April 18, 1943. They seized the opportunity to shoot down the plane, successfully taking out Yamamoto, whose body was found near the wreckage in the Bougainville Jungle. He was strapped upright in his seat and still holding his sword, in a demoralizing loss for the Japanese.

The Americans had two strategies for victory in the Pacific. One, led by Admiral Chester Nimitz, was to concentrate on seizing Japanese-held islands, hopping from one to another and gradually moving north towards Japan on whom they would eventually launch an amphibious attack. The other strategy, led by Supreme Commander Douglas MacArthur, was to move west and attack through the Philippines. Both strategies were employed, and with the Japanese Empire so spread out, US interceptions of supply ships would mean that certain islands would become completely cut off. The US sometimes chose not to bother invading one island, simply moving on to one beyond it and leaving the isolated one to "wither on the vine."

When attacking an island, the Japanese would show tremendous tenacity in defense. The Solomon Islands campaign was the first major amphibious landing that began after Midway in August 1942, and the fighting lasted for six months in hot, humid, mountainous jungle terrain that lacked basic infrastructure. The Japanese warrior code dictated that it was shameful to be taken prisoner, so many would either commit suicide or engage in a mass bayonet charge at the enemy (called a Banzai attack). At the Battle of Saipan in July 1944, after the US had taken two-thirds of the island, the 4,000 Japanese remaining were ordered to participate in a final Banzai attack before daybreak the next morning. They consumed copious amounts of beer and sake before relentlessly charging at the American infantry who, over the course of 12 hours, killed all of them with machine-gun and howitzer fire. The Americans then watched in horror as hundreds of Japanese civilians committed mass suicide by jumping off the island's northern cliffs.

The Battle of Saipan led to the United States gaining a foothold on the Mariana Islands from where they could launch raids on Japan, prompting Tojo, the Japanese Prime Minister, to resign in humiliation. Further island campaigns followed with the Americans using Navajo-speaking Native Americans to send communications,[89] hoping the Japanese would not be able to translate them. Norman Mailer's first novel, *The Naked and the Dead*, vividly depicts the fear the men felt before embarking on an invasion, and Eugene B Sledge's novel *With the Old Breed* describes finding bodies of marines with their severed genitals inserted into their mouths as he struggled to process the brutality of the Japanese.

---

89 Dramatized in the film *Windtalkers* (2002).

The Battle of Leyte Gulf in the Philippines was the largest naval battle in history, conducted in October 1944. Over 200,000 naval personnel fought in waters near the Philippine islands of Leyte, Samar, and Luzon over three days, and at the end of the battle, MacArthur waded ashore to make a radio broadcast: "People of the Philippines," he said, "I have returned!"[90]

Propaganda against the Japanese – who were portrayed as short and slant-eyed, with big teeth and eyeglasses – persisted in the United States itself. The Americans might have appreciated the logic of prioritizing the war in Europe, but the hatred they felt towards the Japanese was more bitter and personal, driven by the events of Pearl Harbor and the Bataan Death March. They braced themselves as the war approached the Japanese mainland in 1944 and 1945.

The iconic photograph taken by Joe Rosenthal of soldiers raising the flag on Iwo Jima.

90　An apocryphal story tells of MacArthur responding to one of his generals who says that he hopes the boat lands close to the shore with "I [also] hope it lands close to the shore, or else the men will see that I can't walk on water."

Japanese resistance stiffened, and they deployed new defensive tactics by camouflaging themselves and hiding out in the jungles and mountains of the surrounding islands. There was no way the Japanese could have won the Battle of Iwo Jima – it had been bombed in advance, was surrounded by ships and planes, and its forces were thoroughly outnumbered (110,000 US men against 21,000 Japanese) – but the Japanese fought so intensely that the Americans suffered over 27,000 casualties. Japanese resistance was finally quelled on March 25 after they launched a final Banzai attack, although holdouts continued to resist. Two people in the island's caves refused to surrender until 1949, four years after the war had ended.

The Okinawa campaign took place between April and June 1945 and was even more costly, as the United States suffered over 60,000 casualties and the Japanese over 110,000. In what was the last major battle of the Second World War, the United States had to contend with the worst kamikaze attacks of the war. Meaning "divine wind" – named after the typhoons that had driven back Kublai Khan's Mongol invasion in 1274 and 1281 – kamikaze attacks began in October 1944 at the Battle of Leyte Gulf, and by the end of the war, a total of around 3,800 kamikaze pilots had died. They were often university students and prepared themselves by holding ceremonials, drinking sake, writing farewell poems, and receiving a "thousand stitch belt" – cloth into which 1,000 women had sewn one stitch as a symbol of unity with the pilot. They would then strap themselves into a plane with 550-pound bombs and fly off with only enough fuel for them to reach their target, and at the Battle of Okinawa, around 1,465 kamikaze fighters attacked the Allied fleet. The destroyer USS *Laffey* was attacked by 20 planes at once as they dove in at 500 miles per hour, spurring the Americans to shoot down as many as they could, shocked and horrified by the nature of these attacks.

The Americans landed on the beach at Okinawa where they initially met no resistance. It was only when they reached Shuri that they found Japanese lying in wait among heavily defended hills, and the Americans fought fierce battles on ridges and hills, suffering the most casualties at Hacksaw Ridge, located atop a 400-foot vertical cliff where thousands were killed and many engaged in hand-to-hand combat.

The ritual suicide of General Ushijima on June 22 effectively ended the Battle of Okinawa, and Japan prepared its citizens to resist the forthcoming American invasion. With significantly depleted resources, they assembled civil defense units (volunteer fighting corps), arming them with pointed bamboo or wood sticks, clubs, truncheons, and bows and arrows before hunkering down. From November 1944, US bombing planes made round-the-clock raids on Japanese cities.

The Tokyo firebombing conducted by 325 B-29 bombers on the night of March 9–10, 1945 was the single most destructive bombing raid in history, leaving an estimated 100,000 civilians dead and 1 million homeless. With buildings tightly packed and made of paper and wood, the fires spread at an extraordinarily destructive rate and exceeded even the death rate caused by the atomic bombing of Nagasaki, estimated to be between 60,000 and 80,000 people.

The Tokyo firebombing was the first in a series of attacks on 64 Japanese cities, and it was still not clear what would bring the war in the Pacific to an end. The war had ended in Europe in May 1945, leaving the US and the world exhausted, but the Japanese showed no sign of giving up. Some experts predicted it might take another million US casualties and continue for a further five years, and America searched for tools they could use to avoid such an outcome.

The Manhattan Project and the End of the War

The science of nuclear physics rapidly developed after Albert Einstein warned Roosevelt in 1939 that the Germans had begun a program to exploit nuclear fission for military purposes. Enrico Fermi, an Italian physicist who had escaped from Mussolini's Italy, proved that a controlled nuclear reaction was possible with an experiment in his laboratory – a squash court under Stagg Field Stadium at the University of Chicago, where he was working. After he succeeded, Fermi sent a coded message to the National Defense Research Committee which said: "The Italian navigator has just arrived in the New World."

In 1942, Roosevelt approved the formation of the Manhattan Project, which was funded with up to $2 billion and overseen by Lieutenant General Leslie Groves. Assigned top secret status, research efforts and facilities were set up in remote locations including Hanford, Washington; Oak Ridge, Tennessee, and Los Alamos, New Mexico. J Robert Oppenheimer led the team of physicists at Los Alamos and tested the first bomb on July 16, 1945. Placed on a 100-foot tower, it was detonated at 5:30 a.m., giving off an explosion four times stronger than anticipated, after which Oppenheimer was moved to quote a passage from the Bhagavad-Gita: "Now I am become Death, the destroyer of worlds."

Several experienced and knowledgeable German Jews and Europeans had worked on the project, prompting the counterfactual questions of what might have happened had they not been forced to leave their home countries;

what might have happened had the Nazis gotten hold of the project, and what might have happened had the United States chosen not to use it.

In 1944, Roosevelt openly sought reelection (for a fourth term) and, due to the circumstances, faced little opposition. The war had turned in the United States' favor, and he comfortably defeated the Republican, Thomas E Dewey. But Roosevelt was in bad health and suffered from high blood pressure, atherosclerosis, and coronary artery disease, and the Democrat convention, knowing there was a strong possibility that Roosevelt might die in office, dropped Henry A Wallace as his running mate and selected Senator Harry S Truman of Missouri instead.

Roosevelt did indeed die before his term was up, of a massive stroke on April 12, 1945, less than a month before the war in Europe ended. He died while sitting for a portrait, and Churchill, as stunned as the rest of the world, described it as comparable to being "struck a physical blow." Hundreds of thousands of people, many with tears in their eyes, lined the train carrying his body from Georgia to Washington, DC and on to New York to pay their final respects.

Harry Truman was sworn in the day Roosevelt died but had no idea of the Manhattan Project until he effectively took office. He was told the bomb was ready and then heard arguments for and against using it. These included whether it was morally justified, the precedent it would set, the destruction it would create, and the uncertainty of the residual damage (the scientific community failed to foresee the awful effects of radiation sickness). Japan was losing, the United States was closing in, and it seemed possible that the war could be won conventionally. But there was no surrender, and Japan had an army of over 2 million in the home islands and was arming civilians. The argument went that the bomb would save not just American lives, but Japanese ones too.

Advisors proposed giving a demonstration of the bomb's potential as a warning, but Truman rejected this on the grounds that it might not guarantee Japanese surrender and that it might not detonate – which would be worse than no demonstration at all. He issued the Potsdam Declaration on July 26, calling for the unconditional surrender of Japanese armed forces with the warning that if they did not, Japan would face "prompt and utter destruction," – to which he received no reply – although the demand for "unconditional" surrender may have generated some hesitation on Japan's part.

In any event, no response was forthcoming, and 11 days later, the *Enola Gay*, a B-29 bomber, dropped an atomic bomb on the city of Hiroshima. Home of the 2nd Army headquarters and an important center of storage and communications, it had not been much damaged during the war – and when the bomb exploded, 70,000 people were instantly killed, with an additional 100,000 dying from wounds and radiation sickness afterwards. Three days later, on August 9, 1945, a second bomb was dropped on Nagasaki where 80,000 people died in total. On August 14, Japan surrendered.

Atomic cloud over Hiroshima, 1945.

Critics argue to this day as to whether dropping the bombs constituted a war crime, but at the time, the American people were jubilant. Few harbored any positive sentiments towards the Japanese, and many felt the same way as Paul Fussell, a 21-year-old Army lieutenant who recalled of his unit: "We cried with relief and joy. We were going to live. We were going to grow up to adulthood after all."

Emperor Hirohito went on national radio for the first time ever to tell his subjects that Japan had surrendered. Japanese aides wept on board the USS *Missouri* in Tokyo Bay as General Umezu signed the surrender of the army and MacArthur became leader of an occupied Japan, tasked with transforming it into a democratic nation. The Japanese public was in shock – bereaved, regretful, and many furious at what they felt had been a terrible deception.

The United States suffered a total of 419,000 military and civilian deaths due to the war. Compared to the three countries that suffered the most – Russia (between 24 to 27 million), China (between 15 and 20 million), and Germany (6.9 to 7.4 million) – this was a tiny number, and the United States emerged as the clear winner of the war, mightier than it had ever been and undamaged at home. The war energized America, ended unemployment, and stimulated productivity. Healthcare improved, American life expectancy rose, and birthrates went up with the postwar baby boom beginning during the war, in 1943.

But the legacy of the war included a global shift in power from Europe to two rival superpowers – the United States and the Soviet Union – and before the war even ended, they began jostling for supremacy. The two new superpowers would face off against each other in the Cold War, which continued for the next 45 years.

## PART SIX

POST WAR TO THE END OF THE COLD WAR

CHAPTER 17

POST-WAR ERA (1945–1964)

Security after the Second World War

The United States and the Soviet Union employed radically different systems of government. Roosevelt, and then Truman, wanted the newly liberated countries of Eastern Europe to have free, democratic elections. But Stalin, furious at the carnage the Soviet Union had endured in the war, wanted a pro-Soviet eastern bloc to protect his country from any risk of another invasion, and with his armies already in place, he was well positioned to enforce his demands.

Mistrust among The Big Three (Roosevelt, Churchill, and Stalin) was already evident during their wartime meetings in Tehran (1943), Yalta (1945), and Potsdam (1945). At the Tehran Conference, Stalin assured Roosevelt that the Republics of Lithuania, Latvia, and Estonia would be reincorporated into the Soviet Union only after the citizens of each republic had voted in a referendum. But he was quick to add that the matter would have to be resolved "in accordance with the Soviet constitution" and that he would not consent to any international control over the elections.

Roosevelt was reluctant to heed the warnings of Churchill and wanted to trust Stalin. He enjoyed Churchill's company socially, but Churchill's passionate defense of the British Empire conflicted with Roosevelt's anti-imperialist views, and when Churchill suggested that the pair of them meet prior to the Yalta Conference to strategize on how to deal with Stalin, Roosevelt refused to do so.

At Yalta, it was agreed that Germany and Berlin would be divided into four zones of occupation between the US, Britain, France, and the Soviet Union. Stalin also agreed that Poland would be reorganized under a communist provisional government and that free elections would be held later. But once the pro-Soviet government was installed in 1945, it had any anti-communist leaders assassinated and sent thousands of others to the gulag. The Soviets employed the same methods in Bulgaria and Romania, with Churchill noting drily on March 5, 1946, that "from Stettin in the Baltic to Trieste in the Adriatic, an iron curtain has descended across the continent."

Eastern Germany, Czechoslovakia, Poland, Romania, Bulgaria, and Hungary all became Soviet satellite states, with Yugoslavia breaking from the Soviets under the leadership of Josip Broz Tito in 1948. In the decades afterwards, revolts against Soviet rule – such as those in Hungary and Poland in 1956, Czechoslovakia (the Prague Spring) in 1968, and Poland again in 1970 – were brutally suppressed, and the risk of nuclear war was high enough to prevent the United States from intervening.

Economically, growth rates in the Soviet Union and its satellite states were extremely slow. The lack of competition in manufacturing coupled with the centralized planning system paralyzed initiative, with correspondingly low production. The Soviets further placed a focus on heavy industry, such as steel production and machine building which made parts of Poland and Czechoslovakia some of the most polluted places in the world. The Chernobyl disaster in Ukraine in 1986 was a culmination of years of policies that actively ignored damage to the environment to meet state production targets.

Additionally, there was no consumer society comparable to that in the West. Little could be bought freely over the counter, land was allocated rather than purchased, and traveling outside of the country required state approval. People who visited the West, such as sailors, pilots, train drivers, and sportsmen, brought back goods and stories about life there, romanticizing it and stoking feelings of resentment towards their own Soviet rule. In the meantime, the Soviet propaganda machine worked hard to paint the West as decadent and socially unstable.

The end of the war saw a further realignment of world powers in which Britain's future was most uncertain. Economically destroyed by the war, it could no longer maintain its position as a global presence; in addition, Churchill was voted out of power in a landslide victory for Clement Attlee's Labour Party in 1945. Attlee claimed Churchill was ill-suited to leadership during peaceful times and proposed a socialist model of government that included a free national health service (the NHS), the nationalization of many key industries, and decolonization abroad. This directly led to India's (and Pakistan's) independence in 1947 and the termination of its Mandate for Palestine, leading to the creation of Israel in 1948.

Churchill hoped the United States would take on the leadership role vacated by Britain. The first item that needed resolving was whether the US would continue with Britain's provision of military and economic assistance to the anti-communist parties in Greece and Turkey. Truman agreed to, in light of the deteriorating relationship between the US and the Soviet Union. He presented the "Truman Doctrine" to Congress in 1947, saying that it was "the policy of the United States to support free peoples who are resisting attempted subjugation by armed minorities or by outside pressures." Even though the Greek and Turkish regimes were not explicitly democratic, they were anti-communist – and that was enough at this juncture to gain US support.

George Kennan, an influential Foreign Service Officer, described the US policy as one of "containment" in an anonymously published telegram in an issue of *Foreign Affairs* magazine. It was a brilliant analysis that explained why the leaders of the Soviet Union viewed the ideals of the West as fundamentally incompatible with its own, how any expression of political dissent was considered a threat, and how the Soviet Union's experience in the Second World War had left them suspicious of the West. It recommended that the US adopt a patient, long-term approach.

In an acknowledgement of how the strategy of punishment employed at the Treaty of Versailles had been a failure, the Economic Recovery Program of 1948 (known as the Marshall Plan after Secretary of State George Marshall) was developed to provide aid to Western Europe. It was designed to rebuild cities, industries, and infrastructure, and provided $13.6 billion for reconstruction. But it was not entirely motivated by charity and stated that one of its goals was a halt to the spread of communism on the European continent. It needed strong partners.

Implementation of the Marshall Plan has been cited as the beginning of the Cold War, casting Germany as an ally and the Soviet Union as an enemy. But it invited all European countries to participate, including the Soviet Union itself and its satellite states. Stalin refused the aid, however, afraid of losing control of those states who accepted it, and he created his own economic plan for those in Eastern Europe: the Molotov Plan. But economic growth in the countries that received Marshall Plan funds was much greater than in those that did not, and by 1950 they had even surpassed pre-war growth levels.

The United States' commitment to its allies was put to the test with the Berlin Airlift incident of 1948–1949. Germany had been divided into a Soviet-occupied zone and a Western-occupied zone, and with Berlin located deep within the Soviet-occupied zone, it was also split four ways. The Russians believed they could gain full control of Berlin and set about blockading roads and water access to Allied-controlled areas of the city. But the US responded by airlifting food and fuel to Berlin from airbases in West Germany, carrying over 2.3 million tons of cargo into West Berlin over the course of a year. The crisis ended as it became clear the West Berliners were not going to reject their US allies, and the Soviet forces lifted the blockade in May 1949.

In the meantime, ties between the Western countries strengthened. These were reinforced in 1949 with the creation of the North Atlantic Treaty Organization (NATO), which committed each of its 12 member states[91] to share responsibility in providing collective security against the Soviet Union. But certain compromises had to be made to gain agreement from every member. France demanded the alliance be applied beyond Europe, conscious that its colonies (including Vietnam, part of French Indochina) were vulnerable to Soviet influence. Truman agreed despite his misgivings, and there was no way that he could have foreseen the ramifications that decision would have in the years to come.

---

91   The 12 member states were the United States, the United Kingdom, Belgium, Canada, Denmark, France, Iceland, Italy, Luxembourg, the Netherlands, Norway, and Portugal.

Another awkward decision had to be made when the Egyptian president, Gamal Abdel Nasser, nationalized the Suez Canal. At the time, the canal was being run by a joint British-French organization, and Britain, France, and Israel joined forces to forcibly retake it. But Egypt was supported by the Soviet Union, and Khrushchev began talking about using nuclear weapons. Eisenhower promptly demanded the British and French withdraw, threatening economic sanctions if they did not. Reluctantly they did, but it humiliatingly underlined their new subordinate role to the United States.

Development of nuclear weapons after the war continued and became a decisive factor in the postwar geopolitical situation. In 1949, the Soviets tested their first atomic bomb in Kazakhstan, and in 1952, the US detonated a hydrogen bomb – 1,000 times more powerful than an atomic bomb[92] – in the Pacific, vaporizing an entire island. In the 1950s, the development of ballistic missiles and jet airplanes (culminating with the B-52 bomber in 1955) improved delivery systems and increased a bomb's range. When the Soviets developed the Sputnik satellite in 1957, the United States reacted by urgently developing their own, triggering the "space race" which was partly driven by the acknowledgement that these satellites could carry nuclear warheads.

The appeal of nuclear weapons was that they were comparatively cheap and contained extraordinarily destructive capabilities. By contrast, maintenance of a conventional army was expensive, and if a government could reduce taxes – on defense spending in this case – it would have a higher chance of reelection and money to spend elsewhere. "Bigger

---

92 Atomic bombs work through nuclear fission, splitting large atoms like uranium or plutonium into small ones. Hydrogen bombs utilize both atomic fission and nuclear fusion (the process of taking two separate atoms and putting them together to form a third atom) to create an explosion.

bang for the buck," as Eisenhower called it. Russia's political system meant that it was not constrained by vote-seeking, and it spent money on both a nuclear arsenal and a conventional army and so usually had many more active soldiers in the military.

The disadvantage of nuclear weapons was how destructive they were. It was very difficult to justify their use, and it resulted in a 45-year stand-off. By the mid-1960s, both the US and the Soviet Union had enough nuclear power to obliterate the other, and films such as *Dr. Strangelove*, *Failsafe*, and *Wargames* all imagined scenarios wherein nuclear weapons were deployed either by mistake or through poorly conceived security protocols.

The principle of mutually assured destruction (MAD) was founded on the notion that if one country struck, the other would counterattack so ferociously that both attacker and defender would be annihilated. The acknowledgement that nuclear radiation caused illnesses such as certain cancers and cardiovascular diseases led to the Partial Nuclear Test Ban Treaty of 1963, which stipulated that all nuclear testing be conducted underground, and antinuclear movements developed that condemned the brutal nature of the weapons. Nuclear confrontation percolated every foreign policy decision made during the Cold War and only receded once it ended.

Yet the risk of a nation leveraging the power of its nuclear weapons has never been fully extinguished. In 2022, Vladimir Putin, the leader of Russia since 2000, took a leaf out of the Cold War playbook when he pronounced the West would face "consequences greater than any of you have faced in history" if it took military action against Russia's invasion of Ukraine. Russia still owns the largest arsenal of nuclear weapons in the world, although justification for their use remains hard to find.

Red Scare

Concerns over nuclear bombs led to fears of infiltration by communist spies who might have their own agenda. People looked askance at one another, and their paranoia seemed justified when Julius and Ethel Rosenberg were arrested and sentenced to death in 1951 for conspiring to pass US atomic secrets to the Soviet Union. The two had been members of the Young Communist League and vigorously protested their innocence, but Ethel's younger brother, David Greenglass, had worked as a machinist at Los Alamos and testified against his sister and brother-in-law.

The couple became the first American civilians to be executed for such charges and the first to receive that penalty during peacetime, leading to denunciations at home and abroad. Some argued that at the time of the Manhattan Project, Russia had been a US ally, so their activity could not be adjudged adversarial, although others argued that the information had been highly classified and was therefore a violation of national security.

In China, Chiang Kai Shek's Chinese Nationalists were defeated by Mao's communists in 1949. China had been in turmoil for years after the Manchu-led Qing dynasty was ousted in 1911, and a series of rival armies and warlords had vied for control of the country, with Chiang Kai Shek's Nationalist army seemingly taking full control by the late 1920s. But Mao's communists fought back, and after a break in hostilities due to the Japanese invasion in the Second World War, Mao finally forced the Nationalists out of China and onto the island of Taiwan, which the Nationalists defended with the help of the US Navy. Chiang Kai Shek's Nationalists had been a client state of the United States and had been provided with huge financial support, but large-scale government corruption and defection of troops to Mao's communists contributed to their defeat. Many anti-communists in the United States begrudged Truman his "loss of China."[93]

Communism, which had never even existed before 1917, appeared to be growing steadily across the world, prompting Truman to order loyalty checks[94] to be conducted on federal employees in 1947. In 1948, Whittaker Chambers, a former member of the US Communist Party, testified to the House of Un-American Activities (HUAC) that a respected former State Department official, Alger Hiss, was a spy for the Communist Party. He claimed that Hiss had given him State Department documents in the 1930s that he had passed on to a Soviet official. Hiss categorically denied it, but California Congressman Richard Nixon pushed Chambers into providing more details, so the latter produced a package of microfilm containing images in Hiss's handwriting that Chambers had hidden inside a pumpkin on his farm in Maryland. Hiss was convicted in 1950 and sentenced to five years in prison, although he continued to deny the story for the rest of his life. Hiss has, however, since been proven guilty after decrypted Soviet cables released in 1996 referred to one of their agent's travels and interactions that matched Hiss's own.

---

93 The United States signed an agreement with Taiwan in 1955 guaranteeing its defense, and it was not until 1979 that the United States recognized the People's Republic of China.
94 Joseph Heller wrote *Catch 22* in 1953 which was about the Second World War but captured the paranoid mood of the 1950s with the "Glorious Loyalty Oath Crusade" initiated by one of the characters in the novel.

In a climate of unmatched paranoia, the FBI reviewed 5 million government employees between 1947 and 1956, ultimately leading to 2,700 dismissals and around 12,000 voluntary resignations. The voluntary resignations were so high because people were required to provide the names of others in the same communist cell (i.e., to "name names"), and many simply chose to resign rather than do so, treating their own membership in the Communist Party as nothing more than a youthful indiscretion. The Wall Street Crash and the Depression had seen memberships rise in the Communist Party, but the brutal purges conducted by Stalin in the 1930s along with the cynical alliance he had made with Hitler before the war badly damaged the party's credibility and membership declined significantly on its own, although HUAC was determined to view it as something more sinister.

Senator Joseph McCarthy in 1954.

The entertainment and education industries became hotbeds of suspicion, and the Republican senator from Wisconsin, Joseph McCarthy, saw an opportunity to make headlines and guarantee his reelection to the Senate. In a speech in West Virginia, he claimed that he knew of 205 communists actively working in the State Department, and waved a piece of paper implying that he had their names. But he refused to provide them, and the public were left with a deep sense of unease.

Arthur Miller used the witch hunts that followed as an allegory for his play *The Crucible* (1953), and McCarthy went on a rampage, claiming communist penetration of the White House and the State Department. His approach initially resonated well with the voters, and many Republicans were tempted to let him carry on, but when McCarthy accused the US Army, it soon became clear that he had overreached.

The Secretary of the Army had refused to give preferential treatment to one of McCarthy's former aides, and McCarthy responded by accusing the Army of harboring communists and formed a committee to investigate. The Army-McCarthy hearings of 1954 were broadcast live on national television (an exciting new source of information and entertainment), and the public was appalled when McCarthy accused Joseph Welch, the US Army's lawyer, of having ties to communist organizations. Welch responded by saying, "Until this moment, Senator, I think I never really gauged your cruelty or your recklessness," and the Senate passed a motion of censure against McCarthy. Poll after poll indicated American disapproval of his behavior and McCarthy, plagued with poor health and alcoholism, died a broken man three years later at only 48 years old.

The Korean War

It was not long before American forces were back at war in Asia. This time to prevent the spread of communism in Korea which had been partitioned after the Second World War between the United States and the Soviet Union. When Dean Acheson, the US secretary of state, gave a speech in January 1950 that appeared to exclude South Korea from the US "defense perimeter," it was rushed to Stalin's desk for consideration, and Kim Il-Sung, North Korea's communist dictator, received Stalin's approval to invade South Korea two weeks later.

It was the first time that the United States's containment policy would be put to the test. Americans watched some 75,000 North Korean troops pouring across the 38th parallel into the South, and conscious of the failures of appeasement that had been attempted prior to the Second World War, the US obtained a United Nations resolution to repel the invasion.[95] MacArthur took command.

The war started badly. South Korean troops were frightened, confused, and prone to fleeing, and many American soldiers, lacking enough water to drink, contracted illnesses by drinking from rice fields fertilized with human waste. But MacArthur ordered a surprise amphibious landing at Inch'on in September 1950, which had the effect of breaking the supply lines to the North Koreans who were in Seoul and forcing them into a headlong retreat. MacArthur then went on the offensive and headed north, prompting Mao to send troops to North Korea and issue a stern warning to the US to stay away from the boundary between North Korea and China unless it wanted a full-scale war.

---

95 Russia was not seated at the UN Security Council, boycotting it because the UN would not seat a member from Communist China.

The Americans pulled back to the 38th parallel, but MacArthur advocated direct attacks on the Chinese mainland, potentially using nuclear weapons to fully roll back the communist threat. This was wild rhetoric that led to Omar Bradley, general of the US Army, rebuking MacArthur and declaring such an approach to be the "wrong war, at the wrong place, at the wrong time, and with the wrong enemy." When Truman agreed, MacArthur's frustration boiled over, and he publicly criticized the president, to which Truman responded by firing him for insubordination on April 11, 1951.

The news upset many Americans. MacArthur was a Pacific War hero and retained a huge amount of political support, but there was a strong tradition of generals being subordinate to politicians, and MacArthur's challenge to that precedent was one he could not win. He was replaced with General Matthew Ridgway, and the war descended into a stalemate around the 38th parallel. Peace negotiations ensued but were held up for two years by Syngman Rhee's (the leader of South Korea) demands for the unification of Korea under his leadership and his abject refusal to accept a cease-fire, but finally, an armistice was signed in July 1953. This time, there was no victor and no peace treaty, and a 2.5-mile-wide demilitarized zone was created that remains an area of tension even today.

It was an exceptionally bloody war that saw nearly 5 million people killed, including 40,000 Americans. MacArthur, for his part, returned to the United States for the first time since before the Second World War and gave a speech to Congress which he ended sullenly, saying, "And like an old soldier of that ballad, I now close my military career and just fade away – an old soldier who tried to do his duty as God gave him the light to see that duty. Goodbye."

Growth of the Consumer Society

Domestically, anxiety about communism in the US was offset by a society that was growing into enormous wealth and luxury. The gross national product more than doubled between 1945 and 1960 and fears the Depression would resume after the economic boom of wartime proved unfounded.

The GI Bill of Rights was passed in 1944, establishing new hospitals and providing money to veterans for college tuition, low-cost mortgages, low-interest loans to start businesses, and a year of unemployment compensation. By 1951, nearly 8 million veterans had received educational and training benefits, and 2.4 million had received $13 billion in federal loans for homes, farms, and businesses. The Bill was later adjusted to include veterans of the Korean and Vietnam wars and has since been expanded to cover everyone who has served in the Armed Forces.

"Levittowns," named after its founder, William J Levitt, were suburban towns that were built for returning veterans and their new families. Standard homes could be constructed in one day (at the peak of construction, a house could be built in 16 minutes) and were built in New York, Pennsylvania, New Jersey, and Puerto Rico. Houses included a white picket fence, a green lawn, and modern appliances and were so similar in appearance that some residents reported walking into the wrong one by accident. The towns themselves included parks, swimming pools, veterans' clubs, and community centers.

Many new towns and cities with low populations were expanded thanks to the automobile, and cities such as Los Angeles, San Diego, Dallas, Houston, Phoenix, and Miami grew as the construction of interstate highways enabled homeowners to commute to work. The availability of air conditioning – once a luxury – became a necessity to make living in the desert heat bearable. Shopping malls were built near towns with vast spaces for parking, and the inclusion of recreation areas turned shopping into a leisure activity. Fueled by the baby boom and improvements in medical care, the nation's population grew from 140 million in 1945 to 200 million by 1970.

Children were raised in absolute luxury compared to their parents, many of whom grew up in the Depression, and advertisers directly targeted children and adolescents. Walt Disney's amusement park, dubbed Disneyland, opened in July 1955 in Anaheim, California, and catered primarily to children. But it also served adults with its reproductions of Main Street and Frontierland, which were designed for visitors to reminisce about a more simple, idealistic American past.

The adult entertainment business grew alongside it. In 1946, Bugsy Siegel opened the Flamingo Hotel and Casino in Las Vegas, Nevada, the only state where gambling was legal. It was built as close to the border of California as it could get, and over 8 million people were visiting Las Vegas annually by 1954, providing a useful measure for just how much disposable income people now had.

Airline travel boomed in the 1950s, and for the first time in history, more US passengers traveled by air than by train. It was expensive (an air hostess job was a coveted position), but with increased wages and the extension of consumer credit, more and more people could afford it. Many families could even rely on a single wage earner, with many mothers staying at home to look after the children.

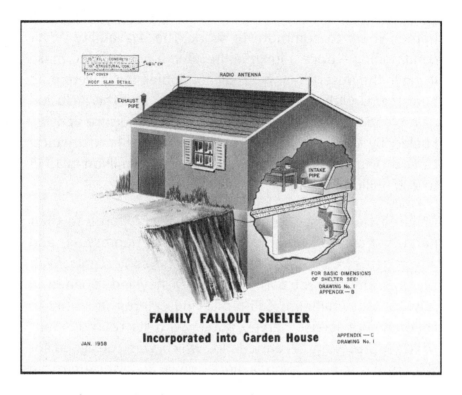

Diagram showing how a family fallout shelter can be incorporated into a home.

However, external threats were never far from people's minds. Children were drilled at school about how to shelter themselves in case of a bomb strike ("duck and cover"), and companies started selling fallout shelters which could be constructed by the consumer themselves and filled with nonperishable canned food and water.

After the Korean War, certain American POWs began confessing to crimes they had not committed. They admitted to germ warfare, dropping anthrax and the plague, and 21 American soldiers refused repatriation. These men had, in fact, been tortured in captivity and repeatedly exposed to communist propaganda, and while the US military denied the charges the soldiers had "confessed" to, they could not explain how they had been coerced into it.

Conformity, control, and institutional thinking were common themes at the time, explored in books like *The Lonely Crowd* (1950) by David Riesman and *The Hidden Persuaders* (1957) by Vance Packard. Packard described how advertisers used depth psychology and subliminal tactics to induce a desire for their products, and films like *The Wild One* (1953) and *Rebel Without a Cause* (1955) imagined young men breaking away from societal conventions of their own volition.

Literature, art, music, and film all grew in global prestige in the 1950s, and the country's architecture broke from tradition. Walter Gropius and Mies van der Rohe applied Bauhaus architectural designs to skyscrapers in New York (the Seagram and the Metlife buildings) and Chicago (the AMA Plaza and Promontory Apartments). American travelers could find their products sold throughout the world, including Coca-Cola, Kodak, Levi's, and Ford. The economist John Kenneth Galbraith called this new America "the affluent society," but almost 10 percent of US citizens – the African Americans – were left out. It would not be long before the country heard their voice.

CHAPTER 18

THE CIVIL RIGHTS ERA (1965–1980)

Build up to the Civil Rights Movement

Blacks had been marginalized in American society ever since the country's inception. Millions of Africans had been forcibly brought to the US as slaves, and after the Civil War, Jim Crow laws were enacted in the South to segregate Black people in work and society. Those laws had not been adopted in the North, but Black people still experienced discrimination in sectors such as housing, education, and employment. Under pressure in 1941, President Roosevelt issued an executive order that banned discriminatory employment practices by companies engaged in war-related work, and was the first presidential directive on race since Reconstruction. It provided a reason for African Americans to switch their traditional Republican vote to the Democrat Party.

Throughout the Second World War, civil rights organizations fought to end discrimination in the armed forces. Segregation was brought into sharp focus after Isaac Woodward, an African American Second World War veteran, was beaten to permanent blindness in a racially motivated attack in 1946. The public was outraged, and President Truman issued an executive order in 1948 to abolish the segregation of races in the military. Following that, Blacks and whites fought together in the Korean War (they fought separately in the Second World War).

At the Democratic National Convention in 1948, Minneapolis Mayor Hubert Humphrey made a passionate speech in favor of civil rights reforms. He urged the party to "get out of the shadow of states' rights and walk forthrightly into the bright sunshine of human rights," which alienated many Southern Democrats, including Mississippi's, whose entire delegation walked out of the convention. This was followed by part of Alabama's, and they eventually formed their own party, the States' Rights Democratic Party ("Dixiecrats"), and nominated Strom Thurmond for president.

"Dewey defeats Truman," as headlined in the
Chicago Daily Tribune on November 4, 1948.

A further split, this time to the left within the Democrat Party, occurred when Henry Wallace founded the Progressive Party. He had been vice president under Roosevelt and was far less antagonistic towards the Soviet Union (even accused in some quarters of being a communist himself), and he ran on a platform of establishing a national health insurance service and further expansion of the welfare system. Everything pointed towards a Republican victory under Thomas Dewey, and the *Chicago Daily Tribune* even printed its early edition the day after the election was held, with the headline "Dewey defeats Truman." But in a huge upset, Truman won, and he gleefully posed with a copy of said newspaper the following day.

Truman's victory proved that Humphrey's pro-civil rights stance was not political suicide, and further progress was made when Jackie Robinson broke the color line in sports in 1947. He became the first African American to play in a Major League Baseball team for the Brooklyn Dodgers and had to overcome racist sentiments from within his own team as well as from opposing ones. But he endured and won the Rookie of the Year Award in 1947 and the Most Valuable Player Award in 1949, the first Black player so honored.

In 1954, a landmark decision by the Supreme Court ruled, in the case of *Brown v Board of Education of Topeka*, that racial segregation in schools was "inherently unequal" and is thereby unconstitutional. Eisenhower had recently appointed a new chief justice, Earl Warren, whom he hoped would not ruffle feathers (he had been attorney general of California when the Japanese Americans had been interned). But he presided over a major shift of the Court towards a liberal direction, and in the *Brown* case, used psychological studies to show that Black girls in segregated schools had low self-esteem and were more likely to develop inferiority complexes. The Court issued directives to proceed with desegregation "with all deliberate speed," although the word "deliberate" remained open to interpretation.

Southern leaders condemned the decision. James Eastland, a senator from Mississippi, declared that "the South will not abide by nor obey this legislative decision by a political body," and Senator Byrd of Virginia issued a call for "Massive Resistance" – a series of laws including one that eliminated state funding for any public school that integrated Black and white children in its classes.

But the momentum was against them. Segregation on inter-state bus travel had been struck down by the Supreme Court in 1946, and a civil rights group called the Congress of Racial Equality (CORE) had put the new law to the test by sending 16 men (eight Black and eight white) on buses from Washington, DC through North Carolina, Tennessee, Kentucky, and Virginia. Several riders were arrested, including the CORE treasurer, Bayard Rustin. But the first "Freedom Ride" had taken place, and awareness of injustice had increased. Many African Americans were emboldened.

Leadership under Martin Luther King

In the summer of 1955, a 14-year-old Black boy, Emmett Till, was brutally murdered in Mississippi. Two white men dragged him out of his uncle's home where he was staying, forced him to carry a cotton gin fan to the Tallahatchie River, and ordered him to take off his clothes. They then beat him, gouged out his eye, shot him in the head, and threw him in the river with the gin fan tied around him with barbed wire – all for allegedly flirting with a white woman a few days earlier.

The two perpetrators were arrested but were acquitted by an all-white jury, bringing the brutality of the Jim Crow segregation laws back to light and generating outrage in the country. Rosa Parks learned of their acquittal at a meeting in a Baptist church in Montgomery, Alabama, and a few days later, she refused on principle to give up her seat in the white section of a bus after it had begun filling up. Parks was a respected member of the NAACP, and when she was arrested and briefly jailed, Black community leaders came together to choose how to respond. They decided that the moment had come to continue the battle against segregation and opted to stage a boycott of the Montgomery bus system.

They looked around for a public spokesman for the cause and settled on the pastor of a local Baptist church who had recently moved to the area from Boston, Massachusetts: Dr. Martin Luther King, Jr. (MLK). King was only 26 at the time and reluctant to lead a movement, but he was known for his public speaking skills and was encouraged by the local Black ministers and community leaders who believed his relative newness to the area would make it easier for him to speak out.

Their biggest concern was that the boycott would not endure. King preached at church meetings to keep people motivated; leaders arranged carpools, and taxi drivers charged only 10 cents (the same as a bus fare) for African American riders. King himself faced death threats and his home was bombed, but he conducted himself with extraordinary decorum, declaring, "Our actions must be guided by the deepest principles of our Christian faith. Love must be our regulating ideal." The media broadcast of the boycott brought King to national attention, and the boycott only ended when the US District Court issued its ruling in *Gayle v Browder*. This outlawed racial segregation on all Montgomery public buses.

Civil rights groups mounted campaigns in places where they knew conflict would arise, aware that the media coverage could be leveraged to serve their cause. A sit-in tactic – of just sitting and waiting – was employed by four Black college students when they were refused service at a whites-only lunch counter in Greensboro, North Carolina in 1960. This was repeated in places across the country. When one group was arrested, another group would take its place, and by the end of the year, over 1,500 Black demonstrators had been arrested.

During the spring of 1961, student activists from CORE picked up the "Freedom Rides" baton, this time taking bus trips through the South to protest segregated bus terminals. Organizers would call journalists ahead of time so they could record any hostile response they encountered – which they often did – from police officers and white protestors.

King's followers all practiced nonaggression, which required incredible self-discipline in the face of violent confrontation. Such a strategy had been successfully employed by Mahatma Gandhi in India after Gandhi believed he could use British conscience regarding colonial possessions against them. King felt he could use American conscience about segregation in the same way, and by using quotes from the Bible and practicing nonviolence, King and his followers retained the moral high ground. They began making inroads, and some politicians, such as Mayor William Hartsfield of Atlanta, declared his city "too busy to hate," urging whites and Blacks to come together peacefully.

John F Kennedy (JFK) had won the 1960 presidential election (by one of the tightest margins in American history) but was reluctant to act. The so-called Solid South had been key to his victory, and although he privately supported the civil rights movement (he had helped secure the release of MLK from jail after he was arrested in Atlanta in 1960), JFK was wary of alienating the South. King actually had a higher opinion of Richard Nixon than of Kennedy.

Firemen turn hoses on demonstrators in
Birmingham, Alabama, in 1963

King brought the movement to Birmingham, Alabama in 1963. He described Birmingham as "the most segregated city in America" and knew that Commissioner of Public Safety Eugene "Bull" Connor would react to a demonstration. Connor, an ardent racist and segregationist, had King arrested and placed in solitary confinement on Good Friday in 1963, and a few weeks later, during a protest, Connor ordered the Birmingham police force to unleash dogs, use clubs, spray tear gas, and unload fire hoses to disperse demonstrators. Hundreds were arrested, and images on television and in the newspapers sparked yet more public fury. King wrote "Letter from a Birmingham Jail" while incarcerated, in which he quoted Jesus, Thomas Aquinas, Socrates, and St. Augustine and described how the denial of justice to one person threatens justice for all, and that people have a moral obligation to disobey unjust laws.

In the summer of 1963, King made his "I Have a Dream" speech in Washington, DC in front of over 250,000 people. He incorporated references to the Founding Fathers and the Bible and employed universal themes of freedom and equality to depict the struggles of Black people in America in one of the most famous speeches in the country's history. Repeating the mantra "I have a dream," he offered up hope that his "four little children will one day live in a nation where they will not be judged by the color of their skin but by the content of their character" and that one day they would be able to sing the words, "Free at last! Free at last! Thank God Almighty, we are free at last!"

The next month, a bomb planted by a member of the Ku Klux Klan killed four Black girls aged between 11 and 14 in a church in Birmingham, Alabama. This galvanized the Kennedy administration into action, and Robert Kennedy, the attorney general and John F Kennedy's brother, worked hard to build bipartisan support for a civil rights bill. Abroad, the US was being derided by the Soviet Union for citizens' supposed "freedoms," and as Africa became decolonized, the United States grew concerned that client states might be hard to come by.

The Civil Rights Act was signed into law in 1965, surviving strong opposition from southern congressmen, and legally sanctioned segregation disappeared quickly. The act prevented employment discrimination and outlawed segregation in hotels, motels, restaurants, and other public places. The Voting Rights Act of 1965 followed, preventing literacy tests from being a voting requirement, and the "Freedom

Summer" of 1964 witnessed Black and white students registering Black voters in Mississippi.

But income disparities and de facto segregation remained,
and Black people's frustrations began to boil over. Race riots
in 150 cities broke out across the country between 1964 and
1968, including a five-day riot in the Watts section of Los
Angeles in 1965, which saw 34 people die and thousands
injured. A 1966 riot in Detroit led to 43 deaths. White people
moved out of areas where racially integrated schools were
being established, and successful Black people now had the
opportunity to move out as well, which had the unfortunate
effect of leaving the poorest Black people in communities
with fewer strong role models.

Martin Luther King at the Lorraine Motel in Memphis
on the day he was shot in 1968.

Martin Luther King himself was assassinated in 1968 in
Memphis, Tennessee at the age of 39. He was struck by a
single bullet on the lower right side of his face as he was
standing on the balcony of the Lorraine Hotel. It had been
fired by James Earl Ray, a racist and small-time criminal, and

in the biggest investigation of its time, Ray was eventually captured at London's Heathrow Airport after an intensive two-month search. The assassination led to major outbreaks of racial violence in over 100 American cities, causing 40 deaths and extensive property damage. Many Black people saw King's assassination as a breach of the nonviolent resistance policy he had championed, and the Black Power movement and the Black Panther Party gained prominence in the late 1960s and early 1970s, engaging in numerous violent encounters with the police.

President Lyndon B Johnson created a set of policies and practices in 1965 that aimed to promote diversity and reduce discrimination in areas such as education and employment. Known as affirmative action programs, they were intended to encourage opportunities for Black people, but his initiatives were met with pushback in the white community.

White students challenged the constitutionality of affirmative action in the cases of *Regents of the University of California v Bakke* (1978) and *Grutter v Bollinger* (2003), but the Court held that race could be used as one factor of many in the college admissions process. However, it overruled those decisions in 2023 when it agreed that Asian American students were being discriminated against in favor of white applicants (*Students for Fair Admissions (SFFA) v Harvard*), and held that affirmative action in college admissions violated the Equal Protection Clause of the 14th Amendment. One of the dissenting judges, Justice Sonia Sotomayor, argued that the US remains a segregated society and "is not, and has never been colorblind," and the question of how to heal the wounds of the past persists.

The African American population remained less affluent than many groups in the United States, including first-generation immigrants from Europe and Asia. It continues to be one of the United States' most intractable problems and occasionally prompts other countries to reflect on their own struggles with integration. In 2020, cities in England, France, Australia, and Mexico all held demonstrations against racism and inequality by leveraging the Black Lives Matter movement.

Malcolm X

An alternative approach to civil rights inequality was offered by Elijah Muhammed and his most powerful spokesman, Malcolm X. Malcolm X was born Malcolm Little in Omaha, Nebraska to a Baptist preacher who was murdered by a white supremacist group when Malcolm was six years old. After his mother had a nervous breakdown, Malcolm was sent to live in various foster homes and reform schools. Then, at 22, he was arrested for burglary and sent to jail.

There he encountered the Nation of Islam (NOI), a socio-re-ligious group that urged fellow Black Americans to protect themselves against white aggression "by any means necessary." The NOI believed in a sort of inverse white supremacy – that the first humans were Black (the Tribe of Shabazz) and that a Black scientist called Yakub had created the white race 6,600 years ago through a form of selective breeding. This white race was inherently violent, and it overthrew the Tribe of Shabazz and achieved global domination.

NOI members could not eat pork, smoke tobacco, drink alcohol, or take illicit drugs and were urged to assert themselves economically by developing Black-owned businesses. They were encouraged to drop their "slave" names, which Malcolm did by replacing "Little" with "X," and when he was released from jail in 1952, he went on an intensive recruiting campaign, growing NOI membership from 400 in 1952 to 40,000 by 1960.

A brilliant speaker, Malcolm became the organization's most influential voice for over ten years. He called Martin Luther King a "chump" and criticized him for his emphasis on nonviolence and racial integration, advocating instead for the complete separation of African Americans from whites (whom he called "devils") and proposing that African Americans either return to Africa or live in a separate country in America.

His friends and followers included Cassius Clay (renamed Muhammad Ali by Elijah Muhammad), Gordon Parks (director of the film *Shaft*), and writer James Baldwin. But Malcolm X became disillusioned with the NOI after Elijah Muhammad's character was called into question. Elijah Muhammad had been found to have violated many of his own teachings by having numerous affairs and many illegitimate children, and Malcolm X split from the NOI in 1964. He embarked on a tour of North Africa and the Middle East and made a pilgrimage to Mecca in Saudi Arabia. He changed his name to El-Hajj Malik El-Shabazz and converted to traditional Sunni Islam.

He returned to the US with a softer, more optimistic attitude. "The true brotherhood I had seen [in Mecca] had influenced me to recognize that anger can blind human vision," he said. "America is the first country... that can actually have a bloodless revolution." But his conflict with the NOI intensified, and he received several death threats before his assassination at the age of 39. He was shot six times in the chest as he took to the stage in New York by three NOI members in February 1965.

After his death, commentators largely ignored his more recent message of collaboration and criticized how he had promoted violence and aggression while part of the NOI. But after his memoir was released posthumously, a more sympathetic view of him took shape. In *The Autobiography of Malcolm X*, he described the events that influenced his life, his struggles with self-discovery and identity, and his singular determination to make a difference. "Power in defense of freedom is greater than power on behalf of tyranny and oppression," he wrote. "Because power, real power, comes from our conviction which produces action, uncompromising action." The memoir remains a modern classic.

JFK

John F Kennedy's personal attributes and political connections made him an attractive candidate for the presidency. His father, Joseph, was a successful politician and businessman and was very ambitious for himself and his sons. Descended from Irish immigrants, Joseph Kennedy had grown up in Boston, Massachusetts, and had made his money through investing in the stock market, reorganizing several Hollywood studios, and owning distribution rights for Scotch Whisky (some of which was sold illegitimately during Prohibition). He was appointed as ambassador to Britain by FDR just before the war broke out in 1938, from where he fought bitterly with the president to keep the US out of the conflict, believing that Britain would eventually be defeated.

Joseph had nine children (four sons), and he placed his focus initially on the success of his eldest son, Joe Kennedy, Jr. But Joe was killed in a plane crash in the war at age 29, so he shifted his focus to his second son, John, and with his father's keen understanding of image and public profile, John made rapid political progress.

JFK on the right, with (from left) Robert and Ted.

JFK was educated at Harvard and joined the Navy in 1941. During the war, his motor torpedo boat PT 109 was rammed and sunk by a Japanese vessel at the Battle of the Solomon Islands, throwing him and his men into the water. He helped some onto a raft and kept them all safe by leading them to a nearby island, swimming for 3 miles while towing an injured crew member behind him by holding the man's life jacket strap in his teeth.[96]

John subsequently earned the Navy and Marine Corps Medal for heroism, and he leveraged the incident and his hero status to obtain a Massachusetts Congressional seat.

96 A film, *PT 109*, was made in 1963 about the incident with Cliff Robertson starring as Kennedy.

He became the junior senator for Massachusetts after three terms in Congress and married Jacqueline Bouvier, the daughter of a prominent New York family, in 1953. She, like Eleanor Roosevelt before her, had to tolerate her husband's philandering nature, and the press, just as they had done for FDR, turned a blind eye, although JFK was well known to have a propensity for prostitutes and risqué sexual encounters. He also suffered from physical illnesses including Addison's disease and recurring back problems which – again like FDR – he managed to conceal from the public.

In 1956, Kennedy wrote *Profiles in Courage*, a volume of short biographies describing specific acts of courage and integrity by eight US senators. It won the Pulitzer Prize, although the journalist Drew Pearson drily noted that the book had been ghostwritten and that Kennedy was known in the Senate for having "more profile than courage." This infuriated Joseph Kennedy to such an extent that he threatened to sue the network for 50 million dollars.

Kennedy was nominated as the Democrat candidate and had to overcome people's fears of his Catholicism. He addressed it by emphasizing the importance of the separation of church and state and by saying that he would not take any direction from the Vatican or any other religious authority while making decisions as president. He was also helped indirectly by the Catholic Church itself when Pope John Paul's Second Vatican Council of 1962 stressed harmonious relations between other religions, describing Protestants as "separated children" rather than heretics.

JFK defeated Richard Nixon in 1960 in one of the closest presidential campaigns in history. He faced off against Nixon in a series of four televised debates, which were the first of their kind, drawing an audience of up to 70 million people.

Kennedy's more photogenic style helped attract voters who could compare him with Nixon, who wore no makeup and whose facial stubble showed on the black-and-white TV screens. Those who had watched the debates felt Kennedy had won, although, conversely, those who had listened to the debates on the radio felt Nixon had won.

On the day of the election, Nixon won 26 states to Kennedy's 22. But Kennedy won in the Electoral College (303 to 219) and the popular vote (by a mere 112,000 votes). The slender margin of loss prompted Nixon's advisors to encourage him to challenge the count, and there were also claims that the mayor of Chicago had arranged with Kennedy's father to ensure Illinois went to the Democrats. But Nixon felt that any challenge would be too destabilizing and alarming for the American people and reluctantly accepted the result.

One of Kennedy's first challenges came in relation to the Cold War. A gap between the number of missiles held by the US compared with those held by the Soviet Union had been growing, and Kennedy felt the US was becoming vulnerable. He supported the anti-communists in South Vietnam and the government of Fulgencio Batista in Cuba, who was forced to flee to the Dominican Republic when the rebel forces of Fidel Castro and Che Guevara attacked Havana. Castro implemented a communist regime, and thousands of Cuban exiles escaped to Florida, leaving the US to consider how they could remove Castro from power.

They decided to support a Cuban counter-invasion and sent over 1,400 paramilitaries to land on the beach in the Bay of Pigs on the south coast. From there, they were to drive into Cuba, draw support from Cuban civilians, and oust the communists from government. But Castro was ready and sent 20,000 troops to the beach to fight back, leading

Kennedy to hesitate and withhold air support, and after three days of fighting, the invaders were forced to surrender. Kennedy took full responsibility for what was a total embarrassment for the United States.

Keenly aware of public relations, the administration looked around for an opportunity to restore some of Kennedy's authority. It did not take long. Nikita Khrushchev, the Premier of the Soviet Union, wanted to establish a missile base on the island of Cuba now that it was a Soviet satellite state, and Kennedy instituted a naval blockade around the island in response. He informed Khrushchev that the US would use military force if it was breached.

The world held its breath as Soviet ships drew closer and closer. No one could be sure how Khrushchev would respond, and nuclear war had never seemed closer – but then, suddenly, the ships withdrew.[97] Khrushchev agreed to dismantle the missile sites from Cuba in return for America's promise not to invade it, and in a separate deal that remained secret for more than 25 years, the US reciprocated by withdrawing its missiles from Turkey.

Calmer relations prevailed thereafter. A direct "hotline" communication link was installed between Washington and Moscow to help defuse any similar situations, and the two countries signed the Atmospheric Test Ban Treaty in 1963. This prohibited testing nuclear weapons in the atmosphere, outer space, and underwater. However, the situation in Vietnam had been gradually escalating, and by the beginning of 1963, the number of military advisors to assist South Vietnam had reached 16,000, joining the 700 that Eisenhower had already authorized. Meanwhile, in Berlin,

---

97 The 2000 film *Thirteen Days* starring Kevin Costner dramatizes the Cuban Missile crisis.

East German troops had begun to erect a wall dividing the city.

Domestically, Kennedy was hampered by his narrow margin of victory and by the strength of the white Southern Democrats to enact much legislation although, at his brother's urging, he became progressively more supportive towards the civil rights movement. After James Meredith, a Black student, was finally admitted to the University of Mississippi (Ole Miss) after he had been rejected twice in 1962, Bobby Kennedy ordered US Marshals to accompany Meredith during his arrival and registration. White protestors rioted, two people died, and dozens were injured, but Meredith registered for class, and a big step towards ending segregation at Ole Miss had been taken.

Kennedy had been president for less than three years when he was assassinated on November 22, 1963. Lee Harvey Oswald, a troubled ex-Marine with pro-Soviet views (he even traveled to the Soviet Union and attempted to become a citizen), fired three shots from the sixth floor of the Texas School Book Depository as the Kennedy motorcade traveled through Dealey Plaza in Dallas. He was struck twice – in the neck and the head – and was pronounced dead shortly after arriving at a nearby hospital.

Unanswered questions remain about the assassination, including whether Oswald was alone in the depository and whether another assassin was shooting on the grassy knoll on the ground. Oswald claimed he was set up, but he was himself murdered two days later by a local nightclub owner, Jack Ruby, captured in a stunning moment on live television in the basement of the Dallas Police headquarters. Ruby's motives are also subject to speculation (he died of a pulmonary embolism in prison), and the Warren Commission was created to investigate all aspects of Kennedy's assassination. It concluded that Oswald had acted alone, but some of its files and records have never been released to the public, and conspiracy theories continue to proliferate.

Kennedy was the second youngest president ever at 43 (Theodore Roosevelt was 42). Combined with his good looks, intelligence, and idealism, his administration was romanticized as the court of "Camelot," and he drove a revolution in US politics that saw style becoming an essential complement to substance. His actual achievements in the White House fell short of his successor's, but his period in charge reflected much of the nation's new sense of confidence about their place in the world and remains a period that is much written about and discussed.

Lyndon B Johnson

Lyndon Johnson being sworn into office on Air Force One, November 22, 1963.

Lyndon Baines Johnson (LBJ) insisted on being sworn in as president on the day Kennedy was killed, and a dramatic photograph shows him aboard Air Force One with his right hand in the air as Jackie Kennedy stands next to him in visible shock with blood on her clothes.

Johnson was a Texan of humble stock. His grandfather, Sam Ealy Johnson, Sr., had been a member of the Populist Party in the 1890s, and Johnson himself had had over 25 years of experience in Washington by the time JFK started on his rise to the presidency, successfully running on a New Deal platform for Congressional representation in 1937. He won a Silver Star for his naval service in the Second World War and was elected to the Senate in 1948, although he was accused of winning fraudulently. It initially seemed that he had lost, but a ballot box mysteriously appeared containing enough votes to push him over the line.

He was beaten out of the Democrat nomination by Kennedy, who then offered him the running mate position. Kennedy believed Johnson would help him attract southern votes where Kennedy was weak, but the two men never became close, and Johnson often felt sidelined by the snobby Harvard-educated Kennedy administration. Yet he worked extraordinarily hard and ultimately achieved far more than Kennedy once in office. First, he signed the Civil Rights Act and the Voting Rights Act into law, and then he signed the Immigration and Nationality Act (1965). This abolished the national origins formula of the 1920s that had de facto discriminated against any race that was not from Northern or Western Europe.

Johnson won the 1964 election by a huge landslide, defeating the Republican Party candidate, Barry Goldwater. Goldwater, a senator from Arizona, had an abrasive and divisive style which had put many people off, although his distaste for the mainstream media, his hawkish foreign policy, and his determination to shrink the size of the government all became popular in the years to come.

Johnson now had a mandate to push through his "great society, a place where the meaning of man's life matches the marvels of man's labor," and he passed many initiatives to fund education, provide healthcare, beautify and develop urban areas, and fight crime and delinquency. He was greatly influenced by Michael Harrington's book *The Other America* (1962), which identified around 20 percent of Americans living in poverty, and he declared a "War on Poverty" in his first State of the Union address. This included programs such as Headstart, Volunteers in Service to America, and TRiO which were designed to help provide educational and employment opportunities for impoverished people. He also pushed through Medicare, which covered hospital and physician costs for the elderly who qualified, and Medicaid, which covered costs for people getting financial assistance from the government.

But poverty was to prove impossible to fully extinguish. Oscar Lewis's social theory of the "culture of poverty" suggested that people in poverty tended to focus on the present, felt hopeless, and spent money as soon as they received it, as opposed to people out of poverty who focused on the future, invested in themselves, and delayed gratification. This was one of the reasons why the War on Poverty failed in its objectives, and today 11.6 percent (37.9 million) of Americans are classified as poor – a reduction from 19 percent in 1964, but nonetheless stubbornly high.

Johnson's agenda was, however, overshadowed by inner-city race riots and the Vietnam War. He was forced to divert funds from the War on Poverty to the war in Vietnam, and Johnson is better remembered as the commander in chief of an unwinnable war in Southeast Asia rather than a champion of the underprivileged and at-risk. Additionally, just as FDR's New Deal had polarized opinions about the reach of the federal government, LBJ's Great Society only polarized them further, pushing US politics onto an increasingly divided path.

The Vietnam War

The Vietnam War lasted almost 20 years and saw more than 3 million people killed, including 58,000 Americans. It had its origins in colonialism but became a war between North and South Vietnam, with the South obtaining most of its support from the United States, which fought to keep communism contained in the North.

French Indochina consisted of a group of French colonies in Southeast Asia they had managed since 1884. Japan had taken control in the Second World War, but after their defeat, Vietnam, Cambodia, and Laos announced their independence in 1945. France, determined to have its possessions back, sent in troops to put down Ho Chi Minh's provisional government of Vietnam, and Ho Chi Minh reacted by initially looking to obtain American support for independence. But the US had agreed to help France at the Potsdam Conference in return for France's cooperation to help rebuild Europe, and although the US held reservations about supporting French recolonization, they justified them by repeating how important it was to contain communism. They were, however, seriously conflicted, and Secretary of State Dean Acheson commented that France's demand was nothing short of "blackmail."

Most people in the United States had no idea where Vietnam was, but fear of communism ran high. The US provided financial aid and equipment to France, although this support could not prevent the French from being decisively defeated by the Viet Minh at the Battle of Dien Bien Phu in 1954. This led to the Geneva Agreements in which France agreed to withdraw all its forces, and a decision to divide Vietnam into North and South sections at the 17th parallel. Elections were planned to be held within two years to reunite the country and choose a president.

An anti-communist South Vietnamese government under Ngo Dinh Diem was established, with its capital in Saigon. The Americans began supporting it with training, military equipment, and CIA intelligence operatives. But Diem himself was corrupt, dictatorial, and deeply unpopular with many in the South, and Viet Minh sympathizers, called Viet Cong (or Viet Communists), emerged within South Vietnam to resist Diem's regime. The promised elections never occurred (which would have resulted in unification under Ho Chi Minh), and Diem tortured and executed thousands of Viet Cong. Further, as a Catholic, he actively repressed Buddhists in a country that was 80 percent Buddhist. The Viet Cong responded by merging with other opponents of Diem's regime to form the National Liberation Front (NLF) in 1960.

In the early days of the war, it was possible to be idealistic about American intervention. Under the Geneva Agreement, Vietnamese citizens could move freely between North and South Vietnam, and Tom Dooley, the US Navy doctor, helped evacuate thousands of Northern Vietnamese on his ship, the USS *Montague*. He wrote a book called *Deliver Us From Evil* that described horrors committed by the Viet Minh that he had witnessed or heard of. These included how thousands of women had been disemboweled, how a Catholic priest had had nails driven into his head in a Viet Minh version of a "Crown of Thorns," and how children had had their ears pierced with chopsticks to prevent them from hearing the Lord's Prayer. Many of his stories have since been discredited, but Dooley became well known for his humanitarian and aid efforts before dying of cancer in 1961.

The Kennedy administration increased American presence in South Vietnam and was challenged with how to stem Diem's unpopularity. Diem's sister-in-law, Madam Nhu, was held in particular contempt as she established the secret police and pushed for "morality laws" based on strict Catholic doctrine. After a Buddhist monk, Thich Quang Duc, burned himself to death at a busy Saigon Road intersection as a protest against Diem's policies, Madame Nhu publicly ridiculed him.

Thich Quang Duc self-immolating in protest against the persecution of the Buddhist monks by the South Vietnamese government in 1963.

Shortly afterwards, US military advisors uncovered a plot to oust Diem, and after Kennedy consulted his ambassador, he agreed to let it go ahead. Diem was captured and killed by a group of soldiers in November 1963, and then, three weeks later, Kennedy himself was killed, leaving the Vietnamese conundrum at its most perilous to date. US advisors hoped Diem's assassination would lead to a more stable government, but it only led to more turbulence as Diem was replaced with a succession of corrupt and unpopular military dictators.

Johnson wanted to prove that he was as anti-communist as his predecessors and his 1964 presidential opponent, Barry Goldwater. He obtained a resolution from Congress that gave him broad powers to "repel any armed attack," and "prevent further aggression," after North Vietnam allegedly attacked two US destroyers, the USS *Maddox* and the USS *Turner Joy* in the Gulf of Tonkin. It later turned out that the attack on the *Turner Joy* had never occurred, and that the attack on the *Maddox* had been after she had ventured into North Vietnamese waters. But it mattered not at the time, as it gave Johnson the authority he needed to increase American presence to bring an end to the conflict.

Privately, Johnson described Vietnam as a "raggedy-ass little fourth-rate country," but he was eager to project power, and US planes began making regular bombing raids the following year. US military presence increased from 16,000 troops at the time of JFK's death to 500,000 by 1968 and, with their experience of fighting in the jungles in the Second World War and their far superior technology and equipment, expectations of success were high. But problems soon became apparent. For one, the military objective was not entirely clear. China had intervened in Korea after MacArthur had pushed too far north, and the US anticipated a similar response if they were to venture too deep into North Vietnam. So they held back and hoped that North Vietnamese morale would simply break down. But this did not happen, and in the end, it was US morale that collapsed instead.

US troops also found retaining possession of villages in the countryside very difficult. When present, they could ensure the cooperation of the villagers, but as soon as they withdrew, the Viet Cong would reappear and take over – putting the villagers themselves in a very vulnerable position. The terrain restricted the use of tanks, and the enemy's guerilla-style warfare, which consisted of nighttime raids, ambushes, and sabotage, was difficult to foresee. Helicopters gave Americans a short-term advantage, but the dense jungles made it tough to secure landing zones, and troops were often inserted and extracted in unpredictable conditions. Finally, winning the hearts and minds of the Vietnamese people – on which, Johnson indicated, victory depended – proved hard to do in practice.

Many journalists accompanied soldiers into combat zones. Michael Herr worked as a war correspondent for *Esquire* magazine from 1967 to 1969, and when he returned to America, intended to write a book about his experiences. But he suffered a nervous breakdown and spent the next five years recovering before he could undertake it. His book, *Dispatches*, was written in the style of New Journalism,[98] bringing a highly personal, subjective perspective on the brutality of the war and the disillusionment felt by the soldiers. He also co-wrote the screenplay for the film *Full*

---

98 New Journalism emerged in the 1960s and 1970s. It is characterized by an immersive and subjective approach to storytelling and was spearheaded by notable journalists such as Tom Wolfe, Truman Capote, and Hunter S Thompson.

Metal Jacket and part of the voiceover delivered by Martin Sheen in *Apocalypse Now*.

A tour of duty for most ground forces lasted one year. This was a way for the US to attempt to keep morale up and prevent battle fatigue, but many could not cope with the uncertainty and pervasive fear of enemy attacks, and it led certain troops to commit atrocities, the worst of which was the My Lai massacre in 1968.

Army commanders had advised the soldiers of Charlie Company that all in the Son My area could be considered Viet Cong or Viet Cong sympathizers and ordered them to destroy the village. But when they arrived, the soldiers – led by Lt. William Calley – found only a quiet village of women, children, and older men preparing their breakfast rice. They were rounded up anyway, and the soldiers were then ordered to shoot them. Some soldiers balked at the command, but suddenly shots rang out, and the massacre began, with Calley himself taking part. Not a single shot was fired back, and the carnage only ended when a US Army helicopter pilot noticed that something was wrong and landed between the retreating villagers and the soldiers. A total of 504 people died – 182 women (17 pregnant) and 173 children including 56 infants – and many young girls and women were raped and mutilated before being killed. The massacre was initially covered up, but when it came out, the public was outraged, and Calley was given a life sentence for his crimes (eventually reduced to ten years). All other participants were acquitted.

As morale declined, another issue was "fragging:" the act of blowing up a "fragmentation grenade" in a superior officer's tent, which would kill him and leave no evidence. Sometimes targets would be given a warning in the form of a grenade with their name painted on it, but other times not, and up to

1,000 fragging incidents are estimated to have taken place in Vietnam, causing 86 deaths.

Drug use and addiction also became major problems. Vietnam and the surrounding countries were hotspots for drug growth and manufacturing, and soldiers took marijuana, heroin, amphetamines, LSD, and prescription pills, among others. A random sample of men returning to the US in 1971 indicated that 20 percent of them were addicted to heroin or opium (opioids) and that almost half of them had tried opioids while there.

Domestic opposition to the war grew after 1966, and many people resisted the draft or demonstrated against the war in the streets. The draft could be avoided by attending college – making higher education suddenly much more appealing – but many could not afford to go to college, leaving the working class and the poor to make up the bulk of those who were drafted. For the first time, it became socially acceptable to oppose the war, which contrasted starkly with the Second World War generation before it. One anti-conscription poster featured the folk singer, Joan Baez, and her sisters, reading "Girls Say Yes to Boys Who Say No," and Martin Luther King, Norman Mailer, and Dr. Spock all spoke out against the war. Other antiwar intellectuals, such as Susan Sontag, actually visited Hanoi to see it for themselves.

The US Army became increasingly frustrated that it was not being given a chance at winning the war. In 1967, General Westmoreland, the senior military commander in Vietnam, returned to Washington and said that he could see "the light at the end of the tunnel." But the following year, the North Vietnamese attempted to foment rebellion among the South Vietnamese and conducted the Tet Offensive – a series of attacks on more than 100 cities and outposts in South Vietnam. It included a raid on the US Embassy in Saigon, and although the offensive ultimately failed, the public was shocked, and shortly afterwards, a beleaguered Johnson declared he would not be running for president again, in a move that was a distinct propaganda victory for North Vietnam.

The election campaign was dominated by the Vietnam issue and created a major split in the Democrat Party. Hubert Humphrey, Johnson's vice president, advocated continuing the war and found himself opposed by Senator Eugene McCarthy, who supported withdrawal and, later in the campaign, Bobby Kennedy. Kennedy appeared to be generating some momentum among voters as he won the California and South Dakota primaries. But he was assassinated in the Ambassador Hotel in Los Angeles by a 24-year-old Palestinian man named Sirhan Sirhan, who held a grudge against Kennedy for sending bombers to Israel.[99] It was a year that also saw the assassination of Martin Luther King, and morale among Americans hit a new low in 1968.

Tens of thousands of protestors rallied against the war at the Democratic convention in Chicago in August of that year. Hubert Humphrey received the party's nomination, but the event was overshadowed by violence outside as police used tear gas and beat protestors with clubs to dispel them from Lincoln Park. Richard Nixon, who had lost to Kennedy in 1960, won the Republican nomination and campaigned on behalf of what he called "the silent majority" as he promised to work towards "peace with honor" in Vietnam. He took advantage of the Democrat split and won the 1968 presidential election.

---

99 You can find more on the assassination of Bobby Kennedy at https://historyinaheartbeat.com/the-assassination-of-robert-f-kennedy/

Peace talks began in Paris that year but stalled almost immediately as the US refused the North's demands to remove the South Vietnamese President Nguyen Van Thieu. Nixon responded by authorizing troops to invade Cambodia in 1970 and to bomb both Cambodia and Laos which were being used as bases and supply lines (the Ho Chi Minh trail) by the North Vietnamese.

This led to fresh demonstrations during which four Kent State University students were killed when members of the Ohio National Guard opened fire on the protestors. Nixon was initially sympathetic to the incident, but after outrage grew and the number of protests increased, he stubbornly declared that "when dissent turns to violence, it invites tragedy."

Nixon had claimed, during the election, that he had a plan to end the war, but it took him five more years to fully disengage the US from Vietnam. He did reduce the number of men that were sent to fight by replacing the draft with a lottery, and he provided the South Vietnamese army with training and improved weaponry so they could take on more fighting themselves (a program termed "Vietnamization"). But his goals of ensuring the security of South Vietnam, withdrawing US troops, and avoiding the perception of a US military defeat were basically impossible.

In late January 1973, a cease-fire agreement was finally signed, and American disengagement was completed later that year. The 17th parallel remained the dividing line between North and South, all foreign troops withdrew, and American POWs were released by the North (although allegations persisted that not all of them were let go).

Neither the North nor the South abided by the cease-fire agreement. The North Vietnamese launched a major new offensive in 1975 after the Watergate scandal, but the unpopularity of the war prevented further American intervention. Saigon fell that year. The American public watched chaotic scenes of people falling to their deaths from airlifts as they desperately tried to escape, and many others crammed onto fishing boats to get away from the reeducation and hard labor camps that the North Vietnamese were imposing. In Cambodia, the genocide committed by Pol Pot's communist Khmer Rouge Party was on such a level of depravity and horror that, after some of the atrocities came to light, many neoconservatives felt justified in America's participation in the war.

The legacy of Vietnam persists today. It generated new divisions within American society, undermined people's faith in the government, and discouraged an internationalist foreign policy. Millions of dollars were spent, and coupled with the increased spending initiatives of the Great Society, a spiral of inflation took hold in the 1970s (the Great Inflation) that affected everyone in the country. Nowadays, any US military engagement is considered with the lessons of Vietnam in mind – the media is kept at a distance, clear goals are identified in advance, engagements should be kept short, and the US death toll must be low. These lessons were top of mind when the country next went to war in the Gulf War of 1990.

The Growth of the Media

The influence of the media increasingly shaped politics and society in the United States. The civil rights movement and demonstrations against the Vietnam War were covered extensively by newspapers, radio, and television and significantly contributed to how people felt about both events. As the century progressed, traditional media outlets were supplemented by information provided independently over the internet, available on computers, cell phones, and tablets.

Newspapers were the first means of communication to have such an impact, led by Joseph Pulitzer and William Randolph Hearst. They reinvented the content of newspapers by employing "yellow journalism" – a style that used big headlines and sensationalized stories – and drove sales by embarking on campaigns and "crusades."

Hearst himself had been expelled from Harvard for general misbehavior and was given the *San Francisco Examiner* by his father who had obtained it as part payment of a poker debt. The younger Hearst had been inspired by Pulitzer's *New York World* and believed he could replicate its success; within three years Hearst saw his newspaper turning a profit and circulation jumping from 5,000 to 55,000. Eventually, his media empire grew to include over 40 publications, and Orson Welles directly based his character of Citizen Kane on him (which Hearst hated, even attempting to shut down production on the film).

Newspapers started to play a bigger role in society at the turn of the 19th century. Hearst and Pulitzer sought to outdo each other in whipping up outrage against Spanish rule in Cuba, both calling for war after the USS *Maine* mysteriously blew up and sank in Havana in 1898. The *New York Journal* ran a headline of "War? Sure?" and the Spanish–American War came to be referred to as the first "media war."

Muckraking journalism – exposés of societal ills and corruption – became a way of driving political and corporation policies. Ida Tarbell exposed the corrupt practices of Standard Oil when she wrote a 19-part series that was published in *McClure's Magazine*, and Ray Stannard Baker's

The Right to Work reported on coal miners and conditions in the mines. Critics claimed that muckrakers were exaggerating and sensationalizing issues, but their work drove the passage of antitrust and food safety legislation which had beneficial effects for everyone.

The development of the radio in the early part of the 20th century extended communication. Ownership of radios soared from zero in 1910 to 12 million by 1930 (the 1930 census was the first to collect data on radio ownership), and individuals began attaining celebrity status. Aimee Semple McPherson was one of the first evangelists to use radio, becoming a household name in the 1920s and 1930s, although her credibility was damaged when her kidnapping was exposed as a stunt, and she was accused of having several extramarital affairs. Politicians jumped on the bandwagon, and before FDR's "fireside chats," Warren G Harding was the first president to broadcast over the radio, at a time when most Americans had never heard the voice of any president.

American radio costs were financed through advertising, which was different to the approach of Britain whose British Broadcasting Corporation charged listeners a license fee.[100] The Federal Radio Commission was set up in 1927 (succeeded by the Federal Communications Commission, FCC) to ensure its programs were "in the public interest, convenience, or necessity," and the types of programs grew more varied; Orson Welles recorded a version of *War of the Worlds* that created a national panic in 1938 when his fictional retelling of an alien invasion was believed by many listeners.

Television intensified radio's effects. It was introduced with a great deal of pomp at the World's Fair in New York City in 1939 by David Sarnoff, an executive at Radio Corporation

---

100   The BBC's first Director General, Lord Reith, believed the radio should be a way of educating the masses, and the early BBC programs reflected that ideology.

of America (RCA), who broadcast the fair's opening ceremonies, including a speech by FDR. Ownership of televisions grew from 7,000 households in 1946 to 50 million by 1960. Spectacles such as *Twenty-One*, a game show in which contestants would stay on if they answered questions correctly, garnered huge audiences, although it was not long before executives realized that more photogenic performers provided better ratings. In this case, executives resorted to rigging the results by giving the questions and answers to the contestants they wanted to win. But they were eventually exposed, and legislation was passed to stop the practice (Robert Redford's *Quiz Show* dramatizes the events in his 1994 film).

Americans were suddenly able to watch politics and justice in action. Senator Estes Kefauver became famous for his televised hearings on organized crime (the "Kefauver Hearings"), viewed by as many as 30 million people in 1951, and Senator Joseph McCarthy was discredited after his performance on television in the Army-McCarthy hearings of 1954.

The televised Kennedy-Nixon debates favored Kennedy, although Nixon had been confident heading into the debates after his televised "Checkers speech" in 1952. On that occasion, after accusations that Nixon had spent political contributions on his personal expenses, Eisenhower asked him to explain himself to the voters, so Nixon went on the air. He duly denied the accusations and then exhibited his political prowess by admitting that he had, in fact, accepted one gift: a black-and-white cocker spaniel named Checkers. The voters loved it. They even sent letters to the Republican Party to demand he stay on the ticket, and Nixon served two terms as Eisenhower's vice president. Later, when Nixon was running for president in 1968, Joe McGinnis highlighted the lengths a public relations team could go to present a presidential candidate attractively in his classic book, *The Selling of the President*. It also showcased some of the marketing skills of Roger Ailes (who founded Fox News in 1996).

Television also enabled viewers to follow events in remote places. The US Army hoped that by giving free rein to the press in Vietnam, people would respond positively to foreign policy. But it had the opposite effect, appalling viewers at the sight of children burned by napalm, dead Vietnamese citizens, and the destruction caused by US bombs. It was the first time the press had shown the bodies of dead soldiers (they had not done so in the Second World War), and when the public was presented with atrocities committed by US troops at My Lai, riots broke out in cities and on university campuses.

In 1969, the first human landing on the moon was so inconceivable to many that they simply refused to believe it was real, and conspiracy theories began to circulate that the whole thing had been filmed in a studio in Hollywood as a propaganda tool in the Cold War. In 1986, viewers were left in shock as they watched the *Challenger* space shuttle explode shortly after takeoff on live television, and plans to send civilians into space were shelved for the next 22 years.

The media was strictly controlled in the Gulf War of 1991. After losing the public relations battle during the Vietnam War, journalists were kept well away from the front lines and were required to submit all their reports and footage to military censors for review before they could be published or broadcast. But some news footage got through, and CNN was catapulted into the national consciousness when it was lucky enough to be the only network in Baghdad when the Coalition bombing campaign began. CNN broadcast live from inside a hotel, resulting in its coverage being watched by over 1 billion viewers worldwide.

The start of the 21st century saw people increasingly turn to the internet for news and information. With recording technologies available to almost everyone, a concurrent rise in the amount of video and news footage occurred, and traditional media outlets were forced to adapt quickly or find themselves out of business. Newspaper circulation declined from over 60 million at its peak in 1984 to under 25 million in 2020, and radio and television channels found themselves competing with podcasts, social media, and streaming services.

Consumers began seeking out media sources whose beliefs or perspectives reflected their own. Well-known journalists openly paraded a bias or point of view to attract them, and multiple mainstream news channels reported on the same events in completely different ways. During the Black Lives Matter demonstrations in 2020, it was possible to watch one news channel that portrayed them as a series of peaceful protests and another that presented them as violent riots. The deliberate polarization of the media today proliferates, and does more to divide the nation than bring it together.

Women's Rights

As newspapers reported on the civil rights movement and the Vietnam War, other movements sought to leverage the media for their own ends. Simone de Beauvoir had written *The Second Sex* in 1949 in which she explored the notion of women being perceived as the "other" sex, and in 1963, Betty Friedan wrote *The Feminine Mystique*, which kickstarted a period known as "second wave" feminism in the US. Women came together to fight against gender roles and discrimination, and for reproductive, workplace, and equality rights.

JFK established the Commission on the Status of Women in 1961, appointing Eleanor Roosevelt as its chairwoman, and the commission found widespread discrimination against women in the workplace and in the law. Women were limited in the number of hours they could work and were prevented from obtaining credit cards or serving on a jury. In addition, the commission noted that women were paid less than men and lacked protections against harassment and abuse, and the commission made several recommendations relating to childcare, maternity leave, and equal pay. The Equal Pay Act was signed into law by Kennedy in 1963 and mandated equal pay for equal work.

Betty Friedan (second from left) and NOW women.

But this was not enough, and in 1966, Betty Friedan cofounded the National Organization for Women (NOW) to lobby for women's full participation in society equal to that of men. Her book introduced the "problem that has no name" – the general dissatisfaction women felt about their rote suburban lives and their desire for more beyond it — and Friedan emphasized the importance of women finding a career (rather than a job) as an outlet for their creativity.

More radical groups began to emerge. The New York Radical Women organization (NYRW) led consciousness-raising groups designed to identify how women were being oppressed. They would choose a topic related to women's experience — husbands, child-rearing, economic dependence, and others — and discuss it in depth, the object being that members would gradually gain awareness of how they were being subjugated by a patriarchal society. In 1968, the NYRW protested at the Miss America Beauty Pageant in Atlanta, where members displayed a "Women's Liberation" banner, describing the event as a cattle auction. They barred men from participating, and some discarded their bras and other "items of oppression" into a "Freedom Trash Can," with one woman chaining herself to a puppet of Miss America "to highlight the ways women were enslaved by beauty standards."

The media delighted in reporting these events, and in 1970, on the fiftieth anniversary of the passage of women's right to vote, up to 50,000 women took to the streets in New York in a Women's Strike for Equality. Sponsored by NOW, they lobbied for reproductive rights, equal opportunity in the workplace, and free childcare, and they paraded satirically charged signs such as "Don't iron while the strike is hot" and "Hardhats for soft broads." It gained national attention and inspired a new generation of women fighting for their rights.

Gloria Steinem, a columnist for *New York* magazine, cofounded a magazine in 1971 called *Ms* and led the charge for legalized abortion and federally-funded daycare centers. As a journalist, she had received attention for her exposé of the mistreatment and exploitation of Playboy Bunny waitresses while working undercover as a Playboy waitress herself. Although she was a very articulate spokeswoman, some of the attention she received from the press was due to how attractive she was, upsetting several of her peers.

Other voices developed radical themes of conflict and struggle against men. Sarah Brownmiller's *Against Our Will: Men, Women, and Rape* (1975) argued that men used the act of rape as a primary tool to oppress and retain power, which led some women to ask why they would ever go to bed with a man. Betty Friedan dismissed this argument and referred to it as the "lavender menace," which drew criticism from certain corners, but she believed that incorporating lesbianism into the feminist agenda would undermine the credibility of the women's movement overall.

The women's movement also caught the wave of the sexual revolution of the 1960s. Alfred Kinsey published his Kinsey Reports in 1948 (male) and 1953 (female), revealing high levels of premarital and extramarital sex and a higher number of homosexuals than expected. *Playboy*, a magazine started by Hugh Hefner in 1953, encouraged women to flaunt their sexuality, and Helen Gurley Brown's *Sex and the Single Girl* (1962) promoted the benefits of women gaining financial independence and experiencing sexual relationships before or without marriage.

The first birth control pill was developed in 1960 and came to be used by more than 80 percent of women of child-bearing age by the beginning of the 1970s. When Pope Paul VI announced Humanae Vitae ("Of Human Life") in 1968 and called birth control "intrinsically wrong,"[101] most Catholics

---

101   He argued that sex was a gift from God and that if you used sex for pleasure rather than procreation, you were turning away from God.

simply ignored it, and the taboo on cohabitation and child-bearing outside marriage broke down, becoming common-place by the mid-1970s.

One of the goals of the movement – the right to an abortion – gained federal legal protection in 1973 in the case of *Roe v Wade*. The debate started when Cherry Finkbine, a pregnant mother of four from Phoenix, Arizona took a sedative that her husband had brought back from Britain which, unbeknown to them, contained a chemical that was linked to severe birth defects. After the couple chose to abort the pregnancy, Finkbine called the local newspaper to warn the community about the dangers of the chemical and a public outcry ensued with many people demanding she give birth anyway.

An intense national debate followed, and when Norma McCorvey found that her right to an abortion was illegal in Texas (other than when necessary to save the mother's life), she filed a lawsuit against her local district attorney, Henry Wade. McCorvey was anonymized under the name Jane Roe, and when the issue came before the Supreme Court, it ruled that the "right to privacy" enshrined within the 14th Amendment of the Constitution protected a woman's right to an abortion. The matter appeared to be settled, but the debate never went away, and in June 2022, the Supreme Court overruled *Roe v Wade*, handing abortion rights back to the states – which may be legally accurate but was generally condemned for the withdrawal of rights that had been in place for 50 years.

An antifeminist backlash occurred in the early 1970s with another woman, Phyllis Schlafly, leading a campaign against the Equal Rights Amendment (Stop-ERA). The Amendment explicitly gave equal rights to women and seemed certain to pass, with 35 of the 38 state legislatures voting in its favor. But Schlafly, a college-educated mother of six, argued that certain biological differences between the sexes precluded them from direct equality. For if women were treated the same as men, they may get called up for the draft (like Russian women in the Second World War), have to endure unisex bathrooms, or lose certain government services and benefits. After lobbying hard, the Amendment was never ratified, falling three votes short.

Women continued to fight diligently for equality, bringing about a third wave of feminism in the 1990s that was more inclusive and celebratory of women's individualism. Sparked by the Anita Hill[102] Senate hearings and the "riot grrrl" punk movement, it embraced female empowerment and sought to raise awareness of how different factors – gender, race, class, sexuality, and religion – can combine to create different types of discrimination ("intersectionality"). It merged into a fourth wave of feminism that occurred around 2012, which focused on violence against women, reaching a high-water mark with the "#MeToo" movement in 2017.

After film producer Harvey Weinstein had been exposed for sexual assault and rape, actress Alyssa Milano posted a message on Twitter requesting other women to post "#MeToo" within their status if they had experienced something similar. Many high-profile actresses and celebrities responded, and a series of solidarity marches took place in January 2018 in cities across the US.

It did attract criticism for a "cancel culture" that followed which, at its height, assumed an accused person's guilt, and stifled debate as participants feared the consequences of making counterarguments. But it prompted more states to

---

102   Anita Hill accused the Supreme Court Justice nominee, Clarence Thomas, of sexual harassment.

sign up for the Equal Rights Amendment, and in 2020, the Amendment gained the 38 state legislatures it needed to become law. The deadline for the signatories, however, had long since expired (in 1982), and it remains unratified.

Ever since the second-wave feminist movement of the 1960s, opportunities for women grew significantly. President Reagan appointed the first woman (Sandra Day O'Connor) to the Supreme Court in 1981,[103] Kamala Harris became the first female vice president in 2021, and 41 women currently hold the CEO position in S&P 500 companies. But many women still find themselves earning less than men and being treated with less respect, and the fight for full equality remains ongoing.

Environmentalism

Another movement that began to take shape in the 1960s was environmentalism. Theodore Roosevelt set a precedent for environmental concerns when he established national parks and reserves, and citizens began to notice the gray air above the cities and the chemical and industrial smells that pervaded them.

A sense of urgency developed after Rachel Carson, a biologist and author, wrote *Silent Spring*, published in 1962. The book highlighted how the pesticide DDT did not just kill the targeted lice and mosquitos but also many more insects besides. Furthermore, its decomposition rate was so slow that it would make its way into the food chain by contaminating birds and fish, which humans would then consume, including mothers who would pass on traces of the chemical when breastfeeding a baby. Since it could potentially cause cancer and genetic defects, people immediately took notice,

103 A further five women have followed: Ruth Bader Ginsburg, Sonia Sotomayor, Elena Kagan, Amy Coney Barrett, and Ketanji Brown Jackson.

and the book became a huge bestseller. The chemical companies howled in indignation.

DDT was initially hailed as a miraculous insecticide (its inventor, Paul Hermann Müller, received the Nobel Prize for its discovery in 1948) and was used extremely effectively by the military in the Second World War. American troops had saved Naples, Italy from an epidemic by dusting more than 1 million Italians with DDT, killing the body lice that spread typhus. They also sprayed it aerially or from a backpack in the Pacific to kill insects spreading diseases, and at home it was applied as pest control to preserve vineyards, orchards, potato fields, and cornfields.

Up until *Silent Spring*, chemical companies had earned themselves a decent reputation, but consumer advocacy developed in the 1960s, and the spotlight was turned towards company practices. Ralph Nader's *Unsafe at Any Speed* (1965) criticized General Motors' decision to reject safety features for its Chevrolet Corvair to make the car more visually attractive, to which GM responded by attempting to find dirt on Nader himself. They tapped his phone and hired prostitutes to catch him in compromising situations, but the strategy backfired spectacularly when Nader found out, and the GM president was forced to apologize and pay $425,000 to Nader for invasion of privacy. Nader then used the money to form a team nicknamed Nader's Raiders, who investigated corporations' safety and health practices.

Bill Anders of the Apollo 8 took this iconic "earthrise" photograph in 1968.

Environmental concerns even managed to bring people together at the end of the 1960s. Amidst a period of deep divisions, the first Earth Day was held on April 22, 1970, after NASA astronauts had taken pictures of the Earth that made people hyper-sensitive to its vulnerability. Millions participated in rallies, marches, and educational programs across the country. Students pushed a brand-new gas guzzler (a Ford Maverick) into a ten-foot-deep trench in San Jose, girl scouts picked trash out of the Potomac River, and thousands marched down a closed Fifth Avenue from Union Square Park to Central Park for an "ecological carnival."

Congressional legislation on environmental matters increased after 1970. The Clean Air Acts (1970) sought to reduce emissions and removed lead compounds – which could lead to brain damage in infants – from gasoline. The Clean Water Act (1972) was passed when the Cuyahoga River in Cleveland, which was terribly polluted and covered in oil slicks, caught fire (not for the first time) after a spark from the train tracks had set it alight. It caused about $50,000 in damage to the railroad bridges and generated genuine concern about the dangers of polluted water.

The Environmental Protection Agency was created in 1970 which required companies to provide an environmental impact statement (EIS) that detailed what damage a proposed project might have on the surrounding environment. This was followed by the Endangered Species Act, which sought to protect ecosystems, although it could be used, arguably cynically, by activists to prevent certain projects from going ahead. When the construction of the Tellico Dam in Tennessee was scheduled to begin, activists claimed the dam would harm the habitat of a tiny southeastern fish called a snail darter. The case made it all the way to the Supreme Court, and the dam was only built after the company collected and transplanted all the snail darters to other rivers.

The Oil Shock of 1973 tested the nation's dedication to environmental causes. An oil embargo was imposed by OPEC members against the US for its support of Israel in the Yom Kippur War, pushing the price of oil up from $2.90 a barrel to $11.65 in four months. The US looked inwards and knew that oil existed on the Arctic Sea coast in northern Alaska. But the ice made it impossible for supertankers to reach it, and when construction of a pipeline to transfer the oil across 800 miles of Alaskan land was first proposed in 1969, it was met with pushback from environmentalists.

After the Yom Kippur War, a renewed effort to pass the legislation was made, and the Trans-Alaska Pipeline Authorization Act squeaked through the Senate after a tiebreaking vote was made in favor by Vice President Spiro Agnew. The construction was an astonishing technical triumph, taking three years to build and employing some 70,000 workers. It crossed permafrost, isolated terrain, and the mountain ranges of Brooks and Chugach in Alaska, and was designed to withstand a magnitude 8.0 earthquake and temperatures from -80 to +95 degrees Fahrenheit. The line-fill volume was huge, at over 9 million barrels (there are 42 gallons in a barrel), and Alaska today accounts for 20 percent of the US's oil supply.

Oil production came with risks, however. In 1989, an oil tanker, the *Exxon Valdez*, left Port Valdez on the south coast of Alaska and struck Bligh Reef, a well-known navigational hazard on the Prince William Sound, tearing open the ship's hull and causing 11 million gallons of oil to spill into the water. It later materialized that the captain was drunk and had altered the navigational course to avoid icebergs, handing the steering to an unlicensed, sleep-deprived third mate. Radar was not working, and with the captain sleeping in his bunk, the ship struck the reef just after midnight in the pitch darkness.

The Deepwater Horizon oil spill in the Gulf of Mexico in 2010 was even worse, leaking 19 times more oil (an estimated 210 million gallons) into the waters off the coast of Louisiana. On that occasion, an explosion occurred on an offshore drilling rig when a surge of natural gas blew through the cement that was built to contain it. It traveled up the rig's riser, igniting when it reached the platform, killing 11 workers while seriously injuring another 17. Both oil spills caused the deaths of millions of birds and fish, the subsequent bankruptcy of many fishermen, and the tremendous suffering of the tourism business.

Nuclear power emerged in the 1950s that appeared to provide a superior alternative to coal-fired and hydroelectric power stations. Nuclear energy originates from the splitting of uranium atoms (a heavy metal) in a process called fission. Fission generates heat and enough steam to spin a turbine and create electricity. Unlike coal, no fuel is burned, so no greenhouse gases are emitted, but concerns about nuclear waste, nuclear proliferation, and accidents gave rise to doubts about the industry's viability.

Initially, the government encouraged nuclear power, and power stations grew in number. But before long, problems started to appear. Thermal pollution – the change in the ambient temperature of natural water sources due to cold water being replaced with warm – caused wildlife and fish to die, and disposing of nuclear fuel rods required special care. They remained radioactive for long periods of time and were often submerged in water for several years before being buried in a disposal site.

The public lost a great deal of faith in nuclear power after the Three-Mile Island accident of 1979 that occurred in Harrisburg, Pennsylvania. A pressure valve failed to close, and operators misread the gauges, leading the core reactor to dangerously overheat to over 4,000 degrees, just 1,000 degrees short of a meltdown. In the case of a meltdown, deadly radiation is released and drifts across the countryside, potentially sickening a great number of people – and when word of the accident leaked, more than 100,000 fled the surrounding towns. Plant workers managed to get the temperature down, and no damage was done. But protests followed, and fears about what could have happened ended the debate about its feasibility.

The accident was far less severe than that of Chernobyl in 1986 or Fukushima in 2011, and nuclear power plants thrive in many other countries in the world. But concerns about the risks – which are extremely low, especially compared with oil or coal mining – make it very difficult for new nuclear power stations to be built (Minnesota has an outright ban on them). But it is likely that, with the political issues intrinsic to the global energy markets, nuclear power stations will make some sort of return in the future.

By the early 1980s, support for the environment was bipartisan, with much of its focus turning towards climate change. George Bush, Sr. declared in 1988 that he would be the "environmental president," and in 1992, Vice President Al Gore brought his environmental concerns to the White House. After he left office, he presented the documentary *An Inconvenient Truth* which specifically highlighted the dangers of global warming. The Obama administration followed up by passing the American Recovery and Reinvestment Act 2009 which invested around $90 billion in clean energy.

The US joined the Paris Agreement of 2015 – an international treaty that aimed to limit global warming to below 2 degrees Celsius (3.6 degrees Fahrenheit) above preindustrial levels. Domestically, Democrat Congresswoman Alexandria Ocasio-Cortez and Senator Ed Markey presented the Green New Deal of 2019, setting a target of bringing US greenhouse gas emissions down to net zero and replacing the entirety of power demand through clean, renewable, and zero-emission energy sources by 2030. The scale of the project was so large and would cost so much (some estimates ranged between $51 trillion and $93 trillion) that it had little chance of becoming law, but it kept environmental concerns high on the agenda. Nowadays, any politician who seeks senior office must outline their plans for the environment, making it one of the biggest changes to have occurred in politics since 1960.

Richard Nixon

Richard Nixon was born into a Quaker family in Southern California in 1913. He encountered some hardship in his youth as he saw two of his five brothers die from tuberculosis, and after the family ranch failed, they were forced to move to Whittier, California where his father opened a grocery store and gas station.

Nixon was educated at Whittier College and Duke University Law School, serving in the US Navy in the Second World War. He entered Congress, like JFK, in 1946, and rose to national attention during the Alger Hiss trial for his continued support of Whittaker Chambers, which ultimately led to Hiss's conviction. He fought off Helen Douglas to win a Senate seat in an aggressive battle during which he implied her having communist sympathies by saying she was "pink right down to her underwear." For his part, he was labeled "Tricky Dick."

Dwight D Eisenhower, who had been sought as a presidential candidate by both the Republicans and the Democrats, eventually chose to run as a Republican and selected the 39-year-old Nixon as his running mate. On the campaign trail, Eisenhower vowed to "clean up the mess in Washington," although one of his biggest challenges came when Nixon was accused of spending campaign money on personal expenses – which Nixon successfully fended off in his Checkers Speech.

Nixon found himself largely underemployed in his role as vice president, in much the same way as Johnson and Truman had been under Kennedy and Roosevelt, respectively. He did step up when Eisenhower had a heart attack in 1955 and obtained his endorsement for the presidency in 1960, but Nixon lost the election narrowly to Kennedy that year. Then, after he ran and lost the race for Governor of California in 1962, many believed his political career was over. He had an intense dislike of the media and made an impromptu speech the morning after that election, declaring, "You won't have Nixon to kick around anymore because, gentlemen, this is my last press conference," upon which he moved to New York City and settled into the life of a practicing attorney.

Nixon stayed out of the 1964 presidential race and gave his support to Barry Goldwater, who lost by a landslide. He was so far removed from the causes of that defeat that he sought to capitalize on it and run for the presidency again in 1967 during a period of major social upheavals in the country. Many white Southerners, who had traditionally supported the Democrats, were against the civil rights movement and had begun aligning themselves with the Republicans, and Nixon set out on his campaign to solidify their support. He also promised to represent the "the silent majority" – by whom he meant those who were not demonstrating in the streets: the blue-collar white folks who worked regular jobs and lived in the suburbs.

He had to fend off the challenges from both Hubert Humphrey of the Democrat Party and George Wallace, the former Democratic Governor of Alabama who had split from the Democrats and ran on a platform of segregationist "law and order," which was similar in many ways to Nixon's. Wallace railed against student radicals, antiwar protestors, and violent Black activists, although in the end, Nixon won the 1968 election, obtaining 30 million votes to Wallace's 10 million.

Nixon and Mao in 1972.

When in office, Nixon received the most acclaim for his foreign relations work, which included visiting Beijing and Moscow in 1972. His National Security Advisor, Henry Kissinger, had worked behind the scenes with Zhou Enlai, China's Premier, to secure a visit, and Nixon spent seven days in China meeting with Chairman Mao Zedong; visiting the Great Wall, Hangzhou, and Shanghai, and partaking in much wining and dining.

Nixon presciently noted, before his visit, that while China may not be great now, it had the potential to be and that it may someday emerge as a major – or even dominant – power. The Sino-Soviet border conflict of 1969 had disproved the notion that Russia and China would have good relations because of their chosen political systems, and he hoped that by fostering good relations with China, Russia would want to follow suit. It did, and a few months later, Nixon became the first ever US president to visit Moscow.[104] He signed two treaties on his trip — the Strategic Arms Limitation Treaty (SALT I) and the Anti-Ballistic Missile Treaty — which were designed to limit the buildup of both nations' nuclear weapons.

Nixon also worked to reduce American presence in Vietnam and by late January 1973, American troops had been reduced from 500,000 to 70,000. The last troops were recalled that year when the draft was abolished, but the war dragged on, making Nixon as hated a figure on the left as Johnson had been. The war ended in a total defeat for South Vietnam in 1975 when the North invaded, and President Gerald Ford refused American reentry.

Domestically, Nixon accepted the legacy of Johnson's Great Society, mostly because his hands were tied by the Democrat-heavy Congress and Senate in his first administration. He caught a wave of goodwill after the moon landings of 1969, comfortably winning reelection in 1972. But then Watergate happened, and within two years, Nixon had resigned in complete disgrace.

The Watergate Scandal

On June 17, 1972, five burglars were caught breaking into the headquarters of the Democratic National Committee at the Watergate Hotel complex in Washington, DC. A security guard noticed that several of the building's door locks had been taped over, and he called the police, who arrived to catch the burglars setting up wiretaps on telephones and stealing documents. One of the burglars was discovered to be the head of Nixon's fundraising organization (known as CREEP), James McCord, and when asked what he was doing,

---

104 FDR had visited the Soviet Union, but not Moscow.

he was quick to deny any link to the White House. Nixon did so too.

At first, the story did not generate much interest, and Nixon won reelection that year in one of the largest landslides of all time. His Democrat opponent, George McGovern, offered up a series of policies on welfare and tax reforms that were far too left-wing to obtain the majority that he needed, and the Democrat Party's other potential candidate, JFK's brother Edward, never ran after becoming a political liability when he crashed his car on the island of Chappaquiddick. It caused the death of the woman riding with him, and instead of immediately calling for help, he fled to his hotel, and the woman was only found the next morning. The 1972 election also saw the attempted assassination of George Wallace, who was shot by a disaffected 21-year-old, Arthur Bremer, permanently paralyzing Wallace from the waist down.

After the initial capture of the burglars at Watergate, two journalists from the *Washington Post,* Bob Woodward and Carl Bernstein, tenaciously pursued the story. Obtaining information from Mark Felt, a high-ranking official at the FBI who remained anonymous for 30 years and who was known in the investigation as "Deep Throat," they uncovered secret payments, hush money, and funds that linked directly back to the White House.

Nixon was in a tough spot. He had to give the impression that he supported the investigation but was, in fact, doing his best to cover it up and make the whole thing disappear. He went on television with a bust of Lincoln on one side and a photograph of his family on the other, saying that he was "appalled at this senseless and illegal action," and that "there can be no whitewash at the White House." Archibald Cox was appointed to prosecute the case, and national hearings took place in 1973 with millions of viewers tuning in to watch them on television. Gradually more and more evidence came out that tied the burglars back to the White House, including a revelation provided by Alexander Butterfield, the former presidential appointments secretary, that Nixon had secretly taped every conversation that occurred in the Oval Office. Prosecutors jumped on it and demanded to hear them.

Nixon initially refused to hand the tapes over, claiming they were protected by executive privilege, but after dragging his feet for as long as he could, even demanding Cox be fired, he was forced to hand them over. The tapes revealed Nixon, days after the break-in, approving a plan suggested by his chief of staff, Bob Halderman, to call the FBI to tell them to "stay the hell out of this... this is, ah, business here we don't want you to go any further on it."

More drama followed in that one of the tapes transcribed by Rose Mary Woods, Nixon's longtime personal secretary, contained an 18.5-minute gap. She claimed she had deleted it by accident, alleging that as she was transcribing it, she took a phone call and pressed the record pedal instead of the stop button. But her reenactment of this showed that such an action was impossible. Questions were then asked as to what the gap contained: maybe it was a direct conversation about the Watergate break-in (Nixon was speaking with Bob Halderman and his assistant for domestic affairs, John Ehrlichman), but it was all hypothesis, and the contents remain unknown to this day. In any event, the public was shocked to hear Nixon's language on the tapes. He called an immigration employee a "kike," and an illegal Mexican a "wetback," told one of his aides to scare the former INS commissioner "to within an inch of his life," and regularly blasphemed and used profanities.

It remains a curiosity as to why Nixon did not destroy the tapes once their existence was revealed. Possibly, he believed destroying them would be too strong an implication of guilt, or he might have believed the tapes would, in fact, vindicate him. He also might simply have thought the tapes would never actually get into the hands of the prosecution – they belonged to him and were protected by executive privilege – and besides, both JFK and FDR had recorded conversations in the Oval Office.

Regardless of his reasons, the reality is that there was no reason for Watergate. Nixon and his team would have known well in advance of election day that he was going to win, so the whole sorry incident was totally unnecessary. But it happened nonetheless, and in 1974, the House Judiciary Committee voted to impeach Nixon for obstruction of justice, abuse of power, criminal cover-up, and several violations of the Constitution. Nixon knew he did not have the votes to win and chose to resign, still denying he had done anything wrong. He died of a stroke in 1994.

Separately, and before Nixon's resignation, Nixon's vice president, Spiro Agnew, had resigned over charges of bribery and tax evasion. So, in an extraordinarily downbeat atmosphere of cynicism and mistrust, the office fell to Gerald Ford – who had only been vice president for eight months – in August 1974. He proceeded to pardon Nixon for any offenses he might have committed against the United States while in office. In total, 40 government officials were indicted or jailed for actions related to the Watergate scandal.

CHAPTER 19

THE JIMMY CARTER AND RONALD REAGAN ERAS (1977–1990)

The Jimmy Carter Administration

The scandal of Watergate painted everyone working in Washington with a sheen of corruption. Gerald Ford was "unelected" and Jimmy Carter, who had never had a role on Capitol Hill (he had held the role of governor of Georgia since 1971), was able to use his distance from it all to his advantage. He comfortably led in the polls in the buildup to the 1976 election, although he gifted Ford a lot back when he gave an interview to *Playboy* magazine in which he said he had committed "adultery in his heart many times," leaving evangelical Protestants somewhat bemused.

Carter's background was unusual, and the press found lots of tidbits to report on. He had grown up outside the small town of Plains, Georgia where his parents, Earl and Lillian Carter, owned a peanut farm. He identified as a "born-again" Christian and occasionally taught Sunday school, and his siblings provided regular fodder for comedians on national television. His sister, Ruth, had appeared in public holding hands with a notorious pornographer claiming she had converted him to Christianity, and his brother, Billy, marketed his own brand of beer ("Billy Beer").

Carter, however, was a dedicated politician. After leaving the US Navy in 1953, he became an activist with the Democrat Party, opposing racial segregation and supporting the civil rights movement, and he served in the Georgia State Senate from 1963–1967. He put human rights high on his agenda when he became governor of Georgia and again when he got into the White House in 1976. He suspended military and economic aid to protest the human rights practices of the governments of Chile, El Salvador, Nicaragua, and Uganda, and tried to mediate peace in the Middle East. His greatest success came with his Israeli-Egypt peace agreement in 1978 (the Camp David Accord).

Israel had recently taken control of the Sinai Peninsula, which had been under Egyptian control, and Carter managed to convince Egypt's president, Anwar Sadat, to come to Israel for talks in 1977. Sadat spoke at a session of the Knesset (the Israeli parliament), which was quite astonishing at the time, and the two leaders then agreed to come together at Camp David to discuss terms for peace. After two weeks, Egypt and Israel agreed on a few points, including Israel's withdrawal from the Sinai Peninsula and recognition of the rights of the Palestinian people. But such a rapprochement did not please everyone, and Sadat was assassinated by an Islamic extremist in 1981. From Carter's perspective, however, it had been the first time since Theodore Roosevelt's efforts to end the Russo–Japanese War in 1905 that a president had so effectively mediated a dispute between two other nations.

Carter also presided over the American relinquishment of the Panama Canal. Built in 1914, it was controlled by the US but had long been considered a symbol of American imperialism by Panama (and other South American countries). The Panama Canal treaties were the subject of significant debate in the Senate, but eventually, they were approved – obtaining the required margin by just one vote.

Domestically, and for the first time in a generation, the economy went through a period of malaise. After American-backed Israel defeated its Arab neighbors in the Yom Kippur War, OPEC retaliated by enacting an embargo on the US, causing oil prices to skyrocket and leading to price increases in everything that required oil, including shipping and airplane expenses. The embargo was lifted as the decade progressed, but OPEC steadily raised prices each year, more than tripling the price of gasoline between 1970 and 1980.

As oil prices rose, the economy slowed, and the Second Oil Crisis – which occurred in the wake of the Iranian Revolution in 1979 – saw oil prices double and panicked consumers rushing to gas stations. A collateral effect was consumers buying fuel-economical cars from Germany and Japan, and the profits of the "Big Three" automakers from Detroit – Ford, Chrysler, and General Motors – suffered correspond-ingly, with Chrysler having to seek a government loan to remain in business. Carter cut taxes and spending, but the inflation rate topped 18 percent in the summer of 1980, and the unemployment rate fluctuated between 6 and 8 percent.

Carter faced a bruising challenge from within his own party for renomination in 1980. Edward Kennedy, whose name remained extremely powerful in Massachusetts, announced his candidacy in November 1979 and won the key states of California and New York. But his profile was hampered by the Chappaquiddick incident, and although he mobilized support from the liberal wing of the party, his campaign stuttered and died. Carter and Mondale were formally nominated for reelection, and Kennedy made his "The Dream Shall Never Die" speech wherein he defended postwar liberal values and advocated for a national healthcare insurance model. He lukewarmly congratulated Carter for his win.

Carter's whole term, however, would be remembered for the Iran Hostage crisis. It was rooted in the US support of the pro-American Shah, Mohammad Reza Shah Pahlavi, whose government was a brutal dictatorship but who provided the US with oil. He was ousted by a radical Islamist group, and Ayatollah Khomeini, who had been in exile in Paris, returned to Iran and was installed as leader. The Shah was exiled to Egypt, but Carter allowed him to come to the US for cancer treatment, which infuriated the Iranian people and prompted a group of pro-Ayatollah students to break into the US Embassy in Tehran and take the 66 employees and diplomats hostage.

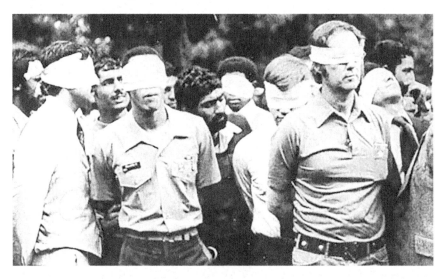

Blindfolded US hostages outside the embassy in Tehran, 1979.

So began their 444 days in captivity,[105] during which they were repeatedly threatened with death and blindfolded

---

105 Six American diplomats evaded capture by hiding in the home of a Canadian diplomat. He issued them Canadian passports, and they escaped, the events of which are dramatized in the films *Escape from Iran: The Canadian Caper* (1981) and *Argo* (2012).

and paraded in front of an angry crowd (and TV cameras) to chants of "Death to America! Death to Carter!" They were disallowed from speaking or reading and were rarely permitted to change clothes. Carter found himself under severe pressure to act. In April 1980, five months after the crisis had begun, he authorized Operation Eagle Claw, a daring military raid that would free the hostages by force. The plan called for helicopters and planes to land in the desert south of Iran and, from there, send a raiding party by helicopter to the embassy to free the hostages. But its execution was a total calamity: severe dust storms disabled two of the eight helicopters, and another crashed, killing eight US servicemen and injuring several more. Without the force deemed necessary to succeed in the rescue, the mission was aborted, and Carter went on television to take responsibility for the failure. With Iran claiming divine intervention, and the US looking weak and incompetent, Carter's popularity and chances of reelection looked bleak.

He was then challenged with how to respond to the Soviet Union's invasion of Afghanistan. Afghan communists had seized control of the country in 1978 but needed support to retain power, and the Soviet Union moved in, installed Babrak Karmal as president, and remained in Afghanistan to prop up the regime. They remained there until 1989 and experienced much of what Americans did in Vietnam, fighting a guerilla war against the mujahideen who evaded defeat by hiding out in the desert and the jagged mountains.

Carter retaliated by refusing to allow American athletes to compete in Moscow for the 1980 Olympic Games and by levying a wheat boycott on the Soviet Union, but many farmers suffered so badly from the latter that the government had to underwrite their losses. In addition, the

SALT II agreement, which Carter had signed with Brezhnev and which limited the number and types of nuclear weapons each country could have, remained unratified in the US. Forecasts of electoral defeat were blinking red for Carter, who lost the 1980 election by a landslide to Ronald Reagan and the Republican Party.

The Ronald Reagan Administrations

An agreement made by Carter led to the release of the hostages in Tehran, although Iran waited until the very day of Reagan's inauguration to actually free them. Reagan, acknowledging all the work Carter had done, sent him as his envoy to receive the hostages when they arrived in West Germany, and a line was finally drawn under the whole sorry business.

Reagan came to power partly by obtaining the support of the evangelical vote headed by Jerry Falwell. Since the Scopes Monkey Trial, evangelicals had retreated from active participation in public life, but Falwell mobilized them into a group he called the Moral Majority and staged "I love America" rallies that denounced such things as the Equal Rights Amendment, homosexuality, pornography, and women's liberation. Despite Carter's strong Christian credentials, evangelicals felt their pro-life positions and traditional family values would be better served by Reagan, even though the latter was the first ever divorced man to become president.

Ronald Reagan in a trailer for Dark Victory (1939).

Reagan was famous before entering politics, having appeared on the radio, in films, and on television. He exuded a calm, relaxed manner which contrasted both with the paranoid Republicans that preceded him and with Carter's stiffness and awkwardness in front of the camera. Reagan was the oldest person ever elected to a first term at 69 and was lucky to survive an assassination attempt shortly after being inaugurated.

He was shot by John Hinckley, Jr., a mentally-ill young man who developed an obsession with the actress Jodie Foster after watching the film *Taxi Driver*. He believed by making a big impression, he would be brought to her attention. Reagan was hit by a .22 long rifle bullet that ricocheted off the side of the presidential limousine and hit him in the left underarm, breaking a rib, puncturing a lung, and causing serious internal bleeding. He was taken to George Washington University Hospital where he was treated and released 12 days later on April 11, 1981. When he returned to the White House, he received standing ovations from his staff and Congress, and his popularity among the public soared.

His persona as well as his policies won him reelection in 1984. The economy had started to take off in 1983, and he faced off against the Democratic candidate, Walter Mondale, who had been Jimmy Carter's vice president. Upon his nomination, Mondale proclaimed (against advice) that he would raise taxes, which doomed his campaign almost immediately, although he displayed some initiative by selecting a woman as his running mate, Geraldine Ferraro.

The other challenge for the Democrats was how to manage the influence of Jesse Jackson, a Baptist minister who had inherited some of Martin Luther King's mantle. He had founded the National Rainbow Coalition and Operation PUSH (People United to Save Humanity) which aimed to bring all minority groups together, but its distinctly left-wing flavor scared many conservative Democrats into voting Republican.

Domestically, Reagan applied the economic theory of supply-side economics. This was a series of dramatic tax cuts and deregulation that assumed more money would be available for reinvestment thereafter, generating more tax revenues for the government. It had been expounded by economists Arthur Laffer and Robert Mundell, and the media termed it "Reaganomics." Reagan found it difficult to reduce the size of the government still further, however, encountering pushback from the employees and officials fearful of losing their jobs. Reagan also did not press for pro-family policy changes, in a blow to the Moral Majority, who went through a process of disillusionment during his two terms.

He took a more aggressive stance towards the Cold War and rapidly escalated the military budget. He recommissioned the Second World War battleship, the USS *Missouri,* and intervened militarily in the Caribbean when rebels on the island of Grenada murdered the Prime Minister and took it over. Many US students were based on the island, and he noted that Cuban laborers were building a new airport which he was concerned would act as a new Soviet beachhead in the region. US forces landed on the island, and within a week, the new government collapsed and was replaced by one friendly to the US.

Reagan used inflammatory rhetoric by describing the Soviet Union as an "evil empire" and supported efforts to keep communism out of Central America. He called the Contra rebels in Nicaragua "freedom fighters" and authorized secret aid to them, but was selective about which countries to help. He refused to send forces to Panama to oust the corrupt dictator, Manual Noriega (this would be carried out by his successor, George H W Bush) and did nothing in Afghanistan. The Reagan administration tried to apply the "Kirkpatrick Doctrine," as espoused by Jeane Kirkpatrick, the US ambassador to the United Nations – which pronounced that the US would support authoritarian regimes if they were anti-communist and were aligned with Washington's goals, even if that regime was antidemocratic or violated certain human rights.

Reagan unveiled a missile defense system called the Strategic Defense Initiative (SDI) which envisioned a shield in outer space to protect the US from incoming missiles. It was an extremely expensive project with no guarantee of success

and could be construed as aggressive rather than defensive –
for if it could shoot down missiles, it could also launch them.
It was derided by critics as "Star Wars," after the movie.

Reagan's "Teflon" image was put to the test with the Iran–
Contra affair. The Boland Amendment prohibited US aid to
the Contras in Nicaragua, which the administration circum-
vented by selling weapons to Iran and using the money to
support the Contras. When questioned, Reagan said he knew
of the sales to Iran but not the diversion of funds, adding that
he believed the sale of arms to Iran was in the best interests
of the US. A press sensation followed with then-unknown
Lieutenant Colonel Oliver North of the National Security
Council explaining how money was diverted to the Contras
for the sake of national security, and a shadow was cast
over the administration's legacy. A poll revealed that only 14
percent of Americans believed the president.

But Reagan was popular, and even though there was some
talk of impeachment for his role in the Iran–Contra affair,
there was little appetite to pursue it. The press was much
gentler with Reagan than with Nixon, partly due to Reagan's
easy manner with them, and when he left office in 1989,
he had the highest approval rating of any president since
Franklin Roosevelt. He died after a battle with Alzheimer's
disease in 2004 at the age of 93.

The End of the Cold War

Despite all the efforts of CIA agents, military personnel,
diplomats, and analysts, no one predicted the Soviet Union
would collapse at the end of the 1980s. Russia had endured
famines, purges, and invasions, all while in a dilapidated state,
so conventional wisdom said it would pull through again. But
the unwinnable war in Afghanistan had intensified hatred

of the Soviet regime – especially in Eastern Europe, where many had experienced communist repression firsthand – and the Soviet economy, heavily influenced by the price of oil, was stagnant.

In 1988, Russia started its withdrawal from Afghanistan. Mikhail Gorbachev then implemented the twin policies of *glasnost* and *perestroika* – political openness, which freed political prisoners and the press; and economic restructuring, which allowed individuals and cooperatives to own businesses and obtain foreign investment. The growth in technologies had made it increasingly difficult to retain a monopoly on access to information, and people heard about the struggles within communist regimes. Movements soon developed to fight against them.

For example, after the new Pope, John Paul II, visited his homeland of Poland in 1979, millions attended open-air masses in Warsaw to hear him speak about human rights and freedom. That moment of spiritual togetherness led to the creation of the Solidarity trade union headed by Lech Walesa which, at its peak, consisted of almost 10 million members including 80 percent of state employees. It set about opposing the repressive nature of the communist government and used nonviolent tactics the Soviet Union struggled to eliminate. In 1988, Gorbachev announced the Soviet Union would no longer defend communism in its satellite states by force, and Poland was opened up to free elections, which the Solidarity Party won resoundingly in September 1989.

The Iron Curtain collapsed that year. East Germany tore down the Berlin Wall in thrilling scenes – today only a few remnants and replicas remain – and Hungary and Czechoslovakia peacefully transitioned to democratic systems of government.

President George H W Bush let events unfold organically, holding back from any temptation to gloat or celebrate, and encouraged Gorbachev's reform efforts when they met in Malta in early December 1989. The furthest he went was to proclaim a "new world order" in the run-up to the Iraq War as he envisaged the broader international community coming together to fight global challenges such as terrorism, nuclear proliferation, and regional conflicts.

One area that resisted democratization was China. Student-led demonstrations occurred in Tiananmen Square in Beijing where they paraded a 10-meter-tall *Goddess of Democracy* statue that had a remarkable likeness to the Statue of Liberty. But as the protest spread to other cities, the Chinese government acted with decisive, brutal force. Tanks and troops flooded Beijing, killing demonstrators and bystanders alike, and deaths and arrests were estimated to be in the thousands. The US would have liked to see democracy succeed in China but also wanted stronger trade relations so chose not to intervene – the result being that the failure of those demonstrations led to one of the most repressive regimes in the world in the 1990s.

At the end of the Cold War, the US hoped that Russia would transform into a democratic, capitalist country complete with individual freedoms and economic prosperity for all. But the reality was that the transition from a command economy to a market one was very difficult, and under the leadership of Boris Yeltsin, a power vacuum developed, and many state-owned assets were transferred to a small group of oligarchs who amassed vast wealth and control. A peaceful transition of power did occur in 2000 when Yeltsin handed the presidency to Vladimir Putin, but since Putin's rule, the government has become more centralized, political freedoms more limited, and nationalism more pronounced.

The legacy of the Cold War persists and revolves around three elements: the development and control of nuclear weapons, the expansion of NATO and the EU, and the lingering effects of military conflicts. The threat of nuclear war continues today, and Russia, Pakistan, India, Israel, and North Korea all practice brinkmanship on some level to gain political advantages. NATO and the EU are rooted in the bipolar superpower era, and the sense of community between them has become a source of envy or menace to those left out. The current conflicts or tensions in Ukraine, Korea, and Afghanistan all have their foundations in the Cold War.

## PART SEVEN

THE NEW WORLD ORDER TO TODAY

CHAPTER 20

POST-COLD WAR ERA (1991–2008)

The First Gulf War

The Cold War was over by 1990. The threat of nuclear war receded, borders opened, and the US took up the mantle of the one undisputed global superpower. But it was not long before it faced its first test – and it emerged in the Middle East.

On August 2, 1990, the Iraqi dictator, Saddam Hussein, invaded Kuwait – a country that provided the US with around 20 percent of its imported oil – and the spot price of oil more than doubled by October. The US placed economic sanctions on Iraq, but these did little, and George H W Bush, after consulting with the international community and forging an unprecedented coalition that included the NATO allies and the Middle Eastern countries of Saudi Arabia, Syria, and Egypt, greenlit Operation Desert Storm which began on January 16, 1991.

The operation was one of the most intensive air bombardments in military history and used smart bombs (guided bombs) for the first time. Iraqi supply lines were cut, their positions were pummeled, and warfare leaflets were dropped to sap morale. The Iraqis still did not withdraw, and US ground forces moved in on February 24. Within 100 hours, Iraq was forced out of Kuwait, and the Iraqis systematically burned and destroyed over 600 Kuwaiti oil fields as they retreated. They dumped 1.5 billion barrels of oil into the Persian Gulf, causing devastating environmental damage.

During the war, Iraq tried to provoke the Middle East into a wider war by firing approximately 42 Scud missiles into Israel. If Israel had retaliated, it could have led to Muslim states rescinding their support to the US, and American diplomats worked closely with Israel to ensure they did not fire back. The missiles killed two people directly and damaged various buildings, but the attack did not merit a direct response from Israel itself although the moment highlighted the continued tension and instability of the area.

Oil wells were set on fire by Iraqi forces as they were ousted in 1990.

Once Iraq was forced out of Kuwait, Bush made the momentous decision to leave Saddam Hussein in power. The military could easily have marched into the capital and ousted the dictator, but Bush decided the US had achieved its objectives and there was no appetite for any kind of "nation-building" that would be required were Hussein removed. The West was quickly left wondering whether they had done the right thing though, as they watched him brutally repress the Shi'ite Muslims and the Kurds, even using chemical weapons against them.

Saddam Hussein accepted peace terms that included recognizing Kuwait's sovereignty and disposing of its weapons of mass destruction. But tensions remained high, and in 1998, he refused to admit entry to United Nations inspectors responsible for overseeing their disarmament. This led to Operation Desert Fox, an intense four-day bombing of Iraqi targets suspected of producing and storing weapons of mass destruction. Hussain's regime remained a source of controversy going into the new millennium when Bush's son took over.

Domestically, military leaders became popular again. Norman Schwarzkopf, the leader of the coalition forces in the war, was affectionately called "Stormin' Norman," and Joint Chief of Staff Colin Powell went on to become George Bush, Jr.'s secretary of state in 2001. Casualties had been low. Only 148 US citizens were killed (another 235 were killed by accidents and friendly fire), and victory was so rapid that there was no time for serious protests. Discipline and morale had been kept high during the war, and there had been no need to reimpose a draft as the US Army recruited through an effective advertising campaign that led with the slogan "Be All You Can Be."

New Threats from Abroad

The US faced its next dilemma in southeastern Europe. Strongman Josep Tito had kept a tight rein on the country of Yugoslavia, but once he died in 1980, ethnic tensions that had previously been suppressed by his communist government returned. Croatia, Slovenia, Serbia, Montenegro, Bosnia, Herzegovina, and North Macedonia all declared independence in the early 1990s, with individual countries participating in "ethnic cleansing" to rid themselves of those minority nationalities within the new nation-state.

The United Nations and the United States tried to stop the bloodshed by employing arms embargoes, sanctions, and peacekeeping missions but were reluctant to get fully involved. There were human rights grounds for involvement but not political ones, which also became the sticking point when intertribal genocide was committed by the Hutus against the Tutsis in Rwanda in Africa.

The other perplexing issue for the United States was the increase in terrorism. Ever since the 1960s, political groups realized the effectiveness of hijacking commercial aircraft, with the standard advice for passengers on board being to do nothing and leave negotiations to trained officials. In 1985, TWA Flight 847 was hijacked shortly after takeoff from Athens, Greece, with the plane held for 17 days. Hijackers tied up and beat several passengers, killing one, and they demanded the release of hundreds of Lebanese from Israeli prisons. In 1988, a commercial flight was destroyed by a bomb planted in the cargo hold by Libyan intelligence agents while flying over Lockerbie, Scotland. It killed all 270 people on board including US government officials and intelligence specialists. Airports began implementing Increased security and screening procedures in response.

In 1993, a car bomb blew up under the World Trade Center in New York, killing six people and injuring another 1,000. The attack had been perpetrated by Muslim terrorists belonging to the group Al-Qaeda, the leader of which expressed no remorse, only voicing his disappointment that one tower had not collapsed into the other. He claimed he wanted to punish the United States for its role in providing aid to Israel and was sentenced to life in prison plus 240 years.

A more lethal, yet homegrown, act occurred in 1995. Timothy McVeigh exploded a car bomb in Oklahoma City, killing 168 people including 19 children, in an act of rebellion against a federal government that he believed had too much power over American people's lives. He cited the events of Ruby Ridge and Waco as examples of how US department officials had killed innocent civilians who had chosen a life outside of regular society, and the bombing pushed individual freedoms and big government back onto the debate table.

The threat of terrorism was costly in time and money. Security businesses became a new, growing industry. Air travel safety now required each flier and each piece of luggage to be carefully checked, but the key question was, if a terrorist were prepared to die in a kamikaze-style attack, how could it be prevented? The answer, ultimately, was that it could not, and the world watched a tragedy unfold in real time on September 11, 2001.

The world was, however, much safer now that the Cold War had ended, and the US radiated an immense cultural influence across the world. People ate McDonald's in Moscow and played baseball in Japan; Hollywood films were watched in Africa, and American rock 'n roll played in bars in Asia. Immigration to the US reached record highs and showed no sign of slowing, and everything the United States did in politics, economics, and civil society had an impact the world over.

The Bill Clinton Administrations

Bill Clinton was a surprising Democratic nomination for the 1992 presidential election. George H W Bush's ratings were high after the Gulf War – at one point, he enjoyed an 89 percent approval rating – and the consensus was that he would win again, with many potential Democrat candidates declining to run.[106] But the United States went into an economic recession in 1992, and Bush, after promising no new taxes (making a famous speech in which he said, "Read my lips: no new taxes"), promptly raised taxes in 1990 and his prestige slid.

Clinton was highly educated. He was a graduate of Georgetown University, a Rhodes Scholar, and held a law degree from Yale. He met his wife, Hillary Rodham, at Yale, and after graduating, he returned to his birthplace of Arkansas where he won the race for governor, becoming one of the nation's youngest governors in history at the age of 32. He was an excellent campaigner, projecting charm and empathy, and had an uncanny ability to remember people's names.

Clinton had two great weaknesses, however, that almost derailed his candidacy. The first was that he had seemingly avoided the draft for the Vietnam War, and the second was that he had a reputation for philandering. Avoidance of the draft might have been reasonable in the 1960s, but since he was running for commander in chief with the power to send others to war, it had the capacity to seriously damage his credibility. He was forced to address it directly by admitting

---

106   These included Mario Cuomo, Jesse Jackson, and Al Gore.

that he only opposed the draft for the Vietnam War but that he was supportive of the draft in the Second World War.

Bill and Hillary Clinton on CBS in 1992.

His reputation for philandering was brought to light by Gennifer Flowers during his presidential campaign. She claimed she had had a 12-year extramarital affair with him, and Clinton went on *60 Minutes* with his wife to refute the charges. Their joint television appearance certainly did a great deal for his own ambitions but ultimately came at a steep cost to Hillary, who came across as a complicated mixture of headstrong, loyal, defensive, and ambitious. It was her first introduction to the public and her political career never fully recovered.

Bill Clinton had to face off against a third contender for the presidency, the billionaire businessman Ross Perot. The practice of negative campaigning between the candidates of the two main parties had significantly increased since the mid-1980s, and Perot sought to take advantage of that by running as an outsider, one step removed from establishment politicians. Journalists discovered that Perot had some eccentricities, however, such as forcing volunteers to sign loyalty oaths and refusing to follow the advice of his campaign managers, and he withdrew his candidacy in July only to reenter the race in October. In the end, Perot received over 19 million votes in the strongest third-party showing in history. His platform included balancing the federal budget and ending the outsourcing of jobs which probably took more votes from Bush than from Clinton, and Clinton was elected as the first Democrat president since Jimmy Carter.

His honeymoon with Congress did not last long, however. A federal court ruling tested his promise to end the exclusion of homosexuals from the military, and a debate ensued, which ended with Clinton proposing a "don't ask, don't tell" policy which satisfied no one, least of all his voters who had been promised something else. Then he tried to implement a major goal of his administration: a national healthcare system.

Clinton sought to provide Americans with basic universal healthcare, something that made the United States an outlier from other Western nations. But his decision to choose the First Lady, Hillary, as leader of the program's task force deviated from precedent and heaped pressure on Hillary herself. She had demonstrated her talents at Yale, but she was combative, worked secretively, and failed to build coalitions with the relevant players involved. The Medical Association, the insurance companies, the pharmaceutical companies, and the Republican Party all opposed various aspects of an extraordinarily complex 1,350-page-long scheme in what was arguably her husband's biggest legislative failure.

By the turn of the century, an estimated 14 percent of the US population – the poorest section of society – did not have any healthcare at all. Also, an anomaly of US healthcare meant that an individual's coverage was almost always tied to their job.[107] This prevented people from changing employers as they were afraid to have their benefits reduced, wait for a period without insurance while they transitioned between roles, or lose their healthcare coverage altogether. In addition, medical research mostly went to illnesses contracted by rich people, since there would be no payoff for designing solutions to illnesses contracted by the poor. Universal healthcare remained a challenging, unsolved issue that was tackled again by Clinton's Democrat successor, Barack Obama.

Dislike of President Clinton, despite an improvement in the economy, led to a Republican victory in the 1994 midterm elections. Both houses ended up in Republican hands for the first time since 1952, and under the leadership of Newt Gingrich, they put forward a legislative agenda called the Contract with America. This consisted of ten points that included balancing the federal budget, cutting taxes, limiting politicians' terms, and improving ethics on Capitol Hill. But divisions between Republicans and Democrats were stark, and Gingrich suffered, much like Hillary Clinton, from a confrontational and uncompromising style – and most of the items on the agenda either did not pass Congress or were substantially altered by the president. The government even shut down in 1995 and 1996 after proposed budget cuts were vetoed by Clinton, prompting Gingrich to threaten

---

107   In the Second World War, US companies competed for workers by offering superior health insurance, and the IRS made employer-based health insurance exempt from taxation. After the Second World War, most countries were devastated by the war and could only provide healthcare to their citizens through the state. But the US economy was booming after the war, so industry was happy to provide it instead.

to refuse to raise the debt limit. The Republicans hoped to present the shutdown as Democratic intransigence, but voters disagreed, and some of the support Clinton had lost came back again.

By the time of the next presidential election in 1996, the economy was booming. Clinton remained unpopular with a large portion of the electorate, and the Republicans had several interesting personalities within their ranks including Pat Buchanan, Steve Forbes, and Colin Powell. But in the end, they selected Bob Dole, who had little charisma or ability to connect with the voters, and Clinton comfortably beat off both the challenges of the Republican Party and Ross Perot's Reform Party to secure a second term.

Relations between the Democrats and Republicans, bitter in 1992, grew wider. An exhaustive investigation into a potential cover-up of financial impropriety by the Clintons was conducted in what became known as the Whitewater scandal. Prosecuted by Kenneth Starr, the incident related to a failed real estate development deal that had been managed by a convicted fraudster and business partner of Clinton's, and although there was no smoking-gun evidence with which to charge Clinton, he was tainted by the whole event.

Then he was accused by Paula Jones of sexual harassment during his time as governor of Arkansas. That investigation kicked off in 1994, and while that was ongoing, he recklessly started another affair with a young White House intern, Monica Lewinsky, in 1995. Clinton's reputation for philandering developed when he was governor, apparently even using Arkansas State Troopers to help him deceive his wife while conducting liaisons behind her back (a controversy that became known as "Troopergate"), so when leaks of his affair with Lewinsky got through to the press, the Republicans were thrilled.

Clinton first denied it, and his wife claimed it was a "vast right-wing conspiracy." But after Lewinsky confessed to a grand jury and DNA evidence had been obtained from a dark blue dress she had worn, Clinton had no choice but to admit it. He went on television on August 17, 1998, to apologize and acknowledged that it was foolish, and in September, Kenneth Starr presented a 445-page report putting forth 11 grounds for impeachment. The House chose to move forward with two – perjury and obstruction of justice.

The press gleefully reported on the aspects of Clinton and Lewinsky's sexual encounters, which included oral sex, phone sex, and various sex games.[108] It was a dramatic departure from how they had chosen to report on prior presidents' extramarital trysts, with partisan politics, a new competitive news environment, and changing social norms all contributing to the new media landscape.

The economic boom in 1998 led to a narrow Democrat midterm victory, and Clinton was acquitted in his impeachment trial in 1999.[109] It was difficult to prove that vital national interests had been at stake, and Democratic support along with some Republican crossover votes enabled him to win acquittal despite evidence to the contrary. Clinton left office with strong public approval ratings – which probably owed more to the strength of the economy than to any forgiveness afforded to him by the electorate – and the son of the man he had beaten in 1992, George W Bush, Jr., took over the presidency in 2000.

---

108 One included inserting a cigar into Lewinsky's vagina and then Clinton putting it in his mouth.

109 He settled the Paula Jones lawsuit for $850,000 but admitted no wrongdoing.

That election had been one of the closest of all time, and the public had to wait for a recount of votes in Florida where Bush's brother was governor. The recount gave Bush victory by a meager 537 votes, which led to questions about whether the ballot design and the paper-based punch card voting machines had confused the voters (some voters claimed that they had meant to vote for one candidate but ended up voting for the other). The Democrat candidate, Al Gore, had won the popular vote by around 500,000, but he had struggled against Bush, who had projected more charisma and personality during the campaign.

The Information Revolution

By the end of the century, a technology revolution occurred that gave rise to inventive ways to communicate, obtain knowledge, and buy and sell products. A new generation of entrepreneurs was afforded a similar status to those of the Gilded Age, and their businesses reached consumers all over the world, with the public and politicians looking at them with a mixture of envy, anger, and fear.

The roots of this revolution come from the growth of the computer industry. The first generation of computers (1940–1956) used vacuum tubes to control electric current flow and were heavy, large, and expensive. But in 1959, Jack Kilby and Robert Noyce invented the microchip, which led to the replacement of vacuum tubes with transistor circuits that fit into a single piece of silicon, eliminating the size, heat, and weight problems of the early computers. From then on, continued advances in miniaturization (integrated circuits and microprocessors) gave rise to new generations of computers and eventually led to user-friendly devices such as personal computers, laptops, and cellphones.

By the late 1980s, what once had been a luxury became a necessity for almost every business and soon for every household. The development of the internet in the 1990s excited people to such an extent that a market bubble formed before crashing in 2000, taking many small companies with it. But the technology was sound enough, and the computers and software used to get online gave rise to whole new industries.

Microsoft, a computer software company, was the biggest company in the United States by the end of the millennium and Bill Gates, its founder, the richest man (worth over $63 billion). By 2020, Microsoft, Apple, Amazon, Google, and Facebook were the top five most valuable companies in the United States, with many of their respective founders – Jeff Bezos of Amazon, Larry Page and Sergey Brin of Google, and Mark Zuckerberg of Facebook (now Meta) – the wealthiest men on the planet.

Sergey Brin and Elon Musk (who cofounded Paypal, SpaceX, and Tesla) both came from foreign countries – Brin from the Soviet Union, and Musk from South Africa – and rose to the top of their fields. Their successes demonstrated how accommodating the United States can be for anyone willing to work hard, and many immigrants to the US today look to them as role models. Certain countries, such as China, Russia, and India, have strict restrictions on foreign ownership and management, and the United States remains a very attractive option for entrepreneurs and businessmen to settle in.

Just like Standard Oil or Carnegie Steel in the Gilded Age, these new technology companies have been accused at various points of monopolistic and anticompetitive practices and of failing to treat their employees humanely. They have also been charged with using tax shelters unconscionably and collecting and sharing their users' private data without consent. But their investment in new technologies, their capacity to create jobs, and their philanthropic activities have made them a vital component of today's economy and an extraordinary success story.

9/11 and the War on Terror

Upon taking office, Bush had planned to implement "compassionate conservatism" – a model that used traditional conservative ideas such as small government and free market principles to meet the social challenges of the time – and was getting to work when everything changed on September 11, 2001. Domestic policies and divisive politics took a backseat, and the country came together in shock and indignation.

Nineteen terrorists hijacked four commercial airplanes, crashing one each into the north and south towers of the World Trade Center in New York and another into the Pentagon in Arlington, Virginia. A fourth plane was heading for Washington, DC – probably targeting the Capitol or the White House – but the hijackers were overpowered by the passengers on board, and it crashed into a field in Pennsylvania. Within two hours of the first plane smashing into the north tower, both towers had collapsed, and part of the Pentagon had been destroyed, leaving the public struggling to process the horror as they watched buildings smoldering on live television and replays running for weeks afterwards.

More than 2,700 people were killed, and just like Pearl Harbor, conspiracy theories immediately began to circulate. These included claims it was an inside job, that the president knew of the attacks but chose to let them go ahead, and that Israel organized it as a false-flag operation. The 9/11 Commission Final Report, released in July 2004, debunked these conspiracy theories, detailing the causes of the attacks and proposing how future ones could be prevented.

The terrorists' willingness to sacrifice their own lives made the attack difficult to prevent or foresee. They came from four different countries (Saudi Arabia, the UAE, Lebanon, and Egypt), which made America's response much more difficult, although Al-Qaeda, whose leader, Osama bin Laden, took responsibility for the attacks, had most recently been based out of Afghanistan, which was governed by the Taliban regime. Bush demanded the Taliban deliver Osama bin Laden and other Al-Qaeda leaders or "share in their fate." When the Taliban refused, the US attacked on October 7, less than a month after 9/11 and with little debate in Congress.

The US called the invasion of Afghanistan "Enduring Freedom," but the difficulties of invading Afghanistan were historically well documented. Britain had been defeated after it invaded Afghanistan between 1838 and 1842, and the Soviet Union remained there for nine years in an unwinnable guerilla war that hastened the decline of its own empire. The mountainous terrain made finding and attacking the enemy extremely difficult, and the country lacked basic infrastructure and a middle class with whom to work and negotiate. Tribal rivalries made many Afghanis in the countryside immune to political incentives, and even with NATO help, they remained inflexible.

It proved impossible to set up a legitimate democracy, and the US only fully exited Afghanistan in 2021 in what had become America's longest-ever war. By that time, it was clear there would be no winning of it in any conventional sense and a deal was made with the Taliban – who had incredibly never been fully defeated – to come back to power and for America to withdraw.

Inside Reach 871 in 2021:

This was all to be in the future, but for now, with the new wisdom being to strike first to prevent future catastrophes, Bush invaded Iraq in 2003. Neoconservative strategists argued that it was the moral duty of the US to intervene and to help oppressed citizens in other nations, and Bush justified the invasion by citing Iraq's refusal to cooperate with UN resolutions. He claimed that Iraq would not give up their weapons of mass destruction and that Saddam Hussein supported terrorism. With Vietnam in mind, Bush's decision led to a vigorous debate about how long the US would have to remain there and how anti-American sentiment would be aroused further.

Dick Cheney, Bush's vice president who had been secretary of defense under his father, said there was no doubt Iraq was amassing weapons of mass destruction, although he, and many others in Bush's government, must have harbored sentiments of unfinished business from the First Gulf War. Bush Jr.'s administration's arguments for invading Iraq were too far-fetched for many, and the United Kingdom was the only ally who agreed to support the US with boots on the ground.

Bush announced Operation Iraqi Freedom on March 19, 2003, and the coalition forces of the US and the UK advanced and captured Baghdad after 22 days of fighting. Bush landed on the aircraft carrier USS *Abraham Lincoln,* which had just returned from the Persian Gulf and was now off the San Diego coast. There he gave a speech with a banner reading "Mission Accomplished" in the background, stating that even though there was still work to do, it was the end of major combat operations in Iraq.

But the US did not find any weapons of mass destruction, and there was no evidence that Saddam Hussain or his Ba'ath Party had supported any Islamic terrorist groups. Iraq lacked any experience in democracy, and a power vacuum developed after the Iraqi army had been dismantled, with guerrilla assaults on the occupying forces and leaders of the new government. Sectarian violence between the rival Shi'a and Sunni militias increased, and Islamic radicals and Al-Qaeda found recruiting easy. Soldiers became vulnerable as soon as they ventured out of the Green Zone – the international sector of Baghdad that was heavily fortified in the center – and suicide attacks, car bombs, kidnappings, and beheadings all became occupational hazards. US military deaths totaled 486 in the year 2003, and the following year, a further 849 soldiers were killed. By the end of 2007, a total of 3,908 US soldiers had been killed.

Comparisons to Vietnam came easily. The US Army was excellent in combat but was ill-equipped to rebuild civil society, and Bush found it impossible to withdraw. But he had no intention of staying permanently, and the costs involved with shipping armies from thousands of miles away swallowed up the peace dividends that had accumulated during the Clinton administrations. Critics appeared from the left – notably from the *New York Times* and the *Washington Post* – and from the right, with traditional conservatives such as Pat Buchanan and Brent Scowcroft arguing for the US to return to isolationism. There was, however, no draft in place, so protests held in New York, Seattle, San Francisco, and Chicago, among others, were more muted than they had been against the Vietnam War.

In 2007, General David Petraeus was appointed to oversee operations, and an increase of 20,000 troops was approved in a controversial plan that became known as "the surge." American troops patrolled cities on foot with members of the Iraqi military to prepare them to step into a more independent role, and after an initial period that saw the highest number of casualties since the war began, things gradually began to quiet down. By the end of 2008, US military and Iraqi civilian deaths had both declined by more than 60 percent, so Bush set a withdrawal date of December 2011, which occurred under his successor, Barack Obama.

Taken together, the wars in Afghanistan and Iraq underlined the predicament the US had to face. It was unconscionable for the US not to have retaliated after 9/11, but it was hard to assign a target, and antagonists knew they had only to wait until US resolve weakened and they withdrew. From the American perspective, however, withdrawal indicated weakness, so they were forced to put it off for as long as they could, even if it was evident there was little to nothing to gain. It was an unresolvable paradox, and it was only under Joe Biden's administration in 2021 that the US finally exited Afghanistan, 20 years and four presidents later.

CHAPTER 21

MODERN DAY
(2008–TODAY)

The Great Financial Crisis

Since the end of the Second World War, the goal of most households was ownership of their own homes. An increasing amount of people achieved this, partly facilitated by low interest rates put in place after the dot-com bubble, a series of corporate accounting scandals, and the September 11 terrorist attacks. Demand for houses was high; the population kept growing, and so house prices kept rising, particularly in and around the big cities. In some areas in the northeast, for example, house prices had doubled between 2000 and 2007, and banks were looking for new ways to attract buyers, including providing loans on conditions that were less stringent than ever before.

Cautious banks had traditionally scrutinized borrowers' income to forecast whether and how easily they could make loan and mortgage payments. But now, some banks were offering mortgages without requiring a down payment and without even asking borrowers to show they were earning any income. Interest rates were often initially set to "teaser" rates, which gave borrowers the illusion that they would be able to afford the payments, but after a period of time (three, five, or seven years), the rates would suddenly skyrocket from that teaser rate of, say, 2 percent to around 8 percent.

Fannie Mae and Freddie Mac[110] – federally-backed home mortgage companies – loaded up on risker and technically prohibited mortgages, such as "subprime" (so-called because the borrowers had low credit ratings), negative amortization (wherein the buyer does not cover the full interest payments each month, meaning the amount of the loan continues to go up), or interest-only mortgages.

Regulatory oversight was slack, and the credit ratings agencies, such as S&P, Moody's, and Fitch, would give the mortgages a low-risk rating. Clever financiers bundled hundreds of thousands of mortgages, including the subprime mortgages, into complicated financial vehicles that were traded between banks, which provided higher returns than government bonds – but only if interest rates stayed low and house prices increased. The day of reckoning came in 2008, however, when thousands of interest rates switched to higher rates, and buyers realized they could not afford the payments.

Entire suburban areas – notably in Florida and Nevada – were depopulated, and as supply swelled, house prices began to sink. Lenders suddenly realized they would not get paid back on the loans they had made and found themselves on the brink of bankruptcy. The stock market fell from 14,164 points in October 2007 to 6,594 points by March 2009, a drop of more than 50 percent.

The crash led to the key question, just as it had in 1929, of whether and to what extent the government should intervene. If it let market forces naturally take their course, many companies would go bankrupt, people would lose

---

110   Fannie Mae and Freddie Mac are both spins on the acronyms of their original names – the Federal National Mortgage Association (Fannie Mae) and the Federal Home Loan Mortgage Association (Freddie Mac).

their jobs, and big banks would collapse. Conservatives in the Bush administration were ideologically opposed to subsidizing failure, and some well-known companies, such as Lehman Brothers, Bear Stearns, and Wachovia, went to the wall. Others, including AIG, Bank of America, and Citigroup were deemed "too big to fail" and were bailed out – with concerns over unemployment, which eventually reached nearly 10 percent in the last years of the Bush administration, shaping that decision.

This was the situation in the presidential election of 2008. Bush had served two terms so was required to step down, and both parties underwent vigorous primary campaigns to select their nominee for leadership. The Republicans nominated John McCain – the Arizona senator who had served as a US Navy pilot and spent seven years in a Hanoi prisoner-of-war camp in the Vietnam War – and the Democrats nominated Barack Obama.

The Barack Obama Administrations

The heir apparent to the Democrat nomination in 2008 had been Hillary Clinton, the former First Lady who was now a senator for New York. She had stood behind her husband during the Lewinsky scandal and held enough name recognition, experience, and contacts to have reasonably expected the nomination. But not everyone agreed.

The Whitewater scandal had implicated her (and her husband, Bill) in some unconscionable real estate dealings and "Travelgate" – an episode wherein seven employees of the White House Travel Office had been fired in 1993 under her orders – had been unpopular. She had an aggressive, didactic style, and the support she gave her husband over his infidelities was perceived by many to have been driven by political ambition rather than personal conviction.

So instead, the Democrats turned to Illinois State Senator Barack Obama. His keynote address speech at the 2004 Democratic National Convention significantly elevated his status and led to the reissue of his memoir, *Dreams of My Father* (originally published in 1995), which was a combination of his feelings about his mixed-race heritage and a narrative of his early life.

Obama grew up the son of a white mother and a Kenyan father, studied at Columbia University and Harvard Law School, and was charismatic and stylish, finding himself ahead in the polls in 2008. McCain tried to counter this by choosing a striking and unusual running mate in Sarah Palin, the telegenic Alaska governor. But in a series of interviews with Katie Couric on CBS, it became clear she had serious liabilities. Palin's responses showed she had virtually no foreign policy experience, read next to nothing, and could not articulate economic policies plainly. She was a gift to the Democrats.

The "Hope" poster used in the Obama election campaign generated a wave of utopian excitement among his supporters. They looked forward to ending the wars in Afghanistan and Iraq, reviving the economy, and providing universal healthcare. He was the first African American in the highest office of the land, a feat that would have been unthinkable 50 years ago, and many felt that America had turned a corner. But with such lofty expectations, he was destined to fall short.

A group of Republicans attempted to discredit Obama by asserting he had not been born in the US ("birthers") and demanded to see his birth certificate; others claimed that his middle name, Hussein, indicated that he was a Muslim convert. But he preserved the dignity and decorum expected of those sitting in the White House, and his administration was untroubled by financial or sexual scandals. He also tried to heal the internal rift in the Democrat Party by appointing Hillary Clinton as secretary of state.

He passed the Affordable Care Act of 2010 (also known as "Obamacare"), which gave healthcare access to millions who could not afford it. Jimmy Carter and Bill Clinton had both failed in efforts to reform the healthcare system, and Obama worked hard in his first administration, when the Democrats held the House and the Senate, to push through this major piece of legislation. He would have preferred to create a system like the United Kingdom's or Canada's wherein access to healthcare was a basic right of citizens, but the lobbying power of insurers, intransigence from the right, and other vested interest parties made this goal unobtainable, resulting in clunky but partly successful legislation.

Republicans objected strenuously to the burdens of making everyone register and increasing taxes, and some Republican governors even refused to carry out their responsibilities under the Act, even if by doing so it meant they were rejecting financial assistance provided by the federal government. They also objected to Obama's stimulus package that injected $787 billion into the economy. The federal budget deficit had been sent soaring above $1 trillion a year, partly due to the American Recovery and Reinvestment Act ("Obama stimulus") which was designed to help the economy recover from the financial crisis of 2008. The stimulus package was a combination of tax cuts, extension of unemployment benefits, and job creation programs.

The expenditures of "Obamacare" and the "Obama stimulus" plans led to protests by the conservatives calling themselves the Tea Party. The name evoked the events of Boston Harbor in 1773 when the protestors rebelled against higher taxation, and Republicans rode the wave of Tea Party momentum into the midterms of 2010. It led to the Democrats losing control of the House – which they never got back for the remainder of the administration – and to deadlock on much legislation.

Obama won reelection in 2012 against the first Mormon candidate, Mitt Romney, but could not carry out the rest of his agenda. Republicans shied away from compromise, and proposed legislation such as the American Jobs Act (which was designed to stimulate the economy through tax cuts, aid, and infrastructure spending) was rejected out of hand, and Republicans threatened to shut down the government unless Obama balanced the federal budget. Such inflexibility brought into question the congressional model of government which, at its best, brings different interest groups together to hammer out agreements that everyone can live with but which, at its worst, prevents any new initiatives from becoming law.

Barack Obama awaits news of Bin Laden in 2011.

On the foreign affairs front, Obama's most conspicuous success was the assassination of Osama bin Laden by Navy SEALs on May 2, 2011, in Pakistan. Pakistan was ostensibly an American ally but was also a haven for terrorists crossing the border from Afghanistan, and a major new threat emerged in the area called the Islamic State. It aimed to expel the Americans from Iraq, restore the ancient caliphate, and institute the strictest form of Sharia law. It became one of the most aggressive opponents of Bashar al-Assad of Syria when civil war broke out there in 2011, renaming itself ISIS, the Islamic State of Iraq and Syria.

Drones were used to bomb and kill specific targets in the Middle East and flown by US operatives based in Nevada, on the other side of the world. The Obama administration was secretive about certain elements of its foreign policy, including its use of drones, whose targets also included Americans sympathetic to Al-Qaeda, eight of whom were killed. He authorized 540 strikes during his two terms and also used drones in non-battlefield settings – namely Yemen, Pakistan, and Somalia.

Obama had signed an order to evacuate the detention center at Guantanamo Bay in Cuba, where suspected terrorists were held without trial for years at a time and where elementary rights protected by the Geneva Convention had been violated. But Republicans and some conservative Democrats wanted to hold some terrorists too dangerous to be put on trial, and when Obama left office eight years later, the prison still held more than 40 men. It remains open to this day.

In 2017, Barack Obama was voted the second-best president since the Second World War (Ronald Reagan was voted the best), with some of that attributed to his dignified style and the symbolic importance of being the first African American in the White House. His achievements were most notable for "Obamacare" and the stimulus packages that he passed to prevent another depression, but compared to the amount of promise he represented when he first took office, his administrations were somewhat underwhelming, although he remains a very popular member of the Democrat Party.

The Donald Trump Administration

With Obama required to step down, the stage appeared to be set for Hillary Clinton who, this time, clinched the nomination for the Democrat Party. But her nomination was still a risk, and although the Republican Party was weak and divided over a new challenger within its ranks – the real estate developer and television star Donald Trump – many remained unconvinced by her.

Ronald Reagan had proven that high office could be obtained by leveraging individual star power, having won the governorship of California twice and the presidency twice. Other stars followed a path into politics, including actor Arnold Schwarzenegger, who was voted Governor of California from 2003–2011, and the wrestler and actor, Jesse Ventura, who became Governor of Minnesota from 1999–2003. Businessmen also ran for office, such as Michael Bloomberg in 2001 and 2019, and Herman Cain in 2012.

Initially, no one gave Donald Trump a chance. He had been the host of *The Apprentice* since 2004 and had significant real estate holdings, mostly in New York and New Jersey. He was abrasive, brash, and contemptuous of the usual proprieties expected of politicians, but he proved popular among people who felt ignored, and they liked that he was not a career politician. He also won the support of white evangelical Christians who preferred him to Clinton's left-wing faction within the Democrat Party that they anticipated would promote abortion rights, gay rights, and feminism.

During the primaries, many Republicans could not tolerate the idea of a Trump presidency and took an "Anyone But Trump" approach, but once he won the nomination, they swallowed their pride and closed ranks behind him. He campaigned under the slogan of "Make America Great Again," (MAGA) hoping to evoke memories of Ronald Reagan's 1980 campaign that used the same slogan, and pointed to illegal immigration, corruption on Capitol Hill, and badly negotiated trade deals as reasons to vote for him.

Right up to election day, there was a prevailing feeling among Americans that Hillary Clinton and the Democrat Party would win. Trump was surely too big a risk: in the run-up to the election, he claimed he paid no taxes, was caught on a hot mic making misogynistic comments, and was later accused of sexual misconduct and assault. No polls or commentators foresaw the result – and when Trump won, albeit by an extremely close margin (he lost the popular vote but prevailed in the Electoral College) – many news networks were left in shock as they were forced to acknowledge that they had been wrong.

Trump had no government or military experience and had no strong alignment with the Republican Party. He had considered running against George Bush, Sr. in 1988 and then ran against Bush, Jr. in 2000 as a candidate of the Reform Party. His success as a businessman was encouraging for those who missed riding the information revolution wave, and his MAGA slogan was intended to appeal to voters who wanted jobs and manufacturing brought back to the US.

Trump's term was characterized by deep partisan divisions. These were mostly reflected on Capitol Hill, where he was impeached twice, and in mainstream media, most of which was left-leaning and supported the Democrat Party. The phenomenon of social media also drove heated discussions and fueled new movements (#MeToo and Black Lives Matter). Barack Obama was the first president to use a social media platform (Twitter) as part of his official communication, but Donald Trump made it his preferred platform to message the public in real-time, sending over 2,600 tweets during his administration. News channels and political commentators eagerly awaited each as they contained spelling mistakes, attacks on individuals and the press, and his own interpretation of events.

Trump had to weather the Covid pandemic that was brought over from China at the end of 2019 and killed over 400,000 Americans while he was in office. His response to it mirrored many other nations': a combination of denial, minimization, fear, fury, and sudden strict lockdowns to prevent contagion. In truth, it was difficult to get the response right as some who caught the virus experienced little to no symptoms at all whereas others died within days. Trump himself caught it and was back at work within three days.

The Democrats hoped that an extensive two-year investigation into Russian interference in the 2016 election would uncover collusion between the Trump campaign and Russian agents. But it did not, and he was then impeached twice – once for requesting the president of Ukraine, Volodymyr Zelensky, launch an investigation into his political opponent, Joe Biden, in return for US military aid; and a second time for "inciting insurrection" after losing the 2020 election.

The Capitol being stormed on January 6th.

He appeared to encourage his supporters to attack the US Capitol on January 6, 2021, after he claimed, without evidence, that he had been fraudulently robbed of victory. Using language such as "if you don't fight like hell, you're not going to have a country anymore," and "we are going to the Capitol," a mob of approximately 10,000 people charged onto Capitol grounds, with 2,000 of them making their way into the building itself. They destroyed property, damaged furniture and artwork, and sent staff scurrying into offices and bunkers to hide. One protestor died, and more than 100 members of law enforcement were injured.

Trump was acquitted on both impeachment cases, although his claims of election fraud seemed to resonate badly with the public as the Republican Party made fewer gains than expected in the midterms of 2022. He has been personally beset by multiple legal troubles since he left office, but is still hoping to make a comeback in 2024.

The Joe Biden Administration

Joe Biden took advantage of Barack Obama's enduring popularity to seek the presidency for himself in 2020. He was nominated by a Democrat Party that had, under the Trump presidency, taken on a more left-wing flavor, and the Party felt Biden's more moderate approach would be the most unifying. He had vast amounts of experience, having worked as vice president to Obama for two terms and as a Delaware senator for 36 years prior to that. But as the oldest president in history at 78, he was visibly slow, often tripping over his words and appearing confused, and many questioned his capacity to meet the demands of the job. He has since announced that he will run for a second term, by which time he will be 82 (and 86 when his term ends).

An early challenge came in the summer of Biden's first term as he set about honoring one of his pledges during the election – pulling US troops out of Afghanistan. He targeted a withdrawal date of August 31, 2021, and as the US forces began pulling out, they were left stunned to see the Taliban recapturing cities and provinces within hours of the troops departing. The Afghanis were incapable of resistance, and Ashraf Ghani's democratically elected government collapsed when the Taliban took hold of Kabul on August 15.

A cascade of Afghani people attempted to leave. As a landlocked country, Kabul airport became a bottleneck for evacuees, and television cameras captured thousands climbing walls, begging and pleading to be allowed through. People were shown handing their babies to US troops, and others clung to aircraft as they took off, only to be thrown to the ground. The area became an enticing target for suicide bombers.

Biden stood squarely behind his decision to leave, presenting the choice in Afghanistan as one to remain indefinitely or to pull out now. But the catastrophic nature of the withdrawal provided isolationists with plenty of ammunition and raised questions as to why it could not have been done more efficiently. The US left behind approximately $7 billion of military equipment together with many foreign nationals and Afghan civilians who had supported the US. They held their breath – along with women, and religious and ethnic minorities – and it seemed that another humanitarian crisis was just around the corner.

Foreign policy remained high on the agenda when, in February 2022, Russia invaded Ukraine. The president of Russia, Vladimir Putin (who has been in power since 2000), spoke in the rhetoric of the Cold War, claiming that any Western intervention would be met with "defeat and ominous consequences should it directly attack [Russia]," leaving the US and most of the West in shock. It came at a time when international cooperation was high and many businesses had outsourced much of their energy and supply chain needs, and a reevaluation of Western reliance on Russian energy and of diplomatic relations with Russia and its allies (notably China) immediately began to take place. Western governments took a moral stance, arguing against unprovoked invasions and for the rights of the Ukrainian people, and they imposed sanctions on Russian individuals and companies. Ukraine was not part of NATO, but they provided military equipment for the Ukrainian army.

The United States, whose military capabilities far outweighed any other Western country, was still reeling from its exit from Afghanistan and refused to provide Ukraine with troops on the ground, even though the case for military engagement was arguably stronger than it had been for the wars in either Iraq or Afghanistan. Putin responded by drafting thousands of men and ordering missiles to rain down on Ukrainian cities including Kyiv, Kharkiv, and Kherson. The situation remains unresolved, but Biden received plaudits for keeping NATO and the West united in their condemnation of Russia.

At home, the Federal Reserve ended its low interest rate policy that had been in place ever since the Great Recession of 2008. Since then, the Fed had kept interest rates low to stimulate the economy, but this had led to inflation, and as soon as interest rates climbed, the S&P 500 tanked by almost 20 percent – its biggest decline since 2008 – as investors worried about how companies and individuals would manage their increased debt load. The US readied itself for a recession and many big technology companies responded by laying off employees, although excitement about the possibilities of artificial intelligence at the beginning of 2023 helped to pick the economy back up.

At the time of writing, uncertainties remain. The trend of globalization and international cooperation seems to have reached a high-water mark, and many American companies are reducing their international presence by repatriating production and manufacturing facilities. This will influence the economy and may undermine foreign relations in the future, with the United States particularly wary of China. China's president, Xi Jinping, is ruling in a more authoritarian way than his predecessors, and military deployments and movements have been detected in the Taiwan Strait. The US will have to use all its tools of diplomacy to ensure stability in the region is maintained.

Looking forward, the presidential candidates are gearing up for the election of 2024. It is shaping up to be another showdown between Biden and Trump - which the public is showing little appetite for – although whoever is nominated will need to make their position clear on a range of issues. These include taming inflation, growing the economy, preserving and developing foreign relations (including how to help conclude the war in Ukraine and how to handle military and economic competition from China), reforming immigration, advancing civil rights, and tackling climate change. It is a daunting list, but if gotten right, will undoubtedly enhance the quality of life for every American.

CONCLUSION
THE USA IN 2023

The United States in 2023 continues to be one of the most attractive countries for people to live, work, and study in, but it has its problems too. Partisan politics, income inequality, racism, immigration, and gun control are all persistent issues that lack easy solutions.

Politics has become increasingly partisan as Republicans and Democrats reflexively support their own party. Because no one is prepared to compromise, proposed legislation often goes nowhere, and the checks and balances system becomes largely ineffective – when a president abuses his power, his party members are unlikely to hold him to account, and he can issue executive orders with little pushback. President Trump obtained his party's support after his attempted coercion of President Zelensky in 2019, and President Biden received support from the Democrats for his botched exit from Afghanistan.

Economically, the country's gross domestic product is the highest in the world, standing at $23 trillion (China's is second at $17 trillion, and Japan's is third at $5 trillion), but over 10 percent of this is driven by the technology sector, much of which is in the hands of a few. Income inequality arguably gives the rich an unfair amount of control in society, often prompting the government to float the idea of taxing them more primarily so that it can finance federal programs. Currently, the Medicare trust will be able to pay only 90 percent of its costs by 2028, and retirees will receive only 76 percent of their Social Security payments by 2037. Other financing options – such as raising income tax, cutting government spending, and implementing austerity measures – are very unappealing to a political party that is trying to win votes. For the time being, the federal debt just keeps rising.

Race relations remain volatile, with rioting and violence occurring every few years after a period of calmness. The year 1992 saw large-scale rioting after a white jury acquitted four police officers for the beating of Rodney King, and in 1995, OJ Simpson was exonerated by a predominantly Black jury despite solid evidence against him. The years 2001, 2014, and 2020 all saw rioting occur in cities across the country due to the deaths of Black men at the hands of white policemen, and the Black Lives Matter movement, while drawing attention to the racism issue, also caused over 1 billion dollars' worth of property damage.

The United States remains an attractive option for immigrants, but for most, it is very difficult to get in. One way is for people to claim asylum once they have arrived in the United States or have otherwise reached the border. With no cap on the number of asylum seekers the United States will accept (the number of refugees, a different status, is established annually by the president is currently capped at 125,000 per year), hundreds of thousands have made their way to the border between Mexico and the United States to claim it. At present, there are over 1.6 million asylum applications awaiting review, which represents a 687 percent increase in cases in ten years. The government continues to struggle with finding an appropriate response.

Gun crime and gun control are unique problems for the United States. The right to bear arms is written into the Constitution and has attained a sacrosanct status, but the high-tech weaponry available for purchase today far exceeds an individual's needs. The year 2020 saw the highest number of Americans killed by a firearm, reaching over 45,000. In the last 30 years, deadly mass shootings have occurred at schools, colleges, shopping centers, nightclubs, concerts, and churches, with the shooter able to claim dozens of lives and injure hundreds more in a matter of minutes. The Obama and Biden administrations both tried to pass gun control legislation after children were shot to death in schools, but opposition from Congress and interest groups such as the National Rifle Association (NRA) stymied their efforts.

***

However, the United States has an incredible abundance of riches to offer its citizens. First, it is politically stable. The American Constitution is the world's oldest written charter of government, and its founding documents nurture and protect individual freedoms, and prevent the concentration of power among its leaders. Such lofty goals are not always met, but they serve as a moral compass for governance and, in contrast to many countries, the peaceful transfer of power is respected. The armed forces do not become directly involved in political life and, although George Washington, Andrew Jackson, and Dwight D Eisenhower were all war heroes who became president, they were voted in or elected according to the law. Radicals or strongmen have never overthrown the government.

Second, the US is exceptionally fortunate in its location. It has access to an incredible range of natural resources and is separated from much of the world by two enormous oceans.

Vast reserves of oil, coal, and gas provide for Americans' energy needs, and the oceans give the US unparalleled security. The only existential threat to its existence has come internally (the US Civil War) rather than externally.

Third, the US has fully embraced capitalism and a market economy. These incentivize entrepreneurs to start businesses and create wealth while providing consumers with a huge array of choices. Capitalism can lead to wealth inequality, exploitation, and market crashes, but the only other real alternative to a market economy is a command economy – such as that employed by the Soviet Union between 1917 and 1990. While this led to rapid industrial expansion, it stifled innovation, limited consumer choices, and fostered corruption.

Finally, the US has been remarkably successful at assimilating and integrating diverse groups of people from all over the world. Ethnic and religious rivalries dominate politics in many countries, and even Canada struggles to assimilate its Québécoise citizens, many of whom speak French and want to secede to preserve their culture. The US is guilty of having treated certain ethnicities unequally – primarily Native Americans and African Americans (and also its Japanese citizens in the Second World War and its Mexican citizens in the Great Depression), but multiculturalism thrives in the US today, and people are free to vote, pray, and protest and they are treated equally and fairly in the eyes of the law.

The term "American exceptionalism" is occasionally used to describe how the US stands apart from other countries in the world. It was first used by Alexis de Tocqueville in 1831 and is closely associated with John Winthrop's notion of the US acting as a beacon for the rest of the world as a "city upon a hill." It naturally invites criticism for its implied message of superiority, but the US is exceptional in that, as the English philosopher and writer G K Chesterton noted, it "is the only nation in the world that is founded on a creed." Most countries began their lives through a common ethnicity, a shared religion, or a communal history – but the US was founded on the principles of freedom, liberty, and equality. You would be hard-pressed to find someone who does not want to live in a world like that.

For more, please sign up for surveys, updates, news, and information about future publications on www.historyina-heartbeat.com/news.

APPENDICES

APPENDIX A

Founding Documents of the United States

Name of Document	Date Ratified
The Declaration of Independence	July 4, 1776
The Constitution	May 29, 1790[111]
The Bill of Rights	December 15, 1791

---

111 This is the date the last state, Rhode Island, ratified the Constitution. Delaware was the first state to ratify it on December 7, 1787.

APPENDIX B

Bill of Rights and Later Amendments

#	Amendment	Date Ratified
1	Freedoms, Petitions, Assembly	December 15, 1791[112]
2	Right to bear arms	December 15, 1791
3	Quartering of soldiers	December 15, 1791
4	Search and arrest	December 15, 1791
5	Rights in criminal cases	December 15, 1791
6	Right to a fair trial	December 15, 1791
7	Rights in civil cases	December 15, 1791
8	Bail, fines, punishment	December 15, 1791
9	Rights retained by the People	December 15, 1791
10	States' rights	December 15, 1791
11	Lawsuits against states	February 7, 1795
12	Presidential elections	June 15, 1804
13	Abolition of slavery	December 6, 1865
14	Civil rights	July 9, 1868
15	Black suffrage	February 3, 1870
16	Income taxes	February 3, 1913
17	Senatorial elections	April 8, 1913
18	Prohibition of liquor	January 16, 1919
19	Women's suffrage	August 18, 1920
20	Terms of office	January 23, 1933
21	Repeal of Prohibition	December 5, 1933
22	Term Limits for the Presidency	February 27, 1951
23	Washington, DC, suffrage	March 29, 1961
24	Abolition of poll taxes	January 23, 1964
25	Presidential succession	February 10, 1967
26	18-year-old suffrage	June 30, 1971
27	Congressional pay raises	May 7, 1992

112 The first ten Amendments are part of the Bill of Rights.

APPENDIX C

Founding Fathers of United States

There are many others who contributed to the founding of the United States, but these are considered by most to be the Founding Fathers

#	Name
1	George Washington
2	Thomas Jefferson
3	John Adams
4	Benjamin Franklin
5	Alexander Hamilton
6	John Jay
7	James Madison

APPENDIX D

List of Presidents

List of US Presidents with dates of terms and parties

#	Name	Party	Years in Office
1	George Washington	None	1789–1796
2	John Adams	Federalist	1797–1800
3	Thomas Jefferson	Democratic-Republican	1801–1808
4	James Madison	Democratic-Republican	1809–1816
5	James Monroe	Democratic-Republican	1817–1824
6	John Quincy Adams	Democratic-Republican	1825–1828
7	Andrew Jackson	Democrat	1829–1836
8	Martin Van Buren	Democrat	1837–1840
9	William Henry Harrison	Whig	1841
10	John Tyler	Whig	1841–1844
11	James Polk	Democrat	1845–1848
12	Zachary Taylor	Whig	1849
13	Millard Fillmore	Whig	1849–1852
14	Franklin Pierce	Democrat	1853–1856
15	James Buchanan	Democrat	1857–1860
16	Abraham Lincoln	Republican	1861–1864
17	Andrew Johnson	National Union	1865–1868
18	Ulysses S Grant	Republican	1869–1876
19	Rutherford B Hayes	Republican	1877–1880
20	James Garfield	Republican	1881
21	Chester Arthur	Republican	1881–1884
22	Grover Cleveland	Democrat	1885–1888
23	Benjamin Harrison	Republican	1889–1892

24	Grover Cleveland	Democrat	1893–1896
25	William McKinley	Republican	1897–1900
26	Theodore Roosevelt	Republican	1901–1908
27	William Howard Taft	Republican	1909–1912
28	Woodrow Wilson	Democrat	1913–1920
29	Warren G Harding	Republican	1921–1922
30	Calvin Coolidge	Republican	1923–1928
31	Herbert Hoover	Republican	1929–1932
32	Franklin Roosevelt	Democrat	1933–1944
33	Harry S Truman	Democrat	1945–1952
34	Dwight D Eisenhower	Republican	1953–1960
35	John F Kennedy	Democrat	1961–1962
36	Lyndon B Johnson	Democrat	1962–1968
37	Richard Nixon	Republican	1969–1973
38	Gerald Ford	Republican	1974–1976
39	Jimmy Carter	Democrat	1977–1980
40	Ronald Reagan	Republican	1981–1988
41	George Bush	Republican	1989–1992
42	Bill Clinton	Democrat	1993–2000
43	George W Bush	Republican	2001–2008
44	Barack Obama	Democrat	2009–2016
45	Donald Trump	Republican	2017–2020
46	Joe Biden	Democrat	2021–

APPENDIX E

List of States

List of States with date of admission into the Union

#	State	Abbreviation	State Capital	Year of Admission
1	Delaware	DE	Dover	1787
2	Pennsylvania	PA	Harrisburg	1787
3	New Jersey	NJ	Trenton	1787
4	Georgia	GA	Atlanta	1788
5	Connecticut	CT	Hartford	1788
6	Massachusetts	MA	Boston	1788
7	Maryland	MD	Annapolis	1788
8	South Carolina	SC	Columbia	1788
9	New Hampshire	NH	Concord	1788
10	Virginia	VA	Richmond	1788
11	New York	NY	Albany	1788
12	North Carolina	NC	Raleigh	1789
13	Rhode Island	RI	Providence	1790
14	Vermont	VT	Montpelier	1791
15	Kentucky	KY	Frankfort	1792
16	Tennessee	TN	Nashville	1796
17	Ohio	OH	Columbus	1803
18	Louisiana	LA	Baton Rouge	1812
19	Indiana	IN	Indianapolis	1816
20	Mississippi	MS	Jackson	1817
21	Illinois	IL	Springfield	1818
22	Alabama	AL	Montgomery	1819

23	Maine	ME	Augusta	1820
24	Missouri	MO	Jefferson City	1821
25	Arkansas	AR	Little Rock	1836
26	Michigan	MI	Lansing	1837
27	Florida	FL	Tallahassee	1845
28	Texas	TX	Austin	1845
29	Iowa	IA	Des Moines	1846
30	Wisconsin	WI	Madison	1848
31	California	CA	Sacramento	1850
32	Minnesota	MN	Saint Paul	1858
33	Oregon	OR	Salem	1859
34	Kansas	KS	Topeka	1861
35	West Virginia	WV	Charleston	1863
36	Nevada	NV	Carson City	1864
37	Nebraska	NE	Lincoln	1867
38	Colorado	CO	Denver	1876
39	North Dakota	ND	Bismarck	1889
40	South Dakota	SD	Pierre	1889
41	Montana	MT	Helena	1889
42	Washington	WA	Olympia	1889
43	Idaho	ID	Boise	1890
44	Wyoming	WY	Cheyenne	1890
45	Utah	UT	Salt Lake City	1896
46	Oklahoma	OK	Oklahoma City	1907
47	New Mexico	NM	Santa Fe	1912
48	Arizona	AZ	Phoenix	1912
49	Alaska	AK	Juneau	1959
50	Hawaii	HI	Honolulu	1959

APPENDIX F

Largest Cities in the US by Population Size (2023)

#	City	State	Population Size (m)
1	New York City	NY	8.992
2	Los Angeles	CA	3.898
3	Chicago	IL	2.761
4	Houston	TX	2.366
5	Phoenix	AZ	1.656
6	Philadelphia	PA	1.627
7	San Antonio	TX	1.466
8	San Diego	CA	1.410
9	Dallas	TX	1.336
10	San Jose	CA	1.033
11	Austin	TX	1.013
12	Jacksonville	FL	0.987
13	Fort Worth	TX	0.972
14	Columbus	OH	0.941
15	Charlotte	NC	0.917
16	Indianapolis	IN	0.907
17	San Francisco	CA	0.894
18	Seattle	WA	0.775
19	Denver	CO	0.750
20	Nashville	TN	0.715

APPENDIX G

National Parks by Size

There are 424 national park sites in the US. These are categorized into different types including National Battlefields, National Historical Sites, National Memorials, and National Monuments.

There are 63 parks that include the term "National Park" in their name. These are listed below by size:

#	National Park Name	State	Size (sq miles)
1	Wrangell–St. Elias	AL	20,587
2	Gates of the Arctic	AL	13,238
3	Denali	AL	9,446
4	Katmai	AL	6,395
5	Lake Clark	AL	6,297
6	Death Valley	CA | NV	5,269
7	Glacier Bay	AL	5,037
8	Yellowstone	WY | MT	3,472
9	Kobuk Valley	AL	2,735
10	Everglades	FL	2,357
11	Grand Canyon	AZ	1,904
12	Glacier	MT	1,583
13	Olympic	WA	1,442
14	Big Bend	TX	1,252
15	Joshua Tree	CA	1,242
16	Yosemite	CA	1,187
17	Kenai Fjords	AL	1,047
18	Isle Royale	MI	893

19	Great Smoky Mountains	TN	816
20	North Cascades	WA	789
21	Kings Canyon	CA	722
22	Sequoia	CA	631
23	Canyonlands	UT	527
24	Hawaii Volcanoes	HI	505
25	Grand Teton	WY	485
26	Rocky Mountain	CO	415
27	Channel Islands	CA	390
28	Badlands	SD	379
29	Capitol Reef	UT	377
30	Mount Rainier	WA	369
31	Petrified Forest	AZ	346
32	Voyageurs	MN	341
33	Shenandoah	VA	306
34	Crater Lake	OR	286
35	Biscayne	FL	270
36	Great Sand Dunes	CO	233
37	Zion	UT	229
38	White Sands	NM	228
39	Redwood	CA	206
40	Lassen Volcanic	CA	166
41	Saguaro	AZ	143
42	Guadalupe Mountains	TX	135
43	Great Basin	NV	121
44	Arches	UT	119
45	New River George	WV	114
46	Theodore Roosevelt	ND	110
47	Dry Tortugas	FL	101
48	Mammoth Cave	KY	83
49	Mesa Verde	CO	82
50	Acadia	ME	76
51	Carlsbad Caverns	NM	73
52	Bryce Canyon	UT	56
53	Wind Cave	SD	53

54	Haleakala	HI	52
55	Cuyahoga Valley	OH	51
56	Black Canyon of the Gunnison	CO	48
57	Congaree	SC	42
58	Pinnacles	CA	42
59	Indiana Dunes	IN	24
60	Virgin Islands	Virgin Islands, USA	23
61	American Samoa	American Samoa	13
62	Hot Springs	AR	9
63	Gateway Arch	MO	0.14

APPENDIX H

Native American Tribes

There are 574 federally recognized tribes in the US, of which 229 are located in Alaska.

Below is a list of the ten largest by population size:

#	Tribe	Population (2021)
1	Cherokee	819,105
2	Navajo	332,129
3	Choctaw	195,764
4	Chippewa	170,742
5	Sioux	170,110
6	Apache	111,810
7	Blackfeet	105,304
8	Creek (Muscogee)	88,332
9	Iroquois	81,002
10	Lumbee	73,691

APPENDIX I

Federal Holidays

#	Holiday Name	Date
1	New Year's Day	January 1st
2	Martin Luther King Day	3rd Monday in January
3	Washington's Birthday / Presidents' Day	3rd Monday in February
4	Memorial Day	Last Monday in May
5	Juneteenth National Independence Day	June 19th
6	Independence Day	July 4th
7	Labor Day	1st Monday in September
8	Columbus Day	2nd Monday in October
9	Veterans Day	November 11th
10	Thanksgiving Day	4th Thursday in November
11	Christmas Day	December 25th

BIBLIOGRAPHY

INTRODUCTION

"Immigration by Country 2023," accessed July 20, 2023, https://worldpopulation-review.com/country-rankings/immigration-by-country.

PART ONE: ORIGINS

"Late Precambrian, Paleozoic, Mesozoic, and Cenozoic Era Study Guide | Inspirit," accessed August 7, 2022, https://www.inspiritvr.com/general-bio/ecology/late-precambrian-paleozoic-mesozoic-and-cenozoic-era-study-guide.

"This Is What The World Looked Like 300 Million Years Ago," Bored Panda (blog), accessed August 7, 2022, https://www.boredpanda.com/pangea-maps-world-300-million-years-ago/.

"Continental Drift | National Geographic Society," accessed August 7, 2022, https://education.nationalgeographic.org/resource/continental-drift.

"What Was Pangea? | U.S. Geological Survey," accessed August 7, 2022, https://www.usgs.gov/faqs/what-was-pangea.

Laura Geggel, "First Americans May Have Arrived to the Continent 30,000 Years Ago | Live Science," accessed April 19, 2023, https://www.livescience.com/first-north-americans-30000-years-ago.html.

Smithsonian Magazine and Douglas Preston, "The Kennewick Man Finally Freed to Share His Secrets," Smithsonian Magazine, accessed August 7, 2022, https://www.smithsonianmag.com/history/kennewick-man-finally-freed-share-his-secrets-180952462/.

Gordon Willey and Philip Phillips, Method and Theory in American Archaeology, n.d.

"Native American - Native American History | Britannica," accessed August 7, 2022, https://www.britannica.com/topic/Native-American/Native-American-history.

Connie J. Mulligan and Emőke J.E. Szathmáry, "The Peopling of the Americas and the Origin of the Beringian Occupation Model: MULLIGAN and SZATHMÁRY," American Journal of Physical Anthropology 162, no. 3 (March 2017): 403–8, https://doi.org/10.1002/ajpa.23152.

"Cahokia," World History Encyclopedia, accessed August 7, 2022, https://www.world-history.org/cahokia/.

Christopher B. Rodning, "Medieval Mississippians: The Cahokian World," Southeastern Archaeology 38, no. 2 (2018): 161.

"Years In Spain: Columbus Finds a Sponsor | Religious Studies Center," accessed August 8, 2022, https://rsc.byu.edu/christopher-columbus-latter-day-saint-perspective/years-spain-columbus-finds-sponsor.

"The Mariners' Museum | EXPLORATION through the AGES," December 11, 2014, https://web.archive.org/web/20141211112431/http://ageofex.marinersmuseum.org/index.php?type=explorer&id=67.

"Champlain's Fight With the Iroquois, 1609," accessed August 8, 2022, https://www.cwjefferys.ca/champlain-s-fight-with-the-iroquois-1609.

"New France [Ushistory.Org]," accessed August 9, 2022, https://www.ushistory.org/Us/8a.asp.

"The Dutch Economy in the Golden Age (16th – 17th Centuries)," accessed August 9, 2022, https://eh.net/encyclopedia/the-dutch-economy-in-the-golden-age-16th-17th-centuries/.

"Iroquois-Dutch Trade Established: 1614," accessed August 9, 2022, https://www.lermuseum.org/new-france-1600-1730/1600-1649/iroquois-dutch-trade-established-1614.

"The Rise and Fall of New Netherland - Martin Van Buren National Historic Site (U.S. National Park Service)," accessed August 9, 2022, https://www.nps.gov/mava/learn/historyculture/new-netherland.htm.

Owen Jarus, "What Happened to the 'vanished' Colonists at Roanoke?," livescience.com, November 20, 2021, https://www.livescience.com/vanished-colonists-at-roanoke.

"History of Jamestown – Jamestown Rediscovery," November 7, 2015, https://web.archive.org/web/20151107053739/http://www.apva.org/history/.

"Pocahontas: Her Life and Legend - Historic Jamestowne Part of Colonial National Historical Park (U.S. National Park Service)," accessed October 30, 2022, https://www.nps.gov/jame/learn/historyculture/pocahontas-her-life-and-legend.htm.

James Henretta, "Salutary Neglect," Encyclopedia Virginia, accessed April 20, 2023, https://encyclopediavirginia.org/entries/salutary-neglect/.

"Mayflower and Mayflower Compact," Plimoth Patuxet Museums, accessed October 21, 2022, https://plimoth.org/for-students/homework-help/mayflower-and-mayflower-compact.

Terry L. Anderson and Robert Paul Thomas, "White Population, Labor Force and Extensive Growth of the New England Economy in the Seventeenth Century," The Journal of Economic History 33, no. 3 (1973): 634–67.

"History of King Philip's War," History of Massachusetts Blog (blog), accessed August 10, 2022, https://historyofmassachusetts.org/what-was-king-philips-war/.

"Fundamental Constitution of Carolina," South Carolina Encyclopedia (blog), accessed October 21, 2022, https://www.scencyclopedia.org/sce/entries/fundamental-constitution-of-carolina/.

Francis Newton Thorpe, "The Federal and State constitutions, colonial charters, and other organic laws of the state[s], territories, and colonies now or heretofore forming the United States of America /compiled and edited under the Act of Congress of June 30, 1906," Text (Washington, DC: Government Printing Office, 1909, December 18, 1998), https://avalon.law.yale.edu/17th_century/nc05.asp.

"Oglethorpe as a Georgia Trustee," Georgia Historical Society (blog), accessed August 9, 2022, https://georgiahistory.com/education-outreach/online-exhibits/featured-historical-figures/james-edward-oglethorpe/oglethorpe-georgias-trustee/.

"Trustee Georgia, 1732-1752," New Georgia Encyclopedia (blog), accessed October 21, 2022, https://www.georgiaencyclopedia.org/articles/history-archaeology/trustee-georgia-1732-1752/.

Caroine"American Passages, A History of the United States | Interactive Maps," accessed August 10, 2022, https://college.cengage.com/history/us/ayers/am_passages/3e/improve/maps/map05.html.

Evan Andrews, "America's Forgotten Swedish Colony," HISTORY, accessed August 10, 2022, https://www.history.com/news/americas-forgotten-swedish-colony.

Hans Fantel, William Penn: Apostle of Dissent (William Morrow & Co, 1974).

"Early Quaker Families, 1650-1800," Friends Journal, June 1, 2009, https://www.friendsjournal.org/2009060/.

Legislative Data Processing Center, "The Constitution of Pennsylvania," The official website for the Pennsylvania General Assembly., accessed October 21, 2022, https://www.legis.state.pa.us/cfdocs/legis/LI/consCheck.cfm?txtType=HTM&ttl=00&div=0&chpt=6.

"The Last Days of William Penn," Pennsylvania Heritage Magazine, accessed October 21, 2022, http://paheritage.wpengine.com/article/last-days-william-penn/.

"Colonial Economy < A Historical Perspective on the American Economy < Economy 1991 < American History From Revolution To Reconstruction and Beyond," accessed October 21, 2022, http://www.let.rug.nl/usa/outlines/economy-1991/a-historical-perspective-on-the-american-economy/colonial-economy.php.

"Indentured Servants In The U.S. | History Detectives | PBS," accessed August 10, 2022, https://www.pbs.org/opb/historydetectives/feature/indentured-servants-in-the-us/.

"Indentured Servitude in Colonial America," October 22, 2009, https://web.archive.org/web/20091022161033/http:/geocities.com/nai_cilh/servitude.html.

"Property Requirements for Voting in Virginia, 1670-1850," accessed August 10, 2022, http://www.virginiaplaces.org/government/voteproperty.html#three.

"Africans in America/Part 1/Bacon's Rebellion," accessed August 10, 2022, https://www.pbs.org/wgbh/aia/part1/1p274.html.

"The First Africans to Virginia—1619," The Gilder Lehrman Center for the Study of Slavery, Resistance, and Abolition, April 9, 2015, https://glc.yale.edu/first-africans-virginia-1619.

Jessica Millward, "From the Ocean Floor: Death, Memory and the Atlantic Slave Trade," AAIHS, March 8, 2017, https://www.aaihs.org/from-the-ocean-floor-death-memory-and-the-atlantic-slave-trade/.

Brendan Wolfe, "Slave Ships," Encyclopedia Virginia (blog), accessed October 22, 2022, https://encyclopediavirginia.org/entries/slave-ships-and-the-middle-passage/.

"Historical Context: Facts about the Slave Trade and Slavery | Gilder Lehrman Institute of American History," accessed August 10, 2022, https://www.gilderlehrman.org/history-resources/teaching-resource/historical-context-facts-about-slave-trade-and-slavery.

J. David Hacker, "From '20. and Odd' to 10 Million: The Growth of the Slave Population in the United States," Slavery & Abolition 41, no. 4 (2020): 840–55, https://doi.org/10.1080/0144039x.2020.1755502.

US Census Bureau, "The Incandescent Light Bulb (1879): October 22-23, 2022," Census.gov, accessed April 21, 2023, https://www.census.gov/newsroom/stories/incandescent-light-bulb.html.

Smithsonian Magazine, "A Brief History of the Salem Witch Trials," Smithsonian Magazine, accessed August 11, 2022, https://www.smithsonianmag.com/history/a-brief-history-of-the-salem-witch-trials-175162489/.

"Chronology Prior to Salem Trials," Salem Witch Museum, accessed August 11, 2022, https://salemwitchmuseum.com/chronology-prior-to-salem-trials/.

"God In America - People - George Whitefield," God in America, accessed August 12, 2022, http://www.pbs.org/godinamerica/people/george-whitefield.html.

Aaron Sharp, "Unlikely Friends: The Remarkable Story of George Whitefield and Benjamin Franklin," Leben (blog), April 1, 2009, https://leben.us/unlikely-friends/.

Jonathan Edwards and Reiner Smolinski, "Sinners in the Hands of an Angry God. A Sermon Preached at Enfield, July 8th, 1741.," n.d., 35.

"Summary Religious Affections," accessed October 23, 2022, http://individual.utoronto.ca/hayes/edwards/Affections.htm.

"What Was the Great Awakening? Know the Facts & Summary," Christianity.com, accessed August 12, 2022, https://www.christianity.com/church/church-history/timeline/1701-1800/the-great-awakening-11630212.html.

"The Life of George Whitefield," Banner of Truth USA, May 13, 2015, https://banner-oftruth.org/us/resources/articles/2015/life-george-whitefield/.

"Estimated Population of American Colonies," accessed August 12, 2022, https://web.viu.ca/davies/H320/population.colonies.htm.

S. D. Smith, "The Market for Manufactures in the Thirteen Continental Colonies, 1698-1776," The Economic History Review 51, no. 4 (1998): 676–708.

"What Is Mercantilism?," The Balance, accessed August 12, 2022, https://www.thebalance.com/mercantilism-definition-examples-significance-today-4163347.

Rebecca Beatrice Brooks, "What Was the British Policy of Salutary Neglect?," History of Massachusetts Blog (blog), accessed August 12, 2022, https://historyofmassachu-setts.org/what-was-the-british-policy-of-salutary-neglect/.

"French & British Military Conflict (1664-1763) – Lake Champlain Maritime Museum," accessed August 12, 2022, https://www.lcmm.org/explore/lake-champlain-history/french-british-military-conflict-1664-1763/.

"French and Indian War," accessed August 12, 2022, https://www.ushistory.org/declaration/related/frin.html.

"The Mariners' Museum: Birth of the U.S. Navy," accessed August 13, 2022, https://www.marinersmuseum.org/sites/micro/usnavy/02.htm.

"George III by Allan Ramsay, 1762," The American Revolution Institute (blog), accessed August 13, 2022, https://www.americanrevolutioninstitute.org/asset/george-iii-by-allan-ramsay-ca-1761-62/.

"How Did the Treaty of Paris Divide Land in North America? | Socratic," Socratic.org, accessed August 13, 2022, https://socratic.org/questions/how-did-the-treaty-of-paris-divide-land-in-north-america.

OpenStaxCollege, "Confronting the National Debt: The Aftermath of the French and Indian War," May 7, 2014, http://pressbooks-dev.oer.hawaii.edu/ushistory/chapter/confronting-the-national-debt-the-aftermath-of-the-french-and-indian-war/.

"Whigs | Encyclopedia.Com," accessed August 13, 2022, https://www.encyclopedia.com/history/modern-europe/british-and-irish-history/whigs.

"The Mariners' Museum : Birth of the U.S. Navy."

Boston Tea Party Ships & Museum, "Sons of Liberty American History 1765," Boston Tea Party Ships (blog), September 23, 2019, https://www.bostonteapartyship.com/sons-of-liberty.

"Resolutions of the Stamp Act Congress," Teaching American History (blog), accessed August 13, 2022, https://teachingamericanhistory.org/document/resolutions-of-the-stamp-act-congress-2/.

History com Editors, "Stamp Act," HISTORY, accessed August 13, 2022, https://www.history.com/topics/american-revolution/stamp-act.

History.com Editors, "Townshend Acts," HISTORY, accessed August 13, 2022, https://www.history.com/topics/american-revolution/townshend-acts.

"The Tea Act," accessed August 13, 2022, https://www.ushistory.org/declaration/related/teaact.html.

"Milestones: 1750–1775 - Office of the Historian," accessed August 13, 2022, https://history.state.gov/milestones/1750-1775/parliamentary-taxation.

"Lexington and Concord," American Battlefield Trust, accessed August 13, 2022, https://www.battlefields.org/learn/revolutionary-war/battles/lexington-and-concord.

"Continental Army," in Wikipedia, July 31, 2022, https://en.wikipedia.org/w/index.php?title=Continental_Army&oldid=1101440980.

Ross, Tara, "This Day in History: The British Hire Hessians to Fight American Colonists," Tara Ross (blog), April 27, 2022, https://www.taraross.com/post/tdih-british-hessians.

"1776 | Timeline | Articles and Essays | Documents from the Continental Congress and the Constitutional Convention, 1774-1789 | Digital Collections | Library of Congress," web page, Library of Congress, Washington, D.C. 20540 USA, accessed August 14, 2022, https://www.loc.gov/collections/continental-congress-and-constitutional-convention-from-1774-to-1789/articles-and-essays/timeline/1776/.

"Richard Henry Lee Quotes," Quote.org, accessed August 14, 2022, https://quote.org/quote/these-colonies-are-and-of-right-ought-608895.

"Challenges of the Articles of Confederation (Article) | Khan Academy," accessed October 24, 2022, https://www.khanacademy.org/_render.

"Milestones: 1776–1783 - Office of the Historian," accessed August 14, 2022, https://history.state.gov/milestones/1776-1783/secret-committee.

"American Revolutionary War," in Wikipedia, August 13, 2022, https://en.wikipedia.org/w/index.php?title=American_Revolutionary_War&oldid=1104174204.

"Banastre Tarleton," in Wikipedia, August 13, 2022, https://en.wikipedia.org/w/index.php?title=Banastre_Tarleton&oldid=1104143257.

"Horatio Gates," George Washington's Mount Vernon, accessed August 14, 2022, https://www.mountvernon.org/library/digitalhistory/digital-encyclopedia/article/horatio-gates/.

"Kings Mountain," American Battlefield Trust, accessed August 15, 2022, https://www.battlefields.org/learn/revolutionary-war/battles/kings-mountain.

"A Hanging at Sunshine," Remember Cliffside (blog), accessed August 15, 2022, https://remembercliffside.com/the-county/a-hanging-at-sunshine/.

History.com Editors, "Mutiny of the Pennsylvania Line," HISTORY, accessed August 15, 2022, https://www.history.com/this-day-in-history/mutiny-of-the-pennsylvania-line.

T. A. Wellington, "1783: Benjamin Franklin Tries to Claim Canada & Other Quebec Curios," Montreal Rampage, accessed August 15, 2022, https://montrealrampage. com/1783-benjamin-franklin-tries-to-claim-canada-other-quebec-curios/.

"Constitutional Rights Foundation," accessed August 15, 2022, https://www.crf-usa. org/bill-of-rights-in-action/bria-8-1-b-who-voted-in-early-america.

"The Maryland State House," accessed April 21, 2023, https://msa.maryland.gov/msa/ mdstatehouse/html/gwresignation.html.

"A History of the United States, 2nd Edition," accessed September 13, 2023,

https://www.wondrium.com/a-history-of-the-united-states-2nd-edition.

PART TWO: INDEPENDENCE

"After the Revolution | American Experience | PBS," accessed August 15, 2022, https://www.pbs.org/wgbh/americanexperience/features/midwife-after-revolution/.

History.com Editors, "State of Franklin Declares Independence," HISTORY, accessed August 15, 2022, https://www.history.com/this-day-in-history/ state-of-franklin-declares-independence.

"Daniel Shays," in Wikipedia, May 14, 2022, https://en.wikipedia.org/w/index. php?title=Daniel_Shays&oldid=1087735773.

"State Constitutions [Ushistory.Org]," accessed August 15, 2022, https://www. ushistory.org/us/14a.asp.

"Meet the Framers of the Constitution," National Archives, November 2, 2015, https:// www.archives.gov/founding-docs/founding-fathers.

"The Only Unavoidable Subject of Regret," George Washington's Mount Vernon, accessed April 25, 2023, https://www.mountvernon.org/george-washington/slavery/ the-only-unavoidable-subject-of-regret/.

"James Madison and the Bill of Rights," Bill of Rights Institute, accessed April 3, 2023, https://billofrightsinstitute.org/essays/james-madison-and-the-bill-of-rights/.

"Cabinet Members," George Washington's Mount Vernon, accessed August 16, 2022, https://www.mountvernon.org/library/digitalhistory/digital-encyclopedia/article/ cabinet-members/.

"TreasuryDirect KIDS - The History of U.S. Public Debt - The Beginning of U.S. Debt," accessed October 24, 2022, https://www.treasurydirect.gov/kids/history/history.htm.

"First Report on the Public Credit," in Wikipedia, September 6, 2021, https://en.wiki-pedia.org/w/index.php?title=First_Report_on_the_Public_Credit&oldid=1042659267.

"The Report on Public Credit," accessed August 16, 2022, https://www.u-s-history. com/pages/h441.html.

Phil Davies, "The Bank That Hamilton Built | Federal Reserve Bank of Minneapolis," accessed August 16, 2022, https://www.minneapolisfed.org:443/article/2007/ the-bank-that-hamilton-built.

"Alexander Hamilton: A Manufacturing Visionary," NIST, December 5, 2016, https://www.nist.gov/mep/manufacturing-infographics/ alexander-hamilton-manufacturing-visionary.

"Hamilton's Reports | Encyclopedia.Com," accessed August 16, 2022, https:// www.encyclopedia.com/defense/energy-government-and-defense-magazines/ hamiltons-reports.

"The First Bank of the United States | Federal Reserve History," accessed August 16, 2022, https://www.federalreservehistory.org/essays/first-bank-of-the-us.

Robert E. Wright, "Rise of the Corporation Nation," in Founding Choices: American Economic Policy in the 1790s (University of Chicago Press, 2010), 217–58, https://www.nber.org/books-and-chapters/ founding-choices-american-economic-policy-1790s/rise-corporation-nation.

Callum McKelvie and All About History published, "What Was the Reign of Terror?," livescience.com, October 20, 2021, https://www.livescience.com/reign-of-terror.html.

"Whiskey Rebellion," George Washington's Mount Vernon, accessed August 16, 2022, https://www.mountvernon.org/library/digitalhistory/digital-encyclopedia/article/ whiskey-rebellion/.

"Milestones: 1784–1800 - Office of the Historian," accessed August 16, 2022, https:// history.state.gov/milestones/1784-1800/jay-treaty.

History.com Editors, "John Adams," HISTORY, accessed August 16, 2022, https://www. history.com/topics/us-presidents/john-adams.

History.com Editors, "French Revolution," HISTORY, accessed August 16, 2022, https:// www.history.com/topics/france/french-revolution.

"XYZ Affair," Monticello, accessed August 16, 2022, https://www.monticello.org/ research-education/thomas-jefferson-encyclopedia/xyz-affair/.

Caryn E. Neumann, "Matthew Lyon," accessed August 16, 2022, https://www.mtsu. edu/first-amendment/article/1442/matthew-lyon.

"Jedediah Peck," in Wikipedia, April 13, 2022, https://en.wikipedia.org/w/index. php?title=Jedediah_Peck&oldid=1082561240.

"Founders Online: Introductory Note: Letter from Alexander Hamilton, Concerning …" (University of Virginia Press), accessed August 16, 2022, http://founders.archives.gov/ documents/Hamilton/01-25-02-0110-0001.

"The Most Consequential Elections in History: Thomas Jefferson and the Election of 1800," accessed August 17, 2022, https://www.usnews.com/news/ articles/2008/08/13/the-most-consequential-elections-in-history-thomas-jeffer- son-and-the-election-of-1800.

Jon Meacham, Thomas Jefferson : The Art of Power (New York : Random House, 2012), http://archive.org/details/thomasjeffersona0000meac.

"Peaceful Transfer of Power | Miller Center," October 13, 2020, https://millercenter.org/contested-presidential-elections/peaceful-transfer-power.

"Thomas Jefferson: The American Franchise | Miller Center," October 4, 2016, https://millercenter.org/president/jefferson/the-american-franchise.

"Westward Expansion (1807-1912): Land Policy and Speculation," SparkNotes, accessed August 17, 2022, https://www.sparknotes.com/history/american/westwardexpansion/section2/.

Census History Staff US Census Bureau, "1800 Overview - History - U.S. Census Bureau," accessed October 25, 2022, https://www.census.gov/history/www/through_the_decades/overview/1800.html.

"How Did Thomas Jefferson's Punitive Law Backfire?," ThoughtCo, accessed August 17, 2022, https://www.thoughtco.com/embargo-act-of-1807-1773316.

"Digital History," accessed August 17, 2022, https://www.digitalhistory.uh.edu/disp_textbook.cfm?smtID=2&psid=2986.

"The Louisiana Purchase | Articles and Essays | Louisiana: European Explorations and the Louisiana Purchase | Digital Collections | Library of Congress," web page, Library of Congress, Washington, D.C. 20540 USA, accessed August 17, 2022, https://www.loc.gov/collections/louisiana-european-explorations-and-the-louisiana-purchase/articles-and-essays/the-louisiana-purchase/.

History.com Editors, "Lewis and Clark Expedition," HISTORY, accessed August 17, 2022, https://www.history.com/topics/westward-expansion/lewis-and-clark.

"The Burr Conspiracy | American Experience | PBS," accessed August 17, 2022, https://www.pbs.org/wgbh/americanexperience/features/duel-burr-conspiracy/.

"The Burr vs. Hamilton Duel Happened on This Day - National Constitution Center," National Constitution Center – constitutioncenter.org, accessed August 17, 2022, https://constitutioncenter.org/blog/burr-vs-hamilton-behind-the-ultimate-political-feud.

"Burr versus Jefferson versus Marshall," The National Endowment for the Humanities, accessed August 17, 2022, https://www.neh.gov/humanities/2013/mayjune/feature/burr-versus-jefferson-versus-marshall.

"Diversity of Native American Groups [Ushistory.Org]," accessed August 17, 2022, https://www.ushistory.org/us/1a.asp.

"What Constitutes a Tribal Constitution? – Cal Indian Legal Services," accessed August 17, 2022, https://www.calindian.org/what-constitutes-a-tribal-constitution/.

"Cherokee Constitution," accessed August 17, 2022, https://www.digitalhistory.uh.edu/active_learning/explorations/indian_removal/cherokee_constitution.cfm.

"Handsome Lake," in Wikipedia, June 17, 2022, https://en.wikipedia.org/w/index.php?title=Handsome_Lake&oldid=1093520765.

"Ten-Squat-a-Way, The Open Door, Known as The Prophet, Brother of Tecumseh | Smithsonian American Art Museum," accessed August 17, 2022, https://americanart. si.edu/artwork/ten-squat-way-open-door-known-prophet-brother-tecumseh-4301.

"The Sac and Fox Tribe – Legends of America," accessed August 24, 2022, https:// www.legendsofamerica.com/sac-and-fox/.

"May 28, 1830 CE: Indian Removal Act | National Geographic Society," accessed August 24, 2022, https://education.nationalgeographic.org/resource/ indian-removal-act.

"The Indian Removal Act and the Trail of Tears," accessed April 28, 2023, https:// education.nationalgeographic.org/resource/indian-removal-act-and-trail-tears.

History com Editors, "Trail of Tears," HISTORY, accessed August 24, 2022, https://www. history.com/topics/native-american-history/trail-of-tears.

Lawrence Hurley, "U.S. Supreme Court Expands State Power over Native American Tribes," Reuters, June 30, 2022, sec. United States, https://www.reuters.com/world/ us/us-supreme-court-expands-state-power-over-tribes-win-oklahoma-2022-06-29/.

Donald R. Hickey, The War of 1812: A Forgotten Conflict (Urbana : University of Illinois Press, 1989), http://archive.org/details/warof1812forgo00hick.

"Lessons From Speaker Henry Clay, 'The Great Compromiser,'" accessed August 18, 2022, https://www.wbur.org/hereandnow/2015/10/09/house-speaker-henry-clay.

"Factors That Influenced James Madison to Declare the War of 1812," Wondrium Daily, December 1, 2020, https://www.wondriumdaily.com/ factors-that-influenced-james-madison-to-declare-the-war-of-1812/.

"Henry Letters," in Wikipedia, June 3, 2021, https://en.wikipedia.org/w/index. php?title=Henry_letters&oldid=1026671995.

"A Brief Overview of the War of 1812," American Battlefield Trust, March 30, 2017, https://www.battlefields.org/learn/articles/brief-overview-war-1812.

"War of 1812 Overview," USS Constitution Museum (blog), accessed August 18, 2022, https://ussconstitutionmuseum.org/major-events/war-of-1812-overview/.

"Battle of the Queenston Heights," American Battlefield Trust, accessed August 18, 2022, https://www.battlefields.org/learn/war-1812/battles/battle-queenston-heights.

"Plan Your Trip to Fort McHenry Today," Visit Baltimore, accessed August 18, 2022, https://baltimore.org/what-to-do/behind-the-ramparts-of-fort-mchenry/.

Theodore Roosevelt, The Naval War of 1812; the History of the United States Navy during the Last War with Great Britain, to Which Is Appended an Account of the Battle of New Orleans. (New York, The Review of reviews company, 1904), http://archive. org/details/navalwarof1812hist00roos.

W. M. from old catalog Woolivine, Captain John Gordon, of the Spies, 1906, http:// archive.org/details/captainjohngordo00wool.

"James Madison's Proposals and the Second Bank of the United States," Wondrium Daily, December 16, 2020, https://www.wondriumdaily.com/james-madisons-proposals-and-the-second-bank-of-the-united-states/.

"Erie Canalway National Heritage Corridor: History and Culture," accessed August 19, 2022, https://eriecanalway.org/learn/history-culture.

"James Madison's Proposals: Building a Strong Transport Network," Wondrium Daily, December 16, 2020, https://www.wondriumdaily.com/james-madisons-proposals-building-a-strong-transport-network/.

Christopher Klein, "8 Ways the Erie Canal Changed America," HISTORY, accessed August 19, 2022, https://www.history.com/news/8-ways-the-erie-canal-changed-america.

"What We Get Wrong about Taxes and the American Revolution," PBS NewsHour, December 26, 2016, https://www.pbs.org/newshour/economy/what-we-get-wrong-about-taxes-american-revolution.

"Demographic History of the United States," in Wikipedia, July 27, 2022, https://en.wikipedia.org/w/index.php?title=Demographic_history_of_the_United_States&oldid=1100778819.

"Module 7: The First New Nation," accessed August 19, 2022.

"The Fed - Distribution: Distribution of Household Wealth in the U.S. since 1989," accessed April 28, 2023, https://www.federalreserve.gov/releases/z1/dataviz/dfa/distribute/chart/#range:2006.4,2021.4;quarter:129;series:Net%20worth;demographic:networth;population:1,3,5,7,9;units:levels.

"The Second Bank of the United States | Federal Reserve History," accessed August 20, 2022, https://www.federalreservehistory.org/essays/second-bank-of-the-us.

"Wayback Machine," March 20, 2009, https://web.archive.org/web/20090320130208/http://www.mises.org/rothbard/panic1819.pdf.

"Relief Act of 1821," in Wikipedia, January 18, 2021, https://en.wikipedia.org/w/index.php?title=Relief_Act_of_1821&oldid=1001063874.

"US Elections Project - National-1789-Present," accessed April 28, 2023, https://www.electproject.org/national-1789-present.

"Extract from Thomas Jefferson to Nathaniel Macon, 12 Jan. 1819 | Jefferson Quotes & Family Letters," accessed August 19, 2022, https://tjrs.monticello.org/letter/1560.

"The Spinning Mule - Strutts North Mill Museum Belper," https://www.Belpernorthmill.Org.Uk/ (blog), accessed August 21, 2022, https://www.belper-northmill.org.uk/collections/our-favourite-things/the-spinning-mule/.

"Steam Powered Mills," accessed August 21, 2022, https://www.cottontown.org/The%20Cotton%20Industry/Mechanisation%20of%20the%20Mills/Pages/Steam-Powered-Mills.aspx.

"Samuel Slater," in Wikipedia, March 20, 2023, https://en.wikipedia.org/w/index. php?title=Samuel_Slater&oldid=1145622757.

"Lowell Mill Girls," in Wikipedia, July 19, 2022, https://en.wikipedia.org/w/index. php?title=Lowell_mill_girls&oldid=1099276466.

"McCormick Reaper Manufactory II," Chicagology (blog), accessed August 21, 2022, http://chicagology.com/rebuilding/rebuilding151/.

"The Consequences of the Industrial Revolution in America," Wondrium Daily, December 31, 2020, https://www.wondriumdaily.com/ the-consequences-of-the-industrial-revolution-in-america/.

"U.S. Senate: Nominating Presidents," accessed August 22, 2022, https://www.senate. gov/about/origins-foundations/parties-leadership/nominating-presidents.htm.

"Lessons From Speaker Henry Clay, 'The Great Compromiser.'"

"U.S. Senate: Nominating Presidents."

"This Day in History: Future U.S. President Andrew Jackson Kills Charles Dickinson for Publicly Calling Jackson a 'Worthless Scoundrel, a Poltroon and a Coward,'" Today I Found Out (blog), May 31, 2012, https://www.todayifoundout.com/index. php/2012/05/this-day-in-history-future-u-s-president-andrew-jackson-kills-charles-dickinson-for-publicly-calling-jackson-a-worthless-scoundrel-a-poltroon-and--a-coward/.

Bob Diamond, "Historically Yours Andrew Jackson vs. John Quincy Adams," Miami's Community News, September 4, 2020, https://communitynewspapers.com/ aventura-news/historically-yours-andrew-jackson-vs-john-quincy-adams/.

"Not a Ragged Mob; The Inauguration of 1829," WHHA (en-US), accessed August 23, 2022, https://www.whitehousehistory.org/ not-a-ragged-mob-the-inauguration-of-1829.

History.com Editors, "Andrew Jackson Holds 'Open House' at the White House," HISTORY, accessed August 23, 2022, https://www.history.com/this-day-in-history/ jackson-holds-open-house-at-the-white-house.

"Rachel & Andrew Jackson | Rachel's Death," WNPT, accessed August 23, 2022, https://www.wnpt.org/rachel-andrew-jackson/rachels-death/.

"Andrew Jackson: Domestic Affairs | Miller Center," October 4, 2016, https://miller-center.org/president/jackson/domestic-affairs.

"Tariff of 1833, Compromise, Nullification Crisis," American History Central, accessed August 23, 2022, https://www.americanhistorycentral.com/entries/tariff-of-1833/.

"Andrew Jackson's Veto of the National Bank," Bill of Rights Institute, accessed February 20, 2023, https://billofrightsinstitute.org/essays/ andrew-jacksons-veto-of-the-national-bank/.

"The Bank War," accessed August 23, 2022, https://www.archives.gov/exhibits/treasures_of_congress/text/page9_text.html.

"King Andrew the First," still image, 1833, https://www.loc.gov/pictures/item/2008661753/.

"Louis McLane | Museum of American Finance," accessed August 23, 2022, https://www.moaf.org/exhibits/checks_balances/andrew-jackson/mclane.

N. P. R. Staff, "American Lives: Reconsidering Henry Clay," NPR, August 17, 2010, sec. Author Interviews, https://www.npr.org/2010/08/17/129229303/american-lives-reconsidering-henry-clay.

Johnny Fulfer, "Panic of 1857," The Economic Historian (blog), July 6, 2020, https://economic-historian.com/2018/07/panic-of-1857/.

"William Harrison: Campaigns and Elections | Miller Center," October 4, 2016, https://millercenter.org/president/harrison/campaigns-and-elections.

"USA History - 1800-1835 - Second Great Awakening," accessed August 21, 2022, https://www.globalsecurity.org/military/world/usa/history/05-01.htm.

"The Early Nineteenth-Century Newspaper Boom · News in Antebellum America · The News Media and the Making of America, 1730-1865," accessed April 29, 2023, https://americanantiquarian.org/earlyamericannewsmedia/exhibits/show/news-in-antebellum-america/the-newspaper-boom.

"American Prophet: The Story of Joseph Smith," accessed August 21, 2022, https://www.pbs.org/americanprophet/joseph-smith.html.

"The First Age of Reform | AP US History Study Guide from The Gilder Lehrman Institute of American History," March 28, 2012, https://www.gilderlehrman.org/node/303.

Alexis de Tocqueville, Democracy in America, n.d.

"The Missouri Compromise," American Battlefield Trust, January 7, 2019, https://www.battlefields.org/learn/articles/missouri-compromise.

"Missouri Compromise," accessed March 23, 2023, https://lehrmaninstitute.org/history/missouri-compromise.html.

"Fire Bell in the Night (Quotation) | Thomas Jefferson's Monticello," accessed August 25, 2022, https://www.monticello.org/research-education/thomas-jefferson-encyclopedia/fire-bell-night-quotation/.

"The Missouri Compromise."

"Sectionalism - Mr. Meier's Web Page," accessed October 28, 2022, http://jmeier.summit.k12.nj.us/home/u-s-i-period-6/sectionalism.

"Battle of the Alamo," in Wikipedia, August 21, 2022, https://en.wikipedia.org/w/index.php?title=Battle_of_the_Alamo&oldid=1105819407.

"Presidential Election of 1844 - 270toWin," 270toWin.com, accessed April 29, 2023, https://www.270towin.com/1844_Election/.

"Mexico's President Herrera Decries the Annexation of Texas · SHEC: Resources for Teachers," accessed August 26, 2022, https://shec.ashp.cuny.edu/items/show/793.

"Essays: The Mexican Army in 1846| A Continent Divided: The U.S.-Mexico War," accessed August 26, 2022, https://library.uta.edu/usmexicowar/item?content_id=177&format_id=1.

"A History of the United States, 2nd Edition."

PART THREE: CIVIL WAR AND RECONSTRUCTION

"Vermont 1777: Early Steps Against Slavery," National Museum of African American History and Culture, accessed August 25, 2022, https://nmaahc.si.edu/explore/stories/vermont-1777-early-steps-against-slavery.

"Before There Were 'Red' and 'Blue' States, There Were 'Free' States and 'Slave' States" – Marquette University Law School Faculty Blog," accessed August 25, 2022, https://law.marquette.edu/facultyblog/2012/12/before-there-were-red-and-blue-states-there-were-free-states-and-slave-states/.

Heejoon Jeon, "JONATHAN EDWARDS AND THE ANTI-SLAVERY MOVEMENT," n.d., 16.

"Tobacco in Colonial Virginia – Encyclopedia Virginia," accessed August 25, 2022, https://encyclopediavirginia.org/entries/tobacco-in-colonial-virginia/.

"Cotton Gin and the Expansion of Slavery," Digital Public Library of America, accessed August 25, 2022, https://dp.la/primary-source-sets/cotton-gin-and-the-expansion-of-slavery.

"Eli Whitney and the Cotton Gin," Bill of Rights Institute, accessed August 25, 2022, https://live-bri-dos.pantheonsite.io/essays/eli-whitney-and-the-cotton-gin/.

"Cotton Gin and the Expansion of Slavery."

Jack R. Mason and Lynn Hunt, Liberty, Equality, Fraternity: Exploring the French RevolutionLiberty, Equality, Fraternity, Pap/Cdr edition (University Park, Pa: Penn State University Press, 2002).

"The Five Greatest Slave Rebellions in the United States | African American History Blog," The African Americans: Many Rivers to Cross (blog), January 12, 2013, https://www.pbs.org/wnet/african-americans-many-rivers-to-cross/history/did-african-american-slaves-rebel/.

"James Henry Hammond," in Wikipedia, July 27, 2022, https://en.wikipedia.org/w/index.php?title=James_Henry_Hammond&oldid=1100815344.

"Why Non-Slaveholding Southerners Fought," American Battlefield Trust, February 9, 2011, https://www.battlefields.org/learn/articles/why-non-slaveholding-southerners-fought.

"William Lloyd Garrison," Spartacus Educational, accessed August 26, 2022, https://spartacus-educational.com/USASgarrison.htm.

"Milestones: 1830–1860 - Office of the Historian," accessed August 27, 2022, https://history.state.gov/milestones/1830-1860/territorial-expansion.

UShistory.org, "Wilmot's Proviso [Ushistory.Org]," accessed August 28, 2022, https://www.ushistory.org/us/30a.asp.

"The Wilmot Proviso," American Battlefield Trust, January 15, 2019, https://www.battlefields.org/learn/articles/wilmot-proviso.

"The California Gold Rush | American Experience | PBS," accessed August 28, 2022, https://www.pbs.org/wgbh/americanexperience/features/goldrush-california/.

"Zachary Taylor: Domestic Affairs | Miller Center," October 4, 2016, https://miller-center.org/president/taylor/domestic-affairs.

"History of Immigration to the United States," in Wikipedia, July 18, 2022, https://en.wikipedia.org/w/index.php?title=History_of_immigration_to_the_United_States&oldid=1098932017.

Fulfer, "Panic of 1857."

"Harriett Beecher Stowe and Uncle Tom's Cabin," Bill of Rights Institute, accessed August 30, 2022, https://live-bri-dos.pantheonsite.io/essays/harriett-beecher-stowe-and-uncle-toms-cabin/.

"Uncle Tom's Cabin - Essential Civil War Curriculum," accessed August 30, 2022, https://www.essentialcivilwarcurriculum.com/uncle-toms-cabin.html.

"Harriet Beecher Stowe: The Little Woman Who Wrote the Book That Started This Great War. | EHISTORY," accessed March 23, 2023, https://ehistory.osu.edu/articles/harriet-beecher-stowe-little-woman-who-wrote-book-started-great-war.

"Anthony Burns Captured," accessed August 30, 2022, https://www.pbs.org/wgbh/aia/part4/4p2915.html.

"Digital History," accessed August 30, 2022, https://www.digitalhistory.uh.edu/disp_textbook.cfm?smtid=2&psid=3277.

"A History of the Republican Party," Linn County Republican LIVE, accessed August 30, 2022, https://www.linncountyrepublicanparty.org/a_history.

"James Buchanan and the Dred Scott Decision," Bill of Rights Institute, accessed August 31, 2022, https://live-bri-dos.pantheonsite.io/e-lessons/james-buchanan-and-the-dred-scott-decision/.

Smithsonian Magazine and Kat Eschner, "President James Buchanan Directly Influenced the Outcome of the Dred Scott Decision," Smithsonian Magazine, accessed August 31, 2022, https://www.smithsonianmag.com/smart-news/president-james-buchanan-directly-influenced-outcome-dred-scott-decision-180962329/.

"Dred Scott Decision Still Resonates Today | The National Constitution Center," National Constitution Center – constitutioncenter.org, accessed August 31, 2022, https://constitutioncenter.org/blog/dred-scott-decision-still-resonates-today-2.

"Republicans and the Homestead Act," We're History (blog), May 20, 2016, http://werehistory.org/homestead-act/.

"Dred Scott, the Lincoln-Douglas Debates, and the Election of 1860 (Article) | Khan Academy," accessed August 31, 2022, https://www.khanacademy.org/_render.

"Ralph Waldo Emerson Praises Abolitionist John Brown," The Morgan Library & Museum, February 17, 2011, https://www.themorgan.org/blog/ralph-waldo-emerson-praises-abolitionist-john-brown.

"Aftermath," Virginia Museum of History & Culture, accessed August 31, 2022, https://virginiahistory.org/learn/historical-book/chapter/aftermath.

"Breckinridge/Lane Democratic Ticket, Broadside, 1860 · Document Bank of Virginia," accessed September 1, 2022, https://edu.lva.virginia.gov/dbva/items/show/107.

"Republican Party Platform (1860)," Teaching American History (blog), accessed September 1, 2022, https://teachingamericanhistory.org/document/republican-party-platform-of-1860/.

"South Carolina Secedes from the Union | History Today," accessed September 1, 2022, https://www.historytoday.com/archive/months-past/south-carolina-secedes-union.

"Pearce Museum | Civil War Texas Governors," accessed September 1, 2022, https://www.pearcemuseum.com/education/seventh-grade-curriculum/civil-war-texas-governors-2/.

"Does the Constitution Permit the Blue States to Secede?," Findlaw, accessed September 1, 2022, https://supreme.findlaw.com/legal-commentary/does-the-constitution-permit-the-blue-states-to-secede.html.

"On This Day, the Confederate Constitution Is Approved | The National Constitution Center," National Constitution Center – constitutioncenter.org, accessed September 1, 2022, https://constitutioncenter.org/blog/looking-back-at-the-confederate-constitution.

"Cornerstone Speech," American Battlefield Trust, accessed September 1, 2022, https://www.battlefields.org/learn/primary-sources/cornerstone-speech.

"Abraham Lincoln and the Corwin Amendment," accessed September 1, 2022, https://www.lib.niu.edu/2006/ih060934.html.

"Inaugural Addresses of the Presidents of the United States : from George Washington 1789 to George Bush 1989," Text (Washington, D.C. : U.S. G.P.O. : for sale by the Supt. of Docs., U.S. G.P.O., 1989), accessed September 1, 2022, https://avalon.law.yale.edu/19th_century/lincoln1.asp.

"Fort Pickens and Fort Sumter," accessed September 1, 2022, https://www2.tulane.edu/~sumter/Background/BackgroundForts.html.

"Abraham Lincoln - Key Events | Miller Center," October 7, 2016, https://millercenter.org/president/abraham-lincoln/key-events.

"Facts - The Civil War (U.S. National Park Service)," accessed September 1, 2022, https://www.nps.gov/subjects/civilwar/facts.htm.

"Milestones: 1861–1865 - Office of the Historian," accessed September 4, 2022, https://history.state.gov/milestones/1861-1865/trent-affair.

"The Border States (U.S. National Park Service)," accessed September 2, 2022, https://www.nps.gov/articles/the-border-states.htm.

Rich Bernett, "The Anaconda Plan of the American Civil War," Wondrium Daily, April 25, 2020, https://www.wondriumdaily.com/the-anaconda-plan-of-the-american-civil-war/.

"U.S. Senate: Senators Witness the First Battle of Bull Run," accessed September 2, 2022, https://www.senate.gov/artandhistory/history/minute/Witness_Bull_Run.htm.

"Civil War 150: The South Asks for English and French Recognition | Fords Theatre," accessed September 4, 2022, https://www.fords.org/blog/post/civil-war-150-the-south-asks-for-english-and-french-recognition/.

"The American Civil War in Britain - Essential Civil War Curriculum," accessed September 4, 2022, https://www.essentialcivilwarcurriculum.com/the-american-civil-war-in-britain.html.

"Robert E. Lee's Decision to Invade the North in September 1862," American Battlefield Trust, February 6, 2009, https://www.battlefields.org/learn/articles/robert-e-lees-decision-invade-north-september-1862.

History.com Editors, "Union Troops Discover Rebels' Antietam Battle Plan," HISTORY, accessed September 3, 2022, https://www.history.com/this-day-in-history/union-troops-discover-rebels-antietam-battle-plan.

"Antietam," American Battlefield Trust, accessed April 30, 2023, https://www.battlefields.org/learn/civil-war/battles/antietam.

Heather Murphy, "The Battlefield Photos That Changed Everything," Slate, September 17, 2012, https://slate.com/human-interest/2012/09/alexander-gardners-antietam-battlefield-photos-changed-photography-and-war.html.

"Stones River," American Battlefield Trust, accessed April 30, 2023, https://www.battlefields.org/learn/civil-war/battles/stones-river.

"Fredericksburg," American Battlefield Trust, accessed April 30, 2023, https://www.battlefields.org/learn/civil-war/battles/fredericksburg.

"A Worse Place than Hell: The Changing Face of Abraham Lincoln Exhibit | Downtown Ventura," February 12, 2015, https://downtownventura.org/event/a-worse-place-than-hell-the-changing-face-of-abraham-lincoln-exhibit/2015-03-21/, https://downtownventura.org/event/a-worse-place-than-hell-the-changing-face-of-abraham-lincoln-exhibit/2015-03-21/.

"Chancellorsville," American Battlefield Trust, accessed September 4, 2022, https://www.battlefields.org/learn/civil-war/battles/chancellorsville.

JEFFVHC, "Lincoln Reacts to the Union's Massive Defeat at Chancellorsville," Vermont Humanities (blog), April 26, 2013, https://civilwarbookofdays.org/2013/04/26/lincoln-reacts-to-the-unions-massive-defeat-at-chancellorsville/.

"Facts - The Civil War (U.S. National Park Service)."

Stephanie McCurry, "The Confederacy Was an Antidemocratic, Centralized State," The Atlantic, June 21, 2020, https://www.theatlantic.com/ideas/archive/2020/06/confederacy-wasnt-what-you-think/613309/.

"Gettysburg," American Battlefield Trust, accessed September 4, 2022, https://www.battlefields.org/learn/civil-war/battles/gettysburg.

"Why Jefferson Davis Was Loathed in the Confederacy He Led," Washington Post, accessed September 5, 2022, https://www.washingtonpost.com/history/2018/12/08/why-jefferson-davis-was-loathed-confederacy-he-led/.

"Financing the Civil War - Essential Civil War Curriculum," accessed September 4, 2022, https://www.essentialcivilwarcurriculum.com/financing-the-civil-war.html.

"The Southern Homefront [Ushistory.Org]," accessed September 4, 2022, https://www.ushistory.org/us/34d.asp.

Rich Bernett, "The Varied Political Views on Emancipation During the Civil War," Wondrium Daily, October 10, 2020, https://www.wondriumdaily.com/the-varied-political-views-on-emancipation-during-the-civil-war/.

"U.S. Senate: The Civil War: The Senate's Story," accessed April 30, 2023, https://www.senate.gov/artandhistory/history/common/civil_war/MorrillLandGrantCollegeAct_FeaturedDoc.htm.

Donald R. Shaffer, "Slavery Ends in the Territories," Civil War Emancipation (blog), June 19, 2012, https://cwemancipation.wordpress.com/2012/06/19/slavery-ends-in-the-territories/.

"Benjamin Butler," in Wikipedia, September 5, 2022, https://en.wikipedia.org/w/index.php?title=Benjamin_Butler&oldid=1108582564.

"Frémont Attempts to Free Missouri's Slaves | Civil War on the Western Border: The Missouri-Kansas Conflict, 1854-1865," accessed September 6, 2022, https://civil-waronthewesternborder.org/timeline/fr%C3%A9mont-attempts-free-missouris-slaves.

"Proclamation Revoking General David Hunter's General Order No. 11 on Military Emancipation of Slaves, May 19, 1862," IDCA, July 29, 2018, https://iowaculture.gov/history/education/educator-resources/primary-source-sets/african-americans-and-civil-war/david-hunter.

"Slavery during the American Civil War," in Wikipedia, August 12, 2022, https://en.wikipedia.org/w/index.php?title=Slavery_during_the_American_Civil_War&oldid=1104129776.

"Black Soldiers in the U.S. Military During the Civil War," National Archives, August 15, 2016, https://www.archives.gov/education/lessons/blacks-civil-war.

"Saltville Battle and Massacre - Camp Nelson National Monument (U.S. National Park Service)," accessed September 6, 2022, https://www.nps.gov/cane/battle-of-saltville-and-massacre.htm.

History.com Editors, "Confederacy Approves Black Soldiers," HISTORY, accessed September 6, 2022, https://www.history.com/this-day-in-history/confederacy-approves-black-soldiers.

History.com Editors, "President Lincoln Signs Ulysses S. Grant's Commission to Command the U.S. Army," HISTORY, accessed September 6, 2022, https://www.history.com/this-day-in-history/lincoln-signs-ulysses-s-grants-commission-to-command-the-u-s-army.

"The Atlanta Campaign," American Battlefield Trust, May 1, 2014, https://www.battlefields.org/learn/articles/atlanta-campaign.

History.com Editors, "William Tecumseh Sherman," HISTORY, accessed September 6, 2022, https://www.history.com/topics/american-civil-war/william-t-sherman.

"SOUTHERNERS RESIST MONUMENT TO SHERMAN," Sun Sentinel, accessed September 6, 2022, https://www.sun-sentinel.com/news/fl-xpm-1994-07-10-9407050412-story.html.

"Mobile Bay," American Battlefield Trust, accessed September 7, 2022, https://www.battlefields.org/learn/civil-war/battles/mobile-bay.

History.com Editors, "Sherman's March to the Sea," HISTORY, accessed September 7, 2022, https://www.history.com/topics/american-civil-war/shermans-march.

"The Surrender Meeting - Appomattox Court House National Historical Park (U.S. National Park Service)," accessed September 7, 2022, https://www.nps.gov/apco/learn/historyculture/the-surrender-meeting.htm.

"Ulysses S. Grant Quotes," American Civil War Stories, accessed September 7, 2022, http://www.americancivilwarstory.com/ulysses-s-grant-quotes.html.

"United States: War Fatalities 1775-2022," Statista, accessed November 3, 2022, https://www.statista.com/statistics/1009819/total-us-military-fatalities-in-american-wars-1775-present/.

"Thaddeus Stevens," in Wikipedia, September 1, 2022, https://en.wikipedia.org/w/index.php?title=Thaddeus_Stevens&oldid=1107961950.

"The Radical Republicans," American Battlefield Trust, June 30, 2021, https://www.battlefields.org/learn/articles/radical-republicans.

"Wade–Davis Bill," in Wikipedia, May 15, 2022, https://en.wikipedia.org/w/index.php?title=Wade%E2%80%93Davis_Bill&oldid=1087980791.

"Remembering the Craziest First Year for an American President," InsideHook, accessed September 7, 2022, https://www.insidehook.com/article/history/remembering-craziest-first-year-american-president.

"Digital History," accessed September 8, 2022, https://www.digitalhistory.uh.edu/disp_textbook.cfm?smtID=2&psid=3096.

"The Moderate, Conservative, and Radical Republicans of Reconstruction," Fact / Myth, December 22, 2016, http://factmyth.com/the-moderate-conservative-and-radical-republicans-of-reconstruction/.

"The Reconstruction Acts of 1867 | Facing History and Ourselves," accessed September 8, 2022, https://www.facinghistory.org/resource-library/reconstruction-acts-1867.

"Not Even Past: Social Vulnerability and the Legacy of Redlining," accessed September 8, 2022, https://dsl.richmond.edu/socialvulnerability/.

"U.S. Senate: About Impeachment," accessed April 30, 2023, https://www.senate.gov/about/powers-procedures/impeachment.htm.

"Original 33," in Wikipedia, April 6, 2022, https://en.wikipedia.org/w/index.php?title=Original_33&oldid=1081341243#cite_note-reconstruction-georgia-3.

"The Most Racist Presidential Election Ever," Ulysses S. Grant Bicentennial, November 25, 2021, https://usgrant200.com/the-most-racist-presidential-election-ever/.

"Black Voters, White Supremacists, and Voter Suppression in Louisiana's 1868 Presidential Election | The Historic New Orleans Collection," accessed September 9, 2022, https://www.hnoc.org/publications/first-draft/symposium-2021/black-voters-white-supremacists-and-voter-suppression-louisianas-1868.

History.com Editors, "15th Amendment," HISTORY, accessed September 9, 2022, https://www.history.com/topics/black-history/fifteenth-amendment.

"Documenting Reconstruction Violence," Equal Justice Initiative Reports, accessed April 5, 2023, https://eji.org/report/reconstruction-in-america/documenting-reconstruction-violence/.

Smithsonian Magazine and Danny Lewis, "The 1873 Colfax Massacre Crippled the Reconstruction Era," Smithsonian Magazine, accessed September 10, 2022, https://www.smithsonianmag.com/smart-news/1873-colfax-massacre-crippled-reconstruction-180958746/.

"William Gaston," National Governors Association (blog), accessed September 10, 2022, https://www.nga.org/governor/william-gaston/.

"1876 Democratic National Convention," in Wikipedia, June 28, 2022, https://en.wikipedia.org/w/index. php?title=1876_Democratic_National_Convention&oldid=1095411153.

"A History of the United States, 2nd Edition."

PART FOUR: INDUSTRIALIZATION TO 1917

"The Steel Business | American Experience | PBS," accessed September 11, 2022, https://www.pbs.org/wgbh/americanexperience/features/carnegie-steel-business/.

"The Age Of Steel," AMERICAN HERITAGE, accessed September 11, 2022, https://www.americanheritage.com/age-steel.

"Why Whaling Was a Major American Industry In the 1800s," ThoughtCo, accessed September 11, 2022, https://www.thoughtco.com/a-brief-history-of-whaling-1774068.

"Life Aboard - New Bedford Whaling Museum," March 1, 2021, https://www.whaling-museum.org/learn/research-topics/whaling-history/life-aboard/.

"John Stobart - Nantucket Sleigh Ride," Scrimshaw Gallery (blog), accessed November 3, 2022, https://www.scrimshawgallery.com/product/nantucket-sleigh-ride/.

"Oil Fields | Encyclopedia.Com," accessed April 5, 2023, https://www.encyclopedia.com/history/dictionaries-thesauruses-pictures-and-press-releases/oil-fields.

"Oil Tank Wagon for Standard Oil Company, circa 1892 - The Henry Ford," accessed September 11, 2022, https://www.thehenryford.org/collections-and-research/digital-collections/artifact/54533/.

"Fatality Rate in Andrew Carnegie's Steel Mills," Forum post, History Stack Exchange, December 20, 2017, https://history.stackexchange.com/q/42434.

History.com Editors, "Triangle Shirtwaist Factory Fire," HISTORY, March 23, 2021, https://www.history.com/topics/early-20th-century-us/triangle-shirtwaist-fire.

"Child Labor in the Industrial Revolution," HISTORY CRUNCH - History Articles, Biographies, Infographics, Resources and More, accessed September 20, 2022, https://www.historycrunch.com/child-labor-in-the-industrial-revolution.html.

"Colorized Photos of Child Laborers Bring Struggles of the Past to Life," Time, accessed September 20, 2022, https://time.com/4187988/colorized-photos-child-laborers-lewis-hine/.

History.com Editors, "Knights of Labor," HISTORY, accessed September 20, 2022, https://www.history.com/topics/19th-century/knights-of-labor.

"Eugene Debs | American Experience | PBS," accessed September 21, 2022, https://www.pbs.org/wgbh/americanexperience/features/wilson-eugene-debs/.

Carnegie Corporation of New York, "The Gospel of Wealth," Carnegie Corporation of New York, accessed September 11, 2022, https://www.carnegie.org/publications/the-gospel-of-wealth/.

Evan Andrews, "9 Things You May Not Know About William Tecumseh Sherman," HISTORY, November 14, 2019, https://www.history.com/news/9-things-you-may-not-know-about-william-tecumseh-sherman.

"Sod House on the Prairie: Hunter Man's Mother Was Girl in Iconic Homestead Photo," Dickinson Press, October 20, 2017, https://www.thedickinsonpress.com/news/sod-house-on-the-prairie-hunter-mans-mother-was-girl-in-iconic-homestead-photo.

Ellen Q. Jaquette, "LibGuides: Disaster Relief in Minnesota: Grasshopper Plagues," accessed September 14, 2022, https://libguides.mnhs.org/disasterrelief/grasshopper.

"Dividing Line: The Past, Present and Future of the 100th Meridian," accessed September 14, 2022, https://www.earthmagazine.org/article/dividing-line-past-present-and-future-100th-meridian/.

"Plains Indian | History, Culture, Art, Facts, Map, & Tribes | Britannica," accessed September 13, 2022, https://www.britannica.com/topic/Plains-Indian.

Richard Greydanus, "Observing Natives with Francis Parkman," Medium (blog), March 19, 2015, https://medium.com/@rgrydns/observing-natives-with-francis-parkman-73450b49a6d8.

Brett & Kate McKay, "Coming of Age: The Importance of Male Rites of Passage," The Art of Manliness (blog), November 10, 2008, https://www.artofmanliness.com/character/advice/coming-of-age-the-importance-of-male-rites-of-passage/.

"Guns Germs & Steel: Variables. Smallpox | PBS," accessed September 13, 2022, https://www.pbs.org/gunsgermssteel/variables/smallpox.html.

"1872-3slaughterofthe Buffalo," accessed September 13, 2022, http://www.nativeamerican.co.uk/1872-3buffalo.html.

"Rutherford B. Hayes: Domestic Affairs | Miller Center," October 4, 2016, https://millercenter.org/president/hayes/domestic-affairs.

"Chief Joseph (1840–1904)," accessed September 13, 2022, https://www.historylink.org/File/8975.

"American Indians and Alaska Natives - By the Numbers," accessed January 29, 2023, https://www.acf.hhs.gov/ana/fact-sheet/american-indians-and-alaska-natives-numbers.

"The Economics of American Farm Unrest, 1865-1900," accessed September 18, 2022, https://eh.net/encyclopedia/the-economics-of-american-farm-unrest-1865-1900/.

"Populist Party Platform of 1892 | The American Presidency Project," accessed September 18, 2022, https://www.presidency.ucsb.edu/documents/populist-party-platform-1892.

"Bryan's 'Cross of Gold' Speech: Mesmerizing the Masses," accessed May 3, 2023, https://historymatters.gmu.edu/d/5354/.

"The Wizard of Oz as an Allegory for the 1896 Presidential Election - James R. Rogers," Law & Liberty (blog), October 26, 2018, https://lawliberty.org/the-wizard-of-oz-as-an-allegory-for-the-1896-presidential-election/.

Bob Riel, "Was The Wizard of Oz Influenced by the 1896 Presidential Election?," Presidential Fever (blog), March 21, 2022, https://medium.com/presidential-fever/was-the-wizard-of-oz-influenced-by-the-1896-presidential-election-5382daa690ae.

Census History Staff US Census Bureau, "Urban and Rural Areas - History - U.S. Census Bureau," accessed September 18, 2022, https://www.census.gov/history/www/programs/geography/urban_and_rural_areas.html.

Ap, "Farm Population Lowest Since 1850's," The New York Times, July 20, 1988, sec. U.S., https://www.nytimes.com/1988/07/20/us/farm-population-lowest-since-1850-s.html.

"The New South (Article) | Khan Academy," accessed September 15, 2022, https://www.khanacademy.org/_render.

"United States - Civil Rights Legislation | Britannica," accessed May 3, 2023, https://www.britannica.com/place/United-States/Civil-rights-legislation#ref612865.

James R. Belpedio, "John Marshall Harlan I," accessed September 15, 2022, https://www.mtsu.edu/first-amendment/article/1335/john-marshall-harlan-i.

"Sharecropping | Themes | Slavery by Another Name | PBS," Slavery By Another Name, accessed September 15, 2022, https://www.pbs.org/tpt/slavery-by-another-name/themes/sharecropping/.

"History of Lynching in America | NAACP," accessed September 15, 2022, https://naacp.org/find-resources/history-explained/history-lynching-america.

"Booker T & W.e.b | The Two Nations Of Black America," FRONTLINE, accessed September 15, 2022, https://www.pbs.org/wgbh/frontline/article/debate-w-e-b-du-bois-and-booker-t-washington/.

Ryan Taylor, "The Atlanta Compromise Speech Transcript - Booker T. Washington," Rev (blog), accessed May 3, 2023, https://www.rev.com/blog/transcripts/the-atlanta-compromise-speech-transcript-booker-t-washington.

"W. E. B. Du Bois | Daniel Murray: A Collector's Legacy by John Y. Cole | Articles and Essays | African American Perspectives: Materials Selected from the Rare Book Collection | Digital Collections | Library of Congress," web page, Library of Congress, Washington, D.C. 20540 USA, accessed May 3, 2023, https://www.loc.gov/collections/african-american-perspectives-rare-books/articles-and-essays/daniel-murray-a-collectors-legacy/w-e-b-du-bois/.

"The Angel in the House," accessed September 16, 2022, http://academic.brooklyn.cuny.edu/english/melani/novel_19c/thackeray/angel.html.

"Herbert Spencer: Theory & Social Darwinism - Video & Lesson Transcript," study.com, accessed September 16, 2022, https://study.com/academy/lesson/herbert-spencer-theory-social-darwinism.html.

Jack Moore, "Muscular Christianity and American Sport's Undying Love of Violence," The Guardian, May 8, 2015, sec. Sport, https://www.theguardian.com/sport/blog/2015/may/08/muscular-christianity-and-american-sports-undying-love-of-violence.

"A Bulldog For Jesus," accessed May 3, 2023, http://www.zianet.com/maxey/reflx335.htm.

History.com Editors, "Seneca Falls Convention," HISTORY, accessed September 16, 2022, https://www.history.com/topics/womens-rights/seneca-falls-convention.

"The Trial of Lizzie Borden: An Account," accessed September 16, 2022, https://famous-trials.com/lizzieborden/1437-home.

"Immigrants in the Progressive Era | Progressive Era to New Era, 1900-1929 | U.S. History Primary Source Timeline | Classroom Materials at the Library of Congress | Library of Congress," web page, Library of Congress, Washington, D.C. 20540 USA, accessed September 19, 2022, https://www.loc.gov/classroom-materials/united-states-history-primary-source-timeline/progressive-era-to-new-era-1900-1929/immigrants-in-progressive-era/.

"European Emigration," in Wikipedia, August 26, 2022, https://en.wikipedia.org/w/index.php?title=European_emigration&oldid=1106710748.

"Land Grants | History of Railroads and Maps | Articles and Essays | Railroad Maps, 1828-1900 | Digital Collections | Library of Congress," web page, Library of Congress, Washington, D.C. 20540 USA, accessed September 19, 2022, https://www.loc.gov/collections/railroad-maps-1828-to-1900/articles-and-essays/history-of-railroads-and-maps/land-grants/.

"The Digital Tool That Helps Robert Shiller Understand the Past," Yale Insights, accessed September 19, 2022, https://insights.som.yale.edu/insights/the-digital-tool-that-helps-robert-shiller-understand-the-past.

"History Lesson 4: Educating European Immigrant Children Before World War I," accessed September 19, 2022, http://www.crfimmigrationed.org/lessons-for-teachers/143-hl4.

"Challenges Faced by Immigrants in the 19th Century," accessed September 19, 2022, https://www.theclassroom.com/challenges-faced-immigrants-19th-century-9525.html.

"Nativism and Fundamentalism in the 1920s (Article) | Khan Academy," accessed September 19, 2022, https://www.khanacademy.org/_render.

"City Life in the Late 19th Century | Rise of Industrial America, 1876-1900 | U.S. History Primary Source Timeline | Classroom Materials at the Library of Congress | Library of Congress," web page, Library of Congress, Washington, D.C. 20540 USA, accessed September 20, 2022, https://www.loc.gov/classroom-materials/united-states-history-primary-source-timeline/rise-of-industrial-america-1876-1900/city-life-in-late-19th-century/.

Smithsonian Magazine and Jimmy Stamp, "Pioneering Social Reformer Jacob Riis Revealed 'How The Other Half Lives' in America," Smithsonian Magazine, accessed September 20, 2022, https://www.smithsonianmag.com/history/pioneering-social-re-former-jacob-riis-revealed-how-other-half-lives-america-180951546/.

"Chicago Fire of 1871," HISTORY, August 21, 2018, https://www.history.com/topics/natural-disasters-and-environment/great-chicago-fire.

"Classic Quotes That Show You Why 'The Jungle' Changed the Food Industry," ThoughtCo, accessed September 20, 2022, https://www.thoughtco.com/the-jungle-quotes-740317.

"THE JUNGLE," accessed September 20, 2022, https://faculty.uml.edu/sgallagher/jungle.htm.

"Boss Tweed | Biography, Political Machine, Cartoons, & Facts | Britannica," accessed September 20, 2022, https://www.britannica.com/biography/Boss-Tweed.

"Elizabeth Stuart Phelps," History of American Women (blog), December 7, 2011, https://www.womenhistoryblog.com/2011/12/elizabeth-stuart-phelps.html.

Daniel Demers, "Jesus Wine and the Temperance Movement," Catholic Stand (blog), January 18, 2020, https://catholicstand.com/jesus-wine-temperance-movement/.

"Is the Catholic Church the Whore of Babylon?," Catholic Answers, accessed September 17, 2022, https://www.catholic.com/tract/hunting-the-whore-of-babylon.

Jacki Lyden, "The Madonna Of 115th Street Gets A Long-Awaited Makeover," NPR, November 1, 2015, https://www.npr.org/2015/11/01/450889721/the-madonna-of-115th-street-gets-a-long-awaited-makeover.

"This Day in Jewish History The Shellfish That Ushered in a Movement - Jewish World - Haaretz.Com," accessed September 17, 2022, https://www.haaretz.com/jewish/2014-07-11/ty-article/.premium/this-day-the-shellfish-that-ushered-in-a-movement/0000017f-dbfe-d3ff-a7ff-fbfe63f80000.

"Reynolds v. United States," Oyez, accessed September 17, 2022, https://www.oyez.org/cases/1850-1900/98us145.

Facebook et al., "Mind Over Matter," Los Angeles Times, August 22, 1999, https://www.latimes.com/archives/la-xpm-1999-aug-22-bk-2412-story.html.

Travis Mitchell, "Measuring Religion in Pew Research Center's American Trends Panel," Pew Research Center's Religion & Public Life Project (blog), January 14, 2021, https://www.pewresearch.org/religion/2021/01/14/measuring-religion-in-pew-research-centers-american-trends-panel/.

"American Experience. The Presidents. Theodore Roosevelt | PBS," accessed September 21, 2022, http://www.shoppbs.pbs.org/wgbh/amex/presidents/26_t_roosevelt/filmmore/filmscript.html.

"T. R. the Rough Rider: Hero of the Spanish American War - Theodore Roosevelt Birthplace National Historic Site (U.S. National Park Service)," accessed September 21, 2022, https://www.nps.gov/thrb/learn/historyculture/tr-rr-spanamwar.htm.

Gary Hoover, "The Sordid Saga of Mr. Singer and His Sewing Machine," Business History - The American Business History Center (blog), January 14, 2022, https://americanbusinesshistory.org/the-sordid-saga-of-mr-singer-and-his-sewing-machine/.

Ruthann Cooper Schiavone says, "Mr. Singer's Money Machine," The Saturday Evening Post, June 13, 2019, https://www.saturdayeveningpost.com/2019/06/mr-singers-money-machine/.

"The Swift Meatpacking Plant," The Moving Assembly Line: A Blueprint for the Future, accessed September 22, 2022, http://51154787.weebly.com/the-swift-meatpacking-plant.html.

Jeff Haden, "108 Years Ago, Ford Doubled Employee Wages Overnight: If You Don't Believe Higher Pay Makes a Difference, Think Again," Inc.com, May 20, 2022, https://www.inc.com/jeff-haden/108-years-ago-ford-doubled-employee-wages-overnight-business-case-for-higher-pay.html.

Daniel Good, "Principled Management," Make Work Better (blog), January 23, 2019, https://medium.com/make-work-better/principled-management-d732ace3f1bb.

"Elton Mayo: The Hawthorne Experiments Thinker.," The British Library (The British Library), accessed September 22, 2022, https://www.bl.uk/people/elton-mayo.

"U.S. Senator Albert J. Beveridge Speaks on the Philippine Question, U.S. Senate, Washington, D.C., January 9, 1900 | US-China Institute," accessed September 22, 2022, https://china.usc.edu/us-senator-albert-j-beveridge-speaks-philippine-question-us-senate-washington-dc-january-9-1900.

"A History of the United States, 2nd Edition."

PART FIVE: FIRST WORLD WAR TO THE END OF THE SECOND WORLD WAR

"Joint Address to Congress Leading to a Declaration of War Against Germany (1917)," National Archives, September 16, 2021, https://www.archives.gov/milestone-documents/address-to-congress-declaration-of-war-against-germany.

UShistory.org, "America in the First World War [Ushistory.Org]," accessed March 2, 2023, https://www.ushistory.org/us/45.asp.

History.com Editors, "William Jennings Bryan Resigns as U.S. Secretary of State," HISTORY, accessed September 23, 2022, https://www.history.com/this-day-in-history/william-jennings-bryan-resigns-as-u-s-secretary-of-state.

"World War I: Building the American Military," www.army.mil, accessed September 23, 2022, https://www.army.mil/article/185229/world_war_i_building_the_american_military.

"Between Acceptance and Refusal - Soldiers' Attitudes Towards War (USA) | International Encyclopedia of the First World War (WW1)," accessed September 23, 2022, https://encyclopedia.1914-1918-online.net/article/between_acceptance_and_refusal_-_soldiers_attitudes_towards_war_usa.

"Four Minute Men," in Wikipedia, May 2, 2022, https://en.wikipedia.org/w/index.php?title=Four_Minute_Men&oldid=1085701918.

"The Voice in the Desert: Billy Sunday's New York Tabernacle Meetings - World War I Centennial," accessed March 25, 2023, https://www.worldwar1centennial.org/index.php/worship-and-lamentation/the-voice-in-the-desert-billy-sunday-s-new-york-tabernacle-meetings.html.

Smithsonian Magazine and Erick Trickey, "The Forgotten Story of the American Troops Who Got Caught Up in the Russian Civil War," Smithsonian Magazine, accessed September 24, 2022, https://www.smithsonianmag.com/history/forgotten-doughboys-who-died-fighting-russian-civil-war-180971470/.

"WWI: Laying the North Sea Mines," accessed September 24, 2022, http://public2.nhhcaws.local/content/history/museums/nmusn/explore/photography/wwi/wwi-north-sea-mine-barrage/mines/laying-mines.html.

"The Fourteen Points," National WWI Museum and Memorial, accessed September 24, 2022, https://www.theworldwar.org/learn/peace/fourteen-points.

"Treaty of Versailles," accessed July 21, 2023, https://encyclopedia.ushmm.org/content/en/article/treaty-of-versailles.

"Germans Prepare to Protest Versailles Treaty Terms," HISTORY, accessed July 21, 2023, https://www.history.com/this-day-in-history/germans-prepare-to-protest-versailles-treaty-terms.

"Palmer Raids," Page, Federal Bureau of Investigation, accessed September 24, 2022, https://www.fbi.gov/history/famous-cases/palmer-raids.

"Why We Don't Remember Edith Galt Wilson as the 'First Woman President' | History News Network," accessed July 22, 2023, http://hnn.us/article/185162.

"The Economy in the 1920s and What Caused the Great Depression," The Balance, accessed March 2, 2023, https://www.thebalancemoney.com/roaring-twenties-4060511.

"When the President Was the Quietest Man in the Room - Atlas Obscura," accessed September 25, 2022, https://www.atlasobscura.com/articles/when-the-president-was-the-quietest-man-in-the-room.

Elizabeth Putnam Gordon, Women Torch-Bearers; the Story of the Woman's Christian Temperance Union (National Woman's Christian Temperance Union Publishing House, 1924), http://archive.org/details/womentorchbearer00gord.

"Al Capone - Scarface, Alcatraz & Death," HISTORY, April 26, 2021, https://www.history.com/topics/crime/al-capone.

"Benefits of National Prohibition...," accessed March 2, 2023, http://www.prohibitionists.org/Background/Benefits_of_Prohibition.htm.

"The Ku Klux Klan in the 1920s," Bill of Rights Institute, accessed March 3, 2023, https://billofrightsinstitute.org/essays/the-ku-klux-klan-in-the-1920s/.

"The Rise of Fundamentalism, The Twentieth Century, Divining America: Religion in American History, TeacherServe, National Humanities Center," accessed September 25, 2022, http://nationalhumanitiescenter.org/tserve/twenty/tkeyinfo/fundam.htm.

Scott McLemee, "Doing the Lord's Work," Inside Higher Ed, March 1, 2006, https://www.insidehighered.com/views/2006/03/01/doing-lords-work.

"The Fires of Creationism - Los Angeles Times," accessed September 25, 2022, https://www.latimes.com/archives/la-xpm-1985-07-10-me-7689-story.html.

"5 Things You Didn't Know About the Scopes 'Monkey' Trial," accessed March 3, 2023, https://tnmuseum.org/junior-curators/posts/5-things-you-didnt-know-about-the-scopes-monkey-trial?locale=en_us.

"ACLU History: The Scopes 'Monkey Trial,'" American Civil Liberties Union, accessed March 3, 2023, https://www.aclu.org/other/aclu-history-scopes-monkey-trial.

"The Great Migration (1910-1970)," National Archives, May 20, 2021, https://www.archives.gov/research/african-americans/migrations/great-migration.

"Marcus Garvey and the Universal Negro Improvement Association, The Twentieth Century, Divining America: Religion in American History, TeacherServe, National Humanities Center," accessed September 25, 2022, http://nationalhumanitiescenter.org/tserve/twenty/tkeyinfo/garvey.htm.

"Dow Jones Falls to Its Lowest Point, July 8, 1932 - POLITICO," accessed September 25, 2022, https://www.politico.com/story/2013/07/this-day-in-politics-july-8-1932-093787.

"Bernie Madoff," Corporate Finance Institute, accessed May 4, 2023, https://corporatefinanceinstitute.com/resources/capital-markets/bernie-madoff/.

"Lessons From the Other Crash of the 1920s," Liberty Through Wealth (blog), September 15, 2020, https://libertythroughwealth.com/2020/09/15/lessons-from-1920s-florida-property-boom/.

"Florida In The Land Boom Of The 1920's," accessed September 25, 2022, http://floridahistory.org/landboom.htm.

"Letters from the Dust Bowl," University of Oklahoma Press (blog), accessed September 26, 2022, https://www.oupress.com/9780806135403/letters-from-the-dust-bowl/.

"The Stock Market Crash of 1929 | US History II (OS Collection)," accessed March 5, 2023, https://courses.lumenlearning.com/suny-ushistory2os2xmaster/chapter/the-stock-market-crash-of-1929/.

Clive Day, "Keynes' Economic Consequences of the Peace," The American Economic Review 10, no. 2 (1920): 299–312.

Ronald Jones, "5 Facts You Probably Didn't Know About Frank D. Roosevelt," The FD Roosevelt Suite (blog), April 9, 2020, https://fdrsuite.org/5-facts-you-probably-didnt-know-about-frank-d-roosevelt/.

"The Myth of FDR's Secret Disability | TIME.Com," accessed July 22, 2023, https://ideas.time.com/2013/07/12/the-myth-of-fdrs-secret-disability/.

"Franklin D. Roosevelt - State of the Union Address -- 1935," accessed September 27, 2022, https://www.albany.edu/faculty/gz580/his101/su35fdr.html.

History.com Editors, "The Fireside Chats," HISTORY, accessed September 27, 2022, https://www.history.com/topics/great-depression/fireside-chats.

"Reverend Charles E. Coughlin (1891-1979) | American Experience | PBS," accessed September 27, 2022, https://www.pbs.org/wgbh/americanexperience/features/holocaust-coughlin/.

Smithsonian Magazine, "When Franklin Roosevelt Clashed With the Supreme Court–and Lost," Smithsonian Magazine, accessed September 27, 2022, https://www.smithsonianmag.com/history/when-franklin-roosevelt-clashed-with-the-supreme-court-and-lost-78497994/.

"How FDR Lost His Brief War on the Supreme Court | Constitution Center," National Constitution Center – constitutioncenter.org, accessed July 22, 2023, https://constitutioncenter.org/blog/how-fdr-lost-his-brief-war-on-the-supreme-court-2.

"'Final Solution': In Depth," accessed September 28, 2022, https://encyclopedia.ushmm.org/content/en/article/final-solution-in-depth.

"Deportations to Killing Centers," accessed May 4, 2023, https://encyclopedia.ushmm.org/content/en/article/deportations-to-killing-centers.

"USS Reuben James (DD-245)," in Wikipedia, May 21, 2022, https://en.wikipedia.org/w/index.php?title=USS_Reuben_James_(DD-245)&oldid=1089037430.

"What Americans Knew," accessed September 28, 2022, https://exhibitions.ushmm.org/americans-and-the-holocaust/topics/what-americans-knew.

"The Great Debate," The National WWII Museum | New Orleans, accessed September 28, 2022, https://www.nationalww2museum.org/war/articles/great-debate.

"World War II Casualties by Country," accessed September 28, 2022, https://worldpopulationreview.com/country-rankings/world-war-two-casualties-by-country.

"The Path to Pearl Harbor," The National WWII Museum | New Orleans, accessed September 28, 2022, https://www.nationalww2museum.org/war/articles/path-pearl-harbor.

"Japanese American Incarceration," The National WWII Museum | New Orleans, accessed September 28, 2022, https://www.nationalww2museum.org/war/articles/japanese-american-incarceration.

District of Columbia 1800 I. Street NW Washington and Dc 20006, "PolitiFact - U.S. Army Was Smaller than the Army for Portugal before World War II," @politifact, accessed September 28, 2022, https://www.politifact.com/factchecks/2014/jun/13/ken-paxton/us-army-was-smaller-army-portugal-world-war-ii/.

Tiffany Leigh Smith, "Department Of History And Government College Of Arts And Sciences," n.d., 177.

History.com Editors, "General MacArthur Returns to the Philippines," HISTORY, accessed September 28, 2022, https://www.history.com/this-day-in-history/macarthur-returns.

"Milestones: 1937–1945 - Office of the Historian," accessed May 4, 2023, https://history.state.gov/milestones/1937-1945/us-soviet.

U. S. Mission Russia, "World War II Allies: U.S. Lend-Lease to the Soviet Union, 1941-1945," U.S. Embassy & Consulates in Russia, May 10, 2020, https://ru.usembassy.gov/world-war-ii-allies-u-s-lend-lease-to-the-soviet-union-1941-1945/.

Boris Egorov, "How the U.S. Studebaker Became the Soviet 'victory Truck' (PHOTOS)," Russia Beyond, December 17, 2020, https://www.rbth.com/history/333156-how-us-studebaker-became-soviet.

"Aerial Bombing of German Cities Hamburg and Dresden by Allied Forces during World War II | Britannica," accessed September 29, 2022, https://www.britannica.com/video/180237/Allied-bombing-Germany-1943.

"Apocalypse in Dresden, February 1945," The National WWII Museum | New Orleans, accessed September 29, 2022, https://www.nationalww2museum.org/war/articles/apocalypse-dresden-february-1945.

MSW, "Trojan Horse of the Ardennes," Weapons and Warfare (blog), September 22, 2015, https://weaponsandwarfare.com/2015/09/22/trojan-horse-of-the-ardennes/.

History.com Editors, "Battle of the Bulge," HISTORY, accessed September 29, 2022, https://www.history.com/topics/world-war-ii/battle-of-the-bulge.

"The American Doolittle Raid And The Brutal Japanese Reprisals," warhistoryonline, April 10, 2019, https://www.warhistoryonline.com/instant-articles/american-doolittle-raid.html.

Jesse Greenspan, "George H.W. Bush's Dangerous Role in WWII," HISTORY, accessed September 30, 2022, https://www.history.com/news/george-hw-bush-wwii-airman.

"Timeline: Last Days of Imperial Japan," Council on Foreign Relations, accessed September 30, 2022, https://www.cfr.org/timeline/last-days-imperial-japan.

"FERMI The Life of Enrico Fermi | U.S. DOE Office of Science (SC)," July 13, 2010, https://science.osti.gov/fermi/The-Life-of-Enrico-Fermi.

"On This Day, FDR Approves Funding the Manhattan Project | The National Constitution Center," National Constitution Center – constitutioncenter.org, accessed October 1, 2022, https://constitutioncenter.org/blog/on-this-day-fdr-approves-funding-the-manhattan-project.

"Franklin D. Roosevelt: Death of the President | Miller Center," October 4, 2016, https://millercenter.org/president/fdroosevelt/death-of-the-president.

"The Atomic Bombings by Ian W. Toll," The National WWII Museum | New Orleans, accessed October 1, 2022, https://www.nationalww2museum.org/war/articles/atomic-bombings-ian-w-toll.

"Milestones: 1937–1945 - Office of the Historian," accessed October 1, 2022, https://history.state.gov/milestones/1937-1945/tehran-conf.

"A History of the United States, 2nd Edition."

PART SIX: POST WAR TO THE END OF THE COLD WAR

"Communist Ideology | Communist Terror | Communist Crimes," accessed October 1, 2022, https://communistcrimes.org/en.

"Winston Churchill's Iron Curtain Speech–March 5, 1946," The National WWII Museum | New Orleans, accessed October 1, 2022, https://www.nationalww-2museum.org/war/articles/winston-churchills-iron-curtain-speech-march-5-1946.

"On the Verge of an Ecological Catastrophe: The Communist Modernization of Eastern Europe," Polish History, August 22, 2021, https://polishhistory.pl/on-the-verge-of-an-ecological-catastrophe-the-communist-modernization-of-eastern-europe/.

"Effects on the Environment in Czechoslovakia from Soviet Influence during the Cold War," in Wikipedia, May 20, 2022, https://en.wikipedia.org/w/index.php?title=Effects_on_the_environment_in_Czechoslovakia_from_Soviet_influence_during_the_Cold_War&oldid=1088781569.

Lisa Osoba, "The Destruction of the Environment in the Former Soviet Union," Dalhousie Journal of Legal Studies 5 (1996): 167.

Georgy Manaev, "What Was Wrong with Life in the USSR?," Russia Beyond, August 13, 2020, https://www.rbth.com/history/332571-what-was-wrong-with-life-ussr.

Klaus W. Larres, "When a Winner Becomes a Loser: Winston Churchill Was Kicked out of Office in the British Election of 1945," The Conversation, accessed October 1, 2022, http://theconversation.com/when-a-winner-becomes-a-loser-winston-churchill-was-kicked-out-of-office-in-the-british-election-of-1945-129746.

"Milestones: 1945–1952 - Office of the Historian," accessed July 30, 2022, https://history.state.gov/milestones/1945-1952/truman-doctrine.

"The Marshall Plan and Molotov Plan | History of Western Civilization II," accessed October 2, 2022, https://courses.lumenlearning.com/suny-hccc-worldhistory2/chapter/the-marshall-plan-and-molotov-plan/.

"Money Matters, an IMF Exhibit -- The Importance of Global Cooperation, Destruction and Reconstruction (1945-1958), Part 4 of 6," accessed May 6, 2023, https://www.imf.org/external/np/exr/center/mm/eng/mm_dr_03.htm.

Maurice Vaïsse, "France and NATO: An History," Politique étrangère Hors série, no. 5 (2009): 139–50, https://doi.org/10.3917/pe.hs3.0139.

Mia Jankowicz, "Putin Threatens West with 'consequences Greater than Any You Have Faced in History' If It Intervenes in His Invasion of Ukraine," Business Insider, accessed March 7, 2023, https://www.businessinsider.com/putin-threatens-worst-ever-consequences-if-west-intervenes-in-ukraine-2022-2.

History.com Editors, "Julius and Ethel Rosenberg Executed for Espionage," HISTORY, accessed July 30, 2022, https://www.history.com/this-day-in-history/rosenbergs-executed.

"Republic of China (1912–1949)," in Wikipedia, October 3, 2022, https://en.wikipedia.org/w/index.php?title=Republic_of_China_(1912%E2%80%931949)&oldid=1113775105#Post-World_War_II.

"Who Lost China? | Harry S. Truman," accessed October 3, 2022, https://www.trumanlibrary.gov/education/presidential-inquiries/who-lost-china.

"Truman's Loyalty Program | Harry S. Truman," accessed October 3, 2022, https://www.trumanlibrary.gov/education/presidential-inquiries/trumans-loyalty-program.

"McCarthyism, Korea and the Cold War," Wisconsin Historical Society, August 3, 2012, https://www.wisconsinhistory.org/Records/Article/CS420.

"U.S. Senate: 'Have You No Sense of Decency?,'" accessed July 30, 2022, https://www.senate.gov/about/powers-procedures/investigations/mccarthy-hearings/have-you-no-sense-of-decency.htm.

"Green, Yellow, Or Red–What Color Was Dean Acheson's Speech?," Hoover Institution, accessed July 30, 2022, https://www.hoover.org/research/green-yellow-or-red-what-color-was-dean-achesons-speech.

History.com Editors, "Korean War," HISTORY, accessed July 30, 2022, https://www.history.com/topics/korea/korean-war.

"The Firing of MacArthur | Harry S. Truman," accessed July 30, 2022, https://www.trumanlibrary.gov/education/presidential-inquiries/firing-macarthur.

Editors, "Korean War."

"Gen. Douglas MacArthur's 'Old Soldiers Never Die' Address to Congress, 19 April 1951.," image, Library of Congress, Washington, D.C. 20540 USA, accessed October 3, 2022, https://www.loc.gov/item/mcc.034/.

"G.I. Bill of Rights," National Archives Foundation, accessed July 30, 2022, https://www.archivesfoundation.org/documents/g-i-bill-rights/.

"Levittown," in Wikipedia, October 1, 2022, https://en.wikipedia.org/w/index.php?title=Levittown&oldid=1113447374.

"What Is Levittown? | Planopedia," accessed October 4, 2022, https://www.planetizen.com/definition/levittown.

"City and Suburb," National Museum of American History, February 28, 2017, https://americanhistory.si.edu/america-on-the-move/city-and-suburb.

Walt Disney, "The Beat Begins: America in the 1950s The Creation of Disneyland © 2004, Reece Fischer," n.d., 8.

"How Air Travel Has Changed in Every Decade from the 1920s to Today," loveexploring.com, accessed October 4, 2022, https://www.loveexploring.com/galleries/86315/how-air-travel-has-changed-in-every-decade-from-the-1920s-to-today.

"Duck and Cover," image, Library of Congress, Washington, D.C. 20540 USA, accessed October 4, 2022, https://www.loc.gov/item/2022604365/.

"The 1960s: Do You Remember Fallout Shelters?," accessed October 4, 2022, https://highlandcountypress.com/Content/Opinions/Opinion/Article/The-1960s-Do-you-remember-fallout-shelters-/4/22/60985.

Smithsonian Magazine and Lorraine Boissoneault, "The True Story of Brainwashing and How It Shaped America," Smithsonian Magazine, accessed July 30, 2022, https://www.smithsonianmag.com/history/true-story-brainwashing-and-how-it-shaped-america-180963400/.

"The Affluent Society | THE AMERICAN YAWP," accessed July 30, 2022, https://www.americanyawp.com/text/26-the-affluent-society/.

"Executive Order 9981: Desegregation of the Armed Forces (1948)," National Archives, September 28, 2021, https://www.archives.gov/milestone-documents/executive-order-9981.

"1948 Democratic National Convention," in Wikipedia, August 6, 2022, https://en.wikipedia.org/w/index.php?title=1948_Democratic_National_Convention&oldid=1102636269.

"Henry Wallace's Flawed Crusade," Dissent Magazine (blog), accessed October 5, 2022, https://www.dissentmagazine.org/article/henry-wallaces-flawed-crusade.

"Dewey Defeats Truman," in Wikipedia, September 25, 2022, https://en.wikipedia.org/w/index.php?title=Dewey_Defeats_Truman&oldid=1112185469.

"The Supreme Court. Expanding Civil Rights. Landmark Cases. Brown v. Board of Education (1954) | PBS," accessed July 31, 2022, https://www.thirteen.org/wnet/supremecourt/rights/landmark_brown.html.

"The Southern Manifesto and 'Massive Resistance' to Brown v. Board," Legal Defense Fund (blog), accessed March 7, 2023, https://www.naacpldf.org/brown-vs-board/southern-manifesto-massive-resistance-brown/.

"On This Day, Rosa Parks Wouldn't Give up Her Bus Seat | The National Constitution Center," National Constitution Center – constitutioncenter.org, accessed October 5, 2022, https://constitutioncenter.org/blog/it-was-on-this-day-that-rosa-parks-made-history-by-riding-a-bus.

UShistory.org, "The Sit-In Movement [Ushistory.Org]," accessed July 31, 2022, https://www.ushistory.org/us/54d.asp.

"William B. Hartsfield," in Wikipedia, April 16, 2022, https://en.wikipedia.org/w/index.php?title=William_B._Hartsfield&oldid=1083038901#Race.

"The Modern Civil Rights Movement and the Kennedy Administration | JFK Library," accessed July 31, 2022, https://www.jfklibrary.org/learn/about-jfk/jfk-in-history/civil-rights-movement.

Jeffrey Frank, "When Martin Luther King Jr. and Richard Nixon Were Friends," The Daily Beast, January 21, 2013, https://www.thedailybeast.com/articles/2013/01/21/when-martin-luther-king-jr-and-richard-nixon-were-friends.

© Stanford University, Stanford, and California 94305, "Connor, Theophilus Eugene 'Bull,'" The Martin Luther King, Jr., Research and Education Institute, April 25, 2017, https://kinginstitute.stanford.edu/encyclopedia/connor-theophilus-eugene-bull.

"Letter from Birmingham City Jail Themes - ENotes.Com," eNotes, accessed October 5, 2022, https://www.enotes.com/topics/letter-from-birmingham-city-jail/themes.

"The Sixties - The Urban Riots," accessed October 5, 2022, http://scholar.library.miami.edu/sixties/urbanRiots.php.

"Sotomayor and Jackson Slam Idea That U.S. Is 'Colorblind,'" NBC News, June 29, 2023, https://www.nbcnews.com/news/latino/sotomayor-jackson-write-strong-dissents-affirmative-action-rcna91817.

"Malcolm X - Quotes, Movie & Children," Biography, September 2, 2021, https://www.biography.com/activists/malcolm-x.

"Malcolm X - Quotes, Movie & Children."

"How Many Women Did JFK Bed? A Detailed List of the President's Affairs," History Hit, accessed October 6, 2022, https://www.historyhit.com/a-detailed-list-of-jfks-affairs/.

"Profiles in Courage," in Wikipedia, September 4, 2022, https://en.wikipedia.org/w/index.php?title=Profiles_in_Courage&oldid=1108509927#Reception.

N, P, and R, "Transcript: JFK's Speech on His Religion," NPR, December 5, 2007, https://www.npr.org/templates/story/story.php?storyId=16920600.

"Analysis | Here's a Voter Fraud Myth: Richard Daley 'Stole' Illinois for John Kennedy in the 1960 Election," Washington Post, accessed October 6, 2022. https://www.washingtonpost.com/news/monkey-cage/wp/2017/08/08/heres-a-voter-fraud-myth-richard-daley-stole-illinois-for-john-kennedy-in-the-1960-election/.

"The Cold War | JFK Library," accessed July 31, 2022, https://www.jfklibrary.org/learn/about-jfk/jfk-in-history/the-cold-war.

Condé Nast, "The Kennedy Mystique Explained in Ten Words," Vogue, November 11, 2013, https://www.vogue.com/article/the-kennedy-mystique-in-ten-words.

"Trip to Texas: Swearing-in Ceremony Aboard Air Force One, Lyndon B. Johnson (LBJ) as President | JFK Library," accessed October 7, 2022, https://www.jfklibrary.org/asset-viewer/archives/JFKWHP/1963/Month%2011/Day%2022/JFKWHP-1963-11-22-E.

Dan Balz, "THE MYSTERY OF BALLOT BOX 13," Washington Post, March 4, 1990, https://www.washingtonpost.com/archive/entertainment/books/1990/03/04/the-mystery-of-ballot-box-13/70206359-8543-48e3-9ce2-f3c4fdf6da3d/.

"Lyndon B. Johnson," The White House, accessed October 7, 2022, https://www.whitehouse.gov/about-the-white-house/presidents/lyndon-b-johnson/.

"Michael Harrington, The Other America, 1962," accessed October 7, 2022, http://web.mit.edu/21h.102/www/Primary%20source%20collections/Civil%20Rights/Other_America.htm.

"Culture of Poverty Theory & Examples | What Is the Culture of Poverty? - Video & Lesson Transcript," study.com, accessed October 7, 2022, https://study.com/academy/lesson/culture-of-poverty-definition-theory-examples.html.

"U.S. Poverty Statistics," Federal Safety Net (blog), accessed May 7, 2023, https://federalsafetynet.com/poverty-statistics/.

"America`s Vietnam War in Indochina," accessed October 9, 2022, https://www.u-s-history.com/pages/h1888.html.

"Famed Doctor Tom Dooley Secretly Helped CIA," HistoryNet, October 29, 2020, https://www.historynet.com/tom-dooley-cia-agent-vietnam-doctor/.

"Buddhist Crisis," in Wikipedia, July 7, 2022, https://en.wikipedia.org/w/index.php?title=Buddhist_crisis&oldid=1096876630.

"The Diem Coup | Miller Center," September 18, 2017, https://millercenter.org/the-presidency/educational-resources/diem-coup.

History.com Editors, "Gulf of Tonkin Resolution," HISTORY, accessed October 9, 2022, https://www.history.com/topics/vietnam-war/gulf-of-tonkin-resolution-1.

"Haunting Legacy: Vietnam and the American Presidency from Ford to Obama," accessed October 9, 2022, https://www.hks.harvard.edu/publications/haunting-legacy-vietnam-and-american-presidency-ford-obama.

Gina Dimuro, "Fragging: When Soldiers In Vietnam Revolted Against Their Superiors By Murdering Them," All That's Interesting, February 17, 2019, https://allthatsinteresting.com/fragging-vietnam-war.

Lukasz Kamienski, "The Drugs That Built a Super Soldier," The Atlantic, April 8, 2016, https://www.theatlantic.com/health/archive/2016/04/the-drugs-that-built-a-super-soldier/477183/.

Patrick Skerrett, "Lessons Learned – and Lost – from a Vietnam-Era Study of Addiction," STAT (blog), July 19, 2021, https://www.statnews.com/2021/07/19/lessons-learned-and-lost-vietnam-era-addiction-study/.

"The Draft and the Vietnam War," accessed October 9, 2022, https://www.studentsof-history.com/vietnam-war-draft.

Tom Megginson on 25 September 2012 in Activism, Peace, and Conflicts, "'Girls Say Yes to Boys Who Say No' - Joan Baez, 1968," Osocio (blog), September 25, 2012, https://osocio.org/message/girls-say-yes-to-boys-who-say-no-joan-baez-1968/.

Terry H. Anderson, "The Light at the End of the Tunnel: The United States and the Socialist Republic of Vietnam," Diplomatic History 12, no. 4 (October 1, 1988): 443–62, https://doi.org/10.1111/j.1467-7709.1988.tb00036.x.

History.com Editors, "President Nixon Calls on the 'Silent Majority,'" HISTORY, accessed October 9, 2022, https://www.history.com/this-day-in-history/nixon-calls-on-the-silent-majority.

"Paris Peace Talks and the Release of POWs | American Experience | PBS," accessed October 9, 2022, https://www.pbs.org/wgbh/americanexperience/features/honor-paris-peace-talks-and-release-pows/.

History.com Editors, "William Randolph Hearst," HISTORY, accessed October 8, 2022, https://www.history.com/topics/early-20th-century-us/william-randolph-hearst.

Anne Cullison, "William Randolph Hearst: Front Page News for Over 150 Years!," accessed October 8, 2022, https://blog.bookstellyouwhy.com/william-randolph-hearst-front-page-news-for-over-150-years.

Cullison.

"Crucible Of Empire : The Spanish-American War - PBS Online," accessed October 8, 2022, https://www.pbs.org/crucible/frames/_journalism.html.

Smithsonian Magazine and Gilbert King, "The Woman Who Took on the Tycoon," Smithsonian Magazine, accessed August 1, 2022, https://www.smithsonianmag.com/history/the-woman-who-took-on-the-tycoon-651396/.

"Federal Radio Commission," in Wikipedia, March 20, 2022, https://en.wikipedia.org/w/index.php?title=Federal_Radio_Commission&oldid=1078275552.

"Estes Kefauver," The Mob Museum, accessed August 1, 2022, https://themob-museum.org/notable_names/estes-kefauver/.

Jessie Kratz, "Vietnam: The First Television War," Pieces of History (blog), January 25, 2018, https://prologue.blogs.archives.gov/2018/01/25/vietnam-the-first-television-war/.

"Peter Arnett at CNN Broadcasts the First Live Television Coverage of War : History of Information," accessed May 8, 2023, https://historyofinformation.com/detail.php?entryid=4627.

Elizabeth Grieco, "Fast Facts about the Newspaper Industry's Financial Struggles as McClatchy Files for Bankruptcy," Pew Research Center (blog), accessed July 19, 2023, https://www.pewresearch.org/short-reads/2020/02/14/fast-facts-about-the-newspaper-industrys-financial-struggles/.

"Women in the 60's," accessed August 2, 2022, https://www.historycentral.com/sixty/Americans/WOMEN.html.

"5 Things Women Couldn't Do in the 1960s | CNN," accessed April 6, 2023, https://www.cnn.com/2014/08/07/living/sixties-women-5-things/index.html.

"Statement of Purpose | National Organization for Women," February 9, 2014, https://now.org/about/history/statement-of-purpose/.

Betty Friedan, The Feminine Mystique (Norton, n.d.).

"Feminist Consciousness-Raising Groups and Women's History," ThoughtCo, accessed August 2, 2022, https://www.thoughtco.com/feminist-consciousness-raising-groups-3528954.

Smithsonian Magazine and Roxane Gay, "Fifty Years Ago, Protesters Took on the Miss America Pageant and Electrified the Feminist Movement," Smithsonian Magazine, accessed October 10, 2022, https://www.smithsonianmag.com/history/fifty-years-ago-protestors-took-on-miss-america-pageant-electrified-feminist-movement-180967504/.

"The 1970 Women's March for Equality in NYC | New-York Historical Society," accessed October 10, 2022, https://www.nyhistory.org/blogs/march-for-equality-in-nyc.

"Half The Story Gloria Steinem Biographer Manages To Tell Feminist's Colorful Life Story In Dry Black And White, Without Juicy Details | The Spokesman-Review," accessed April 5, 2023, https://www.spokesman.com/stories/1995/oct/15/half-the-story-gloria-steinem-biographer-manages/.

"Lesbian Feminism, 1960s and 1970s · Lesbians in the Twentieth Century, 1900-1999 · OutHistory: It's About Time," accessed August 2, 2022, https://outhistory.org/exhibits/show/lesbians-20th-century/lesbian-feminism.

"Alfred Kinsey: A Brief Summary and Critique," ERLC, accessed August 2, 2022, https://erlc.com/resource-library/articles/alfred-kinsey-a-brief-summary-and-critique/.

"The 1960s: A Decade of Change for Women," accessed August 2, 2022, https://www.usnews.com/news/articles/2010/03/12/the-1960s-a-decade-of-change-for-women.

"Roe v. Wade and Supreme Court Abortion Cases | Brennan Center for Justice," accessed October 10, 2022, https://www.brennancenter.org/our-work/research-reports/roe-v-wade-and-supreme-court-abortion-cases.

"Women CEOs of the S&P 500 (List)," Catalyst (blog), accessed April 5, 2023, https://www.catalyst.org/research/women-ceos-of-the-sp-500/.

"Beyond Silent Spring: An Alternate History of DDT," Science History Institute, February 14, 2017, https://www.sciencehistory.org/distillations/beyond-silent-spring-an-alternate-history-of-ddt.

"The Other Foe: The U.S. Army's Fight against Malaria in the Pacific Theater, 1942-45 — The Campaign for the National Museum of the United States Army," accessed October 12, 2022, https://armyhistory.org/the-other-foe-the-u-s-armys-fight-against-malaria-in-the-pacific-theater-1942-45/.

Hanneke Weitering published, "Earth Day 2019: These Amazing NASA Images Show Earth from Above," Space.com, April 22, 2019, https://www.space.com/earth-day-amazing-nasa-photos.html.

"Maverick: Chronicles of a Death Foretold | SJSU News," accessed October 12, 2022, https://sjsunews.com/article/maverick-chronicles-of-a-death-foretold.

"Today in History - April 22," web page, Library of Congress, Washington, D.C. 20540 USA, accessed October 12, 2022, https://www.loc.gov/item/today-in-history/april-22/.

"History of Earth Day & Arbor Day in Parks : NYC Parks," accessed October 12, 2022, https://www.nycgovparks.org/about/history/earth-day-arbor-day.

Smithsonian Magazine and Lorraine Boissoneault, "The Cuyahoga River Caught Fire at Least a Dozen Times, but No One Cared Until 1969," Smithsonian Magazine, accessed October 12, 2022, https://www.smithsonianmag.com/history/cuyahoga-river-caught-fire-least-dozen-times-no-one-cared-until-1969-180972444/.

"What Is an Environmental Impact Statement?," accessed October 12, 2022, https://www.americanbar.org/groups/public_education/publications/teaching-legal-docs/teaching-legal-docs--what-is-an-environmental-impact-statement-/.

The Associated Press, "A Tiny Fish That Once Caused an Epic Conservation Fight Is No Longer under Threat," NPR, October 4, 2022, sec. Animals, https://www.npr.org/2022/10/04/1126825745/snail-darter-endangered-species-list.

"TAPS Facts," Alyeska Pipeline, accessed October 12, 2022, https://www.alyeska-pipe.com/taps-facts/.

"Oil and Gas," accessed April 6, 2023, https://www.akrdc.org/oil-and-gas.

History.com Editors, "Exxon Valdez Oil Spill," HISTORY, accessed October 12, 2022, https://www.history.com/topics/1980s/exxon-valdez-oil-spill.

History.com Editors, "Nuclear Disaster at Three Mile Island," HISTORY, accessed August 3, 2022, https://www.history.com/this-day-in-history/nuclear-accident-at-three-mile-island.

"States Restrictions on New Nuclear Power Facility Construction," accessed October 12, 2022, https://www.ncsl.org/research/environment-and-natural-resources/states-restrictions-on-new-nuclear-power-facility.aspx.

Jessica McDonald, "How Much Will the 'Green New Deal' Cost?," FactCheck. Org (blog), March 14, 2019, https://www.factcheck.org/2019/03/how-much-will-the-green-new-deal-cost/.

John A. Farrell, Richard Nixon: The Life, n.d.

Facebook et al., "'Pink Right Down to Her Underwear' : Politics: The 1950 Senate Campaign of Richard Nixon against Helen Douglas Reached an Unequaled Low. Comparison Is Unfair to John Van de Kamp.," Los Angeles Times, April 9, 1990, https://www.latimes.com/archives/la-xpm-1990-04-09-me-664-story.html.

"How Richard Nixon Became 'Tricky Dick,'" California's Capitol, November 24, 2011, http://www.californiascapitol.com/2011/11/how-tricky-dick-nixon-became-tricky-dick/.

"Dwight D. Eisenhower: Campaigns and Elections | Miller Center," October 4, 2016, https://millercenter.org/president/eisenhower/campaigns-and-elections.

"Richard Nixon's November 1962 Press Conference," in Wikipedia, August 23, 2022, https://en.wikipedia.org/w/index.php?title=Richard_Nixon%27s_November_1962_press_conference&oldid=1106058178.

A. P. M. Reports, "George C. Wallace - Campaign '68 | APM Reports," accessed October 11, 2022, https://features.apmreports.org/arw/campaign68/d1.html.

Vincent Ni and Vincent Ni China affairs correspondent, "Fifty Years on, 'Nixon in China' Loses Its Sparkle in Beijing and Washington," The Guardian, February 21, 2022, sec. World news, https://www.theguardian.com/world/2022/feb/21/fifty-years-on-nixon-in-china-loses-its-sparkle-in-beijing-and-washington.

"Nixon's 1972 Visit to China at 50 | Wilson Center," accessed October 11, 2022, https://www.wilsoncenter.org/blog-post/nixons-1972-visit-china-50.

"Nixon's China Visit, 50 Years Later," accessed October 11, 2022, https://www.asc.upenn.edu/news-events/news/nixons-china-visit-50-years-later.

"The History Place - Vietnam War 1969-1975," accessed October 11, 2022, https://www.historyplace.com/unitedstates/vietnam/index-1969.html.

"James McCord: The Watergate Burglar Who Cracked" - POLITICO, accessed October 11, 2022, https://www.politico.com/news/magazine/2019/12/29/james-mccord-watergate-burglar-obituary-086480.

"The Watergate Story | The Post Investigates," The Washington Post, accessed October 11, 2022, http://www.washingtonpost.com/wp-srv/politics/special/watergate/part1.html.

"Richard Nixon: 'There Can Be No Whitewash at the White House', First Watergate Speech - 1973," Speakola, accessed October 11, 2022, https://speakola.com/political/richard-nixon-no-whitewash-first-watergate-1973.

"Watergate Scandal," in Wikipedia, October 12, 2022, https://en.wikipedia.org/w/index.php?title=Watergate_scandal&oldid=1115549771#%22Smoking_Gun%22_tape.

"Profanity Heard on Nixon Tapes," AP NEWS, accessed October 11, 2022, https://apnews.com/article/2aba0a3aea8eabe74b8f2cc7e9cbeaf5.

"Watergate Casualties and Convictions," accessed October 11, 2022, https://watergate.info/analysis/casualties-and-convictions.

"The Faith of Jimmy Carter," America Magazine, April 11, 2018, https://www.americamagazine.org/arts-culture/2018/04/11/faith-jimmy-carter.

"Milestones: 1977–1980 - Office of the Historian," accessed October 15, 2022, https://history.state.gov/milestones/1977-1980/panama-canal.

"Christian Right," in Wikipedia, July 25, 2022, https://en.wikipedia.org/w/index. php?title=Christian_right&oldid=1100270319.

History.com Editors, "President Reagan Shot," HISTORY, accessed August 4, 2022, https://www.history.com/this-day-in-history/president-reagan-shot.

"A History of the United States, 2nd Edition."

PART SEVEN: THE NEW WORLD ORDER TO TODAY

Timothy Snyder, "1989: Poland Was First! | Timothy Snyder," The New York Review of Books (blog), accessed August 4, 2022, https://www.nybooks.com/daily/2009/12/09/1989-poland-was-first/.

"Poland's Solidarity Movement (1980-1989)," ICNC (blog), accessed October 17, 2022, https://www.nonviolent-conflict.org/polands-solidarity-movement-1980-1989/.

"1990–1991 Gulf War Leaflets 8-Pc Collection | GovMint.Com," Default Store View, accessed October 17, 2022, https://www.govmint.com/8pc-gulf-war-leaflets-collection.

David Choi, "Watch This Haunting 70mm Clip of Iraqi Forces Burning Oil Wells in a Scorched-Earth Policy," Business Insider, accessed October 17, 2022, https://www.businessinsider.com/haunting-clip-of-iraq-burning-oil-2016-6.

"The Gulf War | Miller Center," May 11, 2020, https://millercenter.org/statecraftmovie/gulf-war.

Randolph Capps, Michael E Fix, and Jeffrey S Passel, "The Dispersal of Immigrants in the 1990s," n.d., 2.

"Oprah Talks to Bill Clinton," Oprah.com, accessed October 18, 2022, https://www.oprah.com/omagazine/oprah-interviews-president-bill-clinton.

"Clinton Leads Race, but Can't Shake Draft Issue," Christian Science Monitor, accessed May 9, 2023, https://www.csmonitor.com/1992/0924/24062.html.

Michael Kruse, "The TV Interview That Haunts Hillary Clinton," POLITICO Magazine, accessed November 10, 2022, https://politi.co/2AdwRdw.

Paul Taylor, "Negative Ads Becoming Powerful Political Force," Washington Post, October 5, 1986, https://www.washingtonpost.com/archive/politics/1986/10/05/negative-ads-becoming-powerful-political-force/201c389d-8742-4fe5-83af-ea951981bdd6/.

US Census Bureau, "Health Insurance Coverage: 2000," Census.gov, accessed October 18, 2022, https://www.census.gov/library/publications/2001/demo/p60-215.html.

Lesley Kennedy, "The 1994 Midterms: When Newt Gingrich Helped Republicans Win Big," HISTORY, accessed October 18, 2022, https://www.history.com/news/midterm-elections-1994-republican-revolution-gingrich-contract-with-america.

"Bob Dole, Longtime Senate Leader and 1996 GOP Presidential Nominee, Dies at 98," POLITICO, accessed October 18, 2022, https://www.politico.com/news/2021/12/05/bob-dole-republican-presidential-nominee-advance-obit-033611.

"Troopergate (Bill Clinton)," in Wikipedia, October 12, 2022, https://en.wikipedia. org/w/index.php?title=Troopergate_(Bill_Clinton)&oldid=1115626843.

"The True Story of the Bill Clinton and Monica Lewinsky Scandal," accessed August 5, 2022, https://sports.yahoo.com/true-story-bill-clinton-monica-082500772.html.

Mark Perry, "Animated Chart of the Day: World's Top 10 Billionaires, 2000 to 2022," American Enterprise Institute - AEI (blog), May 20, 2022, https://www.aei.org/ carpe-diem/animated-chart-of-the-day-worlds-top-ten-billionaires-2000-to-2022/.

Gary Hoover, "Most Valuable Companies: The Last 25 Years," Business History - The American Business History Center, August 20, 2020, https://americanbusinesshistory. org/most-valuable-companies-the-last-25-years/.

"CNN.Com - Bin Laden Calls Sept. 11 Attacks 'blessed Terror' - December 27, 2001," accessed May 9, 2023, https://www.cnn.com/2001/WORLD/asiapcf/central/12/26/ ret.bin.laden.statement/index.html?related.

History.com Editors, "Afghanistan War," HISTORY, accessed August 5, 2022, https:// www.history.com/topics/21st-century/afghanistan-war.

"Iraq War - American Soldiers Killed in Iraq 2020," Statista, accessed February 10, 2023, https://www.statista.com/statistics/263798/american-soldiers-killed-in-iraq/.

U.S. Census Bureau and U.S. Department of Housing and Urban Development, "Average Sales Price of Houses Sold for the Northeast Census Region," FRED, Federal Reserve Bank of St. Louis (FRED, Federal Reserve Bank of St. Louis, January 1, 1975), https://fred.stlouisfed.org/series/ASPNE.

"FRB: Finance and Economics Discussion Series: Screen Reader Version - 200899," accessed August 6, 2022, https://www.federalreserve.gov/pubs/feds/2008/200859/ index.html.

Michael Lewis, The Big Short, n.d.

"United States Unemployment Rates by President, 1948-2020," Research (blog), September 4, 2015, https://historyinpieces.com/research/ us-unemployment-rates-president.

"Barack Obama Religion Conspiracy Theories," in Wikipedia, July 25, 2022, https://en.wikipedia.org/w/index. php?title=Barack_Obama_religion_conspiracy_theories&oldid=1100433903.

"How Did the U.S. National Debt Get So Big?," The Balance, accessed August 6, 2022, https://www.thebalance.com/the-u-s-debt-and-how-it-got-so-big-3305778.

"File:Obama and Biden Await Updates on Bin Laden.Jpg," in Wikipedia, February 24, 2021, https://en.wikipedia.org/w/index.php?title=File:Obama_and_Biden_await_ updates_on_bin_Laden.jpg&oldid=1008621127.

"Obama's Final Drone Strike Data," Council on Foreign Relations, accessed August 6, 2022, https://www.cfr.org/blog/obamas-final-drone-strike-data.

"The Most Popular Democrats in America | Politics | YouGov Ratings," accessed May 8, 2023, https://today.yougov.com/ratings/politics/popularity/Democrats/all.

"Capitol Riots: Did Trump's Words at Rally Incite Violence?," BBC News, January 13, 2021, sec. US & Canada, https://www.bbc.com/news/world-us-canada-55640437.

"Putin's Threat Rekindles Cold War Fears of Nuclear War," PBS NewsHour, February 25, 2022, https://www.pbs.org/newshour/world/putin-waves-nuclear-sword-in-confrontation-with-the-west.

"Medicare Is Not 'Bankrupt' | Center on Budget and Policy Priorities," August 4, 2014, https://www.cbpp.org/research/health/medicare-is-not-bankrupt.

"A History of the United States, 2nd Edition."

"'Not Sittin' Here as Some Little Woman:' Looking Back at Hillary and Bill Clinton's 60 Minutes Interview," Peoplemag, accessed September 14, 2023, https://people.com/politics/looking-back-at-hillary-and-bill-clintons-60-minutes-interview/.

Agence France-Presse, "How the Scramble to Leave Afghanistan Is Unfolding," ABS-CBN News, August 19, 2021, https://news.abs-cbn.com/overseas/08/19/21/how-the-scramble-to-leave-afghanistan-is-unfolding.

TapTheForwardAssist, CC BY-SA 4.0 <https://creativecommons.org/licenses/by-sa/4.0>, via Wikimedia Commons

CONCLUSION: THE USA IN 2023

"Research: The Future Financial Status of the Social Security Program," Social Security Administration Research, Statistics, and Policy Analysis, accessed March 15, 2023, https://www.ssa.gov/policy/docs/ssb/v70n3/v70n3p111.html.

Center for Migration Studies, "President Biden's Executive Actions on Immigration," The Center for Migration Studies of New York (CMS) (blog), February 2, 2021, https://cmsny.org/biden-immigration-executive-actions/.

"A Sober Assessment of the Growing U.S. Asylum Backlog," accessed March 15, 2023, https://trac.syr.edu/reports/705/.

John Gramlich, "What the Data Says about Gun Deaths in the U.S.," Pew Research Center (blog), accessed March 15, 2023, https://www.pewresearch.org/fact-tank/2022/02/03/what-the-data-says-about-gun-deaths-in-the-u-s/.

Mike Gonzalez, "'Founded on a Creed': Understanding America's Unique Beginning," The Heritage Foundation, accessed July 20, 2023, https://www.heritage.org/american-founders/commentary/founded-creed-understanding-americas-unique-beginning.

APPENDICES

Jeanette Centeno, "10 Biggest Native American Tribes Today - PowWows.Com Do You Know the Biggest Tribes?," PowWows.com, March 19, 2021, https://www.powwows.com/10-biggest-native-american-tribes-today/.

FURTHER READING

For further reading and film and documentary recommendations, please visit www.historyinaheartbeat.com/
further-reading

ACKNOWLEDGEMENTS

My editors: I would like to thank my amazing editors Jessica Andersen, Susan Michaud, and Karl French for all your hard work, efficiency, and attention to detail. The book really would not be what it is without you.

My publishing team: Andrew Biernat, Jorge Capuras, and all the SPS for your tireless support through the process. You guys are awesome.

My graphic designer: Ana Krasavina, for your wonderful maps and designs.

My family: My parents, Edward and Caroline Serocold, for all their love and support throughout my life. My uncles David Paterson and Michael Paterson, and my cousin, Elizabeth Sherbrooke. Your advice and support have always been invaluable to me, especially when I chose to move across the pond. And to my wife Alice, whose idea this whole thing was.

My friends: Jules Evans and Louai Al Roumani. Both of you inspired me with your own books, and graciously made time for me when I asked you for it.

Finally, I'd like to acknowledge the authors on whose work I relied so much to write this book. Specifically, Robert Remini, Allen C Guelzo, Gary Gallagher, Ira Berlin, Patrick Allitt, James West Davidson, Howard Zinn, Jill Lepore, Ron Chernow and Hugh Thomas. All your books are incredible, and put a fire in me to have one of my own.

AUTHOR BIO

Charles Serocold was born in London, UK, and studied English at the University of Manchester. He is a UK lawyer and moved to the US in 2009, where he obtained an MBA from Hult International Business School in Boston, Massachusetts. He has lived in New York since 2010, and helps people adjust to their lives in the US by providing them with a foundational knowledge of the country, together with information about the practical and logistical aspects of living here. Please visit his website page www.historyinaheartbeat.com/charlesserocold for more information.

URGENT PLEA!

Thank You For Reading My Book!

I really appreciate all of your feedback and

I love hearing what you have to say.

I need your input to make the next version of this

book and my future books better.

Please take two minutes now to leave a helpful review on
Amazon letting me know what you thought of the book:

Thanks so much!

Charles Serocold

Sign up for News

Sign up for news and updates from History in a Heartbeat. We will provide you with news relating to:

- New publications
- New services and courses
- Blog posts
- Surveys
- Company news

www.historyinaheartbeat.com/news

Printed in Great Britain
by Amazon

52333953R00304